Paul the Jew

Paul the Jew

Rereading the Apostle as a Figure of Second Temple Judaism

Gabriele Boccaccini and Carlos A. Segovia, editors

Cameron J. Doody, associate editor

Fortress Press
Minneapolis

PAUL THE JEW

Rereading the Apostle as a Figure of Second Temple Judaism

Cover design: Laurie Ingram

Library of Congress Cataloging-in-Publication Data

Print ISBN: 978-1-4514-7980-5

eBook ISBN: 978-1-5064-1040-1

The paper used in this publication meets the minimum requirements of American National Standard for Information Sciences — Permanence of Paper for Printed Library Materials, ANSI Z329.48-1984.

Manufactured in the U.S.A.

This book was produced using Pressbooks.com, and PDF rendering was done by PrinceXML.

Contents

Preface

Carlos A. Segovia

Pauline studies have undergone a dramatic paradigm shift in the past decades. On the one hand, we have come to rediscover Paul's Jewishness, which is now being explored afresh from every possible perspective. On the other hand, renewed attention is now also being paid to Paul's critical attitude toward the Roman imperial order. The traditional reading of Paul—shared by many Jews and Christians alike over the past nineteen centuries—contended that he was a theologian who deviated from Judaism. In the 1980s, the so-called New Perspective on Paul went on to present him as a theologian whose aim was not so much to break with, but to reform Judaism. None of these models seem to work anymore, however. For, if we read him carefully, Paul only speaks about the restoration of Israel and the ingathering of the nations in a markedly political context: both Israel and the nations have been subdued by Rome, and against this background, Paul's "theology" aims at subverting the macro- and micro-politics of the Roman Empire by questioning its identity-making strategies.

It seems that, initially, for some reason unknown to us, Paul felt uneasy about the Jesus movement. And that suddenly, for some likewise unknown reason, he felt "called" to follow Jesus and to preach him to the nations. This is all Paul says. How can we interpret his words? It is hard to tell what precisely he had in mind, or what actually happened to him. As Alain Badiou suggests, events imply the appearance of something entirely foreign to what is: they break through the order of things; therefore, we can only recognize them by their effects. But we can easily ascertain what Paul did not mean to say. He did not mean to say that he converted from one religion (Judaism) to a different one (Christianity), as "Christianity" was basically an intra-Jewish phenomenon in Paul's time. He simply became a different kind of man, ready to live a different kind of life within Judaism.

Paul clearly states that God's election of Israel is irrevocable (Rom. 11:1, 29) and that he has been commissioned to bring the gentiles through Christ into God's allegiance (15:16, 18). That is what Paul's "theology" is all about. Yet, at the same time, Paul offers a good example of discursive adaptability. His "sacrificial" metaphors reflect some acquaintance with the language specific to the Greco-Roman mystery religions. He uses them to gain his gentile audience, but he does so by simultaneously deconstructing their ordinary meaning insofar as he re-inscribes them within a specifically Jewish (messianic, apocalyptic) mindset. In short, they prove peripheral rhetorical tools at best, instead of representing—as has often been suggested—the core of his message. How then does Paul negotiate gentile inclusiveness through Christ? Are Paul's gentiles merely to be seen as a "cultic" category, and if so, what would this imply? Did Paul subscribe to the view that there are two different ways of salvation—one for the Jews and another one for the gentiles? How should we interpret Jesus' messianic status in Pauline Christology and Paul's apocalyptic eschatology?

The present volume represents an effort to bring together for the first time Second Temple and Pauline scholars to explore in close dialogue these and other related issues, such as Paul's scriptures, his concept of a faithful "remnant," the particular type of religious community he planned to build, and the implicit connections between Baptism, circumcision, and Torah observance inside the Pauline communities. It focuses too on the relationship between Hellenism and Judaism, on the one hand, and on the intertwining of Jewish law and Roman Empire, on the other, in Paul's thought. Lastly, it tries to offer new insights into the ways in which Paul's message was appropriated, and eventually, transformed into something altogether different in early Christianity and formative Islam.

Most of the chapters that follow were offered first as papers at the Third Nangeroni Meeting of the Enoch Seminar, "Rereading Paul as a Second Temple Jew," which was held at the Valdensian Faculty of Theology (Rome) in June 2014 under the auspices of the Enoch Seminar, the Michigan Center for Early Christian Studies, the Department of Near Eastern Studies of the University of Michigan, and the Alessandro Nangeroni International Endowment. I would like to warmly thank all those scholars who contributed to the conference, and especially, Albert Baumgarten, Gabriele Boccaccini, Daniel Boyarin, William S. Campbell, James Charlesworth, Kathy Ehrensperger, Joshua Garroway, Matthew Goff, Larry Hurtado, Isaac Oliver, Anders Petersen, Jeremy Punt, David Rudolph, and Shayna Sheinfeld for their willingness to have their papers and responses reworked and published in this volume. I am also grateful to Gabriele Boccaccini for asking me to organize the conference and for his helpful advice; to Erik Noffke and Jason Zurawksi for their cooperation and assistance during the conference in Rome; to Neil Elliott for accepting to publish the present volume (together with that edited by Mark D. Nanos and Magnus Zetterholm, *Paul within Judaism: Restoring the First-Century Context to the Apostle* [Minneapolis: Fortress Press, 2015], which includes inter alia some other papers also offered at Rome); to Cameron Doody for handling the copyediting; and to Rodney Caruthers for preparing the index.

Introduction

The Three Paths to Salvation of Paul the Jew

Gabriele Boccaccini (with responses by Albert I. Baumgarten and Daniel Boyarin)

The chapters in this volume began as addresses at an academic conference. This introduction includes Gabriele Boccaccini's opening lecture, which was offered as a statement of the agenda of the conference, followed by two brief responses by Albert Baumgarten and Daniel Boyarin, respectively. We have combined them into an introduction because, together, they admirably set out the questions and options being addressed by all the chapters that follow. We believe, moreover, that presenting them as close as possible to the "oral" form in which they were originally delivered may additionally help the readers to "feel" the dialogical flavor and the excitement of the conference. It is our conviction that historical research offers to Christians and Jews alike a new understanding of Paul the Jew, not as an apostle of intolerance, as he has been presented for centuries, but as a messenger of mercy and forgiveness.

◆ ◆ ◆

The Three Paths to Salvation of Paul the Jew

Gabriele Boccaccini

For centuries, Paul has been praised by Christians, and blamed by Jews, for separating Christianity from Judaism. Paul appeared to Christians as the convert who unmasked and denounced the "weakness" (if not the wickedness) of Judaism, and to Jews as the traitor who made a mockery of the faith of his ancestors.[1] Paul was, at the same time, the advocate of Christian universalism and the major proponent of Christian exclusiveness—everybody is called and welcomed, but there is only one way of salvation in Christ for all humankind.

The New Perspective has tried hard to get rid of the most derogatory aspects of the traditional (Lutheran) reading of Paul (claiming that Judaism also should be regarded as a "respectable" religion based on grace), but has not challenged the view of Paul as the critic of Judaism and the advocate of a new supersessionist model of relations between God and humankind—God's grace "in Christ" superseded the Jewish covenant for both Jews and gentiles by creating a third separate "race."

A new paradigm is emerging today with the Radical New Perspective—a paradigm that aims to fully rediscover the Jewishness of Paul. Paradoxically, "Paul was not a Christian,"[2] since Christianity, at the time of Paul, was nothing else than a Jewish messianic movement, and therefore, Paul should be regarded as nothing other than a Second Temple Jew. What else should he have been? Paul was born a Jew, of Jewish parents, was circumcised, and nothing in his work supports (or even suggests) the idea that he became (or regarded himself as) an apostate.[3] On the contrary, Paul was a member of the early Jesus movement, and with strength and unmistakable clarity, proudly claimed his Jewishness, declaring that God also did not reject God's covenant with the chosen people: "Has God rejected his people? By no means! I myself am an Israelite, a descendant of Abraham, a member of the tribe of Benjamin" (Rom. 11:1; cf. Phil. 3:5).

The goal of this volume is fully to embrace the paradigm of the Radical New Perspective not as the conclusion, but as the starting point of our conversation about Paul. The following chapters, based on papers first presented at the Third Nangeroni Meeting in Rome, share that perspective.

In my opinion, the potential of such an approach has just begun to be manifested. We have still a long way to go before fully understanding all its monumental implications. In order to properly locate Paul the Jew in the context of the diverse world of Second Temple Judaism, we need, first of all, to establish a better communication between New Testament scholars and Second Temple specialists—two fields of studies that, to date, have remained too distant and deaf to each other. This is what our meeting in Rome was about; this is the future of Pauline studies.

Three Caveats about the Jewishness of Paul

Since my remarks focus on the Jewishness of Paul, it is important to clarify, as a premise, what we should not imply by that, in order to avoid common misunderstandings.

1. In order to reclaim the Jewishness of Paul, we do not have to prove that he was a Jew like everybody else, or that he was not an original thinker. It is important not to apply to Paul a different standard than to any other Jew of his time. To claim that finding any idea in Paul that is unparalleled in other Jewish authors makes Paul "non-Jewish" would lead to the paradox that no original thinker of Second Temple Judaism should be considered "Jewish"—certainly not Philo or Josephus or Hillel or the Teacher of Righteousness, all of whom also formulated "original" answers to the common questions of their age. Why should only Paul be considered "non-Jewish" or "no longer Jewish" simply because he developed some original thinking? The very notion of making a distinction within Paul between his Jewish and "non-Jewish" (or "Christian") ideas does not make any sense. Paul was Jewish in his "traditional" ideas and remained such even in his "originality."

Paul was a Jewish thinker and all his ideas (even the most nonconformist) were Jewish.

2. In order to reclaim the Jewishness of Paul, we do not have to downplay the fact that he was a very controversial figure, not only within Second Temple Judaism, but also within the early Jesus movement. The classical interpretation that the controversial nature of Paul (both within and outside his movement) relied on his attempt to separate Christianity from Judaism does not take into consideration the diversity of Second Temple Jewish thought. There was never a monolithic Judaism versus an equally monolithic Christianity. There were many diverse varieties of Judaism (including the early Jesus movement, which, in turn, was also very diverse in its internal components).

3. In order to reclaim the Jewishness of Paul, we do not have to prove that he had nothing to say to Jews and that his mission was aimed only at the inclusion of gentiles. As Daniel Boyarin has reminded us in his work on Paul, a Jew is a Jew, and remains a Jew, even when he or she expresses radical self-criticism toward his or her own religious tradition or against other competitive forms of Judaism.[4] Limiting the entire Pauline theological discourse to the sole issue of the inclusion of gentiles would once again confine Paul the Jew to the fringes of Judaism and overshadow the many implications of his theology in the broader context of Second Temple Jewish thought.

Paul the Convert

As in the case of Jesus, the problem of Paul is not whether he was a Jew or not, but what kind of Jew he was, because in the diverse world of Second Temple Judaism, there were many different ways of being a Jew.[5] According to his own words, Paul was educated as a Pharisee. The idea that he abandoned Judaism when he "converted" to the Jesus movement is simply anachronistic.

Conversion as an experience of radical abandonment of one's religious and ethical identity was indeed known in antiquity (as attested in *Joseph and Aseneth*, and in the works of Philo). But this was *not* the experience of Paul. Christianity at his time was a Jewish messianic movement, not a separate religion. Paul, who was born and raised a Jew, remained such after his "conversion"; nothing changed in his religious and ethical identity. What changed, however, was his view of Judaism. In describing his experience not as a "prophetic call," but as a "heavenly revelation," Paul himself indicated the radicalness of the event. Paul did not abandon Judaism, but "converted" from one variety of Judaism to another. With Alan Segal, I would agree that "Paul was a Pharisaic Jew who converted to a new apocalyptic, Jewish sect."[6]

In no way should we downplay the relevance of the event. It was a move within Judaism, and yet, a radical move that reoriented Paul's entire life and worldview. If, today, a Reform Rabbi became an ultraorthodox Jew, or vice versa, we would also describe such an experience in terms of "conversion." Likewise, Paul's conversion should be understood not as a chapter in the parting of the ways between Christianity and Judaism, but as an occurrence in the context of the diversity of Second Temple Judaism.

Paul the Jesus Follower

Paul was a Pharisee who joined the early Jesus movement. Before being known as the apostle of the gentiles, Paul became a member of the Jesus movement, and then, characterized his apostolate within the Jesus movement as having a particular emphasis on the mission to gentiles. Before Paul the apostle of the gentiles, there was Paul "the Jesus follower." Any inquiry about Paul cannot, therefore, avoid the question of what the early Jesus movement was about in the context of Second Temple Judaism.

We all agree that, at its inception, Christianity was a Jewish messianic movement, but what does that mean exactly? It would be simplistic to reduce the early "Christian" message to a generic announcement about the imminent coming of the kingdom of God and about Jesus as the expected Messiah. And it would be simplistic to imagine Paul as simply a Pharisee to whom the name of the future

Messiah was revealed and who believed himself to be living at the end of times.

As a result of his "conversion," Paul fully embraced the Christian apocalyptic worldview and the claim that Jesus the Messiah had already come (and would return at the end of times). This included the explanation of why the Messiah had come before the end. The early Christians had an answer: Jesus did not come simply to reveal his name and identity. Jesus came as the Son of Man who had "authority on earth to forgive sins" (Mark 2 and parallels).

A Second Temple Jewish Debate

The idea of the Messiah as the forgiver on earth makes perfect sense as a development of the ancient Enochic apocalyptic tradition. The apocalyptic "counternarrative" of 1 Enoch centered on the collapse of the creative order by a cosmic rebellion (the oath and the actions of the fallen angels): "The whole earth has been corrupted by Azazel's teaching of his [own] actions; and write upon him all sin" (1 En. 10:8). It was this cosmic rebellion that produced the catastrophe of the flood, but also the need for a new creation.

The Enochic view of the origin of evil had profound implications in the development of Second Temple Jewish thought. The idea of the "end of times" is today so much ingrained in the Jewish and Christian traditions to make it difficult even to imagine a time when it was not, and to fully comprehend its revolutionary impact when it first emerged. In the words of Genesis, nothing is more perfect than the perfect world, which God himself saw and praised as "very good" (Gen. 1:31). Nobody would change something that "works," unless something went terribly wrong. In apocalyptic thought, eschatology is always the product of protology.

The problem of Enochic Judaism with the Mosaic law was also the product of protology. It did not come from a direct criticism of the law, but from the recognition that the angelic rebellion had made it difficult for people to follow any laws (including the Mosaic Torah) in a universe now disrupted by the presence of superhuman evil. The problem was not the Torah itself, but the incapability of human beings to do good deeds, which affects the human relationship with the Mosaic Torah. The shift of focus was not primarily from Moses to Enoch, but from the trust in human responsibility to the drama of human culpability. While at the center of the Mosaic Torah was the human responsibility to follow God's laws, at the center of Enochic Judaism was now a paradigm of the victimization of all humankind.

This is the reason it would be incorrect to talk of Enochic Judaism as a form of Judaism "against" or "without" the Torah. Enochic Judaism was not "competing wisdom," but more properly, a "theology of complaint." There was no alternative Enochic halakah for this world, no Enochic purity code, no Enochic Torah: every hope of redemption was postponed to the end of times. The Enochians were not competing with Moses—they were merely complaining. In the Enochic Book of Dreams, the chosen people of Israel are promised a future redemption in the world to come, but in this world, Israel is affected by the spread of evil with no divine protection, as are all other nations.

The Enochic view had disturbing implications for the self-understanding of the Jewish people as the people of the covenant. It generated a heated debate within Judaism about the origin and nature of evil.[7] Many (like the Pharisees and the Sadducees) rejected the very idea of the superhuman origin of evil; some explored other paths in order to save human freedom and God's omnipotence—paths that led to alternative solutions, from the *cor malignum* of *4 Ezra* to the rabbinic *yetzer hara'*. Even within apocalyptic circles, there were competing theologies. In the mid-second century BCE, the book of *Jubilees* reacted against this demise of the covenantal relation with God by creating an effective synthesis between Enoch and Moses that most scholars see as the foundation of the Essene movement. While maintaining the Enochic frame of corruption and decay, *Jubilees* reinterpreted the covenant as the "medicine" provided by God to spare the chosen people from the power of evil. The merging of Mosaic and Enochic traditions redefined a space where the people of Israel could now live, protected from the evilness of the world under the boundaries of an alternative halakah as long as they remained faithful to the imposed rules. The covenant was restored as the prerequisite for salvation. In this respect, as Collins says, "Jubilees, which retells the stories of Genesis from a distinctly Mosaic perspective, with explicit halachic interests," stood "in striking contrast" to Enochic tradition.[8] Even more radically, the *Community Rule* would explore predestination as a way to neutralize God's loss of control of the created world and restore God's omnipotence.[9]

Enochic Judaism remained faithful to its own premises (Jews and gentiles are equally affected by evil), but was not insensitive to the criticism of having given too much power to evil, thereby dramatically reducing humanity's chances of being saved. The later Enochic tradition tried to solve the problem by following a different path. In the Parables of Enoch, we read that at the end of times in the last judgment, as expected, God and his Messiah Son of Man will save the righteous and condemn the unrighteous. The righteous have "honor" (merit, good works) and will be victorious in the name of God, while "the sinners" have no honor (no good works) and will not be saved in the name of God. But quite unexpectedly, in chapter 50, a third group emerges at the moment of the judgment. They are called "the others": they are sinners who repent and abandon the works of their hands. "They will have no honor in the presence of the Lord of Spirits, yet through His name they will be saved, and the Lord of Spirits will have mercy on them, for great is His mercy."[10]

In other words, the text explores the relation between the justice and the mercy of God and the role played by these two attributes of God in the judgment. According to the book of Parables, the righteous are saved according to God's justice and mercy, the sinners are condemned according to God's justice and mercy, but those who repent will be saved by God's mercy even though they should not be saved according to God's justice. Repentance makes God's mercy prevail over God's justice.

The Christian idea of the first coming of the Messiah as forgiver is a radical, yet very logical, variant of the Enochic system. The concept of the existence of a time of repentance immediately before the judgment and the prophecy that, at that point, "the sinners" will be divided between "the repentant" (the others) and "the unrepentant," is the necessary "premise" of the missions of John and Jesus, as narrated in the Synoptics.

The imminent coming of the last judgment, when the earth will be cleansed with fire, means urgent repentance and "forgiveness of sins" for those who in this world have "no honor." "Be baptized with water; otherwise, you will be baptized with the fire of judgment by the Son of Man": this seems to be, in essence, the original message of John the Baptist as understood by the Synoptics, an interpretation that does not contradict the interest of the Christian authors to present it as a prophecy of Christian Baptism (by the Holy Spirit).

Similar ideas find an echo also in the *Life of Adam and Eve*—a text generally dated to the first century CE—where the sinner Adam does penance for forty days, immersed in the waters of the Jordan (and it is not by accident that John baptized in the living water of the Jordan). The first man (and first sinner) is driven by one steadfast hope: "Maybe God will have mercy on me" (*L. A.E.* 4:3). His plea to be allowed back in the Garden of Eden will not be accepted, but at the time of his death, his soul will not be handed over to the devil, as his crime deserved, but carried off to heaven; so, God decided in his mercy, despite the complaints of Satan.

In the Christian interpretation, John the Baptist, as the precursor, could only announce the urgency of repentance and express hope in God's mercy. But with Jesus, it was another matter: he was the Son of Man who had authority on earth to forgive sins, who left to his disciples the power of forgiveness through Baptism "with the Holy Spirit," and who will return with the angels to perform the judgment with fire. After all, who can have more authority to forgive than the one whom God has delegated as the eschatological judge?

As the forgiver, Jesus was not sent to "the righteous," but to "sinners," so that they might repent. There is no evidence in the Synoptics of a universal mission of Jesus to every person: Jesus was sent to "the lost sheep of the house of Israel" (Matt. 10:6); the righteous do not need the doctor. Jesus was the doctor sent to heal sinners (Mark 2:17; Matt. 9:13), as Luke makes explicit: "I have come to call not the righteous but sinners to repentance" (Luke 5:32).

Reading the Synoptics in light of the book of Parables of Enoch sheds light also on some parables that the Christian tradition attributed to Jesus. The parable of the lost sheep (Matt. 18:10–14; Luke 15:1–7) defines the relationship between God and "the others"; Luke's parable of the prodigal son (15:11–32) reiterates the theme, but also adds a teaching about the relationship between "the righteous" and "the others"—between those who have honor and are saved because they have never abandoned the house of the Father and those who have no honor, and yet, are saved as well since they have repented and abandoned the works of their hands. The examples could be numerous, but no parable seems more enlightening to me than the one narrated by Matthew on the workers in the vineyard (Matt. 20:1–16). The householder who pays the same salary for different "measures" of work gives the full reward (salvation) to the "righteous" and to the "others," just as chapter 50 of the Parables claim that God will do in the last judgment. God's mercy ("Am I not allowed to do what I choose with what belongs to me? Or do you begrudge my generosity?") bests God's justice, or, as the letter of James will say, "Mercy triumphs over the judgment [κατακαυχᾶται ἔλεος κρίσεως]" (James 2:13).

The contrast with the traditions developed in the rabbinic movement could not be stronger. The rabbis freely discuss the relation between the two *middot*—God's measures of justice and mercy—providing flexible answers to the issue. Mishnah *Sotah* (1:7–9) sticks to the principle "with what measure a man metes it shall be measured to him again," and affirms that "with the same measure," God gives justice when punishing evil deeds and mercy when rewarding good deeds. On the contrary, the parallel text in Tosefta *Sotah* (3:1–4:19) claims that "the measure of Mercy is five hundred times greater than the measure of Justice." But the two divine attributes are never opposed as in the book of Parables and in the early

Christian tradition; on the contrary, their necessarily complementary nature is emphasized. Not accidentally, the "rabbinic" version of the parables will end with different words in which God's mercy is praised, but God's justice is not denied: "This one did more work in two hours than the rest of you did working all day long" (*y. Ber.* 2:8).

Paul the Apocalyptic Thinker

The problems of the origin of evil, the freedom of human will, and the forgiveness of sins are at the center of Paul's thought. As we have seen, these were not Pauline problems, but Second Temple Jewish problems. The originality of Paul was not in the questions, but in the answers.

In the letter to the Romans, Paul wrote to the Christian community of Rome: a Christian community of people—Jews and gentiles—who were former sinners, but who believed that they had received forgiveness of sins through Jesus' death. First of all, Paul reminds his readers that according to God's plan, the moral life of Jews is regulated by the Torah, while the moral life of gentiles is regulated by their own conscience (or the natural law of the universe—an idea that Paul borrowed from Hellenistic Judaism and its emphasis on the creative order as the main means of revelation of God's will). Then, Paul repeats the undisputed Second Temple belief that on the day of judgment, God "will repay according to each one's deeds" (Rom. 2:8). In no way did Paul dispute that if Jews and gentiles follow the Torah and their own conscience, respectively, they will obtain salvation. The problem is not the Mosaic law or the natural law; the problem is sin. With all Second Temple Jews, Paul acknowledges the presence of evil, and he quotes a passage of Scripture (Eccles. 7:2) to stress that evil is a universal problem. Every Second Temple Jew would have agreed. The problems are the implications and the remedies to this situation.

Paul sides with the apocalyptic tradition of a superhuman origin of evil. With the Enochic traditions, he shares a similar context of cosmic battle between the Prince of Light and the Prince of Darkness—"What fellowship is there between light and darkness? What agreement has Christ with Belial?" (2 Cor. 6:15)—as well as the hope for future redemption from the power of the devil: "The God of peace will soon crush Satan under your feet" (Rom. 16:20). What we can notice, however, is a certain—more pessimistic—view of the power of evil. In the Pauline system, the sin of Adam takes the place of the sin of the fallen angels: "Sin came into the world through one man [Adam], and death came through sin, and so death spread to all because all have sinned" (Rom. 5:12). Adam's sin is counterbalanced by the obedience of the "new Adam," Jesus. In order to create the conditions that made necessary the sacrifice of the heavenly Savior, Paul exploits the Enochic view of evil by radicalizing its power. While in Enoch, people (Jews and gentiles alike) are struggling against the influence of evil forces, Paul envisions a postwar scenario where "all, both Jews and Greeks, are under the power of sin" (Rom. 3:9). Adam and Eve have lost the battle against the devil, and as a result, all their descendants have been "enslaved to sin" (Rom. 6:6).

Slavery was an established social institution in the Roman Empire. When Paul was talking of people defeated and enslaved as a result of war, everybody knew exactly what the implications were for them and their children. Once the fight was over, the slaves were expected to resign themselves to their condition. Josephus voices the common sense of his time when he addresses the inhabitants of besieged Jerusalem and reminds them that:

> . . . [F]ighting for liberty is a right thing, but ought to have been done at first . . . To pretend now to shake off the yoke [of the Romans] was the work of such as had a mind to die miserably, not of such as were lovers of liberty . . . It is a strong and fixed law, even among brute beasts, as well as among men, to yield to those that are too strong for them. (J. W. 5.365–67)

The Romans admired and honored those who fought bravely for liberty, but despised rebellious slaves and condemned them to the cross. No one could expect the devil to be weaker than the Romans. Freedom could be regained only through the payment of a ransom.

Does that mean that all "slaves" are evil? Not necessarily. Once again, this was a matter of common experience. Being a slave does not necessarily equate to being "unrighteous." However, slaves are in a very precarious situation since they are not free, and at any moment, they could be commanded by their master to do evil things. Paul never questions the holiness and effectiveness of the Mosaic Torah or implies its failure. On the contrary, he reiterates the "superiority" of the Mosaic Torah and the Jewish covenant that has given to Jews a "a full awareness of the fall" (Rom. 3:10) and the "prophecies" about the coming of the Messiah. It is sin that must be blamed, not the Torah:

> The law is holy, and the commandment is holy and just and good. Did what is good, then, bring death to me? By no means! It was sin, working death in me through what is good, in order that sin might be shown to be sin, and through the commandment might become sinful beyond measure. For we know that the law is spiritual; but I am of the flesh, sold into slavery under sin. I do not understand my own actions. For I do not do what I want, but I do the very thing I hate. Now if I do what I do not want, I agree that the law is good. But in fact it is no longer I that do it, but sin that dwells within me. . . . For I delight in the law of God in my inmost self, but I see in my members another law at war with the law of my mind, making me captive to the law of sin that dwells in my members. Wretched man that I am! Who will rescue me from this body of death? (Rom. 7:12–17, 22–24)

It is this situation of total enslavement, not an intrinsic weakness of the "good" Torah, that leads Paul to do what the book of the Parables of Enoch had already done: that is, to seek hope for sinners not only in an heroic attachment to the law (according to God's justice), but also in an intervention of God's mercy, a gracious offer of forgiveness of sins "apart from the Law" (and God's justice). The evilness of human nature under the power of sin determines that "no human being will be justified by deeds prescribed by the law" (Rom. 3:20), but only by a gracious act of "justification by God's grace as gift, through the redemption that is in Christ Jesus, whom God put forward as a sacrifice of atonement by his blood" (Rom. 3:24–25). God had to react to an extreme situation of distress and counterbalance the action of the devil with an extreme act of mercy:

> For while we were still weak, at the right time Christ died for the ungodly. Indeed, rarely will anyone die for a righteous person—though perhaps for a good person someone might actually dare to die. But God proves his love for us in that while we still were sinners Christ died for us. Much more

surely then, now that we have been justified by his blood, will we be saved through him from the wrath of God. (Rom. 5:6–9)

The entire debate about "justification" and "salvation" in Paul is still too much affected by the framework of Christian theology. As an apocalyptic Jew and a follower of Jesus, Paul claimed that forgiveness of sins was the major accomplishment of Jesus the Messiah for Jews and gentiles alike in the cosmic battle that Jesus fought against demonic forces. Justification provides to sinners (Jews and gentiles alike) an antidote, or at least, much-needed relief, to the overwhelming power of evil—a second chance given to people without hope. They were "enemies," and yet, Christ died for them. In the language of the Parables of Enoch, those Jewish and gentile sinners who have received Baptism have put themselves among the "others" who are neither "righteous" nor "unrighteous," but are now "repented sinners." They have no merits to claim, according to God's justice, but have received justification by the mercy of God.

Paul is confident that those who are justified will also be "saved" in the judgment, but justification does not equal salvation.[11] Being forgiven of their sins is, for the sinners, an important step on the way to salvation, but it is not a guarantee of future salvation at the judgment where only deeds will be assessed. Hence, Paul continually reminds his readers of the necessity of remaining "blameless" after receiving Baptism. Having equated "justification by faith" (which Paul preached) with "(eternal) salvation by faith" (which Paul never preached) is one of the major distortions of the Christian reinterpretation of Paul.

Paul the Controversial Christian vs. James and Peter

Paul was just one voice in a debate that involved and divided the many components of Second Temple Judaism, and his position reflects the general position of the early Jesus movement. We may understand why Paul was viewed with suspicion by other Jews who did not share the apocalyptic idea of the superhuman origin of evil and rejected the Christian emphasis on the mission of forgiveness accomplished by

Jesus the Messiah. So, why was Paul also a controversial figure within the early Jesus movement? The answer cannot be attributed only to a natural suspicion toward a person who was long regarded as an "enemy," and, by his own admission, persecuted the church.

There is something in the theology of Paul that differentiated him from other Christian leaders (such as Peter and James). While other members of the early Jesus movement seem more interested in a perspective of restoration of the twelve tribes of Israel (see the incipit of the letter of James), in Paul, there is a special emphasis on the inclusion of gentiles. It was not a new problem: long before Paul, Jewish-Hellenistic communities had already developed models of inclusion of gentiles into their communities as "God-fearers." Paul, instead, did it in an apocalyptic fashion, along the lines of texts such as the Enochic Book of Dreams, where we read that, in the world to come, the "white sheep" (the righteous Jews) will be united with the "birds of the sky" (the righteous gentiles) to form the new people of God. In the Parables of Enoch, also, the Messiah Son of Man is indicated as the "light" of the gentiles.

Paul never claimed to have been the first to baptize gentiles. What is distinctive is the enthusiasm with which Paul devoted his life to preaching to gentiles. But there is something that is far more controversial. Paul seemed to have pushed for an equal status of gentiles within the new community.

The apparent unanimity reached at the so-called Council of Jerusalem did not solve all the problems related to the presence of gentiles in the church. Despite the fact that baptized gentiles were not required to be circumcised or to keep the Law of Moses, the controversy exploded over the relationship between Jews and gentiles within the community, especially during communal meals. Were they to sit at separate tables or might they join the same table—Jew and gentile, male and female, free and slave?

Paul exploited his pessimistic view about the sinfulness of human nature in order to affirm the "equality in sin" of Jews and gentiles within the church. The parting of Christianity from its Jewish apocalyptic roots would lead later Christian theology to wonder whether justification and forgiveness of sins are the same thing; but in the first-century apocalyptic worldview the two terms are synonymous. The most controversial aspect of Paul's preaching was rather his statement that justification—that is, the gift of forgiveness of sins by the Christ—comes into effect "by faith only." While most of the first Jewish followers of Jesus would talk of sin as a temptation (allowing a larger role to the freedom of human will), the metaphor of slavery leaves room only for a personal "yes" (and makes meaningless the idea of any prerequisites or any claim of "superiority" of the Jews over the gentiles, and therefore, any rationale for a distinction between the two groups within the new community). If only a "yes" is asked of the sinners, there is no room for "works" and justification is "by faith only." If, instead, sin is a temptation and sinners maintain a certain degree of freedom, then they can, and should, be asked to "prove" their faith with some "works." This is the move the letter of James makes by claiming that "a person is justified by works and not by faith alone," and that "faith apart from works is dead" (James 2:19–26). Justification is the result of a synergy between humans and God:

> [God] gives all the more grace; therefore it says, "God opposes the proud, but gives grace to the humble." Submit yourselves therefore to God. Resist the devil, and he will flee from you. Draw near to God, and he will draw near to you. Cleanse your hands, you sinners, and purify your hearts, you double-minded. Lament and mourn and weep. Let your laughter be turned into mourning and your joy into dejection. Humble yourselves before the Lord, and he will exalt you. (James 4:6–10)

Not accidentally, the letter of James does not even mention the death of Jesus; the preaching of Jesus, the "law of liberty" he taught, is the prerequisite for justification. For Paul, instead, the death and sacrifice of Jesus is the only thing that counts as a unilateral and gracious act of mercy: "I do not nullify the grace of God; for if justification comes through the law, then Christ died for nothing" (Gal. 2:21).

The theological dispute had profound practical implications in the life of the church. The incident at Antioch shows that Paul and James had opposite views of how Jews and gentiles should coexist in the church. James opposed the sharing of tables among Jews and gentiles, while Paul favored it. Peter was caught in between. At the beginning, Peter conformed to the practice of the church of Antioch, but after "certain people came from James," he "drew back." Paul reacted vehemently, confronting Peter and accusing him of "hypocrisy." For Paul, there is no distinction between Jewish and gentile church members because they were equally sinners and were equally justified by the grace of God through Jesus. Concerning justification, Jews cannot claim any superiority, unless they deny the grace of God: "I do not nullify the grace of God; for if justification comes through the law, then Christ died for nothing" (Gal. 2:21).

Does that mean that Paul "abolished" the distinction between Jews and gentiles in this world *tout court*? This does not seem to be the case. Very interestingly, Paul's famous saying about the equality between Jews and gentiles comes in a broader context that included "male and female" and "slave and free": "There is no longer Jew or Greek, there is no longer slave or free, there is no longer male and female; for all of you are one in Christ Jesus" (Gal. 3:28). In Paul's view, these categories are somehow altered in this world; there is no longer enmity and opposition in Christ. Yet, none of these categories is abolished. Paul asks Philemon to welcome his fugitive slave Onesimus as a brother in Christ, and yet, does not tell Philemon to free all his slaves, using the argument that in Jesus Christ, there is no longer slave or free. Paul mentions Priscilla before her husband, Aquila, in the ministry of Christ (Rom. 16:3–4), and yet, reiterates that "the head of the woman is the man" (1 Cor. 11:3) when he could have claimed that in Jesus Christ, there is no longer male and female. Paul proclaims the end of any enmity between Jews and gentiles in Christ, and yet . . . Why should he have claimed only in this case that such a distinction is no longer valid? Ironically, traditional Christian theology has stressed the definitive "end" of the distinction between Jews and gentiles as a divine decree and has never taken an equally strong stance about the "abolishment" of any distinction of gender and social status. Either Paul abolished all three categories or he did not abolish any of them.

Summary and Conclusion

Paul was a Second Temple Jew, a former Pharisee who became a member and a leader of the early Jesus movement. Like many Second Temple Jews (also outside the Jesus movement), as a result of his "conversion," Paul embraced the apocalyptic view of the superhuman origin of evil and looked at the sinners not only as people responsible for their own actions, but also as victims of a supernatural evil. Like others, he wished for, and expected, some help from heaven to counterbalance the power of evil.

With the other members of the Christian group, Paul shared the idea that Jesus the Messiah had come to earth as the Son of Man to bring forgiveness to sinners, and he believed that Jesus would soon return to carry out a judgment. More than other members of the early Jesus movement, Paul strongly believed that this message of forgiveness included gentile sinners as well, and he decided to devote his life to preaching to the gentiles. Contrary to other members of the Jesus movement, he refused to accept that baptized gentiles had a different or inferior status within the church, as he could not see any distinction between a Jewish sinner and a gentile sinner: they had both been forgiven "by faith only." This does not mean that he advocated the abolishment of the distinction between Jews and gentiles in this world; on the contrary, as in the case of gender and social distinctions, he accepted it as an inevitable (and perhaps, even providential) reality until the end of times, when these distinctions would eventually disappear.

As a Second Temple Jew, Paul never questioned the validity of the Torah; his only concern was the inability of people to obey the Torah. Paul was a Torah-observant Jew who believed that "justification by faith" was a gift offered through Jesus the Messiah to all "sinners" (not only to gentiles). Does that mean that he believed that Jews should abandon the obedience of the Torah and that no Jew could be saved without Baptism? Not at all. While repeating the common Jewish teaching that "all people are sinners," Paul shared the apocalyptic idea that the judgment will be according to deeds and that humankind is divided between the "righteous" and the "unrighteous." But now that the time of the end has come, the unrighteous have been offered the possibility to repent and receive justification through forgiveness. Paul preached to gentiles, but his message was neither addressed to gentiles only nor uniquely pertinent to them. Exactly the same gospel was announced to Jews and gentiles—the good news of the gift of forgiveness: "I had been entrusted with the task of preaching the gospel to the uncircumcised, just as Peter had been to the circumcised" (Gal. 2:7).

Paul had a much more pessimistic view of the power of evil. He compared the situation of humankind to a population defeated and enslaved by the devil, but he would have shared the principle that only the sick need a doctor. The sick include Jews and gentiles alike, although not all of them. The righteous do not need a doctor.

To say that the Jews have the Torah while the gentiles have Christ does not faithfully represent the position of Paul. In Paul's view, Christ is God's gift not to gentiles, but to sinners. The righteous (Jews and gentiles) will be saved if they have done good deeds. But Paul is conscious of the fact that the power of evil makes it incredibly difficult for all humankind to be righteous: for the Jews to follow the Torah and for the gentiles to follow their own conscience. He preaches the good news that, at the end of times, sinners (Jews and Gentiles alike) are offered the extraordinary possibility to repent and be justified in Christ by God's mercy apart from God's justice. Paul was not Lutheran: he never taught "salvation by faith only" to humankind, but announced to sinners, "justification (that is, forgiveness of past sins) by faith." Paul did not preach only two ways of salvation, but rather three: righteous Jews have the Torah, righteous gentiles have their own conscience, and sinners—Jews and gentiles alike, who have fallen without hope under the power of evil—have Christ the forgiver.

◆◆◆

Paul in an Enochian Context:
Response to Gabriele Boccaccini

Albert I. Baumgarten

Il est admis que la vérité d'un homme, c'est d'abord ce qu'il cache.
—A. Malraux, *Antimémoires*

Gabriele Boccaccini begins his discussion of "Re-Reading Paul as a Second-Temple Jewish Author" by clearing away some of the rubble left by approaches to Paul that have now been successfully challenged and opening the field to a more appropriate appreciation of Paul the Jew. Boccaccini states correctly and emphatically:

> Paul should be regarded as nothing other than a Second Temple Jew. *What else should he have been?* [emphasis mine]. Paul was born a Jew, of Jewish parents, was circumcised, and nothing in his work supports (or even suggests) the idea that he became (or regarded himself as) an apostate.[12] On the contrary, Paul was the member of the early Jesus movement and with strength and unmistakable clarity proudly claimed his Jewishness and declared that God also did not reject God's covenant with the chosen people: "Has God rejected his people? By no means! I myself am an Israelite, a descendant of Abraham, a member of the tribe of Benjamin." (Rom. 11:1; cf. Phil. 3:5)

Yet, once we take Paul through the Second Temple Jewish portal, there are numerous paths down which scholars can allow him to walk. As we have learned from the Dead Sea Scrolls, a renewed appreciation of what was once dubbed "Apocrypha and Pseudepigrapha," and other Second Temple Jewish works preserved in different sources, the world of Second Temple Jews was far from uniform. There were many varieties and alternatives in those days, with the outcome—which varieties would survive and which not, which variety, if any, would become dominant—far from certain. Paul's life, as Boccaccini concludes, was "an occurrence in the context of the diversity of Second Temple Judaism." However, if context in interpreting an author is crucial, we now have a seemingly endless choice of contexts in which to place Paul the Second Temple Jew.

It is at this point that Paul himself is least helpful and that Malraux's comment, in the epigram above, is most pertinent: "the truth of a man is above all what he conceals." There is so much about himself that Paul left hidden and that makes it so hard to establish the context in which he should be placed. I will mention only a few obvious ones. Paul wrote little detail about his life prior to the time he composed his letters. Perhaps the only thing that is clear is that he was a Pharisee who came from the Diaspora and zealously persecuted those who believed in the faith he later proclaimed. Yet, what did it mean for him to be a Diaspora Pharisee? I once heard a colleague claim that Paul received a "typical Diaspora Pharisee education," but I wondered: Do we know anything at all about a Diaspora Pharisee education, and, certainly, can we distinguish between a typical Diaspora Pharisee education, which Paul supposedly received, and an atypical one? Next, exactly what was the nature of the Jesus movement, as Paul first encountered it? How justified are we scholars in calling on the canonical Gospels (or any other Gospels) as providing the key to the message of the Jesus movement that Paul first knew? For example: the account of the Lord's Supper that Paul transmitted as he "received it from the Lord himself" in 1 Cor. 11:23-26 is a beginning that leaves much unspecified. Even more importantly, what was wrong with that Jesus movement that it aroused his zeal? Then, after Paul became "the apostle to the gentiles," just what were the charges on which Paul claimed that he received thirty-nine lashes five times (from Jews) and was beaten with rods (by Romans) three times (2 Cor. 11:24-25)? For what infraction(s) was Paul considered deserving of punishment by these different authorities? What did he mean when he wrote that if he is still advocating circumcision, then why is he still being persecuted (Gal. 5:11)?

———

Boccaccini proposes to fill in some of the missing pieces and resolve some of these uncertainties. He begins by opening an important door: "It would be simplistic to reduce the early 'Christian' message to a generic announcement about the imminent coming of the kingdom of God, and about Jesus as the expected Messiah." To avoid this simplistic understanding, Boccaccini proposes to put the Jesus movement in the context of the Enochic traditions, of the questions asked and answers offered to the meaning of life and Jewish experience in the Enochic literature.

This step is justified by appeal to Mark 2 and parallels, where Jesus is identified as the "Son of Man" who has the authority to forgive sins. Boccaccini then amplifies this idea, which goes back to Dan. 7:13–14, with the help of the Enochic traditions. These traditions developed the notion of evil, ascribing cosmic evil to the rebellion of the fallen angels (1 *Enoch* 10:8, for example). As a result, in a universe afflicted by superhuman evil, human beings could not do good deeds and all humans were sinners. Only the Messiah, at the end of days, could forgive sins.

If this was the nature of the Jesus movement, as Paul knew it, Paul was thus much more than "a Pharisee to whom the name of the future Messiah was revealed and who believed himself to be living at the end of times." He took the Enochic foundations of the message a radical step further. Paul argued that as a result of the sin of Adam and Eve, all humans were enslaved to sin (Rom. 6:6). Freedom from this slavery—as freedom from the usual circumstances of slavery, familiar to all in the ancient world—could only be obtained by payment of a ransom. God's gift, by grace, achieved as a sacrifice of atonement in Christ Jesus, was this ransom (Rom. 3:24–25). It was an antidote to the overwhelming power of evil—a second chance given to people without hope. In Enochic terms, those who have received Baptism are justified by the mercy of God. This allowed Paul to take a further step: if all were slaves to evil and totally hopeless, but then justified by faith, then he could also argue for the equal status of gentiles within the new community. All were equally sinners and were equally justified by the grace of God through Jesus, but this conclusion, then, involved Paul in controversy with other believers, such as James and Peter.

This interpretation allows Boccaccini to offer a reappraisal of Gal. 3:28, according to which, there is "no longer Jew or Greek, there is no longer slave or free, male and female; for all of you are one in Christ Jesus." Boccaccini emphasizes that Paul did not abolish slavery: he did not tell Philemon to free his slaves. All of Galatians 3:28, Boccaccini suggests, must therefore be understood in a more nuanced way that usual. Concerning Jews and Greeks, at most—according to Boccaccini—Paul proclaimed "the end of an enmity between Jews and gentiles in Christ," but the usual understanding, according to which Paul proclaimed the absolute "end" of this distinction, must be reconsidered. As Boccaccini concludes, "[e]ither Paul abolished all three categories or he did not abolish any of them."

———

In the summary of his interpretation above, I have emphasized the Enochic aspects of Boccaccini's interpretation of the Jesus movement, and especially, of Paul. What is critical to Boccaccini's case is his weaving together of Enochic explanations of cosmic evil with Paul's explicit appeal to the responsibility of Adam and Eve for the dismal condition of humanity, making all humans, Jew and gentile alike, victims of a supernatural evil.

However, Michael Stone has argued that there were two parallel and virtually mutually exclusive explanations of evil current among Second Temple Jews:

> Two explanations of the state of the world, the Enochic and the Adamic, contrast with one another. According to the first, the sins committed by and the teachings perpetuated by the fallen angels, the "sons of God," were the source of evil and the cause of the state of the world. Quite different stories, attributing the state of the world to Adam's disobedience in general, or more specifically to Eve's seduction by the serpent, also circulated in Jewish works of the Second Temple period, as well as in the New Testament. The Enochic explanation of the state of the world,

attributing it in one form or another to the fall of the Watchers, occurs almost only in works connected with or used by the Qumran sect. Adam apocrypha and legends are developments of the stories in Genesis 1–3 are strikingly absent from Qumran. In other words, at Qumran, where the Enochic (and Noachic) pattern was prominent, the Adamic explanation is scarcely mentioned. When the Adamic explanation occurs in other contexts, the Enochic-Watchers tradition is in the background or absent. The implications of the complementary distribution of these two ways of explaining the state of the world are weighty.[13]

There can be no doubt that Paul belongs in the Adamic camp. If the two strands of thought are as distinct as Stone suggests, how plausible is it to argue that Paul understood the Jesus movement in Enochic terms and took the Enochic worldview as the basis for his contention for justification by faith, for Jew and gentile alike? Is it so easy to propose, as Boccaccini does, that "in the Pauline system, the sin of Adam takes the place of the sin of the fallen angels"?[14] Some further elaboration, clarification, and engagement with Stone's suggested distinction seem required.

———

These reflections on Boccaccini's remarks indicate the difficulties inherent in finding a convincing context against which to situate Paul as a Second Temple Jewish author. I want to conclude with a caveat.

One of the conventions in the life of figures such as Paul was to claim credibility as a result of their difficulties with the authorities. In the public eye, trouble with the legal institutions of the time somehow made figures such as Paul, who claimed access to the higher powers of the world, seem more believable. In those circumstances, it seemed almost worthwhile for some who did not have easy access to ordinary positions of power in society to provoke the authorities (up to a point) and to seem to have paid some price. This could serve as the best evidence one might bring that one was to be taken seriously. Paradoxical as it might seem at first, to seem to have opposed the regime and to have been punished for it was an asset.

For example, Juvenal noted that:

Nowadays no astrologer has credit unless he has been imprisoned in some distant camp, with chains clanking on either arm; none believe in his powers unless he has been condemned and all but put to death, having just contrived to get deported to a Cyclad, or to escape at last from the diminutive Seriphos. (*Sat.* 6.560–564)

Juvenal exaggerated to make his point, but he was not alone. According to Lucian (*Peregr.* 18), Peregrinus deliberately criticized the authorities in Rome in order to provoke their opposition. It worked as intended: as a result of this behavior, Peregrinus rose high in prestige in the eyes of the masses.

Therefore, can Paul really taken at his word when he claimed that he received thirty-nine lashes five times (from Jews) and was beaten with rods (by Romans) three times (2 Cor. 11:24–25)? Even if this is exaggerated, Paul's punishments at the hands of the authorities should serve us as a warning. Some Jews and/or Romans of the time, who presumably knew more than we ever will about what Paul preached and practiced, considered him deserving of punishment. If Boccaccini's Enochian context for Jesus, and especially, for Paul is taken as meaningful, it should account not only for Paul's message, but also help explain why some Jews and/or Romans of the time found it offensive. This aspect is important for completing the intellectual circle. We should never make Paul such a "good" Second Temple Jew (even in Enochian terms) that we forget that Paul was perceived by others of that era as a "bad" Jew, in trouble with other Jews and/or Romans, and worthy of being punished.

However, Paul was not alone as a Second Temple Jew whose views and practices were denounced by other Jews. As Flusser has suggested, the original curse against separatists (של פורשים), which later became the controversial and much disputed curse of the heretics (ברכת המינים), began as a response to the sort of separatism we now know from 4QMMT.[15] When we re-read Paul as Second Temple Jewish author and identify the Second Temple Jewish context into which he fits best, and then, understand why that message would have been disturbing to other Jews of his time and place, he was far from unique. In every sense, Paul was a Jew of his times.

♦ ♦ ♦

Another Response to Gabriele Boccaccini

Daniel Boyarin

This is a very hard stance for me to respond to. Not because I don't find it valuable or because I disagree with it, but because it seems to me the product of such eminent good sense and perspicacious presentation that I hardly find anything to say, other than *kalos!* But since one must say something, in order to be responsive, I would like to pick a nit—one that I think is of some importance.

Jews do not speak of conversion within Jewishness; conversion, to the extent that it means anything in traditional Jewish parlance, can only mean coming from outside and joining the Jewish people. There is no word for ceasing to be a Jew, once again, in traditional Jewish parlance. It is hard for me to understand, therefore, Boccaccini's claim that:

> If today a Reform Rabbi became an ultraorthodox Jew, or vice versa, we would also describe such an experience in terms of "conversion." Likewise, Paul's conversion should be understood not as a chapter in the parting of the ways between Christianity and Judaism but as an occurrence in the context of the diversity of Second Temple Judaism.

Actually, *we* wouldn't refer to the transformation from Orthodox to Reform as a conversion—never. Depending on perspective, the first would be called "repentance" and the second, becoming a sinner—or the second, becoming enlightened, and the first, returning to the Middle Ages—but no Jew, either of the Orthodox nor of the Reform persuasion, would refer to such an event as a conversion. Unless we adopt, from outside, the notion that conversion is defined by a conversion experience—Segal's option, which Boccaccini implicitly rejects—there is no sense in which Paul's adherence to a radical Jewish apocalyptic sect constitutes a conversion at all. In other words, I agree with Boccaccini—but even more so than he does! Similarly, Boccaccini undermines his own most radical insight—as well as his commitment to a "radical New Perspective" on Paul—when he writes,

> As a result of his "conversion," Paul fully embraced the Christian apocalyptic worldview and the claim that Jesus the Messiah had already come (and would return at the end of times). This included the explanation of why the Messiah had come before the end. The early Christians had an answer; Jesus did not come simply to reveal his name and identity. Jesus came as the Son of Man who had "authority on earth to forgive sins." (Mark 2 and parallels)

This, I'm afraid, is not radical enough after Boccaccini has correctly written that there were no early Christians, and thus, no *Christian apocalyptic worldview*" either; it's a contradiction in logic. This is especially the case since Boccaccini himself, in only the very next sentence, makes the absolutely unassailable point that "[t]he idea of the Messiah as the forgiver on earth makes perfect sense as a development of the ancient Enochic apocalyptic tradition." So, which is it: a "Christian" answer or one that grows entirely within Second Temple Judaic ideas? I go for the latter, which I think is Boccaccini's strongest point. Indeed, what makes the Jesus movement special is its revelation of the name and identity of the Messiah, Son of Man, as Jesus of Nazareth *tout court*.

If we forget entirely the appellation "Christian" until it becomes a native term—long after Paul at any rate—and abandon notions of conversion for Paul, all the rest of Boccaccini's thesis falls into place like the endgame of a successful game of solitaire. Especially brilliant is the recognition that "justification" is not salvation, but acquittal for repentants, the "others" of Enochian tradition. Boccaccini, building on concepts developed by such scholars as Mark D. Nanos and Paula Fredriksen, as well as others, has put together a new and compelling synthesis, and especially, added in and focused on the Enochian context that ought to fundamentally change the way that Paul is taught and preached from now on. But will it?

Notes

1. Magnus Zetterholm, *Approaches to Paul: A Student's Guide to Recent Scholarship* (Minneapolis: Fortress Press, 2009).

2. Pamela Eisenbaum, *Paul Was Not a Christian: The Original Message of a Misunderstood Apostle* (New York: HarperOne, 2009).

3. Gabriele Boccaccini, "James, Paul (and Jesus): Early Christianity and Early Christianities," in *Middle Judaism: Jewish Thought, 300 BCE—200 CE* (Minneapolis: Fortress Press, 1991), 213–28.

4. Daniel Boyarin, *A Radical Jew: Paul and the Politics of Identity* (Berkeley: University of California Press, 1994).

5. Boccaccini, "James, Paul (and Jesus)."

6. Alan F. Segal, *Paul the Convert: The Apostolate and Apostasy of Saul the Pharisee* (New Haven: Yale University Press, 1990).

7. Ishay Rosen-Zvi, *Demonic Desires: "Yetzer Hara" and the Problem of Evil in Late Antiquity* (Philadelphia: University of Pennsylvania Press, 2011); Piero Capelli, *Il male: storia di un'idea nell'ebraismo dalla Bibbia alla Qabbalah* (Florence: Società Editrice Fiorentina, 2012); Miryam T. Brand, *Evil Within and Without: The Source of Sin and Its Nature as Portrayed in Second Temple Literature* (Journal of Ancient Judaism Supplements 9; Göttingen: Vandenhoeck & Ruprecht, 2013).

8. John J. Collins, "How Distinctive Was Enochic Judaism?" in *Meghillot: Studies in the Dead Sea Scrolls V-VI*, ed. Mosheh Bar-Asher and Emanuel Tov (Haifa: University of Haifa, 2007), 17–34.

9. Gabriele Boccaccini, *Beyond the Essene Hypothesis: The Parting of the Ways between Qumran and Enochic Judaism* (Grand Rapids: Eerdmans, 1998).

10. Gabriele Boccaccini, "The Evilness of Human Nature in *1 Enoch, Jubilees*, Paul, and *4 Ezra*: A Second Temple Jewish Debate," in *Fourth Ezra and 2 Baruch: Reconstruction after the Fall*, ed. Matthias Henze, Gabriele Boccaccini, and Jason Zurawski (Leiden: Brill, 2013).

11. Chris VanLandingham, *Judgment and Justification in Early Judaism and the Apostle Paul* (Peabody, MA: Hendrickson, 2006).

12. Boccaccini, *Middle Judaism*.

13. M. E. Stone, *Ancient Judaism: New Visions and Views* (Grand Rapids and Cambridge: Eerdmans, 2011), 32.

14. Although it verges on the academically "heretical" in the context of an Enoch seminar, Stone's conclusions cast a shadow of doubt and a burden of demanding more explicit proof on Carlos A. Segovia's conclusions, circulated at the end of the meeting in Rome, that "connections between Paul's worldview

and that of Enochic Judaism are salient and manifold in spite of their observable differences." At the same time, Paul's explanation of evil in Adamic terms strengthens his connection with *4 Ezra* and *2 Baruch*, as noted by Segovia in his circulated conclusions.

15. D. Flusser, "4QMMT and the Benediction Against the *Minim*," in *Judaism of the Second Temple Period: Qumran and Apocalypticism* (trans. A. Yadin; Grand Rapids: Eerdmans, 2007), 70–118.

PART I

Paul and Scripture/
Paul in Scripture

Who Is the Righteous Remnant in Romans 9–11?

The Concept of Remnant in Early Jewish Literature and Paul's Letter to the Romans

Shayna Sheinfeld

While the idea that the early Jesus followers are the remnant of Israel is scattered throughout the New Testament, usually in reference to their identity over and against other Jews, a direct engagement with the concept in relation to its Jewish context[1] only occurs in Paul's Letter to the Romans: the word λεῖμμα (remnant) is first used in 9:27, and then, again in 11:6. Both times, the term is placed in a larger pericope concerning the salvation of Israel and Paul's defense that God did not abandon God's people. The concept of a righteous remnant echoes the idea as found throughout Jewish Scripture, and is inherited not only by the New Testament and early Christians, but by other early Jewish communities as well. Little work has been done on the notion of a remnant within these texts, and thus, little groundwork has been laid for placing Paul's usage of the term in its contemporaneous literary context.

In this chapter, I explore how Paul's use of the remnant concept intersects with the concept as it appears in other texts from the Second Temple period. In doing so, I propose that Paul's use of remnant language participates in a strategy typical of Jewish groups from this period: Paul uses the language of the remnant in order to convince his audience that his interpretation of Israelite tradition is indeed the correct one. In order to show Paul's participation in the remnant trope, I examine the usage of the remnant concept in two other early Jewish texts—the *Damascus Document* and *4 Ezra*. The *Damascus Document* identifies the remnant as its own sectarian group, separated from the other Israelites through their relocation to Damascus, while *4 Ezra* uses the remnant as a way to convince its audience that they should follow the agenda proposed by the text—that is, Torah observance and belief in the imminent *eschaton*. By establishing Paul's participation in early Jewish uses of the remnant, I show not only how Romans 9–11 acts as the climax to the epistle as a whole, but how this climax is reached through Paul's participation in Judaism, not through the establishment of some new identity.

The use of the concept of the remnant in the early Jewish period—including Paul's own usage—stems from Jewish Scripture.[2] The notion is especially prolific in the Prophets. While the concept of remnant can carry a negative connotation, it most often refers to the Israelites left after divine punishment as a locus for the restoration of the community.[3] Stanley Stowers states this succinctly:

> The Hebrew Bible tells many stories about times when the leaders and a large number of the people acted unfaithfully under particular conditions. These are [. . .] stories of salvation. Some of the faithful remain, and God finds a way to use the remnant to bring Israel back to him. There is never a serious question of God abandoning the covenant and revoking his promises to Israel.[4]

Thus, the basic idea of the remnant in the biblical texts reflects the idea that after divine punishment, which is a direct result of the

Israelites not keeping God's covenant, God will, in fact, continue his covenant with the Israelites through the restoration of the remaining (read: remnant) community, and this restoration is in itself "an act of divine mercy."[5] Within the Hebrew Bible and Septuagint, the remnant idea is most prevalent in the latter prophets, such as Isaiah, and in reference to the Babylonian exile. It was an idea, however, that held great sway in the early Jewish period as well.

The Remnant in the *Damascus Document*

One example of remnant usage from the early Jewish period can be found in the ideology of the Dead Sea Scrolls. The *Damascus Document* is a sectarian text from the early Qumran community's history that relates a description of the origins of the group. The text can be divided into two principal parts: columns 1-8 and 19-20 contain the Admonition, while the intervening columns 9-16 contain legal material.[6] The Admonition contains, among other things, a veiled history of the community through the sectarian perception of their own biblical heritage, connecting their origins in the righteous remnant of the Babylonian exile to the perceived present, and thus, establishing the community as the original righteous remnant from the pre-exilic time.[7] The text begins as follows:

> And now, listen, all those who know justice, and understand the actions of God; for he has a dispute with all flesh and will carry out judgment on all those who spurn him. For when they were unfaithful in forsaking him, he hid his face from Israel and from his sanctuary and delivered them up to the sword. But when he remembered the covenant with the forefathers, he saved a remnant for Israel and did not deliver them up to destruction. And at the period of wrath, three hundred and ninety years after having delivered them up into the hands of Nebuchadnezzar, king of Babylon, he visited them and caused to sprout from Israel and from Aaron a shoot of a plant [. . .]. And God appraised their deeds, because they sought him with an undivided heart, and raised up for them a Teacher of Righteousness, in order to direct them in the path of his heart.[8]

According to this history of the community, the remnant lies dormant until the arrival of the Teacher of Righteousness, who is able to guide the group along the correct path. While the allusion to the remnant does indeed reference the period of the Babylonian exile, the text provides a clear connection between membership in the current community and the exilic remnant, thus alluding positively to a continuation of the remnant community,[9] as well as emphasizing the temporal nature of the remnant.

The continuation of the Admonition is explicit: anyone outside of the community is depicted as rejected by God. This rejection begins, like the community itself, at the time of the Babylonian destruction of the first temple and the exile. Thus, the Israelites are split into two groups—those of the remnant and those who violate the covenant through various ways (I 13–21) and kindle God's wrath against them (II 1). The text calls on those who would enter this community to leave behind their sin (II 2) because God loves those who follow the precepts, but will destroy those who do not, leaving not even one survivor (II 6b–7a). The text again addresses the remnant in II 11–12, discussing how God raises up "men of renown for himself, to leave a remnant for the land and in order to fill the face of the world with their offspring." Following this section is an overview of biblical history, describing Noah, the patriarchs, Jacob's sons, and the Israelites in Egypt and in the desert, identifying, through each description, those who were wicked (the majority) and those few who "remained steadfast in God's precepts" (III 12), teaching them "hidden matters in which all Israel had gone astray" (III 13). Those singled out here act as a precursor to the remnant community at Qumran.

The *Damascus Document* uses the concept of the remnant in order to reinforce the dualism the community expounded. This can be seen in two different ways: first, in II 6b–7a, the total destruction of those outside the community indicates that there is no part of the wicked who will be the saved—no remnant will remain from the evil group. These outsiders are not some foreign "Other," but the rest of Israel who remain outside of the community.[10] The concept of remnant is also used to define the community, those who were saved from the first exile, who sought God and the covenant, and who followed the Teacher of Righteousness. Paul Dinter notes that "despite a certain tendency to use the phrase 'remnant/survivors' generally (though note that the negative epithet is always applied to their enemies), there is also present a consistent identification of the remnant with the Qumran community."[11] That is, while language of remnant may be used in a broad sense, the theologically loaded term is used only in reference to the sectarian community. In the *eschaton*, this remnant will inhabit the land and "fill the face of the world with their offspring" (II 12). The concept of a salvaged remnant that remains true to the covenant and thus is the locus for restoration can be found first in scriptural sources, but the idea that this remnant is temporally located now, immediately before the divine judgment, and that this separation of the remnant from the others is, in fact, an act of divine mercy before the event, is unique to the sectarian literature of Qumran.

In the *Damascus Document*, the use of the concept of the remnant is both traditional and innovative. The documents from Qumran indicate a community that clings to the idea that they represented the true Israel, the elect, and they use remnant language in order to express this idea. As I will explore below, Paul uses the remnant idea similarly in Romans, especially in relation to separating Israel itself into two distinct groups: those of the elect or remnant, and everyone else. The *Damascus Document*, however, also uses the remnant idea in order to refer collectively to those outside of the Qumran community;[12] that the concept is used to refer both to the sectarian community and to their enemies demonstrates that the theological importance of the term is not hinged upon the word itself. Instead, the idea of the remnant is only theologically significant when it is applied to the Qumran community. The *Damascus Document* locates the remnant community as existing before divine punishment occurs, having removed themselves from the other Israelites to "Damascus."

The Remnant in *4 Ezra*

The idea of the remnant in *4 Ezra* is tied intricately to the idea of election.[13] Dated after the destruction of the second temple, usually around 100 CE,[14] *4 Ezra* addresses questions of theodicy relating to the election of Israel and divine punishment in response to the destruction of the second temple.[15] The text comprises seven episodes, the first three containing dialogues between Ezra and the angel Uriel, the fourth transitional episode containing a dialogue and an eschatological vision, the fifth and sixth being eschatological visions, and the seventh, final episode consisting of a re-giving of the Torah, along with other secret books, from God to Ezra.

The idea that Israel is elect is not challenged in *4 Ezra*. Throughout the first three episodes, Israel's election is emphasized through Ezra's arguments against the current degraded status of Israel. In the first dialogue, Ezra reminds God that when the peoples and the nations were sinning, God chose Abraham and "made with him an everlasting covenant, and promised him that you would not forsake his descendants" (3:15).[16] Ezra continues, highlighting the patriarchs to whom God made promises and emphasizing the giving of the law on Mount Sinai (3:19). Ezra's lament is over the evil heart, which God did not take away from Israel (3:20), causing Israel to continue to sin. However, Ezra asks, is Babylon better than Israel, that they should have dominion over her (3:28–36)? Ezra's lament acknowledges Israel's election, but questions why Israel was allowed to sin if she is indeed God's chosen nation. Likewise, in the second dialogue with the angel, Ezra reflects on the chosenness of Israel, selected by God from "all the multitude of people" (5:28), and subsequently, scattered among the nations. Ezra argues that since the people of Israel are God's elect, it should be God who punishes them directly, not the nations (5:30). Again, in the third dialogue, Ezra reiterates Israel's status as the elect:

> All of this I have spoken before you, O Lord, because you have said that it was for us that you created this world. As for the other nations which have descended from Adam, you have said that they are nothing, and that they are like spittle, and you have compared their abundance to a drop from a bucket. And now, O Lord, behold, these nations, which are reputed as nothing, domineer over us and devour us. But we your people, whom you have called your first-born, only begotten, zealous for you, and most dear, have been given into their hands. If the world has indeed been created for us, why do we not posses our world as an inheritance? (6:55–59)

None of Ezra's complaints throughout the first three episodes call into question Israel's status as elect, but they do question God's role in the current political situation in light of Israel's election. In other words, Ezra asks how God could allow the nations of the earth, who are like "spittle," to conquer and rule over Israel.

The angel Uriel responds to Ezra's concerns about the elect of Israel in the third episode, where Uriel notes that the world was made for the sake of Israel, but that the "entrances of this world were made narrow and sorrowful and toilsome; they are few and evil, full of danger and involved in great hardships. But the entrances of the future world are broad and safe, and really yield the fruit of immortality" (7:11-14). Thus, the righteous must first pass through the harsh realities of this world before gaining admittance into the next. This leads to the discussion of the many versus the few: "the Most High made this world for the sake of the many, but the world to come for the sake of only a few" (8:1).[17] The righteous are never defined explicitly as Israel here, but based on Ezra's own concerns with Israel's election, the righteous should indeed be identified with Israel, who must first pass through the hardships of this world.[18]

At no point in these early passages in 4 Ezra is the election of Israel specifically associated with the remnant. It is not until the apocalyptic visions of episodes 5-6 that the remnant is connected with the elect—that is, with Israel. The fifth episode is a vision of an eagle and a lion, reminiscent of Daniel 7, which requires an interpretation from the angel.[19] In the interpretation, the angel tells Ezra that the lion represents the Messiah, who will judge the nations and destroy them, after which "he will deliver in mercy the remnant of my people, those who have been saved throughout my borders, and he will make them joyful until the end comes, the day of judgment, of which I spoke to you at the beginning" (12:34). This interpretation suggests two main points. First, the remnant belongs to the tribe of Israel, in spite of Uriel's universal language from the third episode.[20] Second, the remnant may only derive from those who are within the borders of the land; members of Israel who live in the Diaspora, then, are not to be saved.[21]

Episode 6 contains a vision of the man from the sea, interpreted by Uriel as a messiah figure who will reproach the assembled nations, and subsequently, destroy them. He will then gather together the peaceful multitude which is made up of the "ten tribes which were led away from their own land into captivity in the days of King Hosea, whom Shalmaneser the king of the Assyrians led captive" (13:40), and together with them are the remnant "who are left of your people, who are found within my holy borders" (13:48). Again, the remnant consists of Israelites who remain in the land; it is questionable whether the ten tribes can be considered part of the remnant, since they are counted among those not remaining in the land, and in fact, the ten tribes return to the land from a far away, mythical place beyond the Euphrates River.[22]

The remnant in *4 Ezra*, then, consists of righteous members of Israel who reside in the land at the time that the Messiah comes to judge. However, this remnant does not constitute all of Israel: Uriel makes it clear in the third dialogue that while many will live through the hardships of this world, only a few will be righteous enough to qualify for the world to come. The author of *4 Ezra* thus uses the remnant concept in order to suggest that only a small portion of ethnic Israel will survive. This strategic application of the remnant concept would encourage *4 Ezra*'s audience to follow the program set out in the narrative in order to be included in that final, saved remnant: believe in the imminence of the *eschaton* and follow the law.

Paul and the Remnant in Romans

Just as the authors of the *Damascus Document* and *4 Ezra* repurpose the remnant concept first found in the prophetic literature for their own purposes, so too does Paul participate in the reuse of the concept to fulfill his agenda. Twice in his Letter to the Romans, written around 56–58 CE, Paul refers to the remnant. The first is in Rom. 9:27–28, quoting Isa. 10:22–23: "And Isaiah cries out concerning Israel, 'Though the number of the children of Israel were like the sand of the sea, only a remnant of them will be saved; for the Lord will execute his sentence on the earth quickly and decisively.'"[23] The second time is in 11:5: "So too at the present time there is a remnant, chosen by grace." This verse follows a brief explanation in Rom. 11:1-4 of the current remnant of Israel as well as a conflation of two verses from 1 Kgs. 19:10 and 19:18. Both verses are situated in the larger section of Romans 9–11, which, I argue, serves as the climax to chapters 1–8: the whole of Romans is concerned with carving out space for the gentiles "in Christ," which means that Paul has to locate them in the lineage of Abraham.[24] It is this argument that is played out in the first eight chapters—that is, the adoption of the gentiles into Christ, and thus, into Israel—and which sets the need for 9–11, where Paul discusses how this new relationship "creates a kinship where there was none before, a new relationship sanctioned by God, a merciful solution to the Gentile problem."[25] However, in addressing this question throughout the letter, Paul, perhaps inadvertently, calls into question God's own faithfulness to his people in Israel.[26] While Paul is careful to negate any serious comment against the Jews (see, for instance, 3:1-4), Romans 9–11 returns to address the issue at length, and by extension, connects the new kinship of the gentiles to that of Israel.[27]

Romans 9–11 builds up the argument, somewhat awkwardly, of God's faithfulness toward Israel. The awkwardness comes not from the content, per se, but from Paul's frequent paraphrasing of certain arguments, backtracking to reiterate certain points, or using various yet incomplete comparisons. The difficulties in the interpretation are so extreme, in fact, that "there is no prospect of a consensus view,"[28] although there are several dominant interpretations. A brief outline will be useful in order to make sense of Paul's use of the remnant concept in Romans:

- *Rom. 9:1-5*: verse 1 begins a new section, with little segue from the previous chapter. Paul expresses his sorrow for the Jews, who are the inheritors to all the history, covenants, and patriarchs, in addition to being the progenitors of Christ.

- *Rom. 9:6-13*: Paul seeks to defend the idea that God's word has not failed. He does this through showing that not all who are biologically descended from Israel have belonged to those whom God has chosen. Paul uses the examples of Isaac being one of two children of Abraham, and yet, it is through Isaac that God's promise was passed. So, too, it was with Rebecca's children, with Jacob being chosen and Esau being rejected. Thus, the majority of Israel was never part of the elect.[29]

- *Rom. 9:14-18*: the choice of election does not depend on one's own actions, but on God's mercy: just as God hardens the Pharaoh's heart, the hearts of others can also be hardened—including Israel, which is inferred here.

- *Rom. 9:19-23*: Paul asks how God can still find blame in humans, if God is ultimately responsible for these choices. The answer is a wisdom reply—similar in kind to those seen in the first three dialogues in *4 Ezra*—questioning humanity's right to question God. Paul expresses this conclusion through the example of the potter, who can make either something menial or something beautiful, and the vessel itself does not have a say in its purpose.

- *Rom. 9:24-29*: using several biblical source texts, Paul shows how the gentiles are included in God's calling, to the exclusion of most of the Jews. Here, in 9:27, is the first mention of the remnant.

- *Rom. 9:30-10:21*: Israel has stumbled because it pursued the law via works rather than faith, and ultimately, this law is fulfilled in Christ. The emphasis in this section is on the stumbling of the Jews, and their own quest for righteousness, when righteousness could be found only through Christ.

- *Rom. 11:1-10*: Paul asks if God has rejected his people. The answer is adamantly negative, and Paul can point to himself as an example of a Jew who has not been rejected by God. Here, Paul again turns to the concept of the remnant in order to show that there are some left to whom God has remained faithful, who are the elect. The remaining are those whom God has hardened.

- *Rom. 11:11-24*: Paul again emphasizes the stumbling of Israel, but reiterates that it is a stumbling, and not a complete fall. This stumbling is what allows the gentiles a chance to participate in salvation, and thus, to make at least some of Israel jealous. Paul emphasizes that while the partial hardening is good for the gentiles, the ultimate goal is for the complete inclusion of the hardened, that is, Israel, as well. Paul uses two allegories: that of the dough offering, and that of the olive tree. Both emphasize the holiness of Israel.[30] The allegory of the olive tree encourages gentiles not to become too arrogant since, just as some of Israel has been "broken off," so too could God break off the gentiles.

- *Rom. 11:25-36*: Paul presents here the mystery that the hardening of part of Israel is temporary until the full number of gentiles has been brought in. At that point, all Israel will be saved.

In Rom. 9:27, the use of the remnant concept by Paul both relies upon the surrounding arguments, and in turn, is relied upon by them. Paul is contending that not all of what someone from his time would generally consider "Israel" is, in fact, Israel. He does this through the election motif—for instance, Isaac was elect and Esau was not, although both were children of Abraham—and is, thus, stating that not "all Israel" inherits election. To this end, Paul is both justifying the gentile inclusion and explaining the lack of Jewish participation.

Instead, a remnant is elected from Israel, as Paul, quoting Isaiah, states in 9:27: "And Isaiah cries out on behalf of Israel, 'If the number of the children of Israel be as the sands of the sea, a remnant of them will be saved; for the Lord will execute his sentence on the earth quickly and decisively.'" It is important to note, however, that in this passage, Paul is emphasizing not that *only* a remnant will be saved, as it is translated in the NRSV,[31] but instead, that there will always be *at least* a remnant that remains—a remnant that proves that God keeps his word and his faithfulness to Israel. This remnant, Paul is arguing here, exists not on the basis of the law, but on the basis of faith (9:32).

In Rom. 11:2-6, Paul returns to the remnant idea by drawing on the

Elijah narratives as told in 1 Kings,[32] where God tells Elijah that God has kept a remnant of Israel for himself:

> God has not rejected his people whom he foreknew. Do you not know what the scripture says of Elijah, how he pleads with God against Israel? "Lord, they have killed your prophets, they have demolished your altars; I alone am left, and they are seeking my life." But what is the divine reply to him? "I have kept for myself seven thousand who have not bowed the knee to Baal." So too at the present time there is a remnant, chosen by grace. But if it is by grace, it is no longer on the basis of works, otherwise grace would no longer be grace. (Rom. 11:2–6)

In 1 Kings, God's remnant are those Israelites who have not bowed to Baal, the Canaanite god whom Elijah is constantly proving as false. The difference, of course, between Paul's usage of the text and the actual meaning of the text is clear: God's remnant in the 1 Kings narrative have not bowed to Baal, but have kept God's covenant, while for Paul, the remnant is not identified as those who have kept the covenant, per se, but those who are chosen by grace.

The identity of the remnant—that is, who makes up the remnant—in Romans 11 is uncertain, based on the context. Considering Paul's use of the concept earlier in 9:27, it would seem that Paul is referring in 11:5 to the Israelites. Consider more carefully 11:1, where Paul justifies his question asking whether God has rejected his people with the response "μὴ γένοιτο" ("Certainly not!"). The use of this phrase for Paul "has primarily become a device by which he emphatically denies false conclusions that could be (or were?) drawn from his theology the correction of which he then proceeds to set forth," according to Abraham Malherbe.[33] Paul responds to the idea that God has rejected his people with "μὴ γένοιτο," followed by an example—himself: "I myself am an Israelite, a descendent of Abraham, from the tribe of Benjamin." Thus, Paul is offering himself up as one of the remnant of Israel that has been set aside by God. It is not Paul's ethnic identity as a Jew that makes him part of the remnant, as this would then include all Jews—which is clearly not Paul's intention. Instead, I would argue that this remnant, of which Paul is a part, is made up of the Jewish believers in Jesus as Christ.[34]

This identification works well within the context of Romans 11. In 11:7, Paul writes that "the elect [of Israel] obtained it, but the rest were hardened." To whom could this elect be referring, except the same group as the remnant about which Paul writes in 11:5? In 11:8-9, Paul provides proof texts, first from Isaiah, and then from the Psalms, showing how God hardened their hearts and caused them to stumble. The group now being discussed is no longer the remnant, but those from Israel whose hearts God hardened, those who stumbled, that is, whoever is *not* part of the remnant. Paul then is differentiating between those whose hearts were hardened (or those who stumbled, depending on which allegory you want to choose, but they are the same) and the remnant, those who are elect.

It is the stumbling of these Jews that produces time so that the full number of the gentiles (11:25) can attain salvation:

> So that you may not claim to be wiser than you are, brothers, I want you to understand this mystery [μυστήριον]: a hardening has come upon part of Israel, until the full number of Gentiles has come in. And so all Israel [πᾶς Ἰσραὴλ] will be saved; as it is written, "Out of Zion will come the Delivered; he will banish ungodliness from Jacob."

Paul is careful to reiterate that the time of the stumbling is temporary—that eventually, after the fullness of the gentiles have come in, all Israel (πᾶς Ἰσραὴλ) will be saved (11:26). This is the great μυστήριον to which Paul refers in 11:25. The identification of πᾶς Ἰσραὴλ has been discussed in myriad articles, with arguments tending to fall into one of three camps:

- πᾶς Ἰσραὴλ means all the elect, both Jew and gentile
- πᾶς Ἰσραὴλ refers to the ethnic nation of Israel as a whole; or
- πᾶς Ἰσραὴλ refers to the elect of ethnic Israel throughout time.[35]

When considering Paul's discussion of the remnant and those who have stumbled, however, the identity of πᾶς Ἰσραὴλ seems fairly clear. Paul's great μυστήριον is the inclusion of πᾶς Ἰσραὴλ, that is, *all the Jews*—both those who have stumbled through their refusal to believe and the remnant, the current Jewish believers in Christ. After all, just as God is the cause of the hardening of the hearts of those who refuse to believe, they will not remain hard-hearted forever; once the full number of gentiles has been brought in, those whose hearts had been hardened will then be included in those who will receive salvation. Thus, through the remnant concept in Romans 9–11, Paul creates a response to Romans 1–8, with its concern for carving a space for the gentiles in Christ while God remains steadfast in his faithfulness to Israel. The gentiles are included in Israel because only a remnant of Israel is currently "in Christ." Once the full number of gentiles has been brought in, the rest of Israel—to reach πᾶς Ἰσραὴλ—will be brought in.

Like the *Damascus Document* and *4 Ezra*, Paul's use of the remnant concept within Romans 9–11 participates in the expression of the remnant as used in both Scripture and in the other extracanonical texts examined here. Paul's specific concern is the question of divine punishment: he evaluates the possibility that the hardening of hearts—in other words, the "stumbling" on the part of Israel—represents divine punishment. Certainly, if one understands πᾶς Ἰσραὴλ as referring to all Israel, both the remnant and those with hardened hearts combined, Paul's idea of remnant represents a promise of restoration that will happen just as soon as the full number of gentiles is brought in. Thus, unlike the earlier texts, Paul's strategic usage of remnant is the most liberally applied: the remnant can be identified as the current Jewish believers in Christ, and they will eventually be joined by current Jewish unbelievers to form a new group, πᾶς Ἰσραὴλ.

Conclusion

All three texts analyzed above share a common heritage in the remnant idea, as derived from Israelite literature, and are just a sampling of the literary evidence on the use of the concept of remnant in Second Temple texts. Each has its own unique way of interpreting the concept. The *Damascus Document* locates the remnant in the sectarian community of Qumran, one that is located physically away from the other Jews and also temporally near the end times. *4 Ezra* limits the remnant to only a small portion of ethnic Israel that remains in the land during the *eschaton*. Paul's use of the remnant concept within Romans 9–11 identifies them as the small number of Jewish believers in Christ. This group, to which gentile believers are now being added, will eventually be joined by current Jewish non-believers before the end times so that πᾶς 'Ισραὴλ will be saved. All of these texts repurpose the remnant concept to emphasize why their unique interpretation of contemporaneous events is correct.

What Paul does in Romans, then, is not unique for Jewish texts in the Second Temple period. Räisänen notes that

> in resorting to deceptively positive-sounding language in parts of Romans, Paul is involved in the usual strategy of sectarian movements, which tend to justify novel practices and ideas by claiming that they are in full agreement with the tradition, if only the tradition is understood properly.[36]

While Räisänen refers specifically to Paul's language in Romans, I argue that his conclusion is applicable for all the texts under discussion in this chapter, even those not typically associated with sectarian movements. These texts reappropriate the remnant concept from scriptural sources in order to establish identity boundaries for their own Second Temple groups. Each text applies the concept in order to convince an implied audience of its agenda, that is, that its interpretation of Israelite tradition is the only correct interpretation—a hermeneutic clearly at work in all three texts under analysis in this paper. In the case of Romans 9–11, Paul uses the remnant concept to complete the argument that he sets out in chapters 1–8, that the gentiles are able to be adopted into Christ specifically because there is a Jewish remnant who believe, and once the full number of gentiles believe, the rest of Israel will join. Paul reaches this conclusion not through the development of some new identity, but through his interpretation of the remnant trope, a use that signifies his continued participation in Judaism.

Notes

1. For a discussion of the use of the terms Jewish vs. Judean, see the discussion in Marginalia, "Jew and Judean: A Forum on Politics and Historiography in the Translation of Ancient Texts: Have Scholars Erased the Jews from Antiquity?" *Marginalia Review of Books*, August 26, 2014, http://marginalia .lareviewofbooks.org/jew-judean-forum. In this chapter, I use the terms Jew and Jewish unless referring specifically to an ethnic association.

2. *Scripture* or *Bible*, as used in this chapter, should be defined as authoritative texts from Jewish tradition. Much work has already been done on the connection between Paul's use of remnant in Rom. 9:27 and 11:5, and in the Hebrew Bible/Septuagint. See, for instance, the dissertation of Gerhard F. Hasel, *The Remnant: The History and Theology of the Remnant Idea from Genesis to Isaiah* (Berrien Springs, MI: Andrews University Press, 1972). Cf. R. E. Clements, "'A Remnant Chosen by Grace' (Romans 11:5): The Old Testament Background and Origin of the Remnant Concept," in *Pauline Studies: Essays Presented to Professor F. F. Bruce on his 70th Birthday*, ed. D. A. Hagner and M. J. Harris (Exeter, Devon: Paternoster, 1980), 106–21.

3. Lester V. Meyer, "Remnant," *ABD*, 670.

4. Stanley K. Stowers, *A Rereading of Romans: Justice, Jews and Gentiles* (New Haven, CT: Yale University Press, 1994), 296. The word "always" was removed from the lacuna; it is an accurate statement, as long as it is qualified.

5. Meyer, "Remnant," 670.

6. For a description of the various manuscripts, see C. Hempel, *The Damascus Texts* (Sheffield: Sheffield Academic, 2000), 10–14.

7. A. L. A. Hogeterp, *Expectations of the End: A Comparative Traditio-Historical Study of Eschatological, Apocalyptic and Messianic Ideas in the Dead Sea Scrolls and the New Testament* (Leiden: Brill, 2009), 223n431.

8. CD-A I 1–5; 10–11. Translations from the *Damascus Document* taken from Florentino García Martínez and Eibert J. C. Tigchelaar, eds., *The Dead Sea Scrolls Study Edition.* (2 vols.; Leiden: Brill, 1997), 1:551.

9. See II 14–17. Cf. Mark Adam Elliot, *The Survivors of Israel: Reconsideration of the Theology of Pre-Christian Judaism* (Grand Rapids: Eerdmans, 2000), 117n6.

10. Remnant can refer to either the saved group or part of the "wicked" group that remains in biblical literature. See Paul E. Dinter, "The Remnant of Israel and the Stone of Stumbling in Zion According to Paul (Romans 9–11)" (PhD diss., Union Theological Seminary, 1979), 216.

11. Ibid., 219.

12. Ibid., 216.

13. This is no surprise, as Paul himself uses the two ideas almost interchangeably in Romans. See the next section where I discuss Romans.

14. Michael E. Stone, *Fourth Ezra* (Minneapolis: Fortress Press, 1990), 9–10.

15. As a pseudepigraphon, the literary setting for the narrative is after the destruction of the first temple; however, the text was written in response to the destruction of the second temple.

16. Translations from *4 Ezra* are from Stone, *Fourth Ezra*.

17. Alden Thompson argued that, based on Ezra's poignant laments for the "many" who will perish that take place in the third episode, Ezra was more concerned with general humanity than with the fate of Israel: see A. L. Thompson, *Responsibility for Evil in the Theodicy of 4 Ezra* (Missoula: Scholars Press, 1977), 269. This is an unnecessary conclusion, however. Cf. John J. Collins, "The Idea of Election in 4 Ezra," *JSQ* 16 (2009): 87.

18. Hogan argues that the theology that Uriel puts forth stands in a tradition that uses universal language and creates a dualism based on "ethical, rather than ethnic, lines" (133); that is, it does not specifically address Israel, but all humanity in general. However, while Uriel utilizes universal language and does not highlight the importance of the covenant, the Torah still occupies a place of centrality in Uriel's theology. Karina Martin Hogan, *Theologies in Conflict in 4 Ezra: Wisdom Debate and Apocalyptic Solution* (JSJSup 130; Leiden: Brill, 2008), 126–34, especially 133–34.

19. While not named as such, Benjamin Reynolds has successfully shown that it is indeed the angel who serves as interlocutor here. Benjamin E. Reynolds, "The Otherworldly Mediators in 4 Ezra and 2 Baruch: A Comparison with Angelic Mediators in Ascent Apocalypses and in Daniel, Ezekiel, and Zechariah," in *Fourth Ezra and Second Baruch: Reconstruction after the Fall*, ed. M. Henze and G. Boccaccini (Boston: Brill, 2013), 176–93.

20. See the discussion (and subsequent footnote) above about Uriel's universal language and its application to who forms the righteous; however, in light of the fifth episode, there is no doubt that the righteous from episode 3 should be defined as Israel.

21. But see the discussion of episode 6 below.

22. For a discussion on the Euphrates as a temporal boundary, see my forthcoming article: Shayna Sheinfeld, "The Euphrates as Temporal Marker in 4 Ezra and 2 Baruch," *JSJ* 47 (2016): 1–15.

23. Translations from Romans are my own.

24. And thus, in some inclusive relation to ethnic Judeans—e. g., Romans 4.

25. Caroline Johnson Hodge, "'A Light to the Nations': The Role of Israel in Romans 9–11," in *Reading Paul's Letter to the Romans*, ed. J. L. Sumney (Atlanta: Society of Biblical Literature, 2012), 169–86, here 170.

26. See especially Rom. 2:12–29. J. Bassler, *Navigating Paul: An Introduction to Key Theological Concepts* (Louisville: Westminster John Knox, 2007), 78–79.

27. Bassler, *Navigating*, 78–79; see also Hodge, "'A Light to the Nations,'" 170.

28. Bassler, *Navigating*, 71.

29. Räisänen, "Paul, God, and Israel: Romans 9–11 in Recent Research," in *The Social World of Formative Christianity and Judaism: Essays in Tribute to Howard Clark Kee*, ed. J. Neusner, E. S. Frerichs, P. Borgen, and R. Horsley (Philadelphia: Fortress Press, 1988), 178–206, here 182.

30. There is disagreement as to which part of Israel Paul is referring. Räisänen states "most commentators think that the 'first fruits' and the 'root' refer to the patriarch." Räisänen, "Paul, God, and Israel," 188.

31. The NRSV reads: "And Isaiah cries out concerning Israel, 'Though the number of the children of Israel were like the sand of the sea, *only a remnant of them* will be saved; for the Lord will execute his sentence on the earth quickly and decisively'" (emphasis added). John Paul Heil addresses the issues of recent translations and offers a more accurate one in the first part of his article, "From Remnant to Seed of Hope for Israel: Romans 9:27–29," *CBQ* 64 (2002): 703–20.

32. For a discussion of the use of 1 Kings in Romans 11, see Christopher D. Stanley, "The Significance of Romans 11:3–4 for the Text History of the LXX Book of Kingdoms," *JBL* 112, no. 1 (1993): 43–54.

33. Abraham J. Malherbe, "μὴ γένοιτο in the Diatribe and Paul," *HTR* 73 nos. 1 and 2 (1980): 232.

34. John G. Lodge. *Romans 9-11: A Reader-Response Analysis* (Atlanta: Scholars Press, 1996), 136.

35. For a review of the scholars and literature supporting each option, see Ben L. Merkle, "Romans 11 and the Future of Ethnic Israel," *JETS* 43, no. 4 (2000): 710–11.

36. Heikki Räisänen. "A Controversial Jew and His Conflicting Convictions: *Paul, the Law, and the Jewish People* Twenty Years After" in *Redefining First-Century Jewish and Christian Identities: Essays in Honor of Ed Parish Sanders*, ed. F. Udoh et al. (Notre Dame, IN: University of Notre Dame Press, 2008), 322.

The "Historical Paul" and the Paul of Acts

Which Is More Jewish?

Isaac W. Oliver

By distinguishing the "historical Paul"—that is, the Paul known to us through the undisputed letters—from the Paul of the Acts of the Apostles, a text written sometime after 70 CE, but probably before the Bar Kokhba revolt,[1] I am assuming that the two are obviously not one and the same: that the author of Acts has thoroughly appropriated, reconfigured, and incorporated the figure of Paul into his work in ways that suited his interests. Paul Vielhauer's seminal article, published many decades ago, unsettled the facile assumption that the author of Acts simply transcribed Paul's theological thought without any further modification.[2] Indeed, some even ignore Acts as an historical source for reconstructing Paul's life and thought, given all the methodological problems involved. I would like to revisit the perennial question of continuity and discontinuity between Acts and Paul's undisputed letters by assessing how the Jewishness of Paul is represented in both writings. This issue merits renewed consideration, given the many recent positive assessments of Paul's ongoing Jewishness, as allegedly expressed in his own letters,[3] as well as the growing contention put forward by many scholars, including myself, that the books of Luke and Acts are thoroughly Jewish documents.[4] The book of Acts, particularly, emphasizes the *ongoing* relevance for Jewish followers of Jesus maintaining their Jewish identity through Torah praxis by systematically negating any application of Paul's teachings that would claim otherwise. This inquiry, then, works under the dual assumption that Paul did remain a Jew even after joining the Jesus movement and that the Acts of the Apostles also stands in far greater continuity with its Jewish heritage than many think, particularly in its affirmation of the perpetuity of Torah observance and Jewish identity within the *ekklesia* as envisioned by its author.

How Many "Pauls"?

One caveat, however, should be added: I note greater tensions in the writings penned by Paul (that is, the undisputed letters) vis-à-vis the Torah than in Acts (and the Gospel of Luke), which consistently presents Paul as a faithful Jew who follows Jewish custom. Much has been said about Paul's possible inconsistency or incoherence in thought, as expressed in his own writings.[5] Others deny this possibility, advocating for a coherent Paul, which, undeniably, can serve the needs of those seeking to extract a culturally and theologically relevant message out of Paul's writings.[6] One could alternatively envisage a dynamic and continuous shift in Paul's opinions vis-à-vis his Jewish heritage and relationship with other Jews. That Paul could change his mind over central theological tenets should come as no surprise. He, at least once, radically reconsidered his views on Jesus and the movement surrounding this figure, ceasing to oppose Jesus' followers and even joining their ranks. Could Paul have continued to wrestle with his religious convictions even after joining the Jesus movement? Could he have modified his opinion on certain issues more than once?[7]

It comes as no surprise that those scholars who belong to the so-called Radical New Perspective and maintain that Paul remained

Torah-observant often point to passages from the Letter to the Romans to make their point.[8] Overall, Paul's tone in Romans is friendlier and more accommodating with respect to the observance of Jewish commandments (Rom. 14), the status of the Torah (3:31; 7:7, 12), and Jews in general (3:1; 9–11, especially 9:4; 11:1, 26) than in Galatians (Gal. 3:10, 11; 6:15; and so on). Different audiences and circumstances might account for these apparent discrepancies. But could a reoccurring shift in Paul's thought account for the different portraits presented in both letters? Hopefully, all will agree that Paul at least wrote in a manner that led some Christians, very early on, to interpret his letters as abrogating the Torah. Marcion could represent one extreme understanding of Paul that developed in this direction.[9] Perhaps, the Pastoral Letters might be understood as representing yet another Pauline school of thought that interpreted Paul's letters as condemning all those who held onto Jewish circumcision, Torah observance, Jewish "myths," and other Jewish traditions (for example, Titus 1:10–16; 3:9). Could the so-called deuteropauline Epistles such as Colossians and Ephesians be read along similar lines in tune with Galatians (Col. 1:13–17; Eph. 2:14–16)?[10] The book of Acts, on the contrary, would lie at the other end of the spectrum from Marcion and the Pastorals, applying Paul's thought in a way that aligns itself more closely with the position voiced by the "Paul of Romans." We must admit that Paul's complex writings generated various interpretations concerning the relationship of the Jesus movement with its Jewish fabric, with some early interpreters rearranging their Pauline blocks on a foundation they thought aligned with the spirit of Galatians, while others affirmed a Pauline perspective more conciliatory toward Judaism that is ultimately built upon the cornerstone of the Letter to the Romans.[11] Indeed, I will try to show that the portrait of Paul in Acts stands in greater continuity with the Paul of Romans, insofar as Acts depicts Paul as an ongoing Torah-observant Jew who remains committed to the Jewish people and their ultimate destiny.[12]

Two Takes on the Jewishness of the "Historical Paul" and the Paul of Acts

At least two distinct and opposing views exist on the relationship between Paul's undisputed letters and the Acts of the Apostles as far as their Jewishness is concerned. The first view, which we might dub the "classical" approach, posits that Paul was, at best, indifferent to his Jewish heritage. He ceased being Jewish by abandoning Torah praxis and retained an ambivalent relationship with those followers of Jesus who did insist on keeping the Torah. On the other hand, the author of Acts recast Paul to portray him as utterly faithful to the Torah and the Jewish people. The author of Acts domesticated and re-Judaized Paul, placing him back within the Jewish fold he had supposedly abandoned. Vielhauer represents this position well. Concerning Paul's attitude toward the law, he states that Paul was "free from the Law,"[13] having announced its end.[14] For Paul, "Moses was not a prototype but an antitype of the Messiah and a personification of 'the dispensation of death' and 'of condemnation' (2 Cor. 3:4–18)."[15] Paul believed that "the acknowledgment of circumcision meant the nullification of the redemptive act of Christ on the cross (Gal. 5:1–12)."[16] By contrast, the book of Acts portrays Paul "as the Jewish Christian who is utterly loyal to the law."[17] The motivation in Acts was to show that Paul never said anything affecting Judaism in the very least.

Vielhauer rightly points out that for the author of Acts, the law retains its validity for Jewish followers of Jesus. Accordingly, in Acts, Paul makes conciliatory concessions toward Jewish practices, such as having Timothy circumcised or joining zealous Jews in their purification rites in the temple.[18] Yet, Vielhauer diminishes the importance of Judaism in Acts, claiming that its author esteemed it to be at the same level as "pagan religion": "Acts depicts Paul's attitude toward the ancient religion of the Jews just as positively as the Areopagus speech presents his attitude toward the ancient religion of the Greeks."[19] This position is typical of the classical approach, which acknowledges the Jewish portrait of Paul in Acts only to then reduce its relevance by downplaying the importance Jewish tradition apparently continued to enjoy among many followers of Jesus living after 70 CE, the author of Acts included. The late Conzelmann is perhaps the most influential scholar in this regard.[20] His strategy was to compartmentalize the "salvation history" supposedly present in Luke and Acts into three eras: 1), the period of Israel; 2), the period of Jesus; and 3), the period of the church.[21] The Torah was relevant especially during the first period, but lost its importance when the church arose. The major weakness with Conzelmann's schematization is that it does not align with the narrative of Luke-Acts: the Torah enjoys an elevated status in Luke and Acts *throughout all of the three epochs* he outlined—even after Jesus' ascension (Acts 1:9–11) and the proclamation of the so-called Apostolic Decree in Acts 15. Apparently aware of this quagmire, Conzelmann resorted to dismissing its significance on the grounds that the author of Acts was merely reminiscing about an earlier period of "church history" that necessitated a literary adjustment of Paul as a law-abiding Jew.[22] In other words, the Jewish portraits of Jesus, Paul, and many of the other Jewish protagonists in Luke and Acts carried no significance for contemporary debates about Torah observance. As a supposed "Gentile Christian," ignorant about and indifferent to Judaism, the author of Acts did not care whether Jewish followers of Jesus emulated the Jewish Paul sketched in his work. He was only nostalgically reminiscing of a time when the primitive *ekklesia* could boast of a Jewish hall of fame of Torah-observant believers that included such prominent figures as Paul and James. Surprisingly, the dissonance between the author's narration and worldview has not bothered commentators of Acts who embrace the classical approach.

John Gager, an advocate of the Radical New Perspective on Paul, assesses the Jewishness of Paul in the undisputed letters and in Acts in reverse direction to the classical approach.[23] The historical Paul remained faithful to his Jewish heritage. All of the negative pronouncements he made concerning the Torah only applied to gentiles. Gager commendably argues against the common view that

"Jewish Christianity" quickly disappeared from the historical scene once the first generation of Jesus' Jewish followers passed away. He also perspicaciously critiques the common perception of a rapid and inevitable "parting of the ways" between Judaism and Christianity in late antiquity, going as far as postulating that "Jewish Christianity" could have survived into the Islamic period.[24] A culprit from the past, however, must be found in order to account for the undoing of Jewish Christianity and the painful divorce between Jews and Christians. If neither Jesus nor Paul were responsible for this process, who then should be blamed? Gager condemns the author of Acts for the eventual demise of the Jewish foundation of early Christianity. Concerning the representation of Paul in his own letters and in his depiction in Acts, Gager states:

> Contrary to the portrait in Acts, Paul did not repudiate Judaism—or those whom we call Jewish Christians; instead, he focused entirely on his mission to Gentiles, insisting simply that Gentile believers had no need to observe the customs and practices of the Torah. The author of Acts has deliberately drafted Paul to serve for his own anti-Jewish and anti-Jewish-Christian message.[25]

Gager obviously disagrees with those who uphold the more traditional depiction of Paul as an apostate Jew. However, he believes that Judaism was no longer relevant for the author of Acts, even going a step further by denying that its author recast Paul in Jewish terms as a Torah-observant Pharisee. My point is neither to single out Gager nor to downplay the significant considerations he has raised for our understanding of early Judaism and Christianity: it is only to highlight an unfortunate misunderstanding of Acts that, ironically, depends on an approach to the problem of the "partings of the ways" that Gager so aptly criticizes.[26] The claim that the Paul of Acts repudiates Judaism cannot be sustained when one looks closely at the text of Acts. Its author repeatedly portrays Paul as faithfully attending the synagogue on the Sabbath,[27] keeping Jewish festivals such as Shavuot/Pentecost (20:16) and Yom Kippur (27:9),[28] attending the temple in Jerusalem and partaking in its rituals (21:24), affirming his fidelity to the Torah and Jewish customs (28:17), and even circumcising Timothy (16:3)![29] A different approach, then, seems necessary—one that acknowledges the affirmations concerning Torah and Judaism made by Paul in Romans and the author of Acts, respectively, to which we now turn.

To the Jew First and Then to the Gentile (Rom. 1:16)

Very early in his Letter to the Romans, Paul affirms the primacy of the Jewish people in God's design, declaring: "For I am not ashamed of the gospel; it is the power of God for salvation to everyone who has faith, to the Jew first and also to the Greek" (Rom. 1:16). The privileged standing Jews enjoy, which calls for a higher accountability is formulated in similar terms in 2:9-10: "There will be anguish and distress for everyone who does evil, the Jew first and also the Greek, but glory and honor and peace for everyone who does good, the Jew first and also the Greek."

The book of Acts presents the special status of the Jewish people in God's "salvation history" through numerous reports in which the Jewish people have the privilege of hearing the gospel before the gentiles do. This motif of Israel's primacy is built into the geographical scheme of the commission proclaimed by the resurrected Jesus in Acts 1:8, which centers on the city of Jerusalem: "You will be my witnesses in Jerusalem, in all Judea and Samaria, and to the ends of the earth." The book of Acts closely follows these introductory words, first by relating how the Jewish followers of Jesus announced the crucified and risen Jesus to the many Jews assembled in Jerusalem during the Jewish festival of Pentecost (Acts 2), and then, by having its main protagonist, Paul, continually proclaim this message, first to the Jews, and then, to the gentiles. Thus, right after joining the ranks of Jesus' followers, Paul proclaims Jesus in the Jewish synagogues, purportedly confounding "the Jews who lived in Damascus by proving that Jesus was the Messiah" (Acts 9:22). On their first missionary journey, Paul and Barnabas address the Jews of the synagogue of Salamis, Cyprus. This pattern repeats itself throughout Paul's itinerary across the Mediterranean world. Upon arriving in Antioch of Pisidia, Paul preaches in a synagogue full of Jews, addressing them as his compatriots: "You Israelites, and others who fear God [φοβούμενοι τὸν θεόν], listen" (Acts 13:16).[30] Gentile addressees eventually hear Paul's message (Acts 13:44, 48), but this occurs in the Jewish synagogue that hosts Paul as a speaker and only after Paul has interacted extensively with the local Jews. In the next city they visit, Iconium, Paul and Barnabas go through the same motions, visiting a synagogue and speaking "in such a way that a great number of both Jews and Greeks became believers" (Acts 14:1). Acts phrases this successful proselytizing campaign with the formulation "Jews and Greeks" rather than "Greeks and Jews," subtly conveying again the primacy of the Jewish people as hearers, and in this case, accepters of the good news (see 18:1; 19:10, 17; 20:21).[31] Even in a city such as Athens, the symbolic cradle of Greek civilization, Paul first addresses the Jews in the synagogue before confronting the Athenian philosophers at the Areopagus (17:17). Although, in Acts 18:6, Paul angrily announces to the Jews in Corinth that he will now turn his attention to the gentiles, he continues to address Jews wherever he can. Thus, when Paul leaves Corinth and arrives in Ephesus, the first thing he does is to enter the synagogue and discuss with the Jews (18:19). Other Jewish followers of Jesus in Acts, such as Apollos, also continue to reach out to Jews after Paul's solemn declaration made in Corinth (18:24–28). Until the very end, the Paul of Acts goes out of his way to solicit the attention of the Jews in order to proclaim his beliefs about Jesus. Accordingly, when Paul arrives as a prisoner in Rome, he calls together the local Jewish leaders in order to explain his situation and relate his spiritual convictions (28:17–28). Only after doing so does Acts suggest that Paul preached to gentiles in Rome (28:28–31).[32]

The Law Is Holy, and the Commandment Is Holy and Just and Good (Rom. 7:12)

On more than one occasion in Romans, Paul speaks about the Torah in favorable terms. For Paul, the law is "spiritual" (Rom. 7:14), "holy," and contains just and good commandments (7:12). Paul values circumcision and other oracles inscribed in the Torah: "Then what advantage has the Jew? Or what is the value of circumcision? Much, in every way. For in the first place the Jews were entrusted with the oracles of God" (3:1–2). Paul details the benefits, granting of the Torah included, that God showered upon Israel: "They are Israelites, and to them belong the adoption, the glory, the covenants, the giving of the law, the worship, and the promises; to them belong the patriarchs, and from them, according to the flesh, comes the Messiah, who is over all, God blessed forever" (9:4–5). Paul also avoids the insinuation that his teaching, in some way, does away with the Torah: "Do we then throw the law by this faith? By no means! On the contrary, we uphold the law!" (3:31).

There is only one passage where the Paul of Acts directly touches on the status and role of the Torah. It occurs in a speech Paul delivers on a Sabbath to those attending the synagogue of Pisidian Antioch: "by this Jesus everyone who believes is set free from all those sins from which you could not be freed [δικαιωθῆναι] by the law of Moses" (13:39). The author of Acts is not mounting a critique here against the Torah.[33] Jesus, according to Acts, provides the Jewish people with a clean new slate by providing forgiveness for their corporate sins. This is God's doing. The language used here recalls one of Paul's statements in Romans: "For 'no human being will be justified [δικαιωθήσεται] in his sight' by deeds prescribed by the law" (Rom. 3:20; compare Gal. 2:16). In addition, the law, according to Paul, provides knowledge of sin, but does not aid the human in overcoming sin, since the law is "weakened by the flesh" (Rom. 8:3). Acts 13:39 frames the limitations of the Torah differently. It does not openly claim that the law "is weakened by the flesh" or unable to assist the human in overcoming sin. Rather, the law cannot acquit Israel of its corporate, covenantal shortcomings.

The accent on the failure of Israel to live up to its covenantal calling at the corporate level appears elsewhere in Acts in a small speech attributed to Peter during the so-called Jerusalem Council. Peter tries to persuade the Jewish followers of Jesus not to force gentile males to undergo circumcision, pointing out how the latter have received the spirit of holiness, just like some Jews have. He adds: "Now therefore why are you putting God to the test by placing on the neck of the disciples a yoke that neither our ancestors nor we have been able to bear?" (Acts 15:10). For many, Acts 15:10 represents a gentile perspective on the law, written by someone distant from Judaism: a "pagan," a "Gentile Christian," or a God-fearer insufficiently acquainted with Jewish teachings. Acts 15:10, however, really betrays a rather typical Jewish recognition of Israel's corporate and historical failure to observe the Torah. The Peter of Acts blames *Israel* for failing to fulfill the law, not the supposedly overwhelming stipulations contained in the Mosaic Torah.[34] Romans 9:31 expresses a similar assessment of Israel's performance: "Israel . . . did not succeed in fulfilling that law."

The reference to the law as a yoke in Acts 15:10 is not negative. Interestingly, this metaphor concerning the Torah is matched by a *contemporaneous* Jewish work, *2 Baruch*, overlooked in studies of Acts: "For behold, I see many of your people who separated themselves from your statutes and who have cast away from them the yoke of your Law. Further, I have seen others who left behind their vanity and who have fled under your wings" (*2 Bar.* 41:3–4). The author of *2 Baruch* is aware of the apostasy of some Jews from the Torah and cognizant of the historical failure of Israel as a collective entity to live up to the high covenantal standards expected from a divinely elected people. Nevertheless, the author of *2 Baruch* remains optimistic that, by God's grace, a sufficient number of people among the Jewish people will eventually gather together and successfully carry the yoke of the law: "In you we have put our trust, because, behold, your Law is with us, and we know that we do not fall as long as we keep your statutes. . . . And that Law that is among us will help us" (48:22–24). By contrast, certain passages contained in the book of *4 Ezra* reveal a grim outlook on this issue, suggesting that only a select few will be saved: "The Most High made this world for the sake of many, but the world to come for the sake of few. . . . Many have been created, but few will be saved" (8:1–3). The author of Acts joins the authors of *2 Baruch* and *4 Ezra* as well as other Jewish thinkers of his time in recognizing that history testifies to

Israel's collective failure to follow God's Law. "O look not upon the sins of your people, but at those who have served you in truth" is the cry of a Jewish prayer confessing Israel's sins in the aftermath of the failure of the First Jewish Revolt (4 *Ezra* 9:26). The author of Acts, by contrast, prays that the Jewish people look to the risen Jesus, the heavenly and Davidic messiah reigning high above, who announces release from sins to Israel and the pious gentiles, and will soon return to execute his final judgment upon this world as the vindicated and victorious Son of Man. What Israel needs, according to Acts, is a *supplement* (not a supplanter!) to the Torah to assist it in fulfilling its vocation and destiny.[35]

I Myself Am an Israelite, a Descendant of Abraham, a Member of the Tribe of Benjamin (Rom. 11:1)

In his letters, Paul often boasts of his Jewish heritage (Rom. 11:1; Phil. 3:4-6; Gal. 1:13-14). However, he does not shy away, at least on one occasion, from (hyperbolically?) downplaying his Jewish credentials, counting them as "loss" because of Christ (Phil. 3:7). Galatians 1:13 is ambiguous. The New Revised Standard Version renders it, "You have heard, no doubt, of my earlier life in Judaism," allowing for the possibility that Paul continued to remain Jewish. But why would Paul bring up the word Judaism (which he only uses in this section of his writings) at all to speak of a former attitude? And to what extent does his current way of living in Judaism conform to or depart from his Pharisaic past? Does he, for example, still consider himself a Pharisee, especially when we consider the issue in light of Phil. 3:5?

The perceived tensions in the Pauline Letters concerning Paul's relationship to his Pharisaic heritage and perspective on the Torah do not reappear in the book of Acts. The Paul of Acts clearly remains a Jew *and* a Pharisee throughout. He is Torah-observant and a Pharisee par excellence. As noted, the Paul of Acts attends the synagogue on the Sabbath[36] and keeps Jewish festivals such as Shavuot (20:16) and Yom Kippur (27:9). The Paul of Acts never commits any halakic infringement on the Sabbath or other holy days. He never eats any forbidden foods (for example, swine). His itinerary is even designed in Acts in such a way so as to avoid traveling on the Sabbath or on other holy Jewish festivals.[37] Throughout Acts, Paul affirms his fidelity to the Torah and Jewish customs. The statement in Acts 28:17 suggests that Paul remained Pharisaic in his praxis. Before a delegation of Jews in Rome, Paul denies that he has done anything against the Jewish people or the *"customs of our ancestors"* (τοῖς ἔθεσι τοῖς πατρῴοις). The reference to the "customs of the elders" could suggest compliance with Pharisaic tradition—the author of Acts opting to employ the word ἔθος because of its usage among Jews in the Greco-Roman Diaspora. But it is with respect to the hope of the resurrection that the Paul of Acts most clearly embodies Pharisaism. During his appearance before the Sanhedrin of Jerusalem, Paul testifies before his Sadducean and Pharisaic audience that he *is* a Pharisee: "Brothers, I *am* a Pharisee [ἐγὼ Φαρισαῖός εἰμι], a son of Pharisees. I am on trial concerning the hope of the resurrection of the dead" (Acts 23:6). Here, the Paul of Acts is not simply portrayed as an opportunist who cleverly sees his way out of a dangerous situation. The reality of the risen Jesus for Paul both confirms the doctrine of the resurrection and anticipates the collective restoration of Israel. We might even say that the belief in the resurrection is the central theological tenet of Acts—a very un-Greek belief, to say the least (Acts 17:32). In fact, the author of Acts insinuates that the essential difference existing between the messianic movement known as "The Way" (24:14) and the rest of mainstream Judaism only amounts to a failure on the latter to recognize the veracity of the doctrine of the resurrection as manifested through the risen Jesus. Thus, the Paul of Acts claims that his arrest is merely due to the "hope and resurrection of the dead" he so boldly proclaims (23:6; compare 24:15).[38]

In two instances, the Paul of Acts exemplifies a spirit of accommodation to Jewish sensibilities. Acts 16:1-4 is most remarkable for its presentation of a Paul who concedes to Jewish pressure and has Timothy circumcised. This episode, strategically placed right after the proclamation of the so-called Apostolic Decree, serves as defensive buffer against the rumors circulating during the time of the author of Acts that Paul had taught "all the Jews living among the Gentiles to forsake Moses and . . . *not to circumcise their children* or observe the customs" (21:21). If Paul was willing to circumcise the child of a mixed marriage (Timothy's mother was Jewish; his father Greek), how much more would he affirm the circumcision of children born into Torah-observant Jewish families, so the book of Acts argues. To dispel the rumors about Paul's apostasy, James, the brother of Jesus, advises Paul to assist and accompany some Torah-observant Jewish followers of Jesus in their ritual purification at the temple. The Paul of Acts readily complies, affirming, in this concrete and public way, the value of preserving and transmitting Jewish identity. The Apostolic Decree, with its four stipulations given to *gentile Christians*, also clearly presumes, from the point of view of Acts, that *Jewish* followers of Jesus will continue to observe the Torah in toto.[39] This is the *Doppelgleisigkeit* or "bilateral ecclesiology" so clearly evident in Acts: Jewish followers of Jesus continue observing all of their ancestral customs, while gentiles observe a minimal set of Mosaic requirements.[40] It was important for the author of Acts that a visible, corporate body of Jews retained their distinctive presence within the *ekklesia*. These Jews, however, were not to compel gentiles to become Jews (through circumcision in the case of males). On the contrary, gentile Christians were not to lead their Jewish comrades away from their particular way of living; they were supposed to accommodate to their practices if any *Tischgemeinschaft* and *koinonia* were to occur between Jews and gentiles who believed in Jesus. No other book in the entire New Testament is clearer and more consistent than Acts in making such ecclesiological, ethnic, and halakic distinctions.

And So All Israel Will Be Saved (Rom. 11:26)

Romans 11:26 claims that, one day, all of Israel will be saved. This eschatological and soteriological promise was built upon Paul's conviction concerning Israel's permanent election (Rom. 11:27–28). The Jewish rejection of Jesus as the messiah greatly troubled Paul, who even expressed willingness to "be cut off from Christ" for the sake of his people (11:1). Paul earnestly searched the Scriptures to find the divine anticipation of this unexpected turn of events in Israel's history. For Paul, God predetermined, in some mysterious way (11:33), that Israel's "no" to Jesus would ultimately translate into its own salvation (11:15, 31, 25). A key question is whether the author of Acts also held onto similar views or had given up on the salvation of the Jews. Did God forsake the Jews permanently, according to Acts?

According to Butticaz, the majority of interpreters have responded positively to this question.[41] Nevertheless, this conclusion does not fit well with the concerned pronouncements regarding the fate of Israel that are made throughout Luke-Acts—from the very first chapters of Luke (chapters 1–2) to Paul's numerous speeches made before various audiences after his arrest in Jerusalem.[42] The very beginning of Acts opens with a question raised by the Jewish apostles of Jesus about the future of Israel: "Lord, is this the time when you will restore the kingdom to Israel?" (Acts 1:6) The disciples' question has startled those accustomed to viewing the author of Acts as a Roman-friendly gentile Christian.[43] Here, the disciples of Jesus wonder whether the time has finally arrived for Israel's restoration. Their question has rightly been interpreted as expressing hope for Israel's national liberation from the yoke of Roman occupation.[44] The prevailing judgment that views the disciples' question as representing a misunderstanding of the gospel message is hardly hinted at in Acts. The oblique answer provided in Acts simply advises the disciples not to worry about calculating "the times or periods that the Father has set by his own authority" (1:7). If there is an implicit rebuke to the disciples' question, it has nothing to do with their concern regarding the national restoration of Israel, but with its *timing*. In other words, the disciples should not speculate about the *when*, but focus on how to bring this process about. This includes serving as Jesus' witnesses, starting from Jerusalem to Judea, Samaria, and beyond. In this way, Jesus momentarily turns the attention away from the end of time "to the end of the earth" (1:8) without denying Israel's political hope for national restoration.[45]

The question in Acts 1:6 and the subsequent answer given by its Jesus are entirely compatible with expectations voiced only in the Gospel of Luke concerning the restoration of Israel: "They [those in Judea] will fall by the edge of the sword and be taken away as captives among all nations; and Jerusalem will be trampled on by the Gentiles, *until the times of the Gentiles are fulfilled* [ἄχρι οὗ πληρωθῶσιν καιροὶ ἐθνῶν]" (Luke 21:24). The restoration of Jerusalem will come after the time of the gentiles is fulfilled. In Romans, Paul, who lived before the tragic destruction of the temple of Jerusalem in 70 CE, describes the "time of the gentiles" differently, presenting this period as a window of opportunity for gentiles to be saved: "I want you to understand this mystery: a hardening has come upon part of Israel, *until the full number of the Gentiles has come in*" (Rom. 11:25). The phase of the gentiles is viewed in Romans as a time open for non-Jews to repent from their supposed immorality while Israel remains momentarily "hardened." The author of Acts, however, who wrote his text in the aftermath of the destruction of the temple after many gentiles had been offered numerous opportunities to hear the gospel, views the "time of the gentiles" as a time of oppression for Israel, during which Jerusalem is trampled by Rome.[46]

This state of affairs, however, will not endure forever. The hope for the restoration of Israel is openly announced at the beginning of the Gospel of Luke, and is never explicitly renounced anywhere else in Luke or Acts: "Blessed be the Lord God of Israel, for he has looked favorably on his people and redeemed them [ἐποίησεν λύτρωσιν τῷ λαῷ αὐτοῦ]" (Luke 1:68).[47] At the end of Luke, two disciples on their way to Emmaus lament in resignation after Jesus' crucifixion, ironically not knowing that the risen Jesus is standing in their midst: "we had hoped that he was the one to redeem [λυτροῦσθαι] Israel" (24:21). In his response to the disciples of Emmaus, Jesus, according to Luke, does not openly deny that Israel will eventually be delivered. Instead, he shows them from the Jewish Scriptures how it was necessary (ἔδει) for the messiah to suffer before being glorified (24:26–27). Besides functioning as a rhetorical device to augment the credibility of events reported in the narrative,[48] we note that the impersonal verbal form δεῖ also appears in Luke and Acts to signal the divine anticipation, even fore-ordination, of Jesus' death and resurrection: events viewed as necessary steps in bringing eventual salvation to Israel and the nations.[49] Luke's Jesus seems keenly aware of his fate, yet determined to fulfill his destiny. Thus, already in Luke 9:22, Jesus solemnly warns his disciples that "the Son of Man must [δεῖ] undergo great suffering, and be rejected by the elders, chief priests, and scribes, and be killed, and on the third day be raised." Similarly, when the Pharisees warn Jesus of Herod's plan to kill him, Jesus nevertheless insists that it is necessary (δεῖ) for him to make his final pilgrimage and die in Jerusalem (Luke 13:33).[50] To be sure, these solemn proclamations prepare and condition the reader to accept the credibility of Luke's report concerning Jesus' incredibly shameful death. But they also show how such an unexpected and embarrassing event fit within a greater *Heilsplan* inscribed long ago in the Jewish Scriptures. In line with Jewish tradition, the book of Acts maintains that Jerusalem would be preserved and eventually delivered, even if it had handed its own messiah to be crucified, the divine will anticipating events to occur in this way. Accordingly, when Peter claims in Acts that the Jewish crowd in Jerusalem delivered Jesus to lawless men to be crucified, he states that this event occurred in conformance with God's "definite plan and foreknowledge" (2:23). In Acts 3:17, Peter adds that this act was done out of *ignorance* (κατὰ ἄγνοιαν). Similarly, when Paul delivers a sermon in the synagogue of Pisidian Antioch, he claims that the people of Jerusalem and their rulers, *not knowing* (ἀγνοήσαντες) Jesus or the words of the prophets, unwittingly fulfilled prophecy by condemning Jesus to death (13:27). In unexpected ways, the divine will is fulfilled. Consequently, Acts never claims that "the Jews" should be punished for having Jesus crucified. Rather, a general call to repentance is made to the Jewish addressees who feel remorse after realizing their unintentional wrongdoing. Forgiveness for all sins is now provided in Jesus' name (2:37–38).[51]

The author of Acts does not so much hold the Jews accountable for Jesus' crucifixion as he wishes Israel would be stirred to collective repentance and accept its deliverer so that they might finally receive the promise of restoration made to them long ago (3:19–20). The theological dilemma that really disturbed the author of Acts was not the supposed Jewish crucifixion of Jesus, but a more perplexing and present reality that also agitated the Paul of Romans: namely, the persistent Jewish rejection of the "good news" about God's vindication of Jesus through his resurrection and appointment as messiah of Israel and lord over all creation. This greatly troubled the author of Acts, given his Israel-centric worldview and conviction about the integral role divinely assigned to the Jewish people in "salvation history." Rather than relinquish Israel's central role in the grand scheme of God's redemptive plans, the author of Acts, like many Jews from the Second Temple period, returned to the Jewish Scriptures, searching therein for evidence of the divine anticipation of Israel's rejection of its alleged messiah. Thus, at the end of the book of Acts, Paul, in a final frustrated reply to a Jewish delegation from Rome that remains divided over the message of the gospel (28:24), cites the Septuagintal version of Isaiah 6:9, stating:

> You will hear indeed and not understand at all, and you will indeed see but not perceive at all. For the heart of this people has become thick, and with difficulty do they hear with their ears, and they have closed their eyes, lest they see with their eyes and hear with their ears and understand with their heart and turn back, *and I will heal them*. (Acts 28:26–27; author's translation)

According to Acts, even Israel's continual hardness and failure to perceive God's plan, as purportedly revealed through Jesus, was predicted in Scripture. Making such a prophetic assertion allows the author of Acts to affirm, once again, God's control over history even in the most unexpected of events such as the Messiah's crucifixion and persistent rejection by God's own people. The book of Acts, however, leaves hope for the eventual and collective restoration of Israel. Following Bovon, I have literally translated the last phrase of the Septuagintal version of Isa. 6:9, as cited in Acts 28:27, in the future indicative: "and I will heal them" (καὶ ἰάσομαι αὐτούς).[52] The LXX differs at this point from the Masoretic Text, embracing a more optimistic stance toward Israel's collective restoration, which Acts also holds on to. These observations are in complete harmony with the wider Lukan perspective on divine providence: throughout Luke-Acts, God has always anticipated and adapted to unexpected circumstances in order to fulfill divine promises, especially those made to Israel. The story is not over for Israel in Acts. Jewish restoration remains in view. I find, therefore, that the perspective on Israel's final destiny in Acts is close to Paul's own views as penned in Romans, where he also affirms the eventual salvation of all of Israel (11:26).[53] The author of Acts, however, wrote a generation or more after Paul. While Paul was certain that the present age would pass away within his lifetime, the author of Acts had to deal with the problem of the delay of the Parousia. Paul had asserted that the proclamation of the Gospel to the gentiles would arouse the jealousy of the Jews (11:11). But in the aftermath of 70 CE, the author of Acts and the Jesus movement had reached a new impasse: the Gospel had been proclaimed as far as Rome, yet the Jews still remained divided, if not largely indifferent and opposed to the Jesus movement. The Messiah had still not come back, and the first generation of Jesus' followers had all passed away. How was the Jesus movement, during the delay of the eschaton, to relate to the Jewish people and Jewish custom?

It is remarkable that though the author of Acts seems to have experienced alienation from the Jewish world of his time, he still maintained that Jewish followers of Jesus should retain their distinctive Jewish identity by remaining faithful to the Torah and circumcising their children (16:1–3; 21:21). The large segment of Israel that did not believe in Jesus would continue to remain opposed to the Jesus movement until the end—in conformance with divine will, as prophesied in the Jewish Scriptures—after which God would finally heal them. No one, however, save for God—so Acts claims—would know the exact timing of the consummation of these events.

Conclusion

I noted and discussed a number of points of contact I see between Romans and Acts as far as their treatments of the Torah and the fate of the Jewish people are concerned. The Paul of Acts, I maintain, is just as Jewish as the Paul of Romans, if not more so. A similar accommodating spirit vis-à-vis the Jewish people and their heritage, which can be appreciated in Romans, appears in Acts as well, particularly in the two episodes reporting Paul's circumcision of Timothy (Acts 16:1-3) and in his participation in rituals of purification at the temple of Jerusalem (21:26–27).

In many ways, the differences that emerge between Acts and Romans are due to historical developments and changes in circumstances. Because of his apocalyptic belief in the imminent return of Jesus, the historical Paul did not deal with many of the long-term questions pressing the *ekklesia*, including the question of Torah praxis for future generations of Jewish followers of Jesus. "Was anyone at the time of his call already circumcised? Let him not seek to remove the marks of circumcision. Was anyone at the time of his call uncircumcised? Let him not seek circumcision" (1 Cor. 7:18). These were the words Paul wrote about the question of circumcision, convinced—as he penned in the same letter to Corinth—that the "impending crisis" (1 Cor. 7:26), "the appointed time" (7:29) had drawn near and that the present form of this world was "passing away" (7:31). Caught in this eschatological excitement, Paul did not deal extensively with the question of transmitting Jewish values to *subsequent generations*. Paul agreed that a Jewish follower of Jesus should remain Jewish and a gentile follower of Jesus, gentile. Left unanswered, however, was the long-term, generational issue concerning how Jewish followers of Jesus should raise their children and perpetuate Jewishness: a matter not central to Paul's missiological interests, given his fervent belief in the immediate arrival of the "day of wrath." If anything, Paul believed that followers of Jesus should remain single or "as if" they were unmarried (1 Cor. 7:8, 29). There is little room within such an ideology to deal with the anxieties of marriage and children (7:28, 32). Paul's apocalyptic worldview should never be left out of sight, however important he became for the subsequent development of Christian systematic theology.

As far as the salvation of the Jews was concerned, the Paul of Romans believed that the collective redemption of Israel would happen sooner than later. The hardening of Israel until the number of saved gentiles would reach its full number was not supposed to expand and endure indefinitely, at least not on Paul's clock (Rom. 11:25). Paul supposed that the Jews would only remain momentarily hardened until a number of gentiles (rapidly) joined the ranks of the Jesus movement, after which, all of Israel would be saved. All of this was to occur soon. But Jesus never came back. Paul and all of the first Jewish followers of Jesus passed away. It was up to the author of Acts, therefore—who represents only *one* possible interpretation of Paul's ambiguous and complex thought, and aligns more closely to the views of Paul expressed in the Epistle to the Romans—to tackle, during the delay of the Parousia, some of the persisting questions left unanswered by Paul concerning the relationship between the Jesus movement and mainstream Jewry. In such circumstances, the author of Acts voted on behalf of preserving a Jewish wing within the *ekklesia* that would remain faithful to its distinctive calling and customs. This affirmation is formulated in a clearer and more coherent manner in Acts than in Paul's own scattered writings, which, as noted, generated a variety of interpretations—a reflection of Paul's complex expression.

The historian might wonder, in light of the commonalities noted here between Acts and Romans, how this inquiry affects the larger question regarding the historicity of Acts. Obviously, the Jewish dimension of Acts cannot, by itself, prove the historicity of the events, acts, and sayings attributed to Paul, which must be assessed on an individual basis. This issue is reminiscent of the relationship between Matthew's Jesus and the historical Jesus. Both the historical Jesus and Matthew's Jesus are thoroughly Jewish. But many Matthean scholars recognize that Matthew rewrote Mark's gospel to serve his own theological interests and needs, which included, among other things, a clear desire to uphold the Torah. This is no more manifest than in Matt. 5:17–20, which does not pass the so-called criteria of "multiple independent attestation" and "earliest attestation," used by some scholars of the Jesus Seminar (but discarded by others) to reconstruct the life and ministry of the historical Jesus. But even if the historical Jesus did not actually utter the words inscribed in Matt. 5:17–20, one could argue that he certainly would have approved its contents. As David Sim notes, the Matthean portrait of Jesus, though formulated much after Jesus' time, "presents a much more plausible progression that involves considerable agreement between Jesus and his Galilean followers and different ideas and practices by converts in the post-Easter period."[54] For Sim, Matthew did not simply try to "re-Judaize" Jesus, but also sought to correct aspects about him he thought were theologically incorrect and unhistorical.[55] We might say that the author of Acts was motivated by similar concerns in his recasting of Paul. He framed Paul within a Jewish framework in order to correct what he perceived to be misunderstandings of Paul's comments and actions. Whether the depiction of Paul in Acts corresponds to the historical Paul is another question, which was not the concern of this chapter, set rather on assessing the *Jewishness* of both figures. The Jewish correspondence between the Paul of Acts and the Paul of Romans obviously does not prove that the author of Acts knew Paul personally. What Romans and Acts can really tell us about the early history of the Jesus movement is that many Jewish followers of Jesus continued to remain loyal to their Jewish heritage, both before and after 70 CE: that the relationship between the Jesus movement and Judaism remained a perennial concern for many followers of Jesus who continued to long for Israel's restoration.

Notes

1. The current tendency increasingly dates the Acts of the Apostles sometime in the beginning of the second century CE. See, for example, Richard I. Pervo, *Dating Acts: Between the Evangelist and the Apologists* (Santa Rosa, CA: Polebridge, 2006) and Joseph B. Tyson, *Marcion and Luke-Acts: A Defining Struggle* (Columbia, SC: University of South Carolina Press, 2006). Because I maintain that the Acts of the Apostles is a thoroughly Jewish document revealing concern about the Roman destruction of the temple of Jerusalem (Luke 13:31–35; 19:41–44; 21:24; etc.), I place the *terminus ad quem* for its final composition sometime before the Bar Kokhba Revolt (132 to c. 135 CE), since it evinces no knowledge of this event, which would have been expected, given the author's keen interest in the ultimate fate of Jerusalem (cf. Acts 1:6–8).

2. First published as Philipp Vielhauer, "Zum 'Paulinismus' der Apostelgeschichte," *Evangelische Theologie* 10 (1950–1951): 1–15. The article has more recently been republished in English as "On the 'Paulinism' of Acts" in *Paul and the Heritage of Israel: Paul's Claim upon Israel's Legacy in Luke and Acts in Light of the Pauline Epistles. Volume Two of Luke the Interpreter of Israel*, ed. David P. Moessner, Daniel Marguerat, Mikeal C. Parsons, and Michael Wolter (LNTS 452; London: T&T Clark, 2012), 3–17.

3. I cite here the works of only some of the participants of the Nangeroni Meeting of 2014 on "Re-reading Paul as a Second Temple Jewish author," including Pamela Eisenbaum, *Paul Was Not a Christian: The Real Message of a Misunderstood Apostle* (New York: HarperOne, 2009); Mark D. Nanos, *The Mystery of Romans: The Jewish Context of Paul's Letter* (Minneapolis: Fortress Press, 1996); *The Irony of Galatians: Paul's Letter in First-Century Context* (Minneapolis: Fortress Press, 2002); David J. Rudolph, *A Jew to the Jews: Jewish Contours of Pauline Flexibility in 1 Corinthians 9:19–23* (WUNT 2.304; Tübingen: Mohr Siebeck, 2011); Carlos A. Segovia. *Por una interpretación no cristiana de Pablo de Tarso: El redescubrimiento contemporáneo de un judío mesiánico* (Carlos A. Segovia, 2013).

4. See Isaac W. Oliver, *Torah Praxis after 70 CE: Reading Matthew and Luke-Acts as Jewish Texts* (WUNT 2.355; Tübingen: Mohr Siebeck, 2013). The late Jacob Jervell argued in many of his publications that Acts is a "Jewish Christian" text. See, for example, his *The Theology of the Acts of the Apostles* (Cambridge: Cambridge University Press, 1996). For other interpreters who detect an affirmation of Torah praxis in Luke and Acts, see Matthias Klinghardt, *Gesetz und Volk Gottes* (WUNT 2.32; Tübingen: Mohr Siebeck, 1988); William R. G. Loader, *Jesus' Attitude towards the Law* (WUNT 2.97; Tübingen: Mohr Siebeck, 1997); Matthew Thiessen, *Contesting Conversion: Genealogy, Circumcision, and Identity in Ancient Judaism and Christianity* (Oxford: Oxford University Press, 2011); Jürgen Wehnert, *Die Reinheit des "christlichen Gottesvolkes" aus Juden und Heiden* (FRLANT 173; Göttingen: Vandenhoeck & Ruprecht, 1997).

5. See especially Heikki Räisänen, *Paul and the Law* (WUNT 29; Tübingen: J. C. B. Mohr, 1983).

6. N. T. Wright, *Paul in Fresh Perspective* (Philadelphia: Fortress Press, 2009).

7. James D. G. Dunn, *The Theology of Paul the Apostle* (Grand Rapids: Eerdmans, 1998), 131—though open to the possibility that Paul developed his thoughts on the Law between the time he wrote Galatians and Romans—points to the potentially short span of time lying between the two, estimating Galatians to have been written between late 50 and mid-51 and Romans sometime between 50 and 58.

8. See, for example, the set of "pro-Israel" Pauline statements John Gager lists, mostly from Romans, in his *Reinventing Paul* (Oxford: Oxford University Press, 2000), 6–7. Cf. Eisenbaum, *Paul Was Not a Christian*, 27.

9. Marcion's "anti-Jewish" stance should not be exaggerated and needs nuancing, as pointed out more recently by Markus Vinzent, "Marcion the Jew," *Judaïsme ancien/Ancient Judaism* (2013): 159–201.

10. For a reading of Ephesians that argues against seeing this document as eradicating all differences between Jew and gentile, see Markus Barth, *Ephesians 1–3* (Garden City, NY: Doubleday, 1974); Mark S. Kinzer, *Postmissionary Messianic Judaism: Redefining Christian Engagement with the Jewish People* (Grand Rapids, MI: Brazos, 2005), 165–71; Luke Timothy Johnson, *The Writings of the New Testament* (Philadelphia: Fortress Press, 1986), 378–79.

11. I owe this insight to the Pauline scholar Robert B. Foster, whom I thank for the many personal discussions on this topic. Cf. Jacob Jervell, "Retrospect and Prospect in Luke-Acts Interpretation," in *SBL Seminar Papers, 1991*, ed. Eugene H. Lovering (SBLSP 30; Atlanta: Scholars Press, 1991), 403: "What made the Lucan Paul possible? We have at least three different Pauls: the Paul of the Pauline letters, the Paul of Acts, and the Paul of the deuteropauline letters and the Pastorals. Not only by going into the second century and later do we see the ramified tradition on the apostle to the Gentiles. Is it possible to trace the various pictures back to the same source, namely Paul himself, even if we know only fragments of him, namely from his letters? It should be possible to make some progress in analyzing the relation between Paul's theology and thinking on the one hand, and his acts, practice and way of life on the other. In the tradition of Judaism behavior (according or not according to the law!) had theological significance. Halakah was normative, not haggadah. What made the Lucan Jewish and law-observant Paul necessary? It seems that this Paul is as necessary for the Lucan outline as the opposite is for the Pastorals. It would be promising to study the Lucan Paul as part of the history of the Pauline tradition."

12. I accept Pervo's arguments in *Dating Acts*, 51–147, that the author of Acts knew a number of Pauline Letters. Differences between Acts and the Pauline Letters are due, in part, to the different nature and genre of the documents in question:

at least, the undisputed Pauline Letters are epistles and situational in their orientation, while Acts, on the contrary, contains a well-developed historiographical report that relates Pauline tradition in narrative form. On this matter, see Odile Flichy, "The Paul of Luke: A Survey of Research," pp. 18–34 and Daniel Marguerat, "Paul after Paul: A (Hi)story of Reception," pp. 70–89 in Moessner et al., eds., *Paul and the Heritage of Israel*.

13. Vielhauer, "On the 'Paulinism' of Acts," 8–9.

14. Ibid., 11–12.

15. Ibid., 9.

16. Ibid., 9.

17. Ibid., 8.

18. Ibid., 10.

19. Ibid., 7.

20. The earlier and influential work of Franz Overbeck, *Kurze Erklärung der Apostelgeschichte*, ed. W. M. L. De Wett (Kurzgefasstes exegetisches Handbuch zum Neuen Testament I/4; Leipzig: Hirzel, 1870), xxix–xxxv, should be noted here as well.

21. Hans Conzelmann, *The Theology of St Luke*, trans. Geoffrey Buswell (London: Faber and Faber, 1969), 16–17.

22. Ibid., 147.

23. John G. Gager, "Did Jewish Christians See the Rise of Islam?," in *The Ways That Never Parted*, ed. Adam H. Becker and Annette Yoshiko Reed (Minneapolis: Fortress Press, 2007), 361–72.

24. Ibid., 361–72. It is best, however, not to posit that Islam rose out of "Jewish Christian" sects that managed to survive till the seventh century CE, as Pines and Schoeps, among others, have claimed. Rather, Islam emerged out of a Jewish *and* Christian milieu, that scholars such as Carlos A. Segovia are now exploring from a historical-critical approach—a scholarly pursuit in Islamic studies still in its infant stages, due mainly to political factors rather than sound academic argumentation. See Hans-Joachim Schoeps, *Jewish Christianity: Factional Disputes in the Early Church*, trans. Douglas R. A. Hare (Philadelphia: Fortress Press, 1969), 140: "According to Islamic doctrine, the Ebionite combination of Moses and Jesus found its fulfillment in Mohammed; the two elements, through the agency of Jewish Christianity, were, in Hegelian terms, 'taken up' in Islam"; Shlomo Pines, "The Jewish Christians of the Early Centuries of Christianity according to a New Source," *Proceedings of the Israel Academy of Sciences and Humanities* 2 (1966): 237–310. By contrast, see now Carlos A. Segovia, *The Quranic Noah and the Making of the Islamic Prophet: A Study of Intertextuality and Religious Identity Formation in Late Antiquity* (Judaism,

Christianity, and Islam—Tension, Transmission, Transformation 4; De Gruyter, forthcoming).

25. Gager, "Did Jewish Christians See the Rise of Islam?," 367.

26. A scholar of the Radical New Perspective more open to seeing points of continuity between Romans and Acts would be Nanos, *The Mystery of Romans*, 28n13. Eisenbaum, *Paul Was Not a Christian*, 41–43, claims that the Acts of the Apostles played an integral role in forming the traditional image of Paul the convert, the former Jew who became a Christian. Acts, however, does not present Paul as converting from one religion to another, even if it recounts the episode on the road to Damascus three times. In Acts 22:3, as Paul relates his formative journey up to Damascus, he identifies himself as an ongoing Jew: "I am a Jew, born in Tarsus in Cilicia, but brought up in this city at the feet of Gamaliel, educated strictly according to our ancestral law, being zealous for God, just as all of you are today." In Acts 24:5, at his appearance before the Roman governor Felix, Paul is not presented as a Christian or former Jew, but as a leader of the Jewish faction (αἵρεσις) of the Nazarenes, the same term Josephus uses to describe the main groups he identified within Judean society (i. e., Pharisees, Sadducees, and Essenes).

27. Acts 13:14–15; 14:1; 17:1, 10, 17; 18:4, 19, 26; 19:8.

28. On the observance of Yom Kippur by the author of Acts, see Daniel Stökl Ben Ezra, *The Impact of Yom Kippur on Early Christianity* (WUNT 163; Tübingen: Mohr Siebeck, 2003).

29. On Timothy's circumcision, see Oliver, *Torah Praxis after 70*, 430–35.

30. The words φοβούμενοι τὸν θεόν probably refer to full converts to Judaism, since they are later addressed as brothers and descendants of Abraham in 13:26: Ἄνδρες ἀδελφοί, υἱοὶ γένους Ἀβραὰμ καὶ οἱ ἐν ὑμῖν φοβούμενοι τὸν θεόν.

31. Notice Acts 14:5, where it states that the "Gentiles and Jews" (rather than "Jews and Gentiles") sought to mistreat and stone Paul and Barnabas.

32. Cf. Nanos, *Mystery of Romans*, 28n13: ". . . features of Luke's presentation of Paul's view of Law-respectful behavior and his two-step missionary pattern are to be noted in the Paul we meet in the text of Romans."

33. Ernst Haenchen, *The Acts of the Apostles: A Commentary* (trans. Bernard Noble, Gerald Shinn, Hugh Anderson, and R. McL. Wilson; Oxford: Blackwell, 1971), 446n3: "Here however we have the law seen through Hellenistic Gentile Christian eyes, as a mass of commandments and prohibitions which no man can fulfil. Luke here is obviously speaking for himself and transmitting the view of his age and milieu." Richard I. Pervo, *A Commentary* (Hermeneia; Minneapolis: Fortress, 2009), 374, follows in the steps of Hans Conzelmann, *Acts of the Apostles* (Hermeneia; trans. James Limburg, A. Thomas Kraabel, and Donald H. Juel; Philadelphia: Fortress, 1987), 117: "It expresses the view of a Christian at a time when the separation from Judaism already lies in the past." Conzelmann

continues on the same page: "On this basis we can also understand why Luke does not draw the conclusion which logic demands, that this yoke should also be removed from Jewish Christians. For Luke Jewish Christianity no longer has any present significance, but it is of fundamental significance in terms of salvation history." Gerhard Schneider, *Die Apostelgeschichte* (2 vols.; HTKNT 5; Freiburg im Breisgau: Herder, 1980–1982), 2:181, following Haenchen and Conzelmann: "Lukas denkt dabei wohl an die Vielzahl der gesetzlichen Verpflichtungen." Similarly, Alfons Weiser, *Die Apostelgeschichte* (2 vols.; Ökumenischer Taschenbuch-Kommentar zum Neuen Testament 5.1–2; Gütersloh: Gütersloher Verlagshaus Gerd Mohn, 1982–1985), 2:381.

34. For an interesting view on Acts 15:10, see John Nolland, "A Fresh Look at Acts 15.10," *NTS* 27 (1980): 105–15.

35. In this case, my perspective matches Vielhauer's comment made long ago that "justification," so to speak, is only *complementary* for Jews, according to Acts. See Vielhauer, "On the 'Paulinism' of Acts," 10–11. Cf. Joseph A. Fitzmyer, *Luke the Theologian: Aspects of His Teaching* (New York: Paulist Press, 1989), 187: "The gospel that Paul is preaching is understood once again as a *supplement* to the law."

36. He doesn't do so simply to proselytize. See Oliver, *Torah Praxis after 70*, 72–73.

37. Ibid., 230–33.

38. The presentation of Paul as a Pharisee fits with the larger and more nuanced portrait of the Pharisees penciled in Luke-Acts. The Pharisees are not systematically presented as a monolithic group opposed to or even divorced from the Jesus movement. According to Acts, scores of Pharisees, besides Paul, belonged to the Jesus movement (15:5). Even Pharisees who do not belong to the Jesus movement intervene on behalf of its followers. Thus, Gamaliel, a prominent Pharisee, succeeds in convincing the Sanhedrin to release some Jewish disciples of Jesus from custody (5:33–39), just like the Pharisees later defend Paul during a similar hearing (23:7–10) and previously did on behalf of Jesus, warning him about Herod's intents to have him killed (Luke 13:31–33). The prominence of the Pharisees, their nuanced portrait, and the positive depiction of Paul and other followers of Jesus as Pharisees in Acts are remarkable. On the Pharisees in Luke and Acts, see John A. Ziesler, "Luke and the Pharisees," *NTS* 25 (1978–79): 146–57.

39. With Jacob Jervell, *Die Apostelgeschichte* (KKNT Meyer-Kommentar; Göttingen: Vandenhoeck & Ruprecht, 1998), 399, I concur that the Apostolic Decree *does* impose (a partial) submission of the Torah upon gentile Christians, since this legislation is grounded on the Torah (Acts 15:21). Daniel Marguerat, "Paul et la Torah dans les Actes des Apôtres," in *Reception of Paulinism in Acts / Réception du paulinisme dans les Actes des Apôtres*, ed. Marguerat (BETL 229; Leuven: Peeters, 2009), 81–100 (93), denies this interpretation by stating that the author of Acts conceives of the apostolic legislation "comme une *didaché* apostolique

legitimée par l'Esprit saint." However, because of Acts 15:21, Marguerat must acknowledge that the Apostolic Decree "correspond simultanément aux plus anciennes prescriptions de Moïse" (94).

40. David Flusser and Shmuel Safrai, "Das Aposteldekret und die Noachitischen Gebote," in *"Wer Tora vermehrt, mehrt Leben." Festgabe für Heinz Kremers zum 60. Geburtstag*, ed. Edna Brocke and Hans-Joachim Barkenings (Neukirchen-Vluyn: Neukirchener, 1986), 173–92, use the term *Doppelgleisigkeit* to speak of the halakic differentiation made in the earliest history of the Jesus movement between Jewish and gentile followers of Jesus, citing the English deist John Tolland (*Nazarenus or Jewish. Gentile and Mahometan Christianity* [1718]) as well as Moses Mendelssohn (*Schriften zum Judentum* [1930]). Tolland states: "It follows indeed that the Jews, whether becoming Christians or not, are for ever bound to the Law of Moses, as not limited; and he that thinks they were absolved from the observation of it by Jesus, or that it is a fault in them still to adhere to it, does err not knowing the Scriptures" (VI). Similarly, Mendelssohn: "Der Stifter der christlichen Religion hat niemals mit ausdrücklichen Worten gesagt, daß er das Mosaische Gesetz aufheben und die Juden dispensieren wolle. Ich habe dies in allen Evangelisten nicht gefunden. Die Apostel und die Jünger sind sogar lange nachher noch im Zweifel gewesen, ob nicht Heiden, die sich bekehrten, auch das Mosaische Gesetz annehmen und sich beschneiden müßten. Allein es wurde beschlossen, *den Heiden keine zu große* Last *aufzulegen* (Apostelgeschichte). Vollkommen nach der Lehre der Rabbinen, die ich in meinem Schreiben an Lavater angeführt. Aber für Juden, und wenn sie auch das Christenthum annehmen, finde ich im N. T. keine gegründete Dispensation von dem Mosaischen Gesetze. Vielmehr hat der Apostel selbst Timotheus beschnitten. Man räume mir also ein, daß es für mich kein Mittel gibt, mich von dem Mosaischen Gesetz zu befreien" (1:303). The term "bilateral ecclesiology" is coined by Kinzer, *Postmissionary Messianic Judaism*.

41. Butticaz, "'Has God Rejected His People?' (Romans 11.1). The Salvation of Israel in Acts: Narrative Claim of a Pauline Legacy," in Moessner et al., eds., *Paul and the Heritage of Israel*, 148–64 (163). Cf. Michael J. Cook, "The Mission to the Jews in Acts: Unraveling Luke's "Myth of the 'Myriads'", in *Luke-Acts and the Jewish People: Eight Critical Perspectives*, ed. Joseph B. Tyson (Minneapolis: Augsburg, 1988), 123: "There is, additionally, still other tragic irony in Romans 11, where Paul is apprehensive that Gentiles would boast and, becoming proud, no longer stand in awe and respect of Jews in their midst (Rom. 11:18ff.)—not only Jews in theory but also Jews in reality, perhaps in Rome itself. Paul's real apprehension of Gentile attitudes towards Jews ironically and tragically became fulfilled in the person of what some might term his unauthorized biographer, Luke. That indeed is not only ironic; it became tragic for Jews—and for relations between Jews and Christians—throughout history." Needless to say, I disagree with Cook's claim and assumption about the gentile background of the author of Acts.

42. See Robert C. Tannehill, *The Narrative Unity of Luke-Acts: A Literary Interpretation. Volume Two: The Acts of the Apostles* (Minneapolis: Fortress Press, 1994), 288–90, 319–20, 344, and especially, Vittorio Fusco, "Luke-Acts and the Future of Israel," *NovT* 38 (1996): 1–17, for a comprehensive and excellent analysis of the problem.

43. Franz Mussner, *Apostelgeschichte* (NEBNT 5; Würzburg: Echter, 1984), 16: "klingt überraschend und fast seltsam."

44. Frederick F. Bruce, *Commentary on the Book of Acts* (NICNT; Grand Rapids, MI: Eerdmans, 1968), 38: "The apostles maintained their interest in the hope of seeing the kingdom of God realized in the restoration of Israel's national independence."

45. On the author's hope for the restoration of Jerusalem as implied in Acts 1:6–8, see Le Cornu and Shulam, *A Commentary on the Jewish Roots of Acts* (2 vols.; Jerusalem: Academon, 2003), 1:15: "Jesus' answer to the Apostles does not delegitimate their question but merely places it beyond the scope of human knowledge"; Jervell, *Die Apostelgeschichte*, 114: "Es wird nicht danach gefragt, ob das Reich für Israel wiederhergestellt werden soll, denn das ist selbstverständlich. Dies wird ja auch in der Antwort Jesu nicht korrigiert"; Loader, *Jesus' Attitude towards the Law*, 381–82. Cf. Serge Ruzer, "Jesus' Crucifixion in Luke and Acts: The Search for a Meaning vis-à-vis the Biblical Pattern of Persecuted Prophet," in *Judaistik und neutestamentliche Wissenschaft*, ed. Lutz Doering, Hans-Günther Waubke, and Florian Wilk (FRLANT 226; Göttingen: Vandenhoeck & Ruprecht, 2008), 174: "This passage . . . clearly indicates that the author does not wish to abrogate the hope for Israel's redemption, which seems to be presented as having also political overtones."

46. Those who interpret Luke 21:24 as referring to Roman rule (and by implication its end) include Erich Grässer, *Das Problem der Parusieverzögerung in den synoptischen Evangelien und in der Apostelgeschichte* (3d ed.; Berlin, 1977), 162; Gerhard Schneider, *Das Evangelium nach Lukas* (2 vols.; 2d ed.; Gütersloh; Würzburg: Mohn, 1984), 424; Eduard Schweizer, *The Good News according to Luke*, trans. David E. Green (Atlanta: John Knox, 1984), 317; J. Bradley Chance, *Jerusalem, the Temple, and the New Age in Luke-Acts* (Macon, GA: Mercer University Press, 1988), 135 (Luke hints at the restoration of Jerusalem); Fusco, "Luke-Acts and the Future of Israel," 14–15 (Luke assumes Jerusalem will be restored here and throughout); Michael Wolter, "Israel's Future and the Delay of the Parousia," in *Luke the Interpreter of Israel*, ed. David P. Moessner and David L. Tiede (vol. 1 of *Jesus and the Heritage of Israel: Luke's Narrative Claim upon Israel's Legacy*, ed. David P. Moessner; Harrisburg, PA: Trinity Press International, 1999), 307–24 (309).

47. "At that moment she came, and began to praise God and to speak about the child to all who were looking for the *redemption of Jerusalem* [λύτρωσιν Ἰερουσαλήμ]" (Luke 2:38). Cf. Luke 1:16; 1:54–55; 2:25 (the "consolation of

Israel"). The Hebrew equivalents גאולת ישראל and חרות ישראל appear on Jewish coins from the two Jewish Revolts against Rome. While Luke was certainly no zealot calling for followers of Jesus to bear arms against Rome, there is no need to exclude that λύτρωσις in Acts can refer to the hope for the eventual dismantlement of Rome and the restoration of Israel. Cf. David Flusser, *The Sage from Galilee: Rediscovering Jesus' Genius* (4th ed.; Grand Rapids, MI: Eerdmans, 2007), 126–27.

48. Clare K. Rothschild, *Luke-Acts and the Rhetoric of History* (WUNT 2.175; Tübingen: Mohr Siebeck, 2003), provides a very important corrective, demonstrating how the usage of δεῖ was rather standard in Hellenistic historiographical writings and functions rhetorically in Luke-Acts to authenticate the presentation of its version of reported events. Undoubtedly, previous scholarship has lost itself in fine theological discussions about Luke's views on fate and predestination, wondering whether he was indebted to Greek or Jewish beliefs on this matter. But can Luke's rhetorical enterprise be reduced solely to authenticating *historical* truth? This seems unlikely, especially when δεῖ is read with other key terms and passages (e. g., Acts 4:28: βουλή προώρισεν; 13:36; etc.) that wrestle with the embarrassment of the cross and the Jewish rejection of the Jesus movement: problems that were embedded in Pauline letters such as Romans and also preoccupied the author of Acts. Rothschild's fine study is unfortunately built upon the assumption that Luke is ignorant about Judaism (168n71) and no longer interested in the question of the final restoration of the Jewish people (107n27), and consequently, overlooks what the narration in Acts might tell us about Luke's distinctive perspective on Jewish-Christian relations.

49. On the various usages of δεῖ, see Charles Cosgrove, "The Divine Δει in Luke-Acts: Investigations into the Lukan Understanding of God's Providence," *NovT* 26 (1984): 168–90.

50. Cf. ibid., 179: "Jesus, ever cognizant that the divine δεῖ bids him suffer and rejected on his way to exaltation, virtually engineers his own passion."

51. The fact that the Jews in Jerusalem, according to Acts, accomplished this unknowingly makes them less guilty than Judas who was an informed disciple of Jesus (see Luke 22:3; Acts 1:16–20; cf. Luke 12:47; 23:24).

52. François Bovon, "Studies in Luke-Acts: Retrospect and Prospect," *HTR* 85 (1992): 189–90 (175–96). Cf. Helmut Merkel, "Israel im lukanischen Werk," *NTS* 40 (1994): 371–98 (397).

53. Cf. Richard B. Hays, "The Paulinism of Acts, Intertextuality Reconsidered," in Moessner et al., eds., *Paul and the Heritage of Israel*, 35–48 (46): "For both of our authors, the unbelief of many in Israel when offered the good news of the gospel constitutes a significant theological challenge. In both cases, this challenge is met through appeal to the prophecies of Isaiah concerning Israel's blindness and deafness. Thus, this anomalous state of affairs is also attributed to the mysterious will and working of God. Paul, more clearly than

Luke, envisions an eschatological redemption in which all Israel will be saved; nonetheless, Luke holds open the possibility of a future time when God will restore the kingdom to Israel (Acts 1.6–7, perhaps also 3.21), and he continues to refer to the gospel message as 'the hope of Israel' (28.20; cf. Luke 24.21a)."

54. David C. Sim, "Matthew and Jesus of Nazareth," in *Matthew and His Christian Contemporaries*, ed. Sim and Boris Repschinski (LNTS 333. London: T&T Clark, 2008), 155–72 (172).

55. Ibid.

PART II

Paul and Second
Temple Apocalypticism

3

Paul, the Jewish Apocalypses, and Apocalyptic Eschatology

James H. Charlesworth

In the nineteenth century, Pauline specialists sought to understand Paul in light of Greek and Roman culture. Focusing on Paul's ability to write Greek, his origins in the Diaspora, and being a missionary to the gentiles, they found the background for Paul's theology in the mystery religions and the *Kyrios* cults.[1] The turning point in research and the perception that Paul lived in the world of Jewish apocalyptic eschatology came at the beginning of the twentieth century with H. St. John Thackeray's *St. Paul and Contemporary Jewish Theology* (1900) and with Albert Schweitzer's *Paul and His Interpreters* (1911 [German], 1912) and his *The Mysticism of Paul the Apostle* (written in 1906 and published in 1930 [German], 1931). Subsequently, due to the stellar publications by William D. Davies,[2] Hans J. Schoeps,[3] Frederick C. Grant,[4] and

William C. van Unnik,[5] many New Testament scholars assumed the focal point for Paul's theology was the world of Second Temple Judaism.[6] No scholar prior to 1947, and the discovery of the Dead Sea Scrolls, could have imagined what we now know: the vibrant, creative, and marvelous symbolic culture of Palestinian Judaism before 70 CE.

In present research, scholars in most countries recognize that if there is any consensus in Pauline studies, it is that Paul's theology was deeply formed not only by Jewish thought,[7] but especially, by Jewish apocalyptic eschatology.[8] N. T. Wright admits that many Pauline specialists are confused by the concept of "apocalyptic" and that "salvation-history" and "apocalyptic" can be "uncomfortable categories," but he wisely affirms that "apocalyptic" denotes "something which Paul really does seem to have made central."[9] Wright wisely perceives that apocalyptic eschatology involves both a radical newness and a continuous flow of history (so clear in *4 Ezra* and Gal. 4:4–5). John J. Collins rightly points out that the Jewish literary apocalypses should take precedence in studying Paul, and that in 1 Cor. 7:29–31, Paul, under the influence of apocalyptic eschatology, argues that social distinctions have lost their significance.[10] Dale C. Allison claims that Paul, in 1 Corinthians 7, is indebted to Jewish "apocalyptic celibacy."[11] Adela Yarbro Collins rightly points out that Paul is influenced by the typical Jewish apocalyptic contrast between this age and the age to come (*4 Ezra* 8:1–3) when he mentions "the present evil age" (Gal. 1:4).[12] Paul both inherits from Jewish apocalyptic thought and compositions and appeals to his own apocalyptic experiences (as in Gal. 1:12; 2:2, and especially, in 2 Corinthians 12).[13]

This consensus influences the Academy to such an extent that one may consider it to be the *vade mecum* of most books on Paul's life and thought.[14] As Martinus C. de Boer wisely assesses the *status quaestionis*: "It is thus difficult, nay impossible, to discuss Paul's apocalyptic eschatology apart from Jewish apocalyptic eschatology and what scholars have said about the latter since the time of Schweitzer."[15] Thus, Paul's apocalyptic eschatology can be comprehended in more depth by studying the Jewish apocalyptic works and apocalypses that are roughly contemporaneous with him. Within this consensus resides another agreement. It has two dimensions.

First, Paul must be understood within Second Temple Judaism, and specifically, with Jewish apocalyptic eschatology. The Pauline scholars who introduced the claim that Paul's theology was fundamentally built upon Jewish apocalyptic thought are Ernst Käsemann and J. Christiaan Beker. In 1960, Käsemann announced: "Die Apokalyptik ist die Mutter aller christlichen Theologie."[16] Käsemann was focusing on Jesus research when he made this famous claim. Other scholars, notably Peter Stuhlmacher and I. Baumgarten, shifted the focus to Paul, claiming that Paul was deeply influenced by Jewish apocalyptic thought.[17]

Twenty years later, in 1980, J. Christiaan Beker rightly pointed out that Rudolf Bultmann interpreted Paul "via Johannine categories," and thereby, "undercuts Paul's reflections on Israel's destiny, his apocalyptic eschatology, social solidarity, and cosmic theological horizon."[18] In essence, what had been missing in Pauline studies was Paul's solidarity with Israel, his firm conviction that all Israel will be saved, and the fundamental theocentric foundation on "apocalyptic eschatology." Beker was convinced of Paul's position within Jewish apocalypticism; note this insight:

> Paul is heavily indebted to the apocalyptic ideology of his time because he had been an apocalyptic Diaspora Pharisee before his conversion. Apocalyptic is for Paul the bearer of prophecy in new circumstances. It keeps alive the prophetic promises about a new act of God in the future that will surpass God's acts in the past and bring about a transformed creation.[19]

Second, neither of these brilliant New Testament scholars, Käsemann or Beker, showed any real interest in mastering, reading, or comprehending the complex world of the Jewish apocalypses.[20] They did not give us a clear understanding of Jewish apocalyptic thought and how, and in what ways, it is distinguished from prophecy, mysticism, and that elusive category called "Gnosticism."

The purpose of this chapter is, thus, to affirm the consensus that

Paul's theology is fundamentally developed from Jewish apocalyptic eschatology and to bring the Jewish apocalypses and apocalyptic writings into better focus for Pauline studies. Focus will be directed to Paul's seven undisputed letters: Romans, 1 and 2 Corinthians, Galatians, Philippians, 1 Thessalonians, and Philemon. At the outset, let us define three terms: an apocalypse, apocalypticism, and apocalyptic eschatology.

Defining the Key Terms

Since the 1970s, those in the SBL Pseudepigrapha Group have come to a consensus regarding the three key terms. First, "apocalypse" is a genre of literature that appeared within Palestinian Judaism sometime after 300 BCE. Suffice it to quote John J. Collins:

> An "apocalypse" was defined as a genre of revelatory literature with a narrative framework, in which a revelation is mediated by an otherworldly being to a human recipient, disclosing a transcendent reality which is both temporal, insofar as it envisages eschatological salvation, and spatial as it involves another supernatural world.[21]

Second, apocalypticism is the social setting in which the Jewish apocalypses and apocalyptic works first emerged. The fact of being subjugated by Persians, Greeks, and Romans often led to the perception that God was no longer working through history (*Heilsgeschichte*); God had withdrawn to appear at the end time, when God will bring all evil to an end and reward the righteous and faithful Jews.

Third, under the distress of occupation, Jews created apocalyptic eschatology that assumes that time has meaning and is linear. The end time will be a return to the beginning of time, when humans walked in the cool of the evening with God, could talk to animals, and were at peace with themselves in a pleasant land. The concept of paradise was inherited from Persia and "the island of the blessed ones" from the Greeks; as these ideas blended, they influenced the conception of Eden that had long before been developed within ancient Israel. Eventually, Eden was imagined as a garden in which it would be possible to be at one with all, especially the Loving Creator.

To these definitions must be added the phenomenological dimension of the apocalypse, apocalyticism, and apocalyptic eschatology. What happened when a first-century Jew read an apocalypse? Two phenomena occurred.[22] First, the person was transported from this horrible world to the heavenly world above, spatially, or beyond time. That means all conceptions and hope were transferred to another realm in which peace and harmony could be found. Oneness was once again achieved as imagined in the story of Eden.

How was the early Jew enabled to transcend? Sometimes, it is by vision, as in *1 Enoch*, or by a literal trip into the heavens guided by an angel, as in *2 Enoch*. To help the reader to image such transference, an author sometimes provides a means and a command. A good example of a means and invitation is found in Revelation:

> After this I looked, and lo, in heaven *an open door*. And the first voice, which I had heard speaking to me like a trumpet, said, *"Come up hither*, and I will show you what must take place after this." (4:1; italics mine)

The second phenomenon that occurred was "redefinition." The poor were revealed to be the rich. The conquered were disclosed to be the conquerors. The lost were the found. Thus, the faithful Jews who refused to obey the edicts of the Seleucid kings and Roman governors were willing to be martyred. To be obedient and to die for God and country was to live eternally. Virtually all was redefined by an apocalyptic perception of space and time and this redefinition often, depending on one's own antecedent beliefs, led to a heightened awareness of the need to live moral lives as the judgment was near.[23]

Not all apocalyptic thought is eschatology, that is, focused on the end of things or end time. It may be primarily spatial, focusing our attention on the heavens above or on far-off and ideal sacred spaces such as Eden, paradise, and the isle of the blessed ones.[24] The noun "eschatology" should be reserved to discuss and comprehend concepts and terms that are shaped by time and the end of time.[25]

The Continuum of Apocalypses

The extent of the early Jewish apocalypses and Jewish traditions in apocalypses is vast. It can be organized into four categories. These works, an apocalyptic document or an apocalypse, are included in the list because of their apocalyptic nature—that is, they contain an apocalyptic (revelatory) vision, journey, or message that is often spatial or eschatological. The origin of the message is God and it is often transmitted through an archangel.

I) The first category is the apocalyptic writings and the one apocalypse in the Hebrew Scriptures:

Proto-apocalyptic

- Isaiah 24–27; 33; 34–35
- Jeremiah 33:14–26
- Ezekiel 38–39
- Joel 3:9–17
- Zechariah 12–14

Apocalypse in the Hebrew-Aramaic Scriptures

- Daniel 7–12

II) The second category lists the early quasi-apocalypses and the full-blown apocalypses; these date from 300 BCE to the Mishnah (c. 200–225 CE). The list is impressive:

- *The Books of Enoch* (= *1 Enoch*)
- *2 Enoch*
- *3 Enoch* (later with early traditions)
- *Sibylline Oracles*

- *Treatise of Shem*
- *Apocryphon of Ezekiel*
- *Apocalypse of Abraham*[26]
- *Apocalypse of Adam*
- *2 Baruch (Syriac)*
- *3 Baruch (Greek)*
- *Apocalypse of Elchasai*
- *Apocalypse of Elijah*
- *4 Ezra*[27]
- *Greek* Apocalypse of Ezra (second–ninth century CE)
- *Questions of Ezra* (date unclear)
- *Gabriel's Revelation*
- Apocalypse of Lamech (lost)
- *Apocalypse of Moses*
- *Apocalypse of Zephaniah*
- Apocalypse of Zerubbabel (Byzantine but with early traditions)
- *Apocalypse of Sedrach* (second–ninth century CE)
- 4QMessianic Apocalypse (= On Resurrection [4Q521])[28]
- The Jewish apocalypses excerpted in the Cologne Mani Codex

III) The third category is devoted to the "Testaments"; these often contain visions, apocalypses, and apocalyptic sections; they date from the second century BCE (with interpolations [both by Jews and Christians]) to the fifth century CE. They are the following:

- *Testaments of the Twelve Patriarchs*
- *Testament of Job*
- *Testaments of the Three Patriarchs* (Abraham, Isaac, Jacob)

- *Testament of Moses*
- *Testament of Solomon*
- *Testament of Adam*

IV) The fourth category is the Jewish dimension of the Apocalypse of John in the New Testament.

Depending on the date of the traditions preserved in them, these apocalyptic compositions and "apocalypses" are fundamental to understanding the world of early Judaism (300 BCE to 200 CE) in which Paul lived and thought.[29] Since Paul's fundamental presuppositions were Jesus' messianic status, the efficaciousness of Jesus' death and resurrection, and apocalyptic eschatology, these apocalyptic compositions and apocalypses provide insight into Paul's mind.[30] Yet, no one has illustrated how Paul may have been influenced by these texts and the worldview they represent.

Paul and Qumran's Apocalyptic Thought

We know about three apocalyptic communities within Second Temple Judaism, but they are different and should be distinguished.

I. *The Jews Behind the Books of Enoch.* One is the group of Jews, composed mostly of non-priests, who found self-understanding from ancient traditions preserved in the *Books of Enoch*.[31] At least some of these "books" were composed in Lower Galilee. This corpus is a massive collection of apocalyptic texts dating from about 300 BCE to the time of Hillel and Jesus. Most of these compositions were found in the Qumran caves. The alleged absence of the *Parables of Enoch* from the Qumran caves may be due to the celebration of Enoch in chapters 70–71; the Qumranites revered the Righteous Teacher (1QpHab 7).[32]

II. *The Qumran or Essene Movement.* The second group of Jews, composed of Aaronites, other priests, Levites, and eventually, laymen, settled at Qumran and collected or composed what are called the Dead Sea Scrolls; all the documents were found in eleven caves near

Qumran.[33] Thus, even though the Qumranites did not compose one apocalypse, we can conclude that Qumran was an apocalyptic community. Why?

First, the members of the Qumran community collected apocalypses, like Daniel and the *Books of Enoch*. The Qumranites and Essenes certainly had some contact with the Jews behind the compositions attributed to Enoch. And they were deeply influenced, especially in the early decades, by ideas, perceptions, and beliefs found in the apocalyptic works and apocalypses. They also composed or edited additional apocalyptic creations, such as *Apocalypse* (4Q489), *Apocalypse of Weeks Pesher* (4Q427), the *Apocalyptic Text* (6Q14), *New Jerusalem* (1Q32, 2Q24, 5Q15, 4Q554, 554a, 555, 11Q18), *Pseudo-Daniel* (4Q243-245), and *On Resurrection* (4Q521).

Second, the Qumranites believed that they were living in "the last days." All history had been created for their time. All prophecies were directed to their time and their own special role in salvation history.

Third, only those who follow the Righteous Teacher to Qumran had been given apocalyptic knowledge. They alone knew the meaning of the times and the end time. They alone had been given the Holy Spirit. This divine being helped them interpret Scripture, which included many more revelatory works than those eventually canonized.

Fourth, those in the Qumran community believed that angels worshiped with them, and that the celestial beings, like them, followed the lunar-solar calendar (*Books of Enoch, Jubilees, Angelic Liturgy, Hodayot*). Thus, the community was often perceived as an antechamber of heaven. Temple liturgy had been recast so that the appropriate sacrifice was the "offering of the lips." And the earthly temple in Jerusalem was shifted liturgically and sociologically to Qumran and given a cosmic dimension.

These developments mean that the modified dualism of Qumran (1QS 3.13–4.26) was shifted so that the future broke into the present and heaven touched earth. Thus, time and space were redefined. It seems likely that some at Qumran believed that the eternal planting was being prepared, through the incomparable Righteous Teacher, for the final Eden, in which "the trees of life" received "living water" for eternity (1QHa 16).

Many ideas once perceived to be creations of Paul can be found within this Qumran community. Three observations must now suffice to share. First, all humans sin and fall far short of doing God's will. Second, no human can earn God's forgiveness or acceptance through works, no matter how righteous one was perceived to be. Third, all humans receive forgiveness and acceptance solely through God's gracious covenant loyalty. Such ideas permeate the last two columns of the *Rule of the Community* and appear in most columns of the *Hodayot*.

Note the following excerpts from these *Thanksgiving Hymns*. We hear about the sin into which all are born, and that only by God's goodness and mercies can anyone be justified and saved:[34]

> And what is one born of a woman in all your terrifying works?[35]
>   For he is but a form[36] of dust and mixed[37] water.
>   G[uilt and si]n (is) his foundation, shameless nakedness[38]
>   [and the spring of impu]rity, and a perverted spirit dominates in him.[39]
>   And if he should be wicked,
>   he shall be an eternal [sign][40] and a portent[41]
>   (for) dista[n]t generations of the flesh.
>   Only by his goodness can a human be justified;
>   and in the multitude of [your] mer[cies you will save him]. (5.31–34)
>   And I have no refuge (in) the flesh;
>   [. . .] there (are) no righteous (deeds) to be delivered[42] before [you][43]
>   without forgiveness.
>
> But I, I leaned on the multitude of [your mercies].
>   [And for the greatness of] your loving kindness, I await,
>   to bring forth buds[44] as planting,
>   and to grow a shoot to cause shelter in (your) power,
>   and I[. . .]. (15.20–22)

Furthermore, the Qumranites believed that only by God's goodness and mercies can the human stand upright before God:

> For who is like you among the gods, O Lord?[45]
>   And who is like your truth?
>   And who can be justified before you when he is judged?
>   And no hosts[46] of a spirit can reply to your chastisement.
>   And none can stand before your wrath.

And you allow all the sons of your truth
to come into forgiveness before you,
   purifying them from their transgressions
with the multitude of your goodness,
   and with the abundance of your mercies,
   allowing them to stand before you forever (and) ever.[47] (15.31–34)

III. *The Palestinian Jesus Movement.* The first two groups of apocalyptically inspired Jews antedated Jesus by more than two centuries, but they also were contemporaneous with Jesus. In addition, many Pharisees and other Jews were deeply influenced by apocalypticism, but they were neither in the group behind the *Books of Enoch* or Qumranites (or Essenes).

Jesus also set in motion a new movement. During his time and in the 30s and 40s, major creative developments emerged within Jesus' group. Though the *Self-Glorification Hymn* is influenced by Isaiah 53 in describing one seated among the "divine beings," only Jesus' followers used "the Suffering Servant Messiah" concept to portray the life, death, and resurrection of their "Lord." We know about these pre-Pauline traditions because of the early traditions in Mark and John, as well as the traditions, creedal formulae, resurrection beliefs,[48] and hymns inherited from the PJM (my non-anachronistic term for "the apostolic church" by Paul).

The conclusion to this brief review of Jewish apocalyptic thought at Qumran and elsewhere is this: what had been perceived to be Paul's own creation appeared already within apocalyptic Judaism. His concept of time and space was shaped by apocalyptic eschatology. Obviously, Paul added his own creativity to these cognitive structures. For Paul, Jesus was the Christ, the Messiah, who had died for the sins of all and who was raised by God. Those ideas are not necessarily unique to Paul; he most likely inherited them from Jews who believed in Jesus in the 30s of the first century CE.

Paul added to Qumran perspectives the concept that circumcision was of the heart and that the restrictive dietary laws of strict Jews were no longer mandatory.[49] Though Paul circumcised Timothy, whose mother was a Jewess (Acts 26:1–3), he argued that neither circumcision nor epispasm[50] were relevant to salvation (1 Cor. 7:18–19).[51] Thus, Paul (and perhaps about the same time, Peter, according to Acts) opened up the mission to the gentiles; yet, even here, we find no need to circumcise in Adiabene, with Azates, or in Alexandria, as Philo clarifies (esp. in *QE* 2.2). Even in ancient Palestine, some Jews ate pork, and we can no longer define a village as non-Jewish with the discovery of pig bones. Jews could breed pigs and sell them to the gentiles. Paul's criticism of some Jewish laws does not, in any way, distract from his appreciation and devotion to Torah, Law, as God's gift to all.[52]

Paul's Apocalyptic Theology

Paul's thought can now be recognized as shaped and defined by Jewish apocalyptic thought in numerous fundamental ways. In the following passage, Paul expresses his earliest thoughts:

> For since we believe that Jesus died and rose again, even so, through Jesus, God will bring with him those who have fallen asleep. For this we declare to you by the word of the Lord, that we who are alive, who are left until the coming of the Lord, shall not precede those who have fallen asleep. For the Lord himself will descend from heaven with a cry of command, with the archangel's call, and with the sound of the trumpet of God. And the dead in Christ will rise first; then we who are alive, who are left, shall be caught up together with them in the clouds to meet the Lord in the air; and so we shall always be with the Lord. Therefore comfort one another with these words. (1 Thess. 4:14–18; RSV)

We do not have the oral question or written epistle that explains Paul's response, but surely, some in Thessalonica were worried about those who had died and that Christ had not yet returned to save them. Paul's answer is clear and comforts those who grieve: God will send Jesus from heaven to call all to be with the Lord Jesus for eternity. Paul imagines also that he will be alive when this apocalyptic end arrives. The lightning bolt in Paul's apocalyptic cosmos is 1 Thess. 4; it comes from the storm clouds of Jewish apocalyptic eschatology.

Later, in Romans, Paul will shift from emphasizing apocalyptic visions and imagery to eschatology: "Knowing the time, it is already the hour for you to awake from sleep. For salvation is nearer to us now than when we began to believe" (Rom. 13:11; my translation). For this linear concept of time and eschatology, Paul is indebted to the apocalyptic concept of time that first appeared and was developed in the Jewish apocalyptic compositions and apocalypses.

Paul's Concept of the Fullness of Time

Paul's concept that time can be fulfilled derives from Judaism; Greeks and Romans would find it difficult to comprehend. From the beginning of the Hebrew Bible, creation is within time, not before time, as in most other religions. God reveals his will and purpose in time. Time, thus, has a meaning and a linear dimension. The Jewish apocalyptists developed this concept of time to its fullest extent. God will act decisively in the end of time. Time has a beginning and end. Paul's Christology picks that up and develops it with innuendos of protology and emphatic eschatology: Christ Jesus was at the beginning of time and will be the judge at the end of time.

Paul's exegesis of Scripture is also shaped by time. His method of reading and understanding Scripture is by means of a hermeneutic of fulfillment. That method is best developed in the Qumran Pesharim. Paul may have known Essenes, who used the hermeneutic of fulfillment, but he may have learned it from others as it was not unique to the Essenes. He could have learned it from the earliest followers of Jesus; they also used the hermeneutic of fulfillment.

Paul's Literary Dependence

Did Paul ever quote from or allude to a Jewish apocalyptic work or apocalypses? In 1970, C. W. Fishburne concluded that Paul not only knew, but also used the *Testament of Abraham*.[53] This claim seems unlikely, since the apocalyptic work appears to postdate Paul and is probably influenced by passages in the New Testament.[54]

Paul must be allowed to know and quote from an apocalypse known to him, but no longer extant in a full form perceived by us. Thus, Paul seems to quote from an *Apocalypse of Elijah*. That seems evident from a study of 1 Cor. 2:9. Origen (*Comm. Matt.* 23:37), Jerome (*Comm. Isa.* 17 on 64–66), and Photius (*Quaest. Amphil.* 151), among ancient exegetes, and Dale Allison, among modern scholars, are convinced that Paul is quoting a lost apocalypse that bore the name "Elijah." Most likely, an early Jew shifted Isa. 64:4 ("to those who wait for him") into "to those who love him."[55]

2 Corinthians and its Three-Dimensional Apocalyptic Eschatology

According to 2 Corinthians 12, Paul describes "revelations of the Lord" that he has experienced. Note his description and caution:

> I know a man in Christ who fourteen years ago was caught up to the third heaven—whether in the body or out of the body I do not know, God knows. And I know that this man was caught up into Paradise—whether in the body or out of the body I do not know, God knows—and he heard things that cannot be told, which man may not utter. (2 Cor. 12:2–4; RSV)

Paul is certain that he was taken up into the third heaven, saw paradise, and heard things that can never be revealed. These three concepts are developed within the Jewish apocalypses and apocalyptic writings.[56] *Ascension* dominates in many apocalypses. Two Jewish apocalyptic compositions place *paradise* in the third heaven;[57] the most important one is *2 Enoch*. And within the apocalypses, there are *revealed insights* that can be communicated only to the elect ones, if at all. Paul could have known the traditions that were later incorporated into *2 Enoch*:

> And the men took me from there. They brought me up to the third heaven. And they placed me in the midst of Paradise. And that place has an appearance of pleasantness that has never been seen. Every tree was in full flower. Every fruit was ripe, every food was in yield profusely; every fragrance was pleasant. And the four rivers were flowing past with gentle movement, with every kind of garden producing every kind of good food. And the tree of life is in that place, under which the LORD takes a rest when the LORD takes a walk in Paradise. And that tree is indescribable for pleasantness of fragrance. (2 En. 8:1–3; recension A[58])

As Matthew Goff points out, Paul's theology is indebted to the worldview provided by the heavenly mysteries and otherworldly journeys developed and articulated by the Jewish apocalyptic authors.[59]

Resurrection

For many Christians and within dogmatic theology, the central article in "Christian" faith is the belief that God raised Jesus from the dead. This belief defined the earliest communities of Jews who believed in Jesus,[60] using many titles, but emphasizing one before Paul's first letter: "The Messiah Jesus" or "Jesus Christ." As John J. Collins stated in *The Apocalyptic Imagination* (1984), Paul is credited with making the first written witness to Jesus' resurrection, but it is not an isolated event: Paul bases the belief on the Jewish perception that the dead will be raised.[61] That is, Jesus' resurrection is not an isolated event; it is the beginning of the general resurrection affirmed in many Jewish apocalypses. Jesus' resurrection by God is, then, "the first fruits" (Rom. 8:23; 1 Cor. 15:20, 23).[62] Note the double thrust of 1 Cor. 15:13: "If there is no resurrection of the dead, then Christ has not been raised." This resurrection belief was developed within Judaism and took definite shape within apocalyptic texts and apocalypses.[63] Paul's use of "first fruits" in connection with the belief in resurrection is indebted to the Jewish concept of a general resurrection.[64]

Paul's Christology and the *Self-Glorification Hymn*

One of the most important compositions in early Judaism for a perception of Paul's theology and Christology is the *Self-Glorification Hymn*. Here is my composite translation:[65]

[1][. . .] I, I reckon myself among the gods.
And my abode (is) in the congregation of [2]holiness.

Who is reckoned despicable as me?
And who has been despised like [me]?

[And who] [3]is rejected [(by) men] like me?
[And who bears] evil (so) he compares (to) m[e?]

And no instruction [4]can compare with my teaching;
For I, I sat securely in the dwelling of holi[ness].

[5]Who is like me among the gods?
And who can cut me off when I op[en my mouth]?
And the flow of [6]my speech, who can measure (it)?

Wh[o] with language appoints me?
And (who) can compare with my judgment?

[F]or I (am) [7]the beloved of the King,
a friend of the Holy Ones.
And no one can enter [with me].

[And to] my [glo]ry [8]no one can compare;
F[o]r I, [my] rank, (is) with the gods;
[And] my glory (is) with the sons of the King.

Not [9]with (pure) gold will I cro[wn] myself,
Neither with gold (nor) with precious stones.
Not [with the sons of dec]eit [10][will he] reckon me.

Chant, O beloved ones,
sing to the King of [glory].

[11]VACAT

In this hymn, composed sometime in the second century BCE, a Jew imagined or was allowed to see the heavenly court and the gathering of divine beings, the Elim. Among them is an exalted one who is "the beloved of the King, a friend of the Holy Ones." Many New Testament scholars have not imagined such ideas within Second Temple Judaism; the period is too often miscast as thoroughly monotheistic. This unknown person is exalted, but he remains unnamed. I think the author chose the rhetoric of anonymity to allow others to imagine who was being depicted. The concepts and perceptions in this hymn help us comprehend the Jewish background of Paul's Christology, his portrayal of Jesus' exalted status, and the two pre-Pauline christological hymns in Philippians and Colossians. The author of the *Self-Glorification Hymn* and Paul inherited the concept of the "Suffering Servant" found in Isaiah 53.

Salvation and Cross Christology

Recognizing Paul's indebtedness to Judaism and Jewish apocalyptic eschatology should not lead us to miss Paul's genius and the ideas he developed or united in a unique way. His uniqueness and creativity comes into focus when we ask, as Martin Hengel and Anna Maria Schwemer urge: "[W]hat did he do for us?" That is, what did Christ do for us? Hengel and Schwemer were convinced that we should not seek to discern how Paul's thought evolved, but to recognize that his foundation moment was when he experienced "a personal encounter" with Christ, if we can trust Paul's own words. Note their thought:

> It was the revelation of Christ and nothing else—if we can believe Paul's own words (and if we do not want to, we can only be silent)—which gave a clear direction to his further career. At most a development can be seen in the geographical conception of his mission: Damascus, Arabia, Cilicia and Syria . . . and then in the last third of his activity Asia Minor, Macedonia, Greece and the prospect of Rome and indeed Spain. . . .[66]

For Hengel, the cross is central: "[T]he sinless messiah died for our sins and did so, moreover, as Paul himself often emphasizes in formulae, by crucifixion on the wood of curse and shame."[67]

The frequent Pauline references to "according to Scripture" indicate that Jesus' earliest followers, before Paul's first letter around 50 CE, viewed his death in terms of Isaiah 53 and the Suffering Servant, who was interpreted to be the Messiah. Scholars once were convinced that Paul could not have been influenced by Jewish reflections on Isaiah's "Suffering Servant." Now, it is conceivable that he may have been influenced by the thoughts found in the *Self-Glorification Hymn*. Yet, it is also possible to imagine that it is only in light of Jesus' life and death that Jews who believed in Jesus imagined the fulfillment of Isaiah's prophecy.[68]

Continued focus on the Jewish apocalyptic compositions should not be blind to the many ways Paul could have been influenced also, in a much lesser way, by Greek and Roman rhetoric and thought, ethical reflections, historiography, and Platonic perspectives. All scholars are aware that long before Alexander the Great, as proved by the Samaritan papyri,[69] Jews living in Palestine knew and were influenced by Greek thoughts and myths.[70]

An area deserving more intense study concerns the various ways the argumentation and rhetoric of Jewish apocalyptic thought helped shape Paul's mind and expressions. For example, how and in what ways, if at all, Paul was influenced, not only by early Rabbinic methodology and *halakot*, but apocalyptic use of literary sophisticated methods. such as *enthymeme* (an argument that utilizes two premises and one is assumed as common knowledge or tradition and the other is based on secondary apocalyptic rhetoric).[71]

Conclusion

All scholars know that a text must have a context; otherwise, it can mean anything we wish or nothing at all. The context of Pauline theology and Christology is Jewish apocalypticism and apocalyptic eschatology. In that context, we can explore the meaning of Paul's concept of justification, salvation, reconciliation, expiation, redemption, freedom, sanctification, transformation, new creation, and glorification.[72] Schweitzer accurately perceived that Paul lived in the world of Jewish apocalyptic eschatology. Paul may not have known the Qumran texts, but he probably met Essenes during his many visits to Palestine. He may not have known the *Self-Glorification Hymn*, but he shared many similar ideas and perceptions with its author and may have discussed it in Jerusalem with scholars who knew it. As is widely recognized, Pharisees, such as Paul, could be deeply influenced by Jewish apocalyptic theology. In the twenty-first century, claiming that Paul was influenced by Jewish apocalyptic eschatology and not devoting extensive time to the Jewish apocalypses is like singing Handel's *Messiah* and being tone-deaf.

Notes

1. Apuleius's *Golden Ass*, the magical papyri, and the Hermetica, all postdate Paul. Long ago, D. E. H. Whiteley offered this sage advice: "It is of course true, that so far as chronology is concerned, St. Paul might have borrowed from an earlier form of mystery-religion, but the evidence for this hypothetical earlier form no longer exists, if indeed it ever did." See Whiteley, "St. Paul not indebted to the Mystery Cults," *The Theology of St. Paul* (Philadelphia: Fortress Press, 1966), 2–3 (2).

2. Davies, *Paul and Rabbinic Judaism* (Philadelphia: Fortress Press, 1980 [1948]).

3. Schoeps, *The Theology of the Apostle in the Light of Jewish Religious History*, trans. Harold Knight (London: Lutterworth, 1961).

4. Grant, *Roman Hellenism and the New Testament* (New York: Scribner, 1962). Grant was convinced that diasporic Judaism shaped Paul.

5. W. C. van Unnik, *Tarsus or Jerusalem?*, trans. George Ogg (London: Epworth, 1962). Contra Grant, Van Unnik saw rightly that Paul's cultural background was not Tarsus, but Jerusalem.

6. Paul sought to be faithful to the Jesus traditions that he knew, and as Kathy Ehrensperger states: "Certainly, there must have been some 'bridge' of transmission between Jesus' message and ministry and Paul's theologizing, even if the latter is perceived as having transformed the former to relate it to contexts different from first-century Judea and Galilee." See Ehrensperger in *Jesus Research*, ed. Charlesworth et al. (Grand Rapids and Cambridge: Eerdmans, 2014), 531–50 (532). Also, see Ehrensperger's contribution in the present volume.

7. Some scholars claimed that Paul is critiquing Judaism, but as Lee Keck shows in interpreting Romans 2:17–20, Paul is influenced by the Jewish insights into God's impartiality. L. E. Keck, *Romans* (Nashville: Abingdon, 2005), 88.

8. Certainly, Paul must be understood not only within the church, but also within Judaism, and that also means Hellenistic Judaism and the Greek, Roman, and Persian worlds. See Anders Klostergaard Petersen's contribution in the present volume.

9. Nicholas Thomas Wright, *Paul and the Faithfulness of God* (Minneapolis: Fortress Press, 2013), 40.

10. John J. Collins, "What is Apocalyptic Literature?," in *The Oxford Handbook of Apocalyptic Literature*, ed. John J. Collins (Oxford: OUP, 2014), 6, 13.

11. Dale C. Allison Jr. "Apocalyptic Ethics and Behavior," in *The Oxford Handbook of Apocalyptic Literature*, 301.

12. Adela Yarbro Collins, "Apocalypticism and Christian Origins," in *The Oxford Handbook of Apocalyptic Literature*, 337.

13. Greg Carey calls these two forms of influence on Paul "primary" and "secondary apocalyptic discourse." See his contribution "Early Christian Apocalyptic Rhetoric" in *The Oxford Handbook of Apocalyptic Literature*, 218–34.

14. See, in particular, Mark Nanos, "Paul and the Jewish tradition: The Ideology of the *Shema*," in *Celebrating Paul*, ed. Peter Spitaler (CBQMS 48; Washington: Catholic Biblical Association of America, 2011). Also, see the contributions to this collection of essays by David Aune and William S. Campbell.

15. Martinus C. de Boer, "Paul and Apocalyptic Eschatology," in *The Encyclopedia of Apocalypticism* (New York: Continuum, 1999), 1:347.

16. Ernst Käsemann, "Zum Thema der urchristlichen Apokalyptik," *ZThK* (1962): 257–84. This great mind, Bultmann's most famous and influential student, was one of the most sensitive and thoughtful persons I have met. That became clear during the evening I enjoyed a dinner with him and his wife.

17. Peter Stuhlmacher, *Gottes Gerechtigkeit* (Stuttgart: Calwer, 1991); idem, *Das Paulinische Evangelium* (Göttingen: Vandenhoeck & Ruprecht, 1968); I. Baumgarten, *Paulus und die Apokalyptik* (1975). See also Klaus Koch, *Vor der Wende der Zeiten: Beiträge zur apokalyptischen Literatur* (Neukirchen-Vluyn: Neukirchener Verlag, 1996), 130.

18. J. Christiaan Beker, *Paul the Apostle: The Triumph of God in Life and Thought* (Philadelphia: Fortress, 1980), 35. My colleague for my early years in Princeton, Beker was a creative and independent thinker. He was full of life and insight.

19. Ibid., 345.

20. The gifted and creative New Testament scholar J. Louis Martyn also makes Jewish apocalyptic theology the key to Paul's thought, but Martyn does not delve into the Jewish apocalyptic literature. See his otherwise masterful commentary on Galatians: *Galatians: A New Translation with Introduction and Commentary* (New York: Doubleday, 1997).

21. See Collins, "What is Apocalyptic Literature?," 2.

22. I introduced these concepts in 1987; see "Transference and Redefinition," in Charlesworth, *The New Testament Apocrypha and Pseudepigrapha: A Guide to Publications, with Excursuses on Apocalypses* (Metuchen, NJ; London: Scarecrow Press, 1987), 28–32.

23. See the balanced insights shared by Dale Allison in his "Apocalyptic Ethics and Behavior," 295–311.

24. See esp. Christopher Rowland, *The Open Heaven* (New York: Crossroad, 1982).

25. See Jean Carmignac, *Le mirage de l'eschatologie* (Paris: Letouzey et Ané, 1979).

26. See Carlos A. Segovia's chapter in the present volume.

27. See Juan Carlos Ossandón's and David Arthur DeSilva's contribution in the present volume.

28. Also, please see the following comments about apocalyptic documents preserved near Qumran.

29. Also, see Gerbern S. Oegema's focus on 1 and 2 Maccabees in the present volume.

30. See Larry W. Hurtado's contribution in the present volume.

31. See the publications by Gabriele Boccaccini, namely: *Middle Judaism* (Minneapolis: Fortress Press, 1991), *Il medio giudaismo* (Genova: Marietti, 1993), *Beyond the Essene Hypothesis* (Grand Rapids: Eerdmans, 1998), *Roots of Rabbinic Judaism* (Grand Rapids: Eerdmans, 2002), and *I giudaismi del secondo tempio* (Brescia: Morcelliana, 2008). See also the publications edited by idem et al. *Enoch and Qumran Origins* (Grand Rapids: Eerdmans, 2005), *The Early Enoch Literature* (Leiden, Boston: Brill, 2007), *Enoch and the Messiah Son of Man* (Grand Rapids: Eerdmans, 2007), and *Enoch and the Mosaic Torah* (Grand Rapids: Eerdmans, 2009).

32. See Charlesworth's contributions to *The Parables of Enoch: A Paradigm Shift*, ed. Charlesworth and Darrell L. Bock (London: T&T Clark, 2013).

33. While concluding that a "direct contact of Paul with the writings of the Qumran community" can be denied, Heinz-Wolfgang Kuhn presents a list of informed parallels that lead to the supposition of Paul's "certain acquaintance with traditions of the Qumran community." Kuhn in *The Bible and the Dead Sea Scrolls*, ed. J. H. Charlesworth (Waco, TX: Baylor University Press, 2006), 3:185.

34. The translation is by Charlesworth and is published by Cascade Books, in press.

35. This noun is missed by previous editors.

36. Lit. "construction."

37. Aramaic: "to knead"; Syriac: "to create."

38. Or "genitals." See 9.24, 20.28.

39. The scribe leaves an uninscribed space here. It does not denote a new hymn.

40. See 7.33.

41. Or "wonder," "sign." See 7.33 where the noun also means "portent." For "wonder," see 8.9 and 15.24.

42. The *nip'al* infinitive means "to deliver oneself." The author cannot bring anything to deliver (or save) him (himself).

43. In Semitics, literally "from before [you]." See 1QHa 15.31 and Isa. 63:19.

44. Infinitive of ציץ; not a verb in Biblical Hebrew.

45. The author knows the famous "Song of the Sea" in Exodus 15 and he quotes 15:11.

46. Heb. צבא. See 5.25.

47. As in the final columns of 1QS (the *Rule of the Community*), an emphasis is placed on God's forgiveness and covenant loyalty (loving kindness) for acceptance (or salvation), rejecting any conception that a human can earn God's favor by doing good works.

48. See the publications cited by and the insights offered by James Ware in his "The Resurrection of Jesus in the Pre-Pauline Formula of 1 Cor. 15.3-5," *NTS* 60 (2014): 475-98. I demur from his conclusion that Jesus was raised with a "crucified body." It is in 1 Cor. 15:35-50 that Paul discusses the type of resurrection body, and he makes it clear (at least to me) that he is talking not about a "terrestrial body" (15:40) or "physical body" (15:44), but a "celestial body" (15:40) and a "spiritual body" (15:44). I cite Ware for the consensus that Paul has inherited traditions from the early PJM in Jerusalem and Lower Galilee.

49. See the chapters by Mark D. Nanos and Joshua Garroway in the present volume.

50. See J. P. Rubin, "Celsus's Decircumcision Operation," *Urology* (1980): 121-24 and F. M. Hodges, "The Ideal Prepuce in ancient Greece and Rome: Male Genital Aesthetics and their Relation to Lipodermos, Circumcision, Foreskin Restoration, and the Kynodesne," *Bull. Hist. Med.* 75 (2001): 375-405.

51. Not all early Jews concluded that circumcision was fundamental. Philo treated circumcision cavalierly (*Spec. Laws* 2-11 and esp. *QE* 2.2), but the authors of *Pirke Aboth* concurred that circumcision defined Abraham's covenant, and the Talmud judge epispasm to be a transgression (*Yoma* 85b). See the discussion of epispasm by R. Hall in *JSP* 2 (1988): 71-86 and his article in *BR* (1992): 52-57.

52. For a recent discussion of Law in Paul, see David Lincicum, *Paul and the Early Jewish Encounter with Deuteronomy* (Grand Rapids: Baker, 2013).

53. C. W. Fishburne, "I Cor. iii 10-15 and the Testament of Abraham," *NTS* 17 (1970): 109-15.

54. See E. P. Sanders, "Testament of Abraham: A New Translation and Introduction," in *OTP* 1:878.

55. I am indebted here to Dale C. Allison, *Testament of Abraham* (Commentaries on Early Jewish Literature; Berlin; New York: Walter de Gruyter, 2003), 114. Allison, my former student and colleague, is one of the best minds in New Testament research.

56. Lisa Bowens brings in Jewish apocalyptic texts, such as the *Rule of the Community* and the *War Scroll*, in helping us comprehend the contexts and claims of Paul in 2 Corinthians. See her dissertation "Engaging in Battle: Examining Paul's Cosmology, Epistemology, and Anthropology in the Context of Spiritual Warfare in 2 Cor. 12:1-10" (Princeton Theological Seminary, 2014).

57. See esp. the following: *Apoc. Mos.* 37:5, 40:1, and *2 En.* 8.

58. See Andersen's version in *OTP*, 1:115.

59. See Goff's contribution in the present volume.

60. See the chapter in the present book by William S. Campbell.

61. J. J. Collins, *The Apocalyptic Imagination* (New York: Crossroad, 1984), 207.

62. See Carey's insights in his "Early Christian Apocalyptic Rhetoric," 231.

63. See esp. J. H. Charlesworth, *Resurrection* (New York: T&T Clark, 2006).

64. I am indebted to Dale Allison for discussion on this point.

65. This poetic arrangement will appear in the Princeton Dead Sea Scrolls Project, volume 5A, in press.

66. Martin Hengel and Anna Maria Schwemer, *Paul Between Damascus and Antioch: The Unknown Years*, trans. John Bowden (Louisville: Westminster John Knox, 1997), 98. Hengel had the most incredible memory; I will always be indebted to him for decades of nurturing and colleagueship.

67. Ibid., 99.

68. Totally different are the influences from Isaiah 53 on the *Self-Glorification Hymn*.

69. In the seal impressions of the *bullae* (pieces of clay that sealed the scroll) found on manuscripts that date to the period before Alexander the Great and were found in Wadi Daliyeh are seen such non-Jewish images as nude youths, Hermes, Perseus, Herakles, a Satyr, Eros, Achilles, Aphrodite, Zeus, and a dancing Maenad. Notably, see Mary J. Winn Leith, *Wadi Daliyeh I: The Wadi Daliyeh Seal Impressions* (DJD 24; Oxford: Clarendon Press, 1997).

70. Most scholars have been influenced by the insights provided by Martin Hengel in *Judaism and Hellenism: Studies in their Encounter in Palestine During the early Hellenistic Period*, trans. John Bowden (Minneapolis: Fortress Press, 1991).

71. I am impressed by the demonstration of this apocalyptic argumentation in 1 Thessalonians 4 by Carey in "Early Christian Apocalyptic Rhetoric," 231.

72. Joseph A. Fitzmyer has isolated these ten "effects" of the Christ-event according to Paul. See his contribution in *Celebrating Paul*.

4

Paul's Messianic Christology

Larry W. Hurtado

In the following pages, I discuss features of Paul's Christology that I contend comprise a distinctive and noteworthy version of Second Temple Jewish messianism. To use a text-critical analogy: just as there was a textual pluriformity in biblical writings in the Second Temple period (evident in the biblical manuscripts from Qumran), so there was a pluriformity in Jewish messianic hopes and figures, and I contend that Paul's beliefs about Jesus constitute an especially noteworthy instance of that diversity.[1] That is, I propose that Paul's Christology reflects a particular and distinctive "variant-form" of the Jewish messianism of his time.[2] This proposal entails the prior judgment that Jesus' messianic status is integral and important in Paul's christological beliefs and devotional practice. So, I begin by addressing this latter issue, which, in light of an important recent publication, I believe, can be done briefly.

The argument that Jesus' messianic significance was an important factor in Paul's Christology has been strengthened considerably in the excellent study recently published by my Edinburgh colleague, Matthew Novenson: *Christ among the Messiahs*.[3] In this work, he first addresses the much-debated linguistic question of how χριστός functioned in Paul's discourse. A number of scholars have judged that, despite (or even because of) the frequency of Paul's usage of the appellative (270 times in the Pauline corpus), for Paul, χριστός was (or was virtually) a name applied to Jesus, with little (or nothing) of its meaning/usage as "messiah" remaining, or of significance.[4]

But Novenson shows (persuasively to my mind) that in Paul's usage, χριστός should be seen as an example of a particular onomastic category, the "honorific." Novenson defines an honorific as "a word that can function as a stand-in for a personal name but part of whose function is to retain its supernominal associations."[5] That is, Novenson contends that Paul reflects Second Temple Jewish usage of χριστός (and equivalents in other ancient languages) as an appellative for a figure (typically a human) who will act as God's agent of eschatological redemption; but in Paul's usage, the term is applied exclusively and restrictively to Jesus.[6] Indeed, in Paul's usage, the term is tied to Jesus so tightly that it can serve on its own to designate him (about 150 times in the uncontested letters, for example, 1 Cor. 15:3, 12–28). Paul's exclusive association of the term with Jesus is what has misled those who have characterized χριστός in his usage as (merely) a name.[7]

Novenson points to analogies, such as use of the honorific "Augustus" for Octavian, similarly "Epiphanes" uniquely designating Antiochus IV, and, among Jewish examples, Judah "Maccabee," and Shimon "bar Kochba."[8] To cite Novenson's concisely expressed judgement: "Paul's χριστός is an honorific, and it works according to the syntactical rules that govern that onomastic category."[9] As Novenson concludes later in his study, "[i]f χριστός in Paul seems to be not quite a title and not quite a name, this is not because it is on an evolutionary path from the one category to the other but because it is generically something else."[10] Nils Dahl's classic essay, in which he laid out "philological observations" that seemed to lead to "negative conclusions," has served heretofore as the key analysis of Paul's usage of χριστός, but I judge that Novenson's study has superseded it, and must now be regarded as the definitive treatment of the philological question.[11]

Second, in an analysis of a selection of "Christ passages in Paul," Novenson shows that "Paul does all that we normally expect any ancient Jewish or Christian text to do to count as a messiah text and that in no case does he ever disclaim the category of messiahship."[12] There are those (for example, F. C. Baur) who posit a monolithic, "narrow" and ethnocentric Jewish messianism, and portray Paul as negating or transcending it. There are also those who contend that Paul avoided ascribing messianic significance to Jesus (for example, Gaston), because he considered Jesus as Savior for gentiles only, and not as the Jewish Messiah. Then, there is what has been the majority view that, although Paul may well have regarded Jesus as Messiah at some level, this was not an important emphasis in his faith and teaching (for example, Chester).[13] But Novenson builds a strong case that Paul's "Christ language" should be seen as "a case study in early Jewish messiah language," and that Jesus' messianic status and significance form a major factor in the religious convictions of Paul and the early circles of believers (both Jewish and gentile) reflected in his letters.

I admit that my appreciation for Novenson's work is likely conditioned by my perception of it as a more sophisticated articulation, and more thorough defense, of a view that I expressed some years ago.[14] As Novenson grants, to take a view of Paul's Christology as having a strong messianic coloring is to depart from what has been the majority or dominant view among new testament scholars.[15] But there are others as well who have reached a similar conclusion, and Novenson has now given further strong reasons to do so.[16] In light of his work, especially, I do not feel it necessary to argue this point further. Instead, on the recently reinforced premise that Jesus' messianic status was significant for Paul,

I wish to turn now to several features of Paul's messianic Christology that make it a particularly noteworthy variant-form of ancient Jewish messianism.[17]

Distinctives of Paul's Messianic Christology

In referring to "distinctives" of Paul's Christology, I mean features that distinguish the beliefs and devotional stance reflected in Paul's letters from other known expressions of Roman-era Jewish messianism.[18] As indicated already, contrary to some earlier scholars, I do not present Paul's Christology as a departure from a monolithic Jewish messianism, but instead, as a particular variant-form of a diverse and lively Jewish messianism of his time.[19]

One further preliminary note: scholars have frequently portrayed Paul as a massively creative figure (for example, the first Christian theologian).[20] I do not deny that there seem to be some distinctive and creative features in Paul's articulation of his gospel, and that he was impressive in articulating them.[21] Moreover, he certainly appears to have had a particular vision of God's redemptive program, and of his own special calling by God to obtain "the obedience of faith among all the gentiles" (Rom. 1:5) as a/the key component in that program. But I contend that in a number of other matters, including christological beliefs and related devotional practices, in particular, Paul reflected (and intentionally so) a religious stance that he shared with other believers, and that, unlike a professional theologian, Paul did not really devote himself to producing some original programmatic statement of Christian doctrine. In any case, as indicated already, my primary concern here is to treat certain features of the messianic thought *affirmed and advocated by Paul* (that is, what he shared with other early circles of Jesus-believers) as reflecting a novel and distinctive development in the context of the diversity of Second Temple Jewish messianism.

Messiah's Death and Resurrection

It will scarcely require much supporting argumentation to posit that Jesus' death and resurrection are emphases central in Paul's statements of faith (for example, Rom. 4:24-25), in his own preaching (for example, 1 Cor. 2:1-5; Gal. 3:1), and in the traditions that he says he received and shared with his churches (for example, 1 Cor. 15:1-7). Paul refers to Jesus' death frequently and variously: for example, as expressing Jesus' obedience to God (for example, Phil. 2:6-8), Jesus' love (for example, 2 Cor. 5:14-15), and God's redemptive purpose (for example, Rom. 8:31-39), and as the model to be emulated in the behavior of believers (for example, Rom. 6:1-11). Likewise, Jesus' resurrection and exaltation to heavenly glory form the decisive act of God that bestowed on Jesus a unique status now as "Kyrios," as "the Son of God," and as universal ruler (for example, Phil. 2:9-11; Rom. 1:3-4; 1 Cor. 15:20-28). So, these divine actions also serve as the assurance of, and the pattern for, the eschatological (bodily) redemption of believers (for example, Rom. 8:11; 1 Cor. 15:42-49; Phil. 3:21). Obviously, much more could be said, but it is surely unnecessary to argue further the basic point that in Paul's beliefs, Jesus' death and resurrection were hugely important and were thematized in various ways.

Moreover, as Werner Kramer noted decades ago, in Paul's numerous references to Jesus' death and resurrection (as also in other NT writings), the appellative "Christ" is particularly prominent (for example, 1 Cor. 8:11; 15:3; Rom. 5:6, 8; 14:15).[22] This seems to reflect an emphasis on Jesus' death and resurrection in particular as *messianic* acts/events—an emphasis that likely originated in circles of Aramaic-speaking and Greek-speaking Jews and was then echoed and developed by Paul.[23] This emphasis on Jesus' death and resurrection is what other scholars also have often cited as a/the distinctive feature of the messianism affirmed by Paul—the claim that the Messiah had been crucified and that God had raised him from death.

Paula Fredriksen, for example, refers to this claim as "one glaring oddity" in the early "messianic movement" comprised by followers of Jesus.[24] She notes (rightly) that "a crucified messiah was evidently *not* inconceivable: Jews [the early Jewish believers] could and did conceive it." But she judges that the early proclamation of the crucified and resurrected Messiah-Jesus did not succeed with most first-century Jews, because "[a] messiah, crucified or otherwise, was not a messiah in the eyes of Jewish tradition if after his coming the world continued as before."[25] That is to say that for many/most Jews of Paul's time, Jesus was a failed messiah, Jesus' crucifixion "a stumbling block" (Paul's expression, 1 Cor. 1:23) that contradicted any messianic claim.

Similarly, John Collins posits that early christological claims "departed decisively from the Jewish paradigms in many respects," likewise citing as one important such departure, the "notion that the messiah should suffer and die."[26] The term "departed" may, however, be a bit retrospective and anachronistic for the early decades of the Jewish Jesus movement and the time of the Pauline mission. Certainly, it appears that the claim that Jesus' crucifixion was an integral (even divinely ordained) part of his messianic role was without precedent or analogy in the other known versions of Second Temple messianism, and so, was a genuinely innovative notion that also entailed novel readings of biblical texts (for example, Psalms 16; 22; 69; 116). But, to underscore Fredriksen's observation, it was a notion that emerged initially in circles of Aramaic-speaking and Greek-speaking Jews, and in the Jewish homeland. So, instead of referring to early christological claims as a "departure" from Jewish messianic paradigms, it would be more accurate to say that they initially comprised a novel form of Jewish messianism.

Certainly, these earliest Jewish believers did not withdraw from their ethnic ties, and, so far as we can see, they did not understand their messianic claims about Jesus as a "departure" from their ancestral faith. Instead, they engaged fellow Jews declaring their novel messianic claims with the aim of securing acceptance of these claims as the fulfillment of Jewish eschatological/messianic hopes. Granted, these earliest Jewish believers may have met with only limited success in the early decades, and their claims came to be regarded as a Jewish heresy. But this should not prevent the recognition that their claims about Jesus (admittedly somewhat peculiar in the ancient Jewish context) commenced as what we may term a novel variant-form of Jewish messianism.

For the purposes of this discussion, I underscore that this view of their message also characterizes Paul's messianic Christology. Fully recognizing that the proclamation of the crucified Jesus was a difficult "sell" to many/most Jews, Paul, nevertheless, continued to hold that this message is the authentic manifestation of God's redemptive purposes (Rom. 3:21–26), and that Jesus is the Messiah of Israel (Rom. 9:1–5) in whom the Torah finds its eschatological consummation (its τέλος; Rom. 10:4).

Interval and *Parousia*

In early Christian teaching reflected in Paul, the Messiah's death and resurrection entailed another striking feature—an interval between these events and the future consummation of God's redemptive program in which Jesus' return in glory (παρουσία) was central.[27] Moreover, the interval between Jesus' resurrection and *parousia* is itself endowed with special significance as the time for proclamation of the Gospel, to Jews and, especially in Paul's case, to gentiles, making it the time of salvation and giving it a particular eschatological significance. The resulting scheme, in which, first, the Messiah appears and is divinely confirmed (Jesus' resurrection), then followed by this interval in which the message focused on his identity and significance is proclaimed, culminating in his return (*parousia*) and the attendant events that comprise the consummation of God's redemptive purposes (including resurrection of all the elect), seems to be another novel and unprecedented feature of early Christian messianism.

A Cosmic Dimension

A third noteworthy feature of Paul's messianic Christology is the cosmic dimension to Jesus' exaltation and appointed rule. To be sure, among the other various forms of Jewish messianism, there were expectations of a universal dimension to the Messiah's rule. For example, the royal Messiah of *Psalms of Solomon* will redeem Israel and will also exercise sovereignty over all the nations to the ends of the earth (17:30–31).

Of course, various biblical texts posited a worldwide supremacy/sovereignty for the Davidic monarch of Judea (for example, Ps. 2:7–11). Paul also reflects an early Christian reading of Psalm 8 as prefiguring the Messiah, citing, particularly, the reference in this psalm to God's putting "all things" in subjection to Christ (1 Cor. 15:25–28, citing Ps. 8:6). But in Paul's description of Jesus' exaltation and sovereignty, the things to be subjected to Jesus extend beyond the worldwide to encompass all other dimensions of reality as well. Note that in 1 Cor. 15:25–28, Paul even includes death as one of the enemies to be subjugated to Christ and destroyed (verse 26). In the oft-studied passage, widely thought to derive from an early Christian ode, Phil. 2:6–11, Jesus is given "the name above every name," and is to be acclaimed by every being "in heaven and on earth and under the earth" (verses 10–11). This is by no means peculiar to Paul, but is reflected in other NT texts as well, Jesus' supremacy over heavenly powers especially posited (for example, 1 Pet. 3:22; Heb. 1:3–14).

We may come close to an analogy for this cosmic dimension of triumph in the messianic figure of the *Parables of Enoch* who will exercise supremacy over kings and their kingdoms worldwide (*1 Enoch* 46; 48:4–6, 8–10; 52:6–9; 62:3–12), and will even judge "Azazel and all his associates and all his host" (55:4). In another *Parables of Enoch* text, the enthroned Chosen One even seems to judge "all the works of the holy ones in the heights of heaven" (61:8), "holy ones" apparently angelic beings here.[28] Nevertheless, the form of messianism reflected in Paul seems more encompassing, more truly universal on a cosmic scale than, at least, some other expressions of messianic rule, with all dimensions of reality to be subjected to Jesus.

We should also note that Jesus' messianic supremacy is redemptive, not only for Israel, but for the nations as well. Whereas, in some forms of Jewish messianism, the Messiah subdues the nations, and may even inflict punishment upon them, in the vision we have reflected in Paul, Jesus redeems gentiles as well as Israel, enfranchising gentiles into the Abrahamic family (for example, Gal. 3:25–29).

An Affective Emphasis

Still another striking feature of Paul's messianic Christology, and one that is curiously not commented on very frequently, is its strong affective tone. That is, Paul's christological discourse is characterized by a striking intensity in expressing his relationship and that of other believers to Christ. For example, there is Paul's reference to his having been "crucified with Christ," and to his continuing life as entrusting himself to "the Son of God who loved me and gave himself for me" (Gal. 2:20).[29] Or, consider his passionately worded autobiographical passage in Philippians, where he declares the supreme importance of "knowing Christ Jesus my Lord," and posits his single-minded aim "to know Christ and the power of his resurrection and the sharing of his sufferings" (Phil. 3:7–11). Or, note his statement of being motivated strongly by "the love of Christ," whose redemptive death for all should now generate an answering life-commitment to Christ (2 Cor. 5:14–15).[30]

In other statements, Paul also refers to God's love, connecting it strongly with Christ, as in Rom. 8:39, declaring that nothing in all creation "can separate us from the love of God which is in Christ Jesus our Lord."[31] Indeed, there are several references to God's love (typically for believers) in Paul's letters (for example, Rom. 5:5, 8; 2 Cor. 13:11, 14; and in the NT more widely), and also references to loving God in return (for example, Rom. 8:28; 1 Cor. 2:9). This is not typical of religious discourse generally in the Roman religious environment, and so, may well reflect a kind of discourse that Paul inherited from his Jewish and biblical tradition, which features references to YHWH's love for Israel, and Israel's love for YHWH.[32]

But, to underscore my point here, Paul's emphasis on the *love of*

Christ and the strongly affective tone in Paul's references to his relationship to Christ as well, are, to my knowledge, without precedent or analogy in other forms of Second Temple Jewish messianic discourse. One factor helping to account for this might be that Paul's messianic figure is a real, known person of then-living memory, whereas most other types of ancient Jewish messianism projected some future, as yet unidentified, figure.

Moreover, as noted, the closest analogies are in biblical-tradition discourse about God's love and loving God in return, and the expressions of intense devotion found, especially, often in the Psalms. We could say that Paul reflects an incorporation of Jesus into this tradition, perhaps giving us one of a number of expressions of what we may term a "dyadic" pattern, in which Jesus is linked with God uniquely and intimately in early Christian belief and devotional/worship practice (more on the latter in due course).[33] But whatever the factors to invoke as causative for it, this affective tone in Paul's discourse about Jesus is remarkable.

Incorporation in/into Messiah

This affective discourse concerning Jesus seems to be related to the way that Paul refers to the incorporative relationship of believers to Jesus/Christ, which has been labelled variously by scholars as, for example, "union with Christ," "Christ-mysticism," and "participation in Christ."[34] The most well-known, and oft-studied, Pauline expression of this is the ἐν Χριστῷ construction frequent in Paul's letters (56 times in the seven "undisputed" letters).[35] In addition, there are related expressions that are often used with reference to believers vis-à-vis Jesus: εἰς Χριστόν, σὺν Χριστῷ, διὰ Χριστοῦ, and also, ἐν Κυρίῳ.

In the history of scholarship, prompted initially by Adolf Deissmann's 1892 treatise, scholars made various attempts to determine what Paul's references to believers being "in Christ" meant, and what relationship Paul's so-called mysticism may have had to its religious environment. Near the end of the twentieth century, however, Dunn judged that scholarly interest in the subject had

116

"faded" and that the topic had become a "back number" in Pauline studies.[36] It is neither possible nor necessary here to engage the intricacies of that scholarly debate, much less to expound in any adequate manner Paul's discourse about believers as intimately in relationship to Christ. Instead, I simply wish to highlight the integral place occupied by this discourse in Paul's messianic Christology, and to note that this is another distinctive feature of it in comparison to other strands of Second Temple messianism.

Although much more attention historically has been given to the place and meaning of "justification," this emphasis on believers as incorporated in/into Christ is actually very important in Paul's theological discourse. Indeed, Dunn judged it "much more pervasive in [Paul's] writings than his talk of 'God's righteousness'," and Dunn also contended that "study of participation in Christ leads more directly into the rest of Paul's theology than [does] justification."[37] To cite Dunn one further time, he proposed that, as "a fundamental aspect of his thought and speech," Paul's frequent references to being "in Christ/in the Lord" reflect Paul's view that the life of believers, "its source, its identity, and its responsibilities, could be summed up in these phrases."[38]

But we must also note that this centrality of Christ was not at all at the expense of God in Paul's religious thought and practice (nor in other NT writings). Granted, on the one hand, the key distinguishing feature of discourse about God in Paul (and the NT generally) is the prominent place of Jesus. Jesus is "the one by whom believers typically identify themselves, and in their collective devotional practices he is explicit and central" in a degree and manner that is remarkable. On the other hand, however, "in all the various presentations of Jesus' significance, 'God' holds the overarching and crucial place."[39] For Paul, we may say, if adequate discourse about God now requires reference to Jesus, it is also the case that Jesus' significance is expressed consistently with reference to God.

So, Paul's emphasis on believers as "in Christ," in a powerful relationship with Christ, sits comfortably within Paul's larger vision of God's overarching supremacy. Paul also saw Christ as appointed by God as "the Son of God" (the definite article consistently used) and the "Lord" (for example, Rom. 1:3-4; Phil. 2:9-11), and so, the close relationship with Christ that Paul described and affirmed was, for him, the divinely-willed mode by which believers were to enter obediently into *God's* redemptive purposes.[40] Nevertheless, in the context of other forms of Jewish messianism, this centrality of Jesus—in particular, this positing of believers "in Christ"—seems to be another distinguishing mark of the messianic Christology affirmed by Paul.

Devotional Practices

I turn now, finally, to note another feature of Paul's view of Christ. Indeed, to my mind, this is the most striking and distinctive feature of the religious stance reflected in Paul's letters: the exalted Jesus is programmatically treated as the rightful co-recipient of devotional practice (including corporate worship), along with God.[41] Having written on this topic repeatedly over some twenty-five years, I shall (and must) treat only a selection of the data and only briefly here.[42] As in my previous publications, to avoid abstractions, I focus here on specifics of devotional practice, especially those that appear to be features of corporate worship.

We may note first 1 Cor. 1:2, and Paul's concise characterization of believers "in every place" as "all those who call upon the name of our Lord Jesus Christ." The phrasing, τοῖς ἐπικαλουμένοις τὸ ὄνομα τοῦ κυρίου ἡμῶν Ἰησοῦ Χριστοῦ, is obviously an adaptation of a biblical expression used often to describe cultic invocation or worship of YHWH.[43] We can only presume that Paul used this expression in full knowledge of this, and that he refers to some equivalent action of cultic acclamation of "our Lord Jesus Christ." Indeed, to underscore this point, it is this cultic action that he refers to here as itself the sufficient and common description of Jesus-believers.

In Rom. 10:9-13, we likely have another reference to this cultic acclamation of, and ritualized reverence for, the exalted Jesus. Here, Paul refers to uttering the verbal confession, "κύριος Ἰησοῦς" (verse

9), and only a few statements later refers to "calling upon" Jesus (ἐπικαλουμένους, verse 12); then Paul directly quotes the statement from Joel (LXX Joel 3:5; mt 2:32), "whoever calls upon [ἐπικαλέσηται] the name of the Lord shall be saved" (verse 13).[44] Note that, in this reference to the ritual invocation/acclamation of Jesus, Paul uses a biblical statement that originally referred to the cultic invocation/worship of YHWH.

This cultic acclamation of Jesus also seems to be alluded to in 1 Cor. 12:3, and probably in Phil. 2:9-11 as well, as noted earlier, the latter widely thought to derive from an early Christian ode used in worship.[45] Also, the "maranatha" in 1 Cor. 16:22 is now commonly taken as evidence that a similar cultic acclamation/invocation of Jesus featured in Aramaic-speaking circles of Jewish believers as well as in Pauline congregations.[46]

In addition to cultic acclamation/invocation of Jesus and odes celebrating him that were chanted in worship, there is the place of Jesus in the corporate meal of the ekklēsia. Paul refers to this meal as "the Lord's supper" (κυριακὸν δεῖπνον, 1 Cor. 11:20), the risen Christ rather obviously the Lord in question. Indeed, in another passage Paul draws a direct comparison with the cult meals devoted to various Roman-era deities (1 Cor. 10:14-22). Although we should no doubt allow for variations in the specific ways that earliest Christian circles may have understood their common meals, it seems clear that in all extant references, Jesus was central in one way or another, whether as the cult-host of the meal, or in his messianic/redemptive work.[47]

Moreover, Paul's references to prayers include striking instances where Jesus is co-recipient, as in 1 Thess. 3:11-13, where Paul implores God and "our Lord Jesus" jointly on behalf of the Thessalonian believers.[48] Also, Paul's typical letter salutations mentioning both God and Jesus (for example, 1 Thess. 1:1; Phil. 1:2; Gal. 1:3; 1 Cor. 1:3; 2 Cor. 1:2), which are sometimes referred to as "wish prayers" and which may well derive from liturgical formulae, likewise, reflect a striking duality or dyadic devotional stance, in which both God and Jesus are effectively linked as sources of the "grace and peace" invoked upon recipients of the letters. Paul's equally well-known "grace benedictions" that typically end his letters and which also may well reflect early liturgical expressions/practice, further demonstrate the remarkable place of the risen Jesus in the religious life that Paul affirms (for example, 1 Cor. 16:23; Gal. 6:18; 1 Thess. 5:28). Indeed, in 2 Cor. 12:8–9, Paul refers to his own repeated petitions made directly to "the Lord" (who in this context must be Jesus) to remove "a thorn in the flesh."[49]

To cite yet one more item making up the remarkable constellation of devotional actions, the entrance rite for the early circles of Jesus-believers, baptism, appears typically to have been performed "in/into the name" of Jesus (alluded to in 1 Cor. 6:11, for example). Lars Hartman has shown that this likely involved a ritual invocation of Jesus' name over (and/or by) the candidates, signifying that they were now made the property of Jesus.[50] The expression also posits Jesus as the basis of their eschatological salvation.

I trust that these examples will suffice to make the basic point that in Paul's letters, we have a remarkable devotional pattern in which Jesus functions prominently and uniquely along with God, and that this is apparently novel in the context of Second Temple Jewish religion and other known forms of Jewish messianism. Granted, in contexts of worship, the key title Paul applies to Jesus is (ὁ) Κύριος.[51] But in Paul's letters, the one confessed and invoked as Κύριος is also accorded the honorific Χριστός, whose death and resurrection confirm his messianic status. For Paul, Jesus' status as Κύριος does not conflict with or relativize his messianic role, but instead, expresses the particularly exalted nature of Jesus' messianic status.

Conclusion

In the foregoing discussion, I have itemized several key features of the Christology and devotional stance reflected in Paul's letters that are noteworthy individually and that collectively comprise an apparently novel development in Second Temple Jewish religion. To my mind, the most striking of these features is the prominence of the exalted Christ in early Christian devotional practices, the "dyadic" devotional pattern that we have noted.

As noted, perhaps the closest we get to analogous figures are the mysterious Melchizedek (referred to in a few fragmentary Qumran texts, especially 11QMelchizedek) and the messianic figure in the *Parables of Enoch*.[52] But the Melchizedek figure seems to be a high angel projected as acting in the eschatological future essentially as field marshal in the triumph of God's purposes on earth.[53] It is not entirely clear that he should be thought of as a messiah, or how he relates to the messianic expectations found in other Qumran texts. Moreover, he does not seem to play a role in the actual religious life and practices of Qumran or any other circle of Second Temple Jews, and he appears to be more a figure of eschatological dreams.

"The Chosen One" (also known as the "Righteous One," "Anointed One," "that Son of Man") of the *Parables of Enoch* is clearly a messianic figure noted earlier in this discussion, combining several biblical influences, and (as noted earlier) even transcendent qualities.[54] Chosen and named before the creation of the world (*1 Enoch* 48:2–3, 6), it is posited that on some future day, he will be revealed and enthroned and will execute God's judgement, even over "Azazel and all his associates and all his host" (55:4) and other heavenly beings (61:8–9), as well as all the unrighteous people of the earth (62:3–9; 69:26–29).

There surely are interesting similarities between this messianic figure of the *Parables* and the portrayal of Jesus in the letters of Paul and other NT writings. For example, both figures show the combined appropriation of various biblical traditions (the Davidic Messiah, for example, and the "one like a son of man" figure of Daniel 7, the Servant figure of Deutero-Isaiah, and personified Wisdom). But we should not ignore the noteworthy differences as well. As with the Melchizedek of Qumran, the messianic figure in the *Parables of 1 Enoch* is a projection of eschatological hopes and dreams, or perhaps, we should say a product of fervent exegesis of biblical texts, a figure who is yet to be revealed.[55] For Paul, however, the Messiah who has been made ὁ Κύριος is Jesus, a real and recent human figure "born of a woman, born under the Law"

(Gal. 4:4) to whom Paul ascribes extraordinary status and roles (for example, as agent of creation in 1 Cor. 8:4–6).

Moreover (and most significantly in my view), we have no evidence or reason to presume that there were Jewish circles in which the Chosen One of the *Parables* functioned in devotional practices comparably to the ways that Jesus did in the early *ekklēsias*.[56] There is no indication of an equivalent "dyadic" devotional pattern, no programmatic "mutation" in devotional practices/life such as we see reflected (indeed, presumed) in Paul's letters.[57] Note that throughout the *Parables*, it is actually the name of "the Lord of Spirits" (God) that is to be praised (for example, 39:7, 9–11), and through which prayers and intercession are offered (40:6; 45:3, for example). Sinners are those who "deny the name of the Lord of Spirits" (for example, 41:2; 45:1–2; 46:7; 48:10), and the righteous believe in, depend upon, and praise "the name of the Lord of Spirits" (44:4; 46:8; 47:2; 61:11, for example). In this same name (God's), they are saved (48:7; 50:3) and will be blessed (53:6; 58:4); and it is typically God alone to whom cultic worship is given in various scenes (for example, 63:1–7; 69:22–24).[58]

In short, neither Qumran nor the *Parables* explain or account for the distinctive variant-form of messianism that we see affirmed by Paul. Moreover, there seems to me scant evidence to posit some direct influence or significant borrowing from any one of these upon any other.[59] Instead, I suggest that the Melchizedek of Qumran and the Chosen One of the *Parables* offer additional and independent illustrations of the variegated nature of Jewish messianism in the early first century CE, a setting in which Paul's messianic Christology comprises another particularly distinctive, and (in my view) even more remarkable, variant-form.[60]

Notes

1. See, e. g., John J. Collins, *The Scepter and the Star: The Messiahs of the Dead Sea Scrolls and Other Ancient Literature* (New York: Doubleday, 1995), who posits "four distinct messianic paradigms": "king, priest, prophet, and heavenly messiah

or Son of Man" (195). "There were different messianic paradigms, not one composite concept of Messiah" (196). But he also notes that there were occasionally instances of the merging of two or more of these paradigms, forming "a composite figure" (195). See also Adela Yarbro Collins and John J. Collins, *King and Messiah as Son of God: Divine, Human, and Angelic Messianic Figures in Biblical and Related Literature* (Grand Rapids: Eerdmans, 2008); Andrew Chester, *Messiah and Exaltation: Jewish Messianic and Visionary Traditions and New Testament Christology* (WUNT 207; Tübingen: Mohr Siebeck, 2007), esp. 191–327, 329–63, who judged "it is not possible to speak of a single form of messianic expectation or concept . . . ; instead, we have to reckon with a *variety* of different kinds of beliefs and figures" (355).

2. When I presented an earlier form of this chapter in the Rome Nangeroni conference on Paul in 2014, Albert Baumgarten took exception to the use of the term "distinctive," contending that every type of ancient messianism was distinctive, albeit in different ways. I agree. To my mind, therefore, this makes it entirely appropriate to note the particular distinctiveness of Paul's messianic Christology. "Distinctive" here is not an apologetic term, merely a reference to the features that distinguished Paul's stance.

3. Matthew V. Novenson, *Christ among the Messiahs: Christ Language in Paul and Messiah Language in Ancient Judaism* (New York; Oxford: Oxford University Press, 2012).

4. E. g., Chester, "Messianism, Mediators, and Pauline Christology," *Messiah and Exaltation*, 329–96 (see esp. 382–83), who judges that "Christ" in Paul is "mainly bland and apparently insignificant in the way it is used" (383), and queries how it is that Paul "managed to circumvent or ignore" the messianic tradition (and earlier emphasis on Jesus as Messiah) "almost entirely" (384). Note also Magnus Zetterholm, "Paul and the Missing Messiah," in *The Messiah in Early Judaism and Christianity*, ed. Magnus Zetterholm (Minneapolis: Fortress Press, 2007), 33–55, who judged that in Paul, any emphasis on Jesus' messiahship "has vanished into thin air" (37), contending that Paul presented Jesus "in a way that would form an ideological resource for non-Jewish believers in Jesus—the Gospel of Jesus Christ as Lord" (54).

5. Novenson, *Christ among the Messiahs*, 138. I acknowledge that Novenson's case that Paul's use of χριστός is an instance of an "honorific" is a superior way of capturing what I meant in referring to the frequency of Paul's application of the term to Jesus as such that "the term practically functions as a name for Jesus" ("Paul's Christology," in *The Cambridge Companion to St. Paul*, ed. J. D. G. Dunn [Cambridge: Cambridge University Press, 2003], 191), and that χριστός "functions almost like an alternate name" for Jesus (*Lord Jesus Christ: Devotion to Jesus in Earliest Christianity* [Grand Rapids: Eerdmans, 2003], 99). It appears that my phrasing misled Novenson into including me among those who hold

"the axiom that Paul's χριστός is a name, not a title" (*Christ Among the Messiahs*, 66n12).

6. The obvious text regarded as exhibiting Jewish use of χριστός as an appellative for a royal messianic figure is *Pss. Sol.* 17–18. Of course, in the Hebrew Bible and extra-biblical Jewish texts, "anointed (one)" (משיח) can have various applications, and messianic figures may not always be referred to as משיח. To cite Collins (*The Scepter and the Star*, 12), "a messiah is an eschatological figure who sometimes, but not necessarily always, is designated as a משיח in the ancient sources." And for Collins's treatment of *Pss. Sol.*, see 49–56.

7. See, e. g., Martin Hengel's essay, "'Christos' in Paul," in Hengel, *Between Jesus and Paul* (London: SCM, 1983), 65–77 (German original, "Erwägungen zum Sprachgebrauch von Χριστός bei Paulus und in der 'vorpaulinischen' Überlieferung," in *Paul and Paulinism: Essays in Honour of C. K. Barrett*, ed. M. D. Hooker and S. G. Wilson [London: SPCK, 1982], 135–58). Hengel characterized Paul's use of *Christos* as "more of a riddle than a 'key' to a better understanding of Pauline christology" (66). Labelling *Christos* as a "proper name" in Paul's letters (72), nevertheless, Hengel also contended (correctly in my view) that Paul likely explained to his gentile churches what *Christos* meant (73–76).

8. Novenson, *Christ among the Messiahs*, 64–97, esp. 87–97 for his discussion of the category of "honorific." Decades earlier, Earl Richard had observed "interesting parallels" in the Roman usage of imperial titles, e. g., "Imperator Caesar Augustus" and "Lord Jesus Christ"; see his *Jesus: One and Many: The Christological Concept of New Testament Authors* (Wilmington, DE: Michael Glazier, 1988), 326.

9. Novenson, *Christ among the Messiahs*, 97.

10. Ibid., 134.

11. Nils A. Dahl, "Die Messianität Jesu bei Paulus," in *Studia Paulina in honorem Johannis de Zwaan septuagenarii* (Haarlem: Bohn, 1953), 83–95; idem, "The Messiahship of Jesus in Paul," in Dahl, *Jesus the Christ: The Historical Origins of Christological Doctrine*, ed. Donald H. Juel (Minneapolis: Fortress Press, 1991), 15–25. Note also Hengel's view (influenced by Dahl) that in Paul, χριστός functions as a "cognomen": "'Christos' in Paul," 66; and, of course, the oft-cited study by Werner Kramer, *Christ, Lord, Son of God* (SBT 50; Naperville: Alec R. Allenson, 1966), e. g., 42–44. Cf. in distinction Novenson's analysis of "Christ phrases in Paul," where he examines Dahl's philological observations about Paul's use of χριστός: Novenson, *Christ among the Messiahs*, 98–136.

12. Novenson, *Christ among the Messiahs*, 137–73 (citing 138). The passages he examines are Gal. 3:16; 1 Cor. 15:20–28; 2 Cor. 1:21–22; Rom. 9:1–5; Rom. 15:3, 9; 15:7–12; 1 Cor. 1:23; 2 Cor. 5:16–17; Rom. 1:3–4.

13. F. C. Baur, *Paulus, der Apostel Jesu Christi* (Stuttgart: Becher und Müller, 1845; idem, *Paul the Apostle of Jesus Christ* (2 vols.; London: Williams & Norgate, 1845–46; repr. Peabody, MA: Hendrickson, 2003); Lloyd Gaston, "Paul and the

Torah," in *Antisemitism and the Foundations of Christianity*, ed. A. T. Davies (New York: Paulist, 1979), 48–71; repr. in Lloyd Gaston, *Paul and the Torah* (Vancouver: University of British Columbia Press, 1987), 15–34; Andrew Chester, "The Christ of Paul," in *Redemption and Resistance: The Messianic Hopes of Jews and Christians in Antiquity*, ed. Markus Bockmuehl and James Carlton Paget (London: T&T Clark, 2007), 109–21. To cite a more recent work, I cannot find any discussion of the question of whether Paul regarded Jesus as Messiah in Pamela Eisenbaum, *Paul was not a Christian: The Original Message of a Misunderstood Apostle* (New York: HarperOne, 2009). "Messiah" does not even appear in the index. Cf. John Collins's frank appraisal of the views of Gaston and others who claim that Paul did not regard Jesus as Messiah: "The ecumenical intentions of such a claim are transparent and honourable, but also misguided since the claim is so plainly false" (*The Scepter and the Star*, 2).

14. Hurtado, "Paul's Christology," esp. 193; idem, *Lord Jesus Christ*, 98–101.

15. Perhaps the most vocal exception is N. T. Wright, who has insisted in numerous publications that in all of Paul's uses of χριστός there is an intended and strong messianic claim. But I find more dubious Wright's accompanying claim that in ancient Jewish thought "Messiah" typically had a strong incorporative sense: "Messiah" seen as Israel's embodiment. On the basis of this claim, Wright then also contends that in Paul's thought, as Messiah, Jesus embodied/embodies Israel, and through Jesus and the subsequent gospel, thus, "Israel" is transformed to become all those who are joined to Jesus (effectively, the church). Moreover, more recently, Wright claims that Paul also saw Messiah Jesus as "the embodiment of the returning YHWH." Among Wright's publications, see, e. g., *The Climax of the Covenant: Christ and the Law in Pauline Theology* (Minneapolis: Fortress Press, 1991), esp. 18–40, 41–55; and now *Paul and the Faithfulness of God* (2 vols.; London: SPCK, 2013), 2:690–709, 815–911. I find Wright's claims problematic, but I cannot (and need not) engage them here.

16. For somewhat similar views, see, e. g., Collins and Collins, *King and Messiah as Son of God*, 101–22; Edward Adams, "Paul, Jesus, and Christ," in *The Blackwell Companion to Jesus*, ed. Delbert Burkett (London: Blackwell, 2011), 94–110 (esp. 98–99); Ben Witherington III, "Christ," *DPL*, 95–100. Likewise, see Paula Fredriksen, *Jesus of Nazareth, King of the Jews* (New York: Knopf, 2000), 125–37, who contends that Paul's view of Jesus as Messiah was, in fact, closely connected to Paul's gentile mission. For a somewhat similar proposal that for Paul Jesus' messiahship and gentile salvation were connected, see Matthew V. Novenson, "The Jewish Messiahs, the Pauline Christ, and the Gentile Question," *JBL* 128 (2009): 357–73.

17. Cf. Paula Fredriksen's reference to early circles of Jewish Christians as comprising "a variant type of apocalyptic Judaism" (*From Jesus to Christ* [New Haven: Yale University Press, 1988], 167).

18. Cf. Witherington, "Christ," 98, who posited "three elements in [Paul's]

preaching that were without known precedents in early Judaism: (1) Messiah is called God; (2) Messiah is said to have been crucified, and his death is seen as redemptive; (3) Messiah is expected to come to earth again." It is unclear, however, that Paul called Jesus "God," and the following discussion will show additional features that are noteworthy and distinctive to the messianic Christology affirmed by Paul.

19. "In light of the Dead Sea Scrolls, we can now speak of a revival of messianic expectation in Judaism in the Hasmonean and Herodian periods" (Collins and Collins, *King and Messiah*, 63).

20. For treatments of Paul that (over?) emphasize his theological creativity and uniqueness in early Christianity, see, e. g., J. D. G. Dunn, *The Theology of Paul the Apostle* (Grand Rapids: Eerdmans, 1998): "Paul was the first and greatest Christian theologian" (2); and still more so Wright, *Paul and the Faithfulness of God*, passim. Cf., however, the classic (and often overlooked) study by Archibald M. Hunter, *Paul and His Predecessors* (2d ed.; Philadelphia: Westminster, 1961); and my discussion of "Early Pauline Christianity" in *Lord Jesus Christ* (79–153), in which I focus on "beliefs about Jesus that were broadly characteristic of Pauline churches," rather than on "Paul as a theologian" (98).

21. As seems to have been noted among Paul's original readers, who characterized his letters as "weighty and strong" (2 Cor. 10:10).

22. Kramer, *Christ, Lord, Son of God*, 19–38 (citing 35). Kramer sought to identify "pre-Pauline" confessional formulae, with some success in my view. But I also find his tradition-critical analysis faulty at a number of points that need not be discussed here.

23. See, e. g., my discussion of "Judean Christian Traditions in Paul's Letters" in *Lord Jesus Christ*, 167–76.

24. Fredriksen, *From Jesus to Christ*, 142. Note also her statement, "[b]ut for one necessary adjustment in their preaching—explaining why the messiah had been crucified—nothing that the early apostles claimed about Jesus would have been foreign to other Jews" (153). As will be clear from the following discussion, I do not see the emphasis on Jesus' crucifixion and resurrection as the only distinctive, or the most offensive, feature of the earliest Jesus movement to other Jews of the first century CE.

25. Fredriksen, *From Jesus to Christ*, 167–68. She also contends that so long as the church remained predominantly Jewish, gentile adherents were not a problem for Jews, but "as it became more and more Gentile, it compromised its identity as a renewal movement *within* Judaism, and hence its chances for success among Jews" (168). It is not clear to me, however, that a "disproportion of Gentiles to Jews" in early Christian circles developed early enough to account for the "hardening" against the gospel that Paul complained about already in Romans 9–11 (56–57 CE). Cf. W. D. Davies, *The Gospel and the Land: Early Christianity and Jewish Territorial Doctrine* (Berkeley: University of California

Press, 1974), 369–70 (cited approvingly by Fredriksen, *From Jesus to Christ*, 173n75), who claimed that gentiles became the majority "at a very early date." But Jewish believers likely remained dominant, at least as leaders, all across at least the first several decades of the Jesus movement. In any case, I rather suspect that there were other factors in the Jewish large-scale negative response to earliest Christianity. See L. W. Hurtado, *How on Earth Did Jesus Become a God? Historical Questions about Earliest Devotion to Jesus* (Grand Rapids: Eerdmans, 2005), "Early Jewish Opposition to Jesus-Devotion," 152–78; originally published in *JTS* 50 (1999), 35–58.

26. Collins, *The Scepter and the Star*, 208.

27. E. g., 1 Cor. 15:23. In other Pauline texts, Paul refers to the *parousia* of "the/ our Lord Jesus" (e. g., 1 Thess. 2:19; 3:13; 5:23), "the Lord" (1 Thess. 4:15). Other NT writings as well reflect this use of *parousia* (e. g., 2 Thess. 2:1; James 5:7–8; 2 Pet. 3:4; 1 John 2:28; Matt 24:3, 27, 37, 39). Collins has noted this distinctive also (*Scepter and the Star*, 209). Cf. also Paul's use of the term to refer to the return of Titus (2 Cor. 7:6–7) and his own "(bodily) presence" (2 Cor. 10:10; Phil. 1:26; 2:12).

28. See the discussion of this text in George W. E. Nickelsburg and James C. VanderKam, *1 Enoch 2: A Commentary on the Book of 1 Enoch Chapters 37-82* (Hermeneia; Minneapolis: Fortress Press, 2012), 250–51. Cf. Paul's reference to believers judging angels in 1 Cor. 6:3.

29. I take the ἐν πίστει ζῶ as Paul's reference to entrusting himself to Christ. But note the interesting textual variant, ἐν πίστει . . . τοῦ θεοῦ καὶ Χριστοῦ, supported by P46 B D* F G and a few other witnesses. In either reading, however, there is a strong note of close relationship of Paul and Christ.

30. I take "anyone who does not love the Lord" in 1 Cor. 16:22 also as referring to love for Christ as the rightful stance of believers.

31. In the similar assurance in Rom. 8:35, most witnesses refer to τῆς ἀγάπης τοῦ Χριστοῦ, but several witnesses (including ℵ) have τῆς ἀγάπης τοῦ θεοῦ. Vaticanus's reading, τῆς ἀγάπης τοῦ θεοῦ τῆς ἐν Χηριστῷ Ἰησοῦ, seems an obvious harmonization with the wording in 8:39.

32. YHWH's love for Israel (e. g., Isa. 54:8; Jer. 31:3; Zeph. 3:17; and other texts such as the memorable lines in Isa. 49:15–18). Israel's (or devout individuals's) love for YHWH (e. g., Deut. 6:5; 10:12; 11:1; 30:6; Ps. 18:1; 31:23).

33. In earlier publications, I characterized this duality as a "binitarian" devotional pattern, but more recently, I have adopted the term "dyadic," as it is less burdened by theological associations. Cf., e. g., L. W. Hurtado, "The Binitarian Shape of Early Christian Worship," in *The Jewish Roots of Christological Monotheism*, ed. Carey C. Newman, James R. Davila, Gladys S. Lewish (JSJSup 63; Leiden: Brill, 1999), 187–213; idem, *God in New Testament Theology* (Nashville: Abingdon, 2010), esp. 49–71.

34. The recent study by Constantine R. Campbell, *Paul and Union with Christ: An Exegetical and Theological Study* (Grand Rapids: Zondervan, 2012), offers an analysis of Paul's various expressions, ἐν Χριστῷ, εἰς Χριστόν, σὺν Χριστῷ, διὰ Χριστοῦ, and rightly emphasizes the importance of context in grasping Paul's meanings, arguing, e. g., that ἐν Χριστῷ is not a "formula" but, instead, a Pauline "idiom" used with various meanings. He does not, however, distinguish between the undisputed letters and those widely regarded as "deuteropauline." More recently still, Grant Macaskill, *Union with Christ in the New Testament* (Oxford: Oxford University Press, 2013), includes attention to Paul in an analysis of the theological bases and import of NT references to "participation and union" of believers with Christ.

35. This figure does not include the uses of "in him/whom" or the numerous instances of ἐν κυρίῳ (35 in the seven undisputed letters). The latter expression is also used some 24 times in the LXX, all of these, of course, referring to YHWH.

36. Dunn, *The Theology of Paul the Apostle*, 390–412 (citing 393–94), which includes a bibliography of key earlier studies. The classic ones are, of course, Adolf Deissmann, *Die neutestamentliche Formel "in Christo Jesu"* (Marburg: Elwert, 1892; repr. Nabu Public Domain Reprints, 2010); idem, *Paul: A Study in Social and Religious History*, trans. W. E. Wilson (2d ed.; London: Hodder & Stoughton, 1926; German orig. 1911; 2d ed. 1925); Wilhelm Bousset, *Kyrios Christos* (Göttingen: Vandenhoeck & Ruprecht, 1913; 5th ed. 1964; ET: Nashville: Abingdon Press, 1970; repr. Waco: Baylor University Press, 2013); Albert Schweitzer, *The Mysticism of Paul the Apostle*, trans. W. Montgomery (London: A. & C. Black, 1931; German orig. 1929). Already by the date of Deissmann's *Paul*, he could list a full page of publications discussing the topic (140–41, n1). Also note the thoughtful discussion of "The Corporate Christ" in C. F. D. Moule, *The Origin of Christology* (Cambridge: Cambridge University Press, 1977), 47–96.

37. Dunn, *Theology*, 391, 395. Cf., e. g., some 50 uses of δικαιοσύνη in the seven undisputed Paulines, 34 of these uses in Romans.

38. Ibid., 399.

39. Hurtado, *God in New Testament Theology*, 53.

40. I have discussed Paul's references to Jesus as God's Son (infrequent, but very important in his discourse) elsewhere: "Son of God," *DPL*, 900–906; and "Jesus' Divine Sonship in Paul's Epistle to the Romans," in *Romans and the People of God*, ed. Sven K. Soderlund and N. T. Wright (Grand Rapids: Eerdmans, 1999), 217–33.

41. Collins (*Scepter and the Star*, 208) posited that "the most significant Christian departure from Jewish notions of the messiah was the affirmation of the divinity of Christ," comprising "*claims*" that "*eventually* went beyond anything we find in the Jewish texts" (209, emphasis mine). I register two points in response: first, Collins's phrase, "affirmation of the divinity of Christ," is insufficiently clear or precise as to what is meant. It is difficult to tell the

force of rhetoric in ancient texts. Angels can be referred to as "gods," and the mysterious Melchizedek can be identified as the *Elohim* of Ps. 82:1 (11QMelch). The really innovative development in earliest Christian circles, and the far more significant one in its historical context, was the "dyadic" devotional pattern exhibited in a whole constellation of practices. Second, though remarkable and novel, earliest Jewish believers (including Paul) did not apparently intend their Jesus devotion as a "departure" from their Jewish religious matrix.

42. My earlier and fuller discussions include these: *One God, One Lord: Early Christian Devotion and Ancient Jewish Monotheism* (Philadelphia: Fortress Press, 1988; 2d ed., Edinburgh: T&T Clark, 1998); "The Binitarian Shape of Early Christian Worship"; *At the Origins of Christian Worship: The Context and Character of Earliest Christian Devotion* (Carlisle: Paternoster; Grand Rapids: Eerdmans, 1999), esp. 63–97. I continue to be surprised, however, how often scholars downplay or ignore outright the phenomena in question.

43. To "call upon the name of the Lord" (e. g., Gen. 12:8; 13:4; 21:33; cf. 1 Kgs. 18:24–26; Ps. 116[LXX 114]:4, 13[LXX 115:4]); "call upon the Lord" (e. g., 1 Sam. 12:17; Ps. 17[LXX]:4); "call upon your [YHWH's] name" (e. g., Ps. 74[LXX]:2); the reference to Moses and Aaron in Ps. 98(LXX):6–7; and the cultic invitation to "call on me [YHWH]" in Ps. 49(LXX):14–15. Note also, e. g., this phrasing in *Pss. Sol.* 6:1–2. The middle-voice form of the word ἐπικαλέω was also used for invoking other deities in the wider Roman-era environment, and for "magical" incantations as well as reflected in numerous instances in the *Papyri Graecae Magicae*: multiple deities (e. g., PGM VII.601; XII.67, 216), Horus-Harpocrates (e. g., PGM IV.987), Iaô (e. g., PGM XIII.1018), with Sarapis (e. g., PGM XIII.618), with Hermes (e. g., PGM V.187), and with Zeus (e. g., PGM V.469). I thank Paula Fredriksen for pointing me to these specific references. For an excellent introduction and translation of the PGM, see Hans Dieter Betz, ed., *The Greek Magical Papyri, including the Demotic Spells* (Chicago; London: University of Chicago Press, 1986).

44. Carl J. Davis, *The Name and Way of the Lord* (JSNTSup 129; Sheffield: JSOT Press, 1996), discusses the early Christian appropriation of the Joel text.

45. This view of Phil. 2:5–11 originated with Ernst Lohmeyer, *Kyrios Jesus: Eine Untersuchung zu Phil. 2, 5–11* (Heidelberg: Carl Winters Universitätsbuchhandlung, 1928), and has now obtained wide endorsement. Among more recent comments, see Andrew Chester, "High Christology: Whence, When and Why?" *Early Christianity* 2 (2011): 22–50, esp. 39–43. On the importance of odes/hymns as expressions of Jesus devotion, see, e. g., Martin Hengel, "The Song About Christ in Earliest Worship," in *Studies in Early Christology* (Edinburgh: T&T Clark, 1995), 227–91.

46. Wilhelm Bousset's attempts to sidestep the force of 1 Cor. 16:22 did not prove

persuasive. I review the matter briefly in my Introduction to the 2013 reprint of Bousset's *Kyrios Christos*, xii–xiii.

47. Even in *Didache*, Jesus is the occasion for and content of the εὐχαριστία given to God (*Did.* 9:1—10:6).

48. Other examples of similar "wish prayers" in Paul's letters include Rom. 15:5, 13, 33 (in which God alone is invoked). Although scholars remain divided on the question of its authorship, there also examples in 2 Thessalonians (2:16-17, God and Jesus; and 3:5; apparently "the Lord" here is Jesus).

49. On early Christian evidence more broadly, see Paul F. Bradshaw, "The Status of Jesus in Early Christian Prayer Texts," in *Portraits of Jesus: Studies in Christology*, ed. Susan E. Myers (Tübingen: Mohr Siebeck, 2012), 249-60. The classic study is Aleksy Klawek, *Das Gebet zu Jesus. Seine Berechtigung und Übung nach den Schriften des Neuen Testaments: Eine biblisch-theologische Studie* (NTAbh 6/5; Münster: Aschendorffschen Verlagsbuchhandlung, 1921).

50. Lars Hartman, *'Into the Name of the Lord Jesus': Baptism in the Early Church* (Edinburgh: T&T Clark, 1997).

51. On Paul's use of Κύριος, see, e. g., L. W. Hurtado, "Lord," *DPL*, 560-69.

52. Cf. Collins, *The Scepter and the Star*, 136-53, for a review of various figures (human and/or angelic) given "a throne in the heavens." On the Qumran evidence, see, e. g., L. W. Hurtado, "Monotheism, Principal Angels, and the Background of Christology," *The Oxford Handbook of the Dead Sea Scrolls*, ed. T. H. Lim and J. J. Collins (Oxford: Oxford University Press, 2010), 546-64.

53. See, e. g., my discussion of various "principal angel" figures in *One God, One Lord*, 71-92, including Michael (75-78) and the Melchizedek of Qumran texts (78-79).

54. See now the detailed Excursus in Nickelsburg and VanderKam, *1 Enoch 2*, 113-23, esp. 118-19, noting the "composite" nature of this figure. They judge, however, that "in the Parables, with the exception of 71:14 . . . the figure is not human but transcendent" (115). Likewise, Erik Sjöberg, *Der Menschensohn im äthiopischen Henochbuch* (Lund: Gleerup, 1946) took the figure as "ein himmlisches Wesen" (58), and Collins (*Scepter and the Star*, 208): "If he is not divine, he is clearly more than human."

55. Cf. James A. Waddell, *The Messiah: A Comparative Study of the Enochic Son of Man and the Pauline Kyrios* (London: T&T Clark, 2011), who characterized as "bias" my observation that the references to the Chosen One in the *Parables* comprise "literary phenomena" (8).

56. I consider Waddell's claim that "the 'explosion' of early devotion to Jesus that Hurtado insists upon is really an echo of Enoch devotion to the Son of Man" (*The Messiah*, 10) to be a serious misjudgement. I also regard Waddell's extended discussion of my views (8-13) as seriously distorting, and so, his attempts at refutation widely off the mark.

57. Curiously, Nickelsburg and VanderKam posit that in Rev. 5 the Lamb "stands before God's throne as the Chosen One does in 1 Enoch 49:2," and claim that "the Lamb's relationship to God parallels that of the Chosen One and the Lord of Spirits in 1 Enoch and God's Anointed One and God in Psalm 2" (*1 Enoch 2*, 122). But this is to ignore the astonishing distinctive of Rev. 5, which is that the Lamb receives heavenly worship jointly with God, esp. in vv. 8–14. Cf. the landmark study by Richard J. Bauckham, "The Worship of Jesus in Apocalyptic Christianity," *NTS* 27 (1981): 322–41; idem, "The Worship of Jesus," in *The Climax of Prophecy: Studies on the Book of Revelation* (Edinburgh: T&T Clark, 1993), 118–49; Larry W. Hurtado, "Revelation 4–5 in the Light of Jewish Apocalyptic Analogies," *JSNT* 25 (1985): 105–24.

58. In 48:5, all peoples "will fall down and worship before him," but they "will glorify and bless and sing hymns to the name of the Lord of Spirits." That is, it looks as if the Chosen One, acting as God's representative, is the convenor or occasion of this worship, so to speak, but not its recipient. In 62:5–6, "the kings and mighty and all who possess the land will bless and glorify and exalt him who rules over all," which must refer to "that Son of Man" (the Chosen One). But this looks more like a scene of obeisance of the conquered to the conqueror than cultic worship. Were it the latter, we should expect to see the reverence given by the righteous.

59. Cf. in distinction Waddell, *The Messiah*.

60. Indeed, the historical value of such phenomena as Melchizedek and the Chosen One of the *Parables* is enhanced if they and the early Christology that we see in Paul are all essentially independent developments in the Second Temple Jewish setting. For thereby, they provide multiple examples of the various innovations that could take place in that context.

5

Heavenly Mysteries and Otherworldly Journeys

Interpreting 1 and 2 Corinthians in Relation to Jewish Apocalypticism

Matthew Goff

The letters of Paul are often understood as having an apocalyptic perspective. Paul's apocalypticism, as it is often interpreted, centers upon his belief in the *parousia* of the resurrected Christ, understood as an unique and epoch-changing event that heralded God's ultimate victory over sin and death.[1] When scholars of Paul relate his writings to Jewish apocalyptic literature, the comparison is often made to emphasize the difference between the two. Beker, for example, conceptualizes Jewish apocalypticism in terms of a concept of two ages, an eschatological dualism that fundamentally separates the present age from the world to come. In this perspective, the cross not only serves as the fulcrum point between the two ages. It blurs the distinction between them, since the crucifixion, for Paul, occurred in the past while also signaling the coming *parousia*.[2] It is not at all clear, however, that Jewish apocalypticism should be defined as having a "two ages" doctrine.[3] The conception of Pauline apocalypticism put forward by de Boer also strongly distinguishes it from Jewish apocalypticism. For de Boer, who also espouses the "two ages" theme, Jewish apocalypticism distinguishes between two types of eschatology—a "cosmological" mode, in which the present age is overwhelmed by evil, supernatural powers that will be defeated at the final judgment, and a "forensic" type that stresses not evil cosmological forces, but rather, the individual and his personal battle against sin.[4] De Boer appeals to Judaism to provide a false dichotomy that Paul sublimates. For the apostle, God's final defeat over death and sin has a cosmological aspect (for example, 2 Cor. 4:4; 6:15), while also connected to the individual and his struggle against sin (Rom. 5:12–21).[5] De Boer's two modes of apocalyptic eschatology are rooted in traditional debates about Paul among New Testament scholars. Bultmann argued that Paul's eschatology is "forensic," while Käsemann considered it to be "cosmological."[6] As de Boer himself observes, however, his two types of Jewish apocalyptic eschatology are not clearly demarcated in the Dead Sea Scrolls.[7] He does not, it seems to me, understand the full significance of this realization—his conception of Pauline apocalypticism is grounded in New Testament scholarship that appeared long before the scrolls were fully published. The scrolls problematize dominant paradigms in Pauline scholarship. But they nevertheless persist.

These reflections highlight the importance of understanding Paul in relation to Jewish apocalypticism. This chapter undertakes this task. In particular, I concentrate on 1 and 2 Corinthians. When these texts are interpreted in the context of Jewish apocalyptic literature, the overall impression is not that Paul radically reconfigures Jewish apocalypticism, but is, rather, to a great extent in continuity with it.

Jewish Apocalypticism

Apocalypticism is often defined among scholars of early Judaism quite differently than by Pauline scholars. There is no emphasis on "forensic" and "cosmological" types of apocalyptic eschatology. Eschatology is understood as important, but not the central issue. Collins stresses that a claim of divine revelation is central to the Jewish apocalypses.[8] According to his definition of the genre *apocalypse*, it constitutes a type of "revelatory literature with a narrative framework."[9] The word "apocalypse" itself stresses this theme, derived from the Greek ἀποκαλύπτω, "to uncover." In apocalypses, someone typically claims to have received knowledge from a heavenly source, such as a vision or direct interaction with angels (for example, Daniel, Ezra). While apocalyptic texts are often eschatological, they are not necessarily so. Eschatology is not prominent, for example, in the earliest extant examples of the genre apocalypse, the *Book of the Watchers* and the *Astronomical Book* of *1 Enoch*, both from the third century BCE.[10] Moreover, in apocalypses, eschatology often underscores the importance of the theme of revelation, since their eschatological content is typically presented as heavenly knowledge that has been revealed to a seer in a vision (for example, Daniel, Revelation).

The Revelation and Transmission of Heavenly Mysteries in 1 Corinthians

A claim of divine revelation stands at the center of 1 Corinthians. Paul asserts in this letter to have experienced some form of divine revelation, most likely a vision of the resurrected Christ (15:3-8). He employs forms of the word ἀποκαλύπτω to make this point (1:7; Gal. 1:12). He, in turn, conveys the heavenly knowledge that he obtained to the communities he founded. Paul employs "mystery" language to describe the heavenly knowledge that he imparts.[11] Such language is especially abundant in 1 Cor. 1-4. Paul claims to give the Corinthians "God's wisdom, secret and hidden (literally "wisdom hidden in mystery"), which God decreed before the ages for our glory" (2:7). He goes on to assert that one should "think of us in this way, as servants of Christ and stewards of God's mysteries (οἰκονόμους μυστηρίων θεοῦ)"

(4:1; cf. 2:1; 3:19). The term "mystery" denotes knowledge of God's wisdom, a comprehensive, deterministic divine scheme which guides the unfolding of history and creation, presented to the Corinthians as a revealed truth.[12] For the Corinthians, understanding this mystery requires Paul's teaching and guidance, which he provides through his letters and visits (3:1-2; cf. 4:20). There is a pedagogical dimension to Paul's heavenly mysteries.

The Dead Sea Scrolls indicate that the apostle's characterization of revealed knowledge as a "mystery" is in strong continuity with Jewish tradition.[13] The term רז, "mystery," in the scrolls frequently signifies supernatural revelation. The *Habakkuk Pesher*, for example, asserts that God disclosed to the Teacher of Righteousness "all the mysteries of the words of his servants, the prophets" (7:5; cf. 1QH 9:21, 10:13; CD 3:18). In the Dead Sea Scrolls, the word "mystery" can signify supernatural revelation in the apocalypses. The Aramaic version of *1 Enoch* 106:19 (4Q204 5 II, 26–27), for example, reads: "I know the mysteries of (רזי) [the Lord which] the holy ones have revealed and shown to me."[14] 4QInstruction, a wisdom text that shows extensive influence from the apocalyptic tradition, repeatedly asks a student-addressee to study the רז נהיה, the mystery that is to be. This expression denotes a form of supernatural revelation that provides insight into God's deterministic plan, according to which, history and creation unfold (4Q417 1 I, 3–4, 8–9).[15] Appreciating the early Jewish background of Paul's mystery language helps us conceive of the apostle as both a recipient and source of divine revelation, who transmits this special knowledge, the mysteries, to his communities. The members of these groups can be understood like the addressees of 4QInstruction, as students who are to contemplate and reflect upon the esoteric knowledge imparted by their teacher.[16]

The *Parousia* of a Messiah:
1 Corinthians 15 vis-à-vis Contemporary Jewish Apocalypses

One of the most important mysteries that Paul teaches is that the regular flow of history will culminate in a final, dramatic moment:

"Listen I will tell you a mystery! We will not all die, but we will all be changed, in a moment, in the twinkling of an eye, at the last trumpet. For the trumpet will sound and we will be changed" (15:51; cf. 7:26–31; 1 Thess. 4:16). The theme of resurrection is at the center of Paul's gospel (cf. Rom. 6:5–11). For him, the death and resurrection of Christ signaled a transformation of the world, the beginning of the full sovereignty of God on earth, unfettered by any evil or demonic power. Christ is "the first fruits of those who have died" (1 Cor. 15:20). His resurrection is considered unique, but also the beginning of a paradigm. The faithful are to receive eternal life after death, as Jesus did after his crucifixion. Paul employs an Adam/Christ typology when making this claim: "For since death came through a human being, the resurrection of the dead has also come through a human being" (verse 21; cf. verses 43–49).[17] While God introduced death through Adam, the apostle's argument goes, he established (eternal) life through Christ.

Paul continues by putting forward an eschatological scenario. First Corinthians 15:23 claims that initially come the first fruits (the resurrection of Christ) and "then at his coming (ἐν τῇ παρουσίᾳ αὐτοῦ) those who belong to Christ." The *parousia* denotes the return of the resurrected Christ, at which point, the faithful will be resurrected.[18] After this, according to Paul, "then comes the end (τὸ τέλος), when (ὅταν) he hands over the kingdom to God the Father, after (ὅταν) he has destroyed every ruler and every authority and power" (verse 24).[19] Paul does not envision merely the defeat of political leaders, but rather, a more comprehensive overthrow of wickedness, sin, and even death (verses 26, 54–55; cf. Rom. 8:38). After their downfall, God's dominion, the heavenly kingdom, exerts full control over the world. The eschatological events Paul promulgates in 1 Corinthians 15 have a threefold sequence. The first, for Paul, had already happened, the resurrection of Christ. The second is the *parousia*, which leads to the resurrection of the faithful and the overthrow of the worldly powers. The third is the *telos*, the final stage of God's plan, which comprises the return of divine rule from Christ to the Lord—the full dominion of God's sovereignty.

The scope of Paul's eschatological claims is impressive. But the devil is in the details. Christ receives some type of control over God's kingdom, which he relinquishes once evil has been defeated (15:28). This means, although it is not stated explicitly in the letter, that the resurrected Christ becomes a king or at least some sort of representative of God's kingdom on earth, not unlike the "one like a son of man" in Daniel 7. First Corinthians does not state, however, when exactly Christ is to obtain this exalted status and acquire the power with which he conquers evil (1 Cor. 15:24). Based on the evidence of the letter itself, it could take place at his resurrection or his *parousia*.[20]

Paul's eschatological proclamation in 1 Corinthians 15 can be better understood through comparison with Jewish apocalypses that are approximately contemporary. I focus on the *Similitudes of Enoch* and *2 Baruch*, both of which were composed during the second half of the first century CE (note also *4 Ezra*). They are preserved, respectively, in Ethiopic and Syriac. In the *Similitudes*, eschatological judgment is not carried out by God in heaven, but by the Son of Man (*walda be'si*), the title of a messianic figure (in contrast to Daniel 7) who sits upon a throne on earth (*1 En.* 46:2-3; cf. 61:8; 69:29). The Son of Man will judge and conquer worldly powers: "all the kings and the mighty and the exalted and those who rule the land will fall on their faces in his presence" (62:9), as well as sinners and the unrighteous in general (verse 2; cf. *4 Ezra* 12:32-33). The eschatological scenario includes a disruptive and radical transformation of the earth, in which the "mountains will leap like rams" (*1 En.* 51:4). There will also be a resurrection of the dead (verse 1).

Paul's presentation of the resurrected Christ as a heavenly being who descends to overthrow kings has much in common with the *Similitudes*. In the Pauline text, as in the Enochic booklet, a messiah represents a manifestation on earth of God's heavenly dominion. In both writings, a messiah defeats worldly powers, which signify not simply political rulers, but wickedness in a broader sense. The messianic scenario in the *Similitudes* may also suggest an answer to something that Paul leaves rather unclear in 1 Corinthians 15—when Christ is to acquire the divine authority which he gives back to God in 1 Cor. 15:24: not at the moment of Christ's resurrection, but after this, when the resurrected Christ is to come down from heaven to judge, not unlike the Son of Man in the *Similitudes*.

2 Baruch envisages a messianic and eschatological scenario that exhibits even more similarities with 1 Corinthians 15.[21] This work describes the future tribulation (*2 Bar.* 26–30). The advent of this cataclysm is inaugurated by the appearance of a messiah:

> That which will happen at that time bears upon the whole earth. Therefore, all who live will notice it. For at that time I shall only protect those found in this land at this time. And it will happen that when all that which should come to pass in these parts has been accomplished, the Anointed One will begin to be revealed. (29:1–3; cf. *4 Ezra* 7:28–33)

The crops, according to *2 Baruch*, will become abundant and only enjoyed by the righteous of Israel (*2 Bar.* 29:5). Everyone else will have been eliminated (verse 2). Chapter 29 proclaims that the emergence of a messiah is the beginning of this scenario, although this figure himself plays a rather passive role in the eschatological scene. Elsewhere, however, *2 Baruch* asserts that the messiah is to wield great power on the earth and overthrow worldly powers, much like the resurrected Christ of 1 Corinthians or the Son of Man in the *Similitudes of Enoch* (*2 Bar.* 39:7–40:1). That the messiah of *2 Baruch* will "begin to be revealed" suggests he existed prior to this moment, although his location or the duration of this prior existence are not clear (cf. *4 Ezra* 12:32; 13:26, 52).

Second Baruch 30 clarifies the importance of the messiah: "And it will happen after these things when the time of the appearance of the Anointed One has been fulfilled and he returns with glory that then all who sleep in hope of him will rise" (verse 1; cf. 50:1). The Syriac for "appearance" is ܡܐܬܝܬܐ (*m'tyt'*). This term corresponds in the Syriac New Testament to the Greek *parousia*, used in 1 Cor. 15:23 and elsewhere.[22] The statement "the appearance of the Anointed One has been fulfilled" is reasonably understood as parallel to the phrase that follows, "he returns with glory." So interpreted, they comprise two different ways of stating that the messiah, once he initially appears, shall re-emerge upon the earth.[23] The return of the messiah signals not a general resurrection of the dead, but rather, only of those who "sleep in hope of him"[24] (ܟܡܣܒܪܗ). The most immediate antecedent of the key pronoun "him" is not God, but rather, the anointed one. Those who are faithful to the messiah are to be rewarded with eternal life.

Second Baruch puts forward a form of messianic expectation that is extremely close to that of 1 Corinthians 15. Both texts describe an eschatological scenario that starts with the advent of a messiah. This is followed, according to both compositions, by the *parousia* of a messiah, at which point, the resurrection is to occur, for those who were devoted to him. Additionally, *2 Baruch* and 1 Corinthians describe not only a physical resurrection, but rather, the ultimate exaltation of the righteous, who acquire a heavenly, eternal form of existence. Both texts discuss the physical transformation they shall experience when this occurs.[25]

Comparison with *2 Baruch* and the *Similitudes of Enoch* establishes that, when assessing 1 Corinthians 15 in relation to Jewish apocalypticism, the issue is not simply one of Paul drawing upon an older Jewish "heritage" or "background." Apocalypticism was a vibrant and creative complex of traditions during the apostle's lifetime. The ideas in these apocalyptic texts should not be reduced to simplistic modes of thought (that is, cosmological versus forensic). Different authors appropriated a common body of traditions in different ways. Jewish apocalypticism does not comprise a discourse that Paul radically transformed. Rather, he was a participant in it. Contemporary Jewish apocalyptic traditions helped him understand the death of Jesus. Apocalypses from the first century CE, especially *2 Baruch*, help explain why Paul believed, as did other followers of Jesus at the time, that the resurrected Christ would come back in glory (his *parousia*) to resurrect the righteous and bestow upon them eternal life.

Heavenly Ascension in 2 Corinthians

Second Corinthians can also be profitably interpreted against the background of Jewish apocalypticism. This is evident, for example, in 2 Cor. 6:14–15, which attests a dualistic pairing of light and darkness, followed by one that opposes Christ and Belial: "What fellowship is there between light and darkness? What agreement does Christ have with Beliar?" Belial (or Beliar) is a supernatural figure of evil who appears repeatedly in the Dead Sea Scrolls (e. g., 1QM 13:10–11; CD 5:18).[26] Second Corinthians's pairing of an opposition between Christ and Belial with another between light and darkness may indicate that Paul was shaped by Jewish dualistic traditions, such as those evident in the *Treatise of the Two Spirits*. This composition distinguishes between good and evil divine powers that guide human behavior who are associated, respectively, with either light or darkness (1QS 3:13–4:26).

The pericope of 2 Corinthians, however, that most clearly connects with the Jewish apocalyptic tradition is 2 Cor. 12:1–10.[27] The first four verses of this passage read:

> It is necessary to boast; nothing is to be gained by it, but I will go on to visions and revelations of the Lord (ὀπτασίας καὶ ἀποκαλύψεις κυρίου). I know a person in Christ who fourteen years ago was caught up to the third heaven—whether in the body or out of the body I do not know; God knows. And I know that such a person—whether in the body or out of the body I do not know; God knows—was caught up into paradise and heard things that are not to be told, that no mortal is permitted to repeat.

Paul mentions a visionary experience that he attributes to someone else. It is evident, however, that he is talking about himself (verses 7–9). The text uses the verb ἁρπάζω, "to be caught up," two times in reference to the vision (cf. 1 Thess. 4:17).[28] This language suggests that the vision is one of heavenly ascent. He alludes to the possibility that he may have left his body (verses 2–3). Paul is also vague about the content of the vision. It may have involved an image of the resurrected Christ (perhaps sitting upon a heavenly throne), since elsewhere, he claims to have seen an "apocalypse" of Christ (for example, 1 Cor. 15:8). However, in 2 Corinthians 12, while the visionary describes himself as "in Christ," the content of this vision is not explicitly about Jesus. Rather, it is about the "third heaven" and "paradise" (see further below), tropes that Paul never engages in depth in his letters. In contrast to 1 Corinthians 15, nothing about the heavenly knowledge revealed in 2 Corinthians 12 is eschatological (note, however, 5:1-5).

Second Corinthians 12 has much in common with the Jewish apocalyptic tradition. He uses the language of ἀποκάλυψις to signify the revelations he describes (verse 1). It should be noted, however, that this chapter describes a vision that is quite different from the revelations that are typical in the apocalypses. In 2 Corinthians 12, no visionary is shown cryptic images that are interpreted by an angel. Heavenly ascents are a central component of one of the subtypes of the genre apocalypse demarcated by Collins, the "otherworldly journey." In these apocalypses, which include the *Apocalypse of Zephaniah* and *2 Enoch*, the visionary travels, often accompanied by angels, and secrets about the heavenly world are revealed to him.[29] The Enochic apocalypses contain several examples of such ascents.[30] In *1 Enoch*, when Enoch is lifted up by the angels, they show him, for example, the precise movements of the sun and the moon in the *Astronomical Book* (*1 En.* 72:1; cf. 18:1-5; 106:19). He is transformed by his celestial ascent. The disputed ending of the *Similitudes* asserts that Enoch is the Son of Man (71:14). While this may be a secondary addition, perhaps a Jewish effort to portray Enoch rather than Jesus as the Son of Man, Enoch's new identity may be a result of his mystical transformation that takes places once he ascends to heaven.[31] He goes to heaven and is set before the Lord of Spirits (*1 En.* 70:1). Enoch asserts that in his presence, "my flesh melted and my spirit was transformed" (71:11). In *2 Enoch*, when Enoch travels to the tenth heaven, he also changes: "And I looked at myself, and I had become like one of his glorious ones, and there was no observable difference" (verse 10). The trope of a visionary transformed by his ascent is also prominent in *3 Enoch*. In this text, Metatron, an important, exalted figure in heaven who is known as "the Prince of the Divine Presence" and even "the Lesser Yahweh," is the transformed Enoch (4:3; 12:5).

Second Corinthians resonates powerfully with Enochic ascent traditions in other ways. Paul was taken up to paradise and the third heaven (2 Cor. 12:2, 4). In *2 Enoch* paradise, the ultimate abode of the righteous, designed after the garden of Eden, is likewise in the third heaven.[32] In *3 Enoch*, the visionary who journeys to heaven is not Enoch, but Rabbi Ishmael. He speaks with Enoch/Metatron in heaven. He reveals divine knowledge to the rabbi. Ishmael's goal is "to behold the vision of the chariot" (*3 En.* 1:1). *3 Enoch* is an important example of *merkabah* mysticism, a late antique phenomenon in the context of which rabbis devised various ecstatic techniques one could use to obtain a vision of the "chariot," a reference to God seated upon his heavenly throne.[33] Paul may have used some of these practices to attain the vision mentioned in 2 Corinthians 12.[34]

The remarkable claims made by Enoch in *2 Enoch* and Rabbi Ishmael in *3 Enoch* regarding their experiences in heaven make intelligible why Paul is reluctant to describe what he saw in the third heaven. He states that he glimpsed things that "no mortal is permitted to repeat" (2 Cor. 12:4). Ancient Jewish mystical texts contain similar prohibitions.[35] Paul's reticence testifies to the transcendent nature of the heavenly realities that were seen in the vision. The apostle may have also been of the opinion that the Corinthians, of whose spiritual progress he was critical (for example, 1 Cor. 3:1), were not ready for a full disclosure of his vision.

Paul's assertion about his vision can also be helpfully interpreted in relation to ancient Jewish accounts of heavenly ascents (2 Cor. 12:6). One of the Dead Sea Scrolls, entitled the *Self-Glorification Hymn* (4Q491c), contains an account of someone claiming to have had some sort of experience in heaven that transformed him. He asserts that he is now among the angels. He boasts about his transformed status. He asks "Who is comparable to me in my glory?" (line 8) Moreover, the speaker claims that because of this experience, he is able to endure sorrow and suffering as no one else can (line 9).

Paul has a lot to be modest about. Moreover, he asserts that he was given a thorn in the flesh and torments by Satan, so that he may not become too elated (verse 7). He experiences weakness and hardships, which he gladly boasts about (verses 11–12).[36] Such boasting makes sense in the context of his view, common throughout his letters, that the heavenly world is radically distinguished from the worldly plane of existence. Weakness, like foolishness, for Paul, while bad from a conventional, or one could say "worldly" perspective, become emblems of affinity with heaven (for example, 1 Cor. 1:25–27). Weakness and hardship are, in the mindset of Paul, worthy of boasting. And they, so understood, are not dissimilar to ascent visions, since both signify affinity with the heavenly realm. Paul turns to both his suffering and his ascent to bolster his authority among the Corinthians (2 Cor. 11:7; 12:11). The *Self-Glorification Hymn* suggests Paul's combination of these two themes of suffering and ascension is not simply a topos unique to his thought or social situation. It is compatible with how other Jews in antiquity described their visions of heavenly ascent.

Conclusion

First and Second Corinthians have much in common with the Jewish apocalyptic tradition. This is, above all, evident in the apostle's claim that the gospel he preaches is grounded in divine revelation—an "apocalypse" of the resurrected Christ. This is a mystery from the heavenly world that he received and transmits in his letters. He claims not simply to impart a vision of Christ, but also a broader, more comprehensive revelation of the wisdom of God (1 Cor. 2:7), which provides special knowledge into his dominion over history and creation. Claims of supernatural revelation are a foundational element of Paul's writings. This is also the case in Jewish apocalypses. Paul turned to this tradition, which was an important part of the Judaism of his day, to understand the death of Christ and his *parousia*. Pauline apocalypticism does not constitute a radical reformulation of Jewish apocalypticism, but, on the contrary, is in substantial continuity with it.

Notes

1. See, for example, J. Christaan Beker, *Paul the Apostle: The Triumph of God in Life and Thought* (Philadelphia: Fortress Press, 1984), 204–8; idem, *Paul's Apocalyptic Gospel: The Coming Triumph of God* (Philadelphia: Fortress Press, 1982). Consult also J. Louis Martyn, "Epistemology at the Turn of the Ages: 2 Corinthians 5:16," in *Theological Issues in the Letters of Paul* (Edinburgh: T&T Clark, 1997), 87–110; R. Barry Matlock, *Unveiling the Apocalyptic Paul: Paul's Interpreters and the Rhetoric of Criticism* (JSNTSup 127; Sheffield: Sheffield Academic Press, 1996).

2. Beker, *Paul the Apostle*, 211.

3. The eschatological defeat of evil is often envisaged in Jewish apocalyptic literature not as a profound rupture away from the historical continuum, but rather, a crucial element of God's plan that orchestrates history, from creation to judgment. This is evident, for example, in the *Apocalypse of Weeks* and the *Animal Apocalypse*. See further Loren T. Stuckenbruck, "Overlapping Ages at Qumran and 'Apocalyptic' in Pauline Theology," in *The Dead Sea Scrolls and Pauline Literature*, ed. J.-S. Rey (STDJ 102; Leiden: Brill, 2014), 309–26.

4. For him, an example of the former type is *Testament of Moses* 10 and the latter *4 Ezra* and *2 Baruch*. See Martinus C. de Boer, "Paul and Apocalyptic Eschatology," in *The Encyclopedia of Apocalypticism*, ed. J. J. Collins, B. McGinn and S. Stein (3 vols.; New York: Continuum, 2000), 1:345–83 (359); idem, "Paul and Jewish Apocalyptic Eschatology," in *Apocalyptic and the New Testament: Essays in Honor of J. Louis Martyn*, ed. J. Marcus and M. L. Soards (JSNTSup 24; Sheffield: JSOT Press, 1989), 169–90.

5. De Boer, "Paul and Apocalyptic Eschatology," 360. See also Leander E. Keck, "Paul and Apocalyptic Theology," *Int* 38 (1984): 229–41 (235).

6. De Boer, "Paul and Apocalyptic Eschatology," 361.

7. Ibid., 360. Note, for example, the *Treatise of the Two Spirits* (1QS 3:13–4:26), in which the individual and the ethical decisions he makes are situated against the backdrop of a grand conflict in the cosmos between forces of light and darkness.

8. John J. Collins, *The Apocalyptic Imagination* (2nd ed.; Grand Rapids: Eerdmans, 1998). See also Christopher Rowland, *The Open Heaven: A Study of Apocalyptic in Judaism and Early Christianity* (New York: Crossroad, 1982), 70.

9. Collins, *The Apocalyptic Imagination*, 5. See also Matthew J. Goff, "The Apocalypse and the Sage: Assessing the Contribution of John J. Collins to the Study of Apocalypticism," in *ISBL Vienna volume*, ed. S. White Crawford and C. Wassen (Leiden: Brill, forthcoming).

10. These writings do indeed have eschatological elements (e. g., *1 Enoch* 10, 80). But the knowledge revealed to Enoch in them shows a much greater interest

in other topics, such as the nature of the world during the days of the flood and the regular motion of the moon and sun. Also, numerous texts are eschatological, but not apocalypses, such as the post-exilic prophetic texts of Joel or Isaiah 24–27.

11. Compare Eph. 3:3–4. In this text, Paul asserts that he acquired a mystery through revelation, and then, tries to give the Ephesians a conception of the "mystery of Christ." See also Rom. 11:25; 16:25; Eph. 6:19; Col. 1:26–27; 2:2; 4:3. Consult Markus Bockmuehl, *Revelation and Mystery in Ancient Judaism and Pauline Christianity* (Grand Rapids: Eerdmans, 1990), 158–63.

12. In 1 Cor. 14:2, he presents speaking in tongues as speaking in mysteries (cf. 13:2). First Corinthians 15:51 is examined below.

13. Raymond E. Brown, *The Semitic Background of the Term "Mystery" in the New Testament* (Philadelphia: Fortress Press, 1968); Benjamin Gladd, *Revealing the Mysterion: The Use of Mystery in Daniel and Second Temple Judaism with its Bearing on First Corinthians* (BZNW 160; Berlin: de Gruyter, 2008).

14. Józef T. Milik, *The Books of Enoch: Aramaic Fragments of Qumrân Cave 4* (Oxford: Clarendon, 1976), 210. See also George W.E. Nickelsburg, *1 Enoch: A Commentary on the Book of 1 Enoch, Chapters 1-36, 81-108* (Hermeneia; Minneapolis: Fortress Press, 2001), 537. The term *rāz* also denotes supernatural revelation in the book of Daniel (2:18–19, 27–30, 47 [bis]; 4:6).

15. Matthew J. Goff, *4QInstruction* (WLAW 2; Atlanta: Society of Biblical Literature, 2013), 14–17.

16. First Corinthians may have been influenced by a trajectory of the Jewish wisdom tradition exemplified by 4QInstruction. See Matthew J. Goff, "Being Fleshly or Spiritual: Anthropological Reflection and Exegesis of Genesis 1-3 in 4QInstruction and 1 Corinthians," in *Christian Body, Christian Self: Concepts of Early Christian Personhood*, ed. C. Rothschild and T. Thompson (WUNT 1.284; Tübingen: Mohr Siebeck, 2011), 41–59.

17. Goff, "Being Fleshly or Spiritual," 52–58; Stephen Hultgren, "The Origin of Paul's Doctrine of The Two Adams in 1 Corinthians 15.45-49," *JSNT* 25 (2003): 343–70.

18. For the *parousia*, and its delay, see Jörg Frey, "New Testament Eschatology—an Introduction: Classical Issues, Disputed Themes, and Current Perspectives," in *Eschatology of the New Testament and Some Related Documents*, ed. J. G. van der Watt (WUNT 2.315; Tübingen: Mohr Siebeck, 2011), 3–32 (25–26).

19. In 1 Cor. 15:24, the second ὅταν clause is subordinate to the first. See Hans Conzelmann, *First Corinthians: A Commentary on the First Epistle to the Corinthians* (Hermeneia; Minneapolis: Fortress Press, 1988), 271.

20. See further below. De Boer, "Paul and Apocalyptic Eschatology," 377–78, engages the same problem.

21. Collins, *The Apocalyptic Imagination*, 212–25; Matthias Henze, "'Then the Messiah will begin to be revealed': Resurrection and the Apocalyptic Drama in 1 Corinthians 15 and Second Baruch 29-30, 49-51," in *Anthropologie und Ethik im Frühjudentum und im Neuen Testament. Wechselseitige Wahrnehmungen. Internationales Symposium in Verbindung mit dem Projekt Corpus Judaeo-Hellenisticum Novi Testamenti (CJNHT) 17.-20. Mai 2012, Heidelberg*, ed. M. Konradt and E. Schläpfer (WUNT 1.322; Tübingen: Mohr Siebeck, 2014), 441–62. In this volume, also see Samuel Vollenwieder, "Auferstehung als Verwandlung. Die paulinische Eschatologie von 1Kor 15 im Vergleich mit der syrischen Baruchaokalypse (2Bar)," 463–90. See further, Matthias Henze, *Jewish Apocalypticism in Late First Century Israel: Reading Second Baruch in Context* (TSAJ 142; Tübingen: Mohr Siebeck, 2011), 324–39.

22. Matt. 24:27; 2 Cor. 7:6; 2 Pet. 1:16. See William Jennings, *Lexicon to the Syriac New Testament* (Oxford: Clarendon, 1926), 114; Henze, "Then the Messiah will begin to be revealed," 451.

23. It is not fully clear where the messiah went, in order to return to this world. See Henze, ibid., 452.

24. Daniel M. Gurtner, *Second Baruch: A Critical Edition of the Syriac Text: With Greek and Latin Fragments, English Translation, Introduction, and Concordances* (London: T&T Clark, 2009), 66–67.

25. *2 Baruch* 51:3: "The glory of those who proved to be righteous on account of my law ... their splendor will then be glorified by transformations, and the shape of their face will be changed into the light of their beauty so that they may acquire and receive the undying world which is promised to them." Cf. 1 Cor. 15:35–41.

26. Devorah Dimant, "Between Qumran Sectarian and Qumran Nonsectarian Texts: The Case of Belial and Mastema," in *History, Ideology and Bible Interpretation in the Dead Sea Scrolls* (FAT 90; Tübingen: Mohr Siebeck, 2014), 135–51.

27. Albert Hogeterp, "The Otherworld and This World in 2 Cor. 12:1-10 in Light of Early Jewish Apocalyptic Tradition," in *Other Worlds and Their Relation to This World: Early Jewish and Ancient Christian Traditions*, ed. T. Nicklas et al. (JSJSup 143; Leiden: Brill, 2010), 209–28; Christopher Rowland and Christopher R. A. Morray-Jones, *The Mystery of God: Early Jewish Mysticism and the New Testament* (CRINT 12; Leiden: Brill, 2009), 379–408; Bockmuehl, *Revelation and Mystery*, 170–75.

28. Hogeterp, "The Otherworld and This World in 2 Cor. 12:1-10," 217; Rowland and Morray-Jones, *The Mystery of God*, 141.

29. Martha Himmelfarb, *Ascent to Heaven in Jewish and Christian Apocalypses* (New York: Oxford University Press, 1993).

30. One of the major issues in terms of Paul's knowledge of Enochic traditions is the disputed claim that he shows familiarity with the Watchers myth in 1 Cor. 11:10. This verse claims that women should wear head coverings "because of the angels." It is beyond the scope of this chapter to discuss this issue. See

Loren T. Stuckenbruck, "Why Should Women Cover Their Heads Because of the Angels? (1 Corinthians 11:10)," *Stone-Campbell Journal* 4 (2001): 205–34.

31. For this position, consult James C. VanderKam, "Righteous One, Messiah, Chosen One and Son of Man in 1 Enoch 37-71," in *The Messiah: Developments in Earliest Judaism and Christianity*, ed. J. H. Charlesworth (Minneapolis: Fortress Press, 1992), 169–91. Consult also Collins, *The Apocalyptic Imagination*, 187–91.

32. *Second Enoch* 8:1: "They brought me up to the third heaven. And they placed me in the midst of paradise" [A] (cf. 9:1). The Greek *Life of Adam and Eve* (*Apoc. Moses*) also presents the third heaven as the location of paradise (37:5). See Hogeterp, "The Otherworld," 220; Rowland and Morray-Jones, *The Mystery of God*, 393–96.

33. For an example of such techniques, see *Hekhalot Rabbati* (Schäfer §§204-5). Note Rowland and Morray-Jones, *The Mystery of God*, 235. For an overview of *merkabah* mysticism, consult Ra'anan Boustan, *From Martyr to Mystic: Rabbinic Martyrology and the Making of Merkavah Mysticism* (TSAJ 112; Tübingen: Mohr Siebeck, 2005).

34. So also Christopher R. A. Morray-Jones, "Paradise Revisited (2 Cor. 12:1–12): The Jewish Mystical Background of Paul's Apostolate. Part Two: Paul's Heavenly Ascent and Its Significance," *HTR* 86 (1993): 265–92 (283).

35. For example, according to the well-known rabbinic tale about the four who entered paradise, one may not speak about the *merkabah* with someone else, unless that person is wise (*m. Ḥag* 2.1).

36. Also note that boasting was the context in which he brought up the vision in the first place (2 Cor. 11:16–33; cf. 1:12; 7:14).

PART III

Paul and Gentile Inclusiveness

6

Paul and the Food Laws

A Reassessment of Romans 14:14, 20

David Rudolph

Sometimes, the ecclesial application of a New Testament interpretation is so disturbing that the ethical implications should elicit a full-scale reassessment. This is the case with the traditional reading of Romans 14, which labels Jewish followers of Jesus as "weak in faith" if they observe the Torah, a stigma that ultimately undermines the existence of Jews in the church.[1] As John Barclay, a proponent of the traditional view, puts it, "Paul subverts the basis on which Jewish law-observance is founded . . . his theology introduces into the Roman Christian community a Trojan horse which threatens the integrity of those who sought to live according to the law."[2] The aim of this chapter is to reassess the traditional interpretation of Romans 14 by focusing on Paul's principle at the heart of the chapter—"nothing is unclean in itself; but it is unclean for anyone who thinks it unclean . . . everything is indeed clean" (Rom. 14:14, 20). After summarizing the traditional view, I will seek to demonstrate that Paul's instructions in this passage do not burst the bounds of Judaism. On the contrary, they draw his predominantly gentile audience more deeply into Judaism so that they can better understand the halakhic principles surrounding matters of ritual uncleanness/impurity and defilement.

The Traditional View

The traditional interpretation of Rom. 14:14, 20 considers the Jewish food laws[3] to be "abolished"[4] and "no longer in effect"[5] with the coming of Christ. This conclusion is based on several claims:

1. *Textual argument:* The language of "clean" (καθαρός) and "unclean" (κοινός) in Rom. 14:14, 20 refers to Israel's food laws. Paul's statement in verse 14b ("it is unclean for anyone who thinks it unclean") reflects a law-free approach to these laws.
2. *Contextual argument:* The weak abstain from meat and wine (Rom. 14:2, 21). This confirms that Jewish law observance is in view.
3. *Intertextual argument:* Rom. 14:14, 20 is informed by a tradition that Jesus "declared all foods clean" (Mark 7:19b).

Rereading Paul as a Second Temple Jewish Author in Romans 14

The traditional reading of Rom. 14:14, 20 has been normative for so long that many studies of the passage seem to begin with the assumption that the traditional interpretation has been conclusively established, and then, proceed to make the data conform to this law-free portrait of Paul. Weaknesses in the traditional case are rarely mentioned and references to post-supersessionist approaches are few and far between. In this section, I will take a step in the direction of correcting this imbalance by re-reading Paul in Rom. 14:14, 20 as a Second Temple Jew who thought halakhically and viewed Israel's Leviticus 11 food laws as binding on Jewish followers of Jesus such as himself, but not on gentiles.

"Everything is indeed clean" (Rom. 14:20)

The traditional interpretation of Rom. 14:20 assumes that Paul's words refer to a divine revocation of Israel's food laws. However, this is a narrow way of reading the text, given Paul's predominantly gentile audience.[6] It is more likely that Paul is addressing gentile believers directly in Rom. 14:20, and saying, "Everything is indeed clean [for you]." Kathy Ehrensperger concurs:

> . . . the addressees in this passage are Gentiles. Thus what Paul formulates here is not a general statement about the perception of food, but a specific statement addressed to specific people in a specific context. . . . "For them" the food laws do not apply. Thus, "for them" all food is pure. Paul, in addressing non-Jews, is arguing in a Levitical vein here . . . Paul just confirms that the general Jewish perception concerning these laws in relation to Gentiles applies also to Gentiles who are now in Christ.[7]

A compelling argument can be made that "Everything is indeed clean" was a slogan among the gentile strong.[8] With this in mind, one can read verse 20 with the slogan in quotation marks:

> *"Everything is indeed clean,"* but (πάντα μὲν καθαρά,[9] ἀλλὰ) it is wrong for you to make others fall by what you eat. (Rom. 14:20)

Paul does something similar in 1 Cor. 6:12 and 10:23–27:

> *"All things are lawful for me,"* but (πάντα μοι ἔξεστιν ἀλλ') not all things are beneficial. (1 Cor. 6:12a)
> *"All things are lawful for me,"* but (πάντα μοι ἔξεστιν ἀλλ') I will not be dominated by anything. (1 Cor. 6:12b)
> *"All things are lawful,"* but (πάντα ἔξεστιν ἀλλ') not all things are beneficial. (1 Cor. 10:23a)
> *"All things are lawful,"* but (πάντα ἔξεστιν ἀλλ') not all things build up. (1 Cor. 10:23b)

The many parallels between Rom. 14:19–22 and 1 Cor. 10:23–27 are notable and may suggest that the former is informed by Paul's reflections on the latter, written possibly only a year earlier.[10] If Rom. 14:20 is a slogan representing a gentile perspective on freedom, which

Paul is quoting, then it does not imply that Israel's food laws have been invalidated for Jews.

To sum up, the Torah does not command gentiles to keep Israel's dietary laws. Paul is likely reassuring the gentiles in Rom. 14:20 that they are *not* obligated to observe the Leviticus 11 dietary laws—"Everything is indeed clean [for you gentiles]." He may also be quoting a slogan of the gentile strong. This reading of Rom. 14:20 is consistent with Paul's "rule in all the churches" (1 Cor. 7:17–24),[11] which distinguishes between Jewish and gentile responsibilities in the *ekklesia*.[12] Thus, Rom. 14:20 can be read as a halakhic statement of how Paul applied the Torah's Leviticus 11 dietary laws in a differentiated way to a community of Jesus-believing gentiles and Jews who worshipped the God of Israel and sought to live according to the Scriptures of Israel.

"It is unclean for anyone who thinks it unclean" (Rom. 14:14b)

The traditional interpretation of Rom. 14:14b assumes a law-free Paul, who is indifferent to Israel's food laws. However, given the legal terminology Paul uses in this passage, more room should be made for the possibility that Paul, a student of Gamaliel, viewed the dispute between the weak and strong in halakhic terms, and that his advice to the Messiah followers in Rome was based on halakhic principles. In Rom. 14:14, Paul writes "nothing is unclean (κοινὸν) in itself; but it is unclean (κοινὸν) for anyone who thinks it unclean (κοινὸν)." *It is important to note that Paul uses the term κοινός rather than καθαρά (verse 20) and that he includes the qualifier "in itself" (δι' ἑαυτοῦ).*

Paul appears to understand the dispute in Romans 14 as related to the Jewish legal concept of κοινός. The term κοινός in connection with ritual purity is unattested in non-Jewish Greek literature. It is also absent from the LXX Pentateuch. The first attested usage of κοινός in relation to food is 1 Macc. 1:47, 62 and 4 Macc. 7:6. Recent study of the term has tended to view it as a "synonym for ἀκάθαρτος,"[13] or alternatively, as a technical term for "clean animals which are somehow objectionable *as food*."[14] The lack of attestation in biblical law and its relatively late entry into Jewish legal vocabulary would seem to suggest that κοινός had a meaning "separate and distinct" from ἀκάθαρτος, as J. D. M. Derrett concludes in his *Filología Neotestamentaria* study.[15]

A plausible scenario for its origin in Jewish law is that there was no word in the LXX Pentateuch that adequately described the halakhic category of food under discussion in 1 Macc. 1:47, 62 (that is, it did not fit into the Torah's holy [קדש/ἅγιος] ¦ common [חל/βέβηλος]/pure-clean [טהור/καθαρός] ¦ impure/unclean [טמא/ἀκάθαρτος] grid,[16] but overlapped these categories), and so, the author of 1 Maccabees used κοινός to refer to this grey area. Scholarship has tended to try to force κοινός into the Torah's conceptual framework,[17] like fitting a square peg into a round hole, but in doing so, the word's significance in describing a more grey overlapping area is lost.[18]

The author of 1 Maccabees may have used the term κοινός because the food in question was *associated* with gentiles who practiced idolatry:

> Alternatively, it could be that the author of 1 Macc considers the food prepared by any Gentile or Jewish renegade as κοινά and therefore defiling (in an offensive or moral sense), even if, technically, the food item is permitted for a Jew to eat.... We could add that the term came to be used to designate *any* food prepared by Gentiles. Such a semantic development seems quite understandable, since the associative dimension of *communion* (κοινωνία), which underlines the term κοινός, easily crosses into the realm of dietary practices. After all, the very *raison d'être* for keeping kosher for many Jews in antiquity meant *disassociating* themselves from other ethnic groups, preserving thereby their identity and collective *sanctity*—the very antonym of profaneness. As the Torah "repeats" in Deut the regulations of kashrut, it states: "For you are a holy (ἅγιος/קדוש) people to the LORD your God; and the LORD has chosen you to be a people for His own possession *out of all the peoples* who are on the face of the earth" (Deut. 14:2; emphasis mine). Prolonged association with other peoples could lead, so some Jews believed, to the abandonment of Jewish identity and transformation into the Gentile "other."[19]

To sum up, the legal term κοινός was likely coined in Second Temple Jewish literature to refer to halakhic grey areas related to impurity that did not fit neatly into the category of ἀκάθαρτος, such as food prepared by gentiles.

Returning to Rom. 14:14, it is likely that Paul intentionally used the non-specific term κοινός, rather than a more contextually defined and biblically established term such as ἀκάθαρτος, because he was focusing, in verse 14, on categories of foods that fell into grey areas and were halakhically more open to question: for example, food that was considered "unfit" because of the way it was slaughtered or due to its association with food sacrificed to idols or other perceived contaminants.

Amid the broad spectrum of differing standards of κοινός, first-century Jews such as Paul made personal decisions about what they considered κοινός, and were expected to live by their own standards, hence Paul's statement in Rom. 14:14 that "nothing is unclean in itself; but it is unclean for anyone who thinks it unclean." What was κοινός for one person was not κοινός for another. This is a less common way of reading Rom. 14:14 because New Testament scholars often assume a more monolithic Second Temple Judaism. Recent scholarship, however, has called this assumption into question.

In his essay "'Someone who considers something to be impure—for him it is impure' (Rom. 14:14): Good Manners or Law?," Daniel Schwartz argues that "for many Jews, and certainly for Judaism as it was coming to be in the age of Paul, the important and binding things were those that we undertake upon ourselves in full cognizance of the fact that others do not."[20] The Pharisaic *havurah* had such an approach when it came to ritual purity. Tosefta *Demai* chapter 2 describes the "one who imposes on himself the obligations" and describes the various areas of ritual purity that he takes on.[21] Similarly, in Mishnah *Ḥagigah* 2:5-7, the individual's commitment to ritual purity is related to the particular level he chooses to take on, and his level of responsibility corresponds to his personal intention. In his paper "Impurity and Social Demarcation: Resetting Second Temple Halakhic Traditions in New Contexts," Yair Furstenberg notes how the the active decision to regard something as impure makes it impure for that person:

That rabbinic purification is only a matter of personal will and skill is inferred from Mishna Hagigah. At first, the Mishnah states the conditions for achieving each grade of purity: For example, הטובל לחולין והוחזק לחולין אסור למעשר. "If a man immersed himself to render himself fit to eat of unconsecrated produce, he may not touch [Second] Tithe." According to this translation purity depends only on personal intention and decision. As one immerses he must decide what kind of purity he is accepting upon himself; his care for purity will be shaped accordingly. Someone who chooses to only eat unconsecrated food in purity will not be careful in regard to more severe purities. This interpretation, accepted by all since the Tosefta and both Talmuds, expresses what seems to be the rabbinic notion of purity: there may be various levels of scrupulousness; nonetheless, all levels of purity are accessible to the individual, provided that he is aware of his obligations.[22]

Furstenberg goes on to argue that Paul held a similar perspective on purity in Rom. 14:14 and that the two texts may represent a common stream within early Judaism:

More specifically, verse 14 could be best understood in light of the purity system described in Mishna Hagigah. There we say that things that were completely pure on one level were deemed impure on a higher level. Inevitably, a scrupulous Pharisee (for example) who looked inwards, towards the inner circles where he, his cloths and his foods were all considered to be impure, could not but arrive at Jesus' conclusion. Indeed, he must be careful lest his food turn into a stumbling block for the priest, but as a consequence, a notion of relative impurity must develop, if he is to take seriously the complete split between the various levels of purity. Evidently, the notion of relative impurity, stated clearly by Jesus, was so strong that it has the power to completely split society into discrete groups. In Paul's version, outside this Palestinian purity system, we are left with the mere demand to respect each of the member's intentions. Although the decision to abstain from food, believing it to be impure, has no objective standing, since all is pure, it is the intention that counts. So Paul claims. Interestingly, also in rabbinic literature we can trace the shift from a strictly social conception of purity to an individual realization of purification. We have seen that the same halakhah that initially tied purity to an acknowledged social affiliation was re-read to involve only individual intention. Through similar paths the world of purity was transmitted from Second Temple context to the developing communities in Rabbinic Galilee and Christian Rome.[23]

Halakhic diversity is another factor that likely influenced Paul's approach to purity in Rom. 14:14. In the Pharisaic context, Paul's background, there was not only much diversity, but diversity related to the very principle Paul articulates in Rom. 14:14—halakhah that was more individualistic and that made room for the identification of impurity on the basis of personal intention. In his essay "Impurity Between Intention and Deed," Eric Ottenheijm highlights how the houses of Hillel and Shammai within Pharisaic Judaism differed over the recognition of human intention as a factor in determining the halakhic status of actions or vessels. After tracing the legal logic of how the two houses differed in their view of liquid susceptibility (that is, the ability of liquids to transfer and contract impurity),[24] Ottenheim concludes:

> First century interpretations of the Levitical law of suceptibility to impurity by liquids range from susceptibility by moisture (Qumran) via susceptibility through moistening (Beth Shammai) to susceptibility by human will (Beth Hillel). The pronounced closeness of Beth Shammai to Qumran suggests that the Hillelite concept indeed marked an innovation in Pharisaic Judaism. According to the view of Beth Hillel, impurity became a matter of classification through the human will. The Hillelite logic of intention did, however, not touch on the main sources of impurity: corpse impurity, skin diseases or fluxes and blood-impurity. Nevertheless, human intention is operative here and even decisive in halakhic cases as well. What motivated these disputes in Pharisaic Judaism? . . . The Hillelites appear to represent a tendency toward individualization and rationalization, with an emphasis on individual will power as the heart of halakhic ruling. This concept pervades all halakhic realms. With the Hillelite shift to the human will, the individual moves towards the center of the socio-religious structure. Legendary material attributed to Hillel and his School stress this focus on the individual . . . the Hillelite logic remained heavily disputed and it was only with R. Akiva's refined concept of intention and deed, that the human will as the *locus halakhicus* with regards to purity was accepted.[25]

Against this historical backdrop of a diverse Second Temple Judaism, and a non-uniform Pharisaic Judaism, one can see more clearly how Romans 14 reflects Paul's distinctively Hillelite approach to the impurity of actions and objects. This reading is consistent with Luke's testimony that Paul was trained in Jerusalem by Gamaliel, the son of Hillel[26] ("I am a Jew, born in Tarsus in Cilicia, but brought up in this city *at the feet of Gamaliel*, educated strictly according to our ancestral law, being zealous for God, just as all of you are today" [Acts 22:3]). Paul's training as a Pharisee of Pharisees, and his broad exposure to pluriform Second Temple Judaism, made him into something of a first-century halakhic pluralist who favored the Hillelite emphasis on personal intention when it came to purity issues. Seen in this way, Paul's statement in Rom. 14:14b—"it is unclean for anyone who thinks it unclean"—was not an expression of indifference toward ritual purity,[27] but a claim consistent with the on-the-ground reality of a variegated first-century Judaism.

"Nothing is unclean in itself" (Rom. 14:14a)

An underlying assumption behind the Hillelite view that personal intention can change the purity status of objects and persons is that nothing is unclean in itself. This is consonant with an haggadic tradition[28] about Yochanan ben Zakkai—a Pharisee who was a contemporary of Paul, a successor of Gamaliel and a student of Hillel:[29]

(A) A heathen asked Raban Johanan ben Zakkai and said to him:

These things you do, they look like sorcery. You bring in a cow and slaughter it, and burn it and pound it, and pour water over its ashes and one who is impure because of corpse impurity, you sprinkle on him two, three drops, and you say he is pure.
He said to him: Did ever in your days a spirit of madness enter into this man?
He said to him: No. He said to him: And did you not see another one in whom a spirit of madness entered?
He said to him: Yes.
He said to him: And what did they do?
He said to him: They brought roots and burnt incense under him and sprinkled water over him and it was driven out.
He said to him: Do not your ears hear what your mouth says?
Like this spirit is the spirit of impurity, as it is said: "(I will remove) also the prophets and the spirits of uncleanness" (Zech. 13:2).

(B) And as soon as he left, his disciples asked him:

Rabbi, this one you pushed away with a stick, to us, what do you answer?

He said to them:

By your life, nor does the body make impure, nor does the water make pure, but it is an enactment of the Holy One Blessed be He!

The Holy One Blessed be He said:

A decree have I decreed an enactment have I enacted, and you are not allowed to transgress my enactment, "This is a decree of the law" (Num. 19:1).[30]

Yochanan ben Zakkai's point is that ritual impurity and its antidote do not reflect objective ontological realities:

> The Hillelite rationalized halakhic logic presupposes that impurity is not an external, objective force. . . . Purity halakhah ruling on intention presupposes that impurity be perceived not merely as a "physical power." This negation of inherent impurity is indeed expressed in an agadic tradition about Raban Johanan ben Zakkai. . . . According to the text Raban Johanan ben Zakkai is asked about the presumed magical character of the biblical ritual of the burning of the parah or red cow (Numbers 19). The ashes were needed for purifying extreme forms of impurity such as corpse-impurity. . . . At first sight the polemic against magic or sorcery appears to be the main point. However, the wording of the pupils' question and Raban Johanan's second reply (B) move beyond polemics. *Corpse impurity has nothing to do with inherent powers or demonic danger. Nor is there any inherent meaning in purification.* As corpse impurity constitutes one of the main sources of impurity, the negation in (B) is instructive as to the rabbinic "negative theology of purity." *The exclusive reason for the rules of purity is that they were given by God.*[31]

The *Letter of Aristeas* evidences a similar approach to impurity, viewing it as a divine designation, rather than as an objective ontological category:

> The author of this Jewish work from the Diaspora knows and believes that in the beginning God created "the wild animals of the earth of every kind, and the cattle of every kind, and everything that creeps upon the ground of every kind. And God saw that it was *good*" (Gen. 1:25). Instead of attributing an innate, ontological impurity to forbidden animals such as swine or camel, this Diasporan Jew finds refuge in the usage of allegory, highlighting the moral etiquettes of kashrut *even while affirming the ongoing necessity of keeping kosher*: "By calling them [i. e., forbidden animals] impure, he has thereby indicated that it is the solemn binding duty of those for whom the legislation has been established to practice righteousness" (147). Here the author of the Let. Arist. sees the usage of (im)purity language in the Mosaic legislation more in a functional

than ontological sense. Impurity is imputed, not inherent. His perspective comes close to that of "R. Yohanan b. Zakkai"...[32]

Returning to Rom. 14:14a, it is apparent that Paul was not making a radical statement when he wrote that "nothing is unclean in itself." On the contrary, he was communicating a normative Hillelite perspective on ritual purity that already had a degree of acceptance in the wider Jewish Diaspora.[33] Ehrensperger regards Paul's statement as unspectacular:

> When Paul states that "Nothing is profane in itself but it is only profane for any one who thinks it profane" he tunes in with a general Jewish perception of the world in terms of the profane/holiness distinction. . . . [T]hese categories are not related to any ontological or "natural" qualities but to God's statutes, which are relevant for those who consider themselves in a covenantal relationship with him. . . . If we presuppose that Paul's perception here is embedded in Graeco-Roman and Jewish understandings of purity issues rather than that that he is stating something revolutionary or breathtaking that is foreign to Jewish tradition, then this implies that he merely states what everybody knows anyway. "Everything is indeed pure" refers to Jewish perceptions of purity and impurity as non-ontological categories, but as God's ordinances, his Torah for his people. A tradition attributed to Jochanan ben Zakkai formulates: "In your life, it is not the corpse that defiles . . . and not the water that cleanses . . . it is the ordinance of the King of all Kings." Read in this context, Paul quite unspectacularly merely states what is the Jewish perception in this matter: the Jewish food laws of course are regulations related to God's covenant with the people Israel. That "the earth is the Lord's and all that is in it" (Ps. 25:1) is not questioned in any way by the setting of the laws that regulate which parts of God's creation are at the disposition of the people Israel. The impure animals are impure for the covenant people, as is emphasized in almost mantra-like manner in Leviticus 11: "it is unclean/impure for you" (11:4, 5, 6, 7); "they are unclean for you" (11:8); "they are untouchable for you" (11:10-11, 12, 23) etc. As with other purity regulations, these apply to the covenant partner Israel and not to the nations. Gentiles are not required to keep purity laws, particularly not (all of) those that are related to ritual impurity, as these are only relevant for Jews in their relationship with God.[34]

The textual argument for the traditional interpretation of Rom. 14:14, 20 only appears weighty when the Second Temple Jewish background is disregarded. When this *Sitz im Leben* is factored in, and

Paul is reread as a Second Temple Jew in Rom. 14:14, 20, a compelling case can be made that Paul was speaking from a Hillelite-Pharisaic perspective and was thinking like a Diaspora Jew who, like many other Diaspora Jews, believed that nothing was unclean in itself.[35]

> "Some believe in eating anything, while the weak eat only vegetables.... [I]t is good not to eat meat or drink wine or do anything that makes your brother or sister stumble"
> (Rom. 14:2, 21)

The traditional interpretation of Rom. 14:2, 21 assumes that Paul regarded the Torah-observant as "weak" and the non-Torah-observant as strong. The "weak" were weak in faith because they were unaware of their liberty in Christ to enjoy all things. They remained concerned about ritual purity. By contrast, the strong in faith could eat anything because they understood that the Torah's food and purity laws had been superseded with the coming of Christ. Once again, this is a very narrow way of reading the text.

A more broad-ranging approach would make room for the possibility that *the issue was not purity but people who were purists about purity.*[36] That is, the "weak" were not simply people who were Torah-observant, but individuals who were *judgmental* when they saw others following a standard of Torah observance in relation to purity that was seemingly lower than their own (verses 3–4, 10, 13). *Based on Rom. 14:14, it appears that the "weak" viewed ritual impurity and defilement as objective ontological realities.* A sign of the weakness of the weak was that they easily stumbled because of this ontologically-oriented purist outlook, even to the point of ruin (verse 15). By contrast, *the strong in faith were those who held a non-ontological view of purity. They knew that "nothing" was unclean in itself.* Paul counted himself among the strong (Rom. 15:1) because he had this knowledge.[37] He maintained the normative Hillelite-Pharisaic perspective that intention determined impurity, that individual standards of impurity could vary, and that God can overlook accidental mixtures.

Paul indicates that the weak had concerns about meat and wine, in particular. But since wine is not prohibited in Mosaic law, it may be reasonably assumed that the weak were concerned about gentile contact with meat and wine.[38] They likely worried that the meat at community meals had been tainted by idolatry or mixed with unclean/unfit foods:

> Apart from the ingredients, uncleanness could also be incurred through food preparation. . . . Watson, Ziesler, and others suggest a variation on this theme. They conclude that some Jews practiced "safe eating" through abstinence. The Jews could not trust the level of truth in advertising when the gentile butcher claimed that the meat was free of uncleanness. They avoided contact with meat altogether, rather than risk contamination.[39]

The weak probably had a similar concern about wine.[40]

Paul's stance was more nuanced (not less Jewish) in that he permitted the eating of indeterminate food (1 Cor. 10:14–30). This was consistent with the on-the-ground reality that some Diaspora Jews ate indeterminate food from the *macellum* regularly or on occasion. E. P. Sanders concurs:

> One of Paul's responses as he wrestled with the problem of meat offered to idols was, When a guest, do not raise the question, but do not eat the meat if its origin is pointed out (1 Cor. 10:27–29). This may well have been a common Jewish attitude when dining with pagan friends. Barrett thinks that this is Paul's most unJewish attitude. My own guess is that it too has a home somewhere in Judaism.[41]

Following Sanders, Magnus Zetterholm argues that Paul's approach was consistent with how some mainstream Jews approached the matter of food purchased at the market. Zetterholm suggests that Paul may have relied on a proto-rabbinic halakhah that considered sold objects to be generally "non-sacral" in status:

> The reason Paul finds food bought at the market least problematic is presumably also the lack of an immediate cultic context, and it is not inconceivable that here Paul draws from a local Jewish halakhah concerning food bought at the market in Corinth when creating a set of rules for Gentile Jesus-believers. Rabbinic literature shows that the rabbis discussed the extent to which the act of selling disconnects objects from a ceremonial context. In the Tosefta, R. Jehuda ha-Nasi is said to have advocated the view that selling in general signified a nonsacral status for

an object (see *m. Avodah Zarah* 4:4–5; cf. *t. Avodah Zarah* 5:5).[42] The other rabbis disagreed, but the discussion shows that some Jews could argue in this direction. Therefore, it is not impossible that Corinthian Jews argued that food bought at the market no longer had a ceremonial significance attached to it owing to the act of selling. In fact, Paul's view on this matter might indicate that this was the case.[43]

A corroborating argument that Paul's stance on food sacrificed to idols reflects Jewish contours of halakhic flexibility is the apostle's use of the term σκάνδαλον in Rom. 14:13: "Let us therefore no longer pass judgment on one another, but resolve instead never to put an obstacle (πρόσκομμα) or stumbling block (σκάνδαλον) in the way of another."[44] Notably, the metaphorical use of the noun σκάνδαλον is limited to the Septuagint and New Testament.[45] In the Pauline corpus, this term functions as Jewish Greek:

> Both formally and materially the NT use of σκάνδαλον and σκανδαλίζω is exclusively controlled by the thought and speech of the OT and Judaism.[46]

Given the distinctively Jewish use of σκάνδαλον in the New Testament, it may be reasonably assumed that Paul's use of σκάνδαλον in Rom. 14:13 is rooted in the Torah commandment not to "*put a stumbling block* (LXX: σκάνδαλον; mt: מכשל) before the blind" (Lev. 19:14).[47] In rabbinic literature, "the blind" in Lev. 19:14 is "interpreted metaphorically to represent any person or group that is unaware, unsuspecting, ignorant, or morally blind, and individuals are prohibited from taking advantage of them or tempting them to do wrong. . . . It is also a call to action demanding that society and people do everything possible to help the weak."[48] The application of the Leviticus 19:14 *skandalon* command extends to situations in which one individual tempts another (whether Jew or gentile) to eat forbidden food:

> R. Nathan [mid second century] said: How do we know that a man must not hold out a cup of wine to a Nazirite or the limb of a living animal to the children of Noah? Because it is stated, *thou shalt not put a stumbling-block before the blind*. (Lev. 19:14)[49]

Michael Thompson notes the similarity between Rabbi Nathan's teaching on Leviticus 19:14 and Paul's exhortation not to put a σκάνδαλον before the weak:

> It may be only a coincidence, but the temptations of offering wine to a nazirite or meat with blood in it to a fellow Jew is strikingly similar to the temptation of the weak Christians in Rome to compromise their integrity and follow the example of the strong by drinking wine and eating meat of uncertain origin. This might take on greater significance in light of the early tradition preserved in Eusebius, which depicts James as a nazirite. We have seen that Lev. 19.14 was a very familiar text in rabbinic thought; could it be that the saying attributed to R. Nathan actually preserves an earlier, common Jewish application of the verse—an application which was particularly fitting for the Roman situation? Possibly. Paul certainly knows Leviticus well. He has already quoted a verse from the same chapter in Rom 13.9 (Lev. 19.18; cf. also Gal. 5.14), and if there did exist an early Christian "holiness code" paralleling some elements of the Levitical law of chapter nineteen, the prohibition of putting a σκάνδαλον before another would presumably be familiar to the readers. What is more, whereas the gospels provide no parallel to Paul's τιθέναι σκάνδαλον in Rom. 14.13b, Lev. 19.14 LXX does, although the verb there is προστιθέναι.[50]

The rabbis also applied the *skandalon* command to situations where a stumbling block could cause gentiles to commit idolatry (*b. Ned.* 62b).[51]

In light of the above, it is reasonable to assume that underlying Paul's Rom. 14:13 concern for the weak stumbling are Jewish ethical categories of thought. What are the implications of Paul halakhically applying the Torah's *skandalon* command in Lev. 19:14 to the situation in Romans 14? By addressing the conflict in this way, Paul is implicitly upholding the Torah and not undermining it. Moreover, it is significant that Paul alludes to the *skandalon* command in verse 13 leading up to his comments about κοινός in verse 14. Paul again points to the *skandalon* command in verse 21 immediately after his comment πάντα μὲν καθαρά (verse 20). This would seem to indicate that *Paul is intentionally framing his statements about ritual defilement and purity in a Torah positive context. Or, to put it another way, he is making it loud and clear that his statements should not be taken to mean that he is playing fast and loose with the law.*

Paul regarded the "weak" as weak in faith in Romans 14, not because they were observing the Torah in a normative way, but because they were observing the Torah in a way that was not normative from his perspective. The weak were purists about purity. They viewed impurity and defilement as objective ontological categories, contrary to Paul's Pharisaic-Hillelite view that nothing was "unclean *in itself*" (οὐδὲν κοινὸν δι' ἑαυτοῦ [Rom. 14:14]).[52] They lacked the knowledge and faith to believe that intention determined impurity, that individual standards of impurity could vary, and that God could overlook accidental mixtures.

Paul's approach was similar to the way in which rabbinic Judaism handles questions of intentionality and accidental mixtures today. Consider, for example, how the *Shulchan Aruch* (*Code of Jewish Law*) and the *Tur* answer the question, "What do you do if a small amount of pork inadvertently comes into contact with your food?"[53] While a non-halakhic Jew with an objective ontological perspective might consider pork to be a spiritually deadly substance and discard the whole dish because the food has been contaminated, the halakhah takes a different approach. It returns to the Hillelite principle that pork is not unclean in itself. It has only been assigned an unclean status in the Torah. Thus, there is a legal remedy—nullify the pork, that is, change its status! Nullification of unclean foods is a fundamental aspect of maintaining a kosher kitchen in rabbinic Judaism.[54]

There are two basic ways to nullify unclean foods: *bitul b'rov* (nullification in a majority)[55] and *bitul b'shishim* (nullification in a ratio of sixty).[56] If pork accidentally falls into the traditional Jew's kosher food and the pork constitutes the minority of the food, then under the principle of *bitul b'rov*, the pork may be legally nullified and the food eaten:

> In the opinion of most *Poskim* [legal decisors, heads of *yeshivot* and members of rabbinic courts], when a non-kosher food becomes *batel* [nullified], the mixture may be eaten even by the most scrupulous. Indeed, some authorities soundly censure one who hesitates to eat the mixture, as this shows a heretical reservation about the effectiveness of *bitul* [nullification].[57]

What if the accidental mixture with pork results in the traditional Jew's food tasting like pork? In this case, the whole mixture changes its status to unclean under the principle of *taam k'ikar*, and is now prohibited. If the ratio of clean food to pork is 60:1, however, then the pork and its taste in the mixture is legally nullified through *bitul b'shishim*, and the entire mixture is ruled clean to eat.

How can a traditional Jew in good conscience eat food that contains pieces of pork and tastes like pork? He can do this in good conscience because he does not believe that pork is unclean in itself. The halakhic approach is coherent when one considers the extreme difficulty of keeping clean food separate from agents of uncleanness: for example, unclean smells and residues that are transferred by touch. The more scrupulous one becomes, the more one sees mixtures. Thus, a non-halakhic Jew may experience revulsion at seeing his food mixed with pork and throw it out, thinking it is spiritually corrupted *in toto*. The halakhic Jew handles it with legal precision and may determine that the food in its entirety is clean to eat.

A similar exercise of personal intention to nullify forbidden food is the tradition of *bitul chametz*. After a final search for *chametz* before Passover in order to keep the command to "remove leaven from your houses" (Exod. 12:15), the formula is recited, "All leaven and anything leavened that is in my possession, which I have neither seen nor removed, and about which I am unaware, shall be considered nullified and ownerless as the dust of the earth."[58] Here, the halakhic Jew is aware that crumbs may still exist in his house, but he does not lose sleep over it because he has made a concerted effort to find all leaven in his home and has nullified any remaining leaven through his personal declaration. It is an act of faith because the halakhic Jew trusts that God knows his heart and intention, and that God overlooks what he was unable to find.

Returning to Romans, many exegetes assume that Paul's teaching in Rom. 14:14, 20 reflects his emancipated view of the Jewish food laws. From this perspective, the "weak in faith" are Torah-observant and Paul is not. I contend, however, that Paul is actually more Torah-observant than they are. Paul's training in Pharisaic-Hillelite halakhah led him to ask critical questions about accidental mixtures that the weak in Rome did not ask due to their lack of knowledge. In Romans 14, Paul is echoing a Hillelite understanding that no food is unclean (κοινός) in essence; it is the halakhic designation of it as "unclean" that makes it unclean. I am not arguing that Paul observed a proto-rabbinic *bitul* halakhah comparable to what is in the *Code of Jewish Law*. Rather, it seems that Hillelite Pharisees such as Paul asked the same questions that the later rabbis asked about accidental mixtures, and they arrived at similar conclusions.[59]

Why did the weak view ritual impurity in ontological terms? Perhaps it is because they were mostly from non-Jewish backgrounds.[60] Exegetes often assume that the weak in Romans 14 were predominantly Jews since the weak were concerned about Jewish law observance. However, this logic is faulty.[61] First, gentiles drawn to Judaism are often more zealous about Jewish life than those born Jews.[62] And second, if the congregation in Rome had a larger percentage of gentiles than Jews—which is likely—then it is plausible that gentiles were a majority among the strong *and* the weak.[63] These Jewish-oriented gentiles and/or converts to Judaism who made up the weak may have been influenced by Greco-Roman conceptions of ritual impurity that were associated with magic and superstition,[64] and this may have led to a more objective ontological way of thinking about the Jewish food laws.

"I know and am persuaded in the Lord Jesus . . ." (Rom. 14:14)

Traditional interpreters of Romans 14 often claim that in verses 14 and 20, Paul points to a tradition that Jesus "declared all foods clean" (Mark 7:19b). While this is possible, it is more probable that the words "I know and am persuaded in the Lord Jesus" refer to the apostle's close relationship with Jesus, and how his communion with the Messiah confirmed his Pharisaic-Hillelite convictions about ritual impurity. Notably, the three other times Paul writes "in the Lord Jesus" (ἐν κυρίῳ Ἰησοῦ), he does not allude to a Gospel tradition, but points to his personal identification with Jesus:

I hope *in the Lord Jesus* (ἐν κυρίῳ Ἰησοῦ) to send Timothy to you soon, so that I may be cheered by news of you. (Phil. 2:19)

Finally, brothers and sisters, we ask and urge you *in the Lord Jesus* (ἐν κυρίῳ Ἰησοῦ) that, as you learned from us how you ought to live and to please God (as, in fact, you are doing), you should do so more and more. (1 Thess. 4:1)

Now such persons we command and exhort *in the Lord Jesus Christ* (ἐν κυρίῳ Ἰησοῦ Χριστῷ) to do their work quietly and to earn their own living. (2 Thess. 3:12)

Douglas Moo concedes that the traditional dominical interpretation of ἐν κυρίῳ Ἰησοῦ (verse 14) "reads quite a bit into the phrase," and contends that Paul more likely means: (1) "I know *through my fellowship with the Lord Jesus* . . ." or (2), "I know *through my understanding of the truth revealed in the Lord Jesus*. . . ."[65] Räisänen concurs that many scholars overstate the case for a correlation between Rom. 14:14, 20 and Mark 7:19b: "Paul is not referring to a saying of the historical Jesus. . . . What we have in Rom. 14.14, then, is an insight which Paul obtained from his faith on the basis of his fellowship with Christ."[66]

Assuming that Paul is referring to a dominical tradition in Rom. 14:14, there still remains the question—of which tradition.[67] Since Paul, in Rom. 14:14, is rejecting the objective ontological view of ritual impurity, perhaps he is alluding to Jesus' teaching that food cannot defile (κοινοῖ) a person (Mark 7:14–15, 18–23; cf. Matt. 15:11, 17–20). As Ottenheijm puts it, "Jesus departs from Qumran and agrees with the Hillelite Pharisees in the negation of the inherent power or the merely physical quality of ritual impurity."[68] In his article "Defilement Penetrating the Body: A New Understanding of Contamination in Mark 7.15," Furstenberg underscores that Jesus, in Mark 7:15 and its context, upholds the Torah view that eating κοινός does not cause a person to become ontologically defiled:

Contaminated food does *not* cause the person eating it to become impure. According to the laws that appear in Leviticus 11, only the consumption of prohibited foods, such as the carcass of an animal not ritually slaughtered or a "swarming creature," can cause impurity, and not the consumption of foods that have become contaminated. This fact is articulated explicitly by

Rashi (Rabbi Shlomo Yitzhaki), the authoritative Talmudic commentator, who states: "According to the Torah food does not contaminate the person eating it." Rashi's statement, which summarizes the approach of the Talmud to this issue, is surprisingly similar to Jesus' anti-Pharisaic saying. . . . The dispute with the Pharisees over their custom of hand washing, according to this reading, led Jesus to articulate his disapproval toward their new, non-biblical concern with consumption of ritually contaminated foods. In *halakhic* terms, his saying might be rephrased thus: "Contrary to your *halakhah*, which is unknown in the bible, the body is not defiled by eating contaminated food. Rather, it is defiled by what comes out of it." . . . Jesus' opinion—contrary to that of the Pharisees—is that even food which has been contaminated by defiled hands does not contaminate a person who ingests it.[69]

If Paul, in Rom. 14:14a, is alluding to a dominical tradition, he may be saying that Jesus' teaching on food and defilement (κοινός) validates the Pharisaic-Hillelite view that "nothing is unclean in itself" and confirms his halakhic approach to the situation in Rome. This way of interpreting Rom. 14:14a roots Paul's instructions in a Jesus tradition—a tradition that upholds the continuing authority of the biblical food laws for the people of Israel.[70]

Finally, there are a number of methodological weaknesses in the attempt to link Rom. 14:14a to a Torah-negative understanding of Mark 7:19b. In my article "Jesus and the Food Laws: A Reassessment of Mark 7:19b,"[71] I survey the problems with the traditional law-free interpretation of Jesus' teaching in this passage and offer an alternative reading that is consistent with the rereading of Rom. 14:14, 20 that has been proposed in this chapter. That alternative reading is that *Mark found in Jesus' teaching, a basis for gentile exemption from the Leviticus 11 dietary laws due to the non-ontological nature of defilement.* Mark was probably familiar with Paul's Letter to the Romans and Pauline halakhah on food-related issues. *It is more likely, therefore, that Mark was influenced by Rom. 14:20 in the construction of his editorial comment in Mark 7:19* than that Paul was influenced by a dominical tradition that Jesus had invalidated Leviticus 11 and other key portions of the Torah.[72]

Conclusion

Paul's instructions in Rom. 14:14, 20 do not burst the bounds of Judaism or reflect indifference to Jewish difference, as the traditional interpretation maintains. Rather, *Paul is focused on gentiles and Torah*. He is addressing two groups composed of mostly gentiles who were arguing about whether Jewish ethnic practices, and the Torah's food laws in particular, were obligatory for non-Jews. The weak were purists about purity. They were not simply people who were Torah-observant, but individuals who were judgmental when they saw others following a standard of Torah observance in relation to purity that was seemingly lower than their own (verses 3-4, 10, 13). Based on Rom. 14:14, the Achilles heel of the "weak" was that they regarded ritual impurity and defilement as objective ontological realities. A sign of the weakness of the weak was that they easily stumbled because of this ontologically oriented purist outlook, even to the point of ruin (verse 15).

By contrast, the strong in faith were those who held a non-ontological view of purity. They knew that "nothing" was unclean in itself. Paul counted himself among the strong because he had this knowledge (Rom. 15:1). He maintained the normative Hillelite-Pharisaic perspective that ritual impurity is non-ontological, that intention determines impurity, that individual standards of impurity can vary, and that God can overlook accidental mixtures. In response to this largely intra-gentile debate, Paul reminds the gentiles that they are not obligated to keep Israel's food laws (Rom. 14:20). Gentiles have a choice. And in exercising that choice, they need to prayerfully define their own standards of observance, respect the standards of others, and keep the Torah's *skandalon* command not to put a stumbling block before those who might fall (Lev. 19:14; Rom. 14:13). In doing this, they will be keeping one of the greatest commands of all in Jewish law, "Love your neighbour as yourself" (Lev. 19:18; Rom. 13:9; 14:15).[73]

Notes

1. See Michael Wyschogrod, "A Letter to Cardinal Lustiger," in *Abraham's Promise: Judaism and Jewish-Christian Relations*, ed. R. Kendall Soulen (Grand Rapids: Eerdmans, 2004), 207–8; Matthew A. Tapie, *Aquinas on Israel and the Church: The Question of Supersessionism in the Theology of Thomas Aquinas* (Eugene: Pickwick, 2014), 4, 25–47; Mark S. Kinzer, *Postmissionary Messianic Judaism: Redefining Christian Engagement with the Jewish People* (Grand Rapids: Brazos, 2005), 58; David Rudolph, "Messianic Jews and Christian Theology: Restoring an Historical Voice to the Contemporary Discussion," *Pro Ecclesia* 14, no. 1 (2005): 58–84; idem, "Paul's "Rule in All the Churches" (1 Cor. 7:17–24) and Torah-Defined Ecclesiological Variegation," *Studies in Jewish-Christian Relations* 5 (2010): 1–23; idem, *A Jew to the Jews: Jewish Contours of Pauline Flexibility in 1 Corinthians 9:19–23* (Tübingen: Mohr Siebeck, 2011), 35–44.

2. John M. G. Barclay, "'Do we undermine the Law?': A Study of Romans 14.1–15.6," in idem, *Pauline Churches and Diaspora Jews* (Tübingen: Mohr Siebeck, 2011), 58–59.

3. Studies on Romans 14 often do not make a distinction between the Torah's dietary laws that define clean/unclean animals (Lev. 11; Deut. 14:3–20) and purity legislation (e. g., Lev. 11–15; Num. 19). Due to this lack of precision, "food laws" is used in this chapter as a catchall term for both categories when interacting with the traditional view unless there is a need to be more specific.

4. Peter Stuhlmacher, *Paul's Letter to the Romans: A Commentary*, trans. Scott H. Hafemann (Edinburgh: T&T Clark, 1994), 227.

5. Thomas R. Schreiner, *Romans* (Baker Exegetical Commentary on the New Testament; Grand Rapids: Baker, 1998), 730–31.

6. See Rom. 1:13, "I want you to know, brothers and sisters, that I have often intended to come to you (but thus far have been prevented), in order that I may reap some harvest *among you as I have among the rest of the Gentiles.*" Cf. Rom. 9:3f; 10:1–2; 11:13, 23–31; 15:15–16.

7. Kathy Ehrensperger, "'Called to be Saints'—The Identity-Shaping Dimension of Paul's Priestly Discourse in Romans," in *Reading Paul in Context: Explorations in Identity Formation: Essays in Honour of William S. Campbell*, ed. Kathy Ehrensperger and J. Brian Tucker (London: T&T Clark International, 2010), 106–7. The argument assumes that Paul does not regard clean/unclean distinctions to be objective ontological categories. This will be discussed below.

8. Michael B. Thompson, *Clothed with Christ: The Example and Teaching of Jesus in Romans 12.1–15.13* (Sheffield: Sheffield Academic Press, 1991), 197; C. E. B. Cranfield, *The Epistle to the Romans: A Critical and Exegetical Commentary* (2 vols.; Edinburgh: T&T Clark, 1979), 2:713n2.

9. LXX Lev. 11:46–47 uses καθαρός to refer to animals that are clean for Jews to eat.

10. Parallels include: (1) The πάντα . . . ἀλλά formulas with οἰκοδομή; (2) Hyperbolic statements about freedom, viz. forbidden food in predominantly gentile contexts; (3) Exhortations not to seek one's own advantage but that of the other; (4) Discussions about how to deal with questions of conscience; and (5) weak/strong categories. Paul likely wrote Romans from Corinth (James D. G. Dunn, *Romans 9-16* [Dallas: Word, 1988], 884–907), and the similarity between Rom. 14:19–22 and 1 Cor. 10:23–27 reflects a wider connection between 1 Cor. 8-10 and Rom. 14-15. See Carl N. Toney, *Paul's Inclusive Ethic: Resolving Community Conflicts and Promoting Mission in Romans 14-15* (Tübingen: Mohr Siebeck, 2008), 189–90, 205.

11. Rudolph, "Paul's 'Rule in All the Churches'," 1–23; Anders Runesson, "Paul's Rule in All the *Ekklēsiai*," in *Introduction to Messianic Judaism: Its Ecclesial Context and Biblical Foundations*, ed. David Rudolph and Joel Willitts (Grand Rapids: Zondervan, 2013), 214–23.

12. Cf. Acts 15:1–35.

13. Matthew Thiessen, *Contesting Conversion: Genealogy, Circumcision, and Identity in Ancient Judaism and Christianity* (Oxford: Oxford University Press, 2011), 131; cf. Isaac W. Oliver, *Torah Praxis after 70 CE: Reading Matthew and Luke-Acts as Jewish Texts* (Tübingen: Mohr Siebeck, 2013), 345–38.

14. Clinton Wahlen, "Peter's Vision and Conflicting Definitions of Purity," *NTS* 51 (2005): 512. See David J. Bolton, "Who Are You Calling 'Weak'?: A Short Critique of James Dunn's Reading of Rom 14,1–15,6," in *The Letter to the Romans*, ed. Udo Schnelle (Leuven: Peeters, 2009), 621–23; Jonathan Goldstein, *I Maccabees: A New Translation with Introduction and Commentary* (Garden City: Doubleday, 1976), 222–23; Mikeal C. Parsons, "'Nothing Defiled AND Unclean': The Conjunction's Function in Acts 10:14," *PRSt* 27 (2000): 263–74; Colin House, "Defilement by Association: Some Insights from the Usage of ΚΟΙΝΌΣ/ΚΟΙΝΌΩ in Acts 10 and 11," *Andrews University Seminary Studies* 21 (1983): 147; Ben Witherington, *The Acts of the Apostles: A Socio-Rhetorical Commentary* (Grand Rapids: Eerdmans, 1998), 350n95. Cf. Mishnaic tractate *Demai* for a discussion of food categorized as "doubtful," e. g., *m. Demai* 3.4.

15. J. D. M. Derrett, "κοινός, κοινόω," *Filología Neotestamentaria* 5 (1992): 76.

16. Lev. 10:10.

17. E. g., Richard Bauckham, "Peter, James and the Gentiles," in *The Missions of James, Peter, and Paul: Tensions in Early Christianity*, ed. Bruce Chilton and Craig Evans (Leiden: Brill, 2005), 102–103, renders κοινός as "profane," "impure," or "defiled," depending on the context. Contra Thiessen, *Contesting Conversion*, 131.

18. "Κοινός is not, then, an essential state of halakhic uncleanness, rather it is a grey-zone state, arising due to essentially clean food becoming contaminated" (Bolton, "Who Are You Calling 'Weak'?," 622).

19. Oliver, *Torah Praxis after 70 CE*, 346, 348–49. Cf. Bauckham, "Peter, James and the Gentiles," 91–107; Ehrensperger, "'Called to be Saints'," 98–103.

20. Daniel R. Schwartz, "'Someone who considers something to be impure—for him it is impure' (Rom. 14:14): Good Manners or Law?," in *Paul's Jewish Matrix*, ed. Thomas G. Casey and Justin Taylor (Rome: Gregorian & Biblical, 2011), 303. See Paula Fredriksen, "How Later Contexts Affect Pauline Context, or: Retrospect is the Mother of Anachronism," in *Jews and Christians in the First and Second Centuries: How to Write Their History*, ed. Peter J. Tomson and J. Schwartz (Leiden: Brill, 2014), 33.

21. "Moreover, while the associates did view nonmembers as ritually defiling, the outsiders' ritual impurity resulted not from the commission of some grave sin but simply from the fact that the outsiders did not take upon themselves the same purity obligations that the associates had" (Jonathan Klawans, *Impurity and Sin in Ancient Judaism* [Oxford: Oxford University Press, 2000], 109).

22. Yair Furstenberg, "Impurity and Social Demarcation: Resetting Second Temple Halakhic Traditions in New Contexts" (paper presented at the Thirteenth International Orion Symposium: Tradition, Transmission, and Transformation: From Second Temple Literature through Judaism and Christianity in Late Antiquity, Jerusalem, 23 February 2011), 3. See *m. Hag.* 2.5–7; *t. Hag.* 3.1–3. Note the weight placed on intention in *t. Hag.* 3.2: "He who immerses in order to rise up from uncleanness to cleanness, lo, this person is clean for all purposes. He who immerses—if he had the intention [of becoming clean], he becomes clean. And if not, [he remains] unclean" (Jacob Neusner, *How the Halakhah Unfolds: Volume IV: Hagigah in the Mishnah, Tosefta, Yerushalmi, and Bavli* [Lanham: University Press of America, 2009], 421).

23. Furstenberg, "Impurity and Social Demarcation," 9.

24. See Lev. 11:24, 38.

25. Eric Ottenheijm, "Impurity Between Intention and Deed: Purity Disputes in First Century Judaism and in the New Testament," in *Purity and Holiness: The Heritage of Leviticus*, ed. M. J. H. M. Poorthuis and J. Schwartz (Leiden: Brill, 2000), 141–43. See Howard Eilberg-Schwartz, *The Human Will in Judaism: The Mishnah's Philosophy of Intention* (Atlanta: Brown Judaic Studies, 1986), 95–143; Yitzhak Gilat, "Intention and Deed in the Teachings of the Tanna'im" [Heb.], in *Studies in the Development of Halakhah* (Ramat Gan: Bar Ilan University Press, 2001), 72–83; Joseph Baumgarten, "Liquids and Susceptibility to Defilement in New 4Q Texts," *JQR* 85 (1995): 93; Vered Noam, "The House of Shammai and Sectarian Halakhah" [Heb.], *Jewish Studies* 41 (2002): 55; Ephraim E. Urbach, *The Halakhah: Its Sources and Development* (Tel Aviv: Massada, 1996), 190–93. The Mishnah is replete with statements that reflect the Hillelite focus on human thought as a determinant of impurity; see Mira Balberg, *Purity, Body, and Self in Early Rabbinic Literature* (Berkeley: University of California Press, 2014), 83–87, 91–93.

26. Cf. Acts 5:34. The argument behind Gamaliel being Hillel's grandson is based on

a late source (*b. Shabb.* 15a). It is more likely that he was Hillel's son. See Jacob Neusner, *A Life of Rabban Yohanan Ben Zakkai: Ca. 1-80 C. E.* (Leiden: Brill, 1970), 34.

27. Similarly, Paul's statement in Rom. 14:5 ("One person esteems one day more than another, while another esteems all days alike. Let all be fully convinced in their own minds") was likely not an expression of Pauline indifference toward the biblical calendar as the traditional view maintains. There are five other ways of explaining this text that are more consistent with the context: (1) Paul was indifferent to the ontological weight the weak were placing on the holiness of various days. Note that Paul focuses on the issue of food immediately before and after his discussion of days (vv. 2–4, 6), giving the impression that the principle he espouses in verse 14 applies to both issues; (2) Paul may be speaking specifically to gentiles in Rom. 14:5, as he does in verse 20. The Torah does not command gentiles to keep Israel's festivals. Paul may be reassuring the gentiles in verse 5 that they are not under obligation to observe Israel's holy days; (3) Paul may be referring to festivals and fasts that were not commanded in the Torah, e. g., Nikanor Day, Hanukkah, the fifteenth of Av, and Herod's Days (Esther 9:27–28; 1 Macc. 4; Josephus, *Ant.* 12.7, 10; *J. W.* 2.7; Persius, *Sat.* 5.180); (4) Paul may be referring to grey areas in biblical calendar law that were halakhically more open to question even as Paul used κοινός to refer to indeterminate areas of dietary law. An example of a calendar-related area of dispute in Second Temple Judaism is the dating of Shavuot (the Festival of Weeks/Pentecost). The Pharisees claimed that Shavuot could fall on *various days of the week* while the Sadducees and the Qumran community maintained that Shavuot could fall *only on the day after the weekly Sabbath, i. e., Sunday.* As a Pharisee, Paul would have been aware of the arguments on both sides; and (5) Paul may have in mind the practice of Sabbath fasting, a custom unique to the Roman Jewish community. This interpretation fits well with Rom. 14:5–6 where Paul connects the ethic of esteeming a particular day with abstaining from food. See Margaret H. Williams, "Being a Jew in Rome: Sabbath Fasting as an Expression of Romano-Jewish Identity," in *Jews in a Graeco-Roman Environment* (Tübingen: Mohr Siebeck, 2013), 51–58.

28. This tradition is not necessary to establish my case since the Hillelite view that personal intention can change the purity status of objects and persons presumes that nothing is impure in itself.

29. Neusner, *A Life of Rabban Yohanan Ben Zakkai*, 34–35; idem, *First Century Judaism in Crisis: Yohanan ben Zakkai and the Renaissance of Torah* (New York: Ktav, 1982), 48–49, 54–61.

30. *Pesiq. Rab Kah.* 4:7 (trans. Ottenheijm). Cf. *Pesiq. Rab.* 14:14; *Yal. Shimoni Hukat* 759; *Num. Rab.* 19:8; *Tanḥ. Hukat* 8. See Jacob Neusner, *The Idea of Purity in Ancient Judaism* (Leiden: Brill, 1973), 105; Menachem Kellner, *Maimonides' Confrontation with Mysticism* (Oxford: The Littman Library of Jewish Civilization, 2006), 130;

Yochanan Silman, "Introduction to the Philosophical Analysis of the Normative-Ontological Tension in the Halakha," *Da'at* 31 (1993): 8–10.

31. Ottenheijm, "Impurity Between Intention and Deed," 132, 143–44; emphasis mine. See Kinzer, *Postmissionary Messianic Judaism*, 55–56, 80–81; Bruce Chilton, "The Purity of the Kingdom as Conveyed in Jesus' Meals," in *SBL Seminar Papers, 1992*, ed. Eugene H. Lovering (Atlanta: Scholars, 1992), 485–86; Ephraim E. Urbach, *The Sages: Their Concepts and Beliefs*, trans. Israel Abrahams (2 vols.; Jerusalem: Magnes, 1975), 1:99.

32. Oliver, *Torah Praxis after 70 CE*, 355–56.

33. "As for nothing by itself being pure or impure, even later rabbis construed these as assigned, not innate categories. . . . My main point here is that nothing in these passages about food definitely puts either Paul or his gentiles outside or over-against Jewish observance" (Fredriksen, "How Later Contexts Affect Pauline Context," 33–34).

34. Ehrensperger, "'Called to be Saints'," 101, 105–106. See Mark D. Nanos, *The Mystery of Romans: The Jewish Context of Paul's Letter* (Minneapolis: Fortress Press, 1996), 199–200.

35. "Paul may be repeating here for his gentiles what was a practical *modus vivendi* for diaspora Jews" (Fredriksen, "How Later Contexts Affect Pauline Context," 33).

36. Peter J. Tomson, *Paul and the Jewish Law: Halakha in the Letters of the Apostle to the Gentiles* (Minneapolis: Fortress Press, 1990), 244–45, describes the weak as "hyper-halakhic" and "oversensitive."

37. Cf. 1 Cor. 8:4–7 where the strong are those who have knowledge that an idol is "nothing" (οὐδὲν). See Kathy Ehrensperger, *Paul at the Crossroads of Cultures: Theologizing in the Space Between* (London: Bloomsbury, 2013), 194–96; idem, "To Eat or Not to Eat—Is this the Question?," in *Decisive Meals: Table Politics in Biblical Literature*, ed. Ehrensperger, Nathan MacDonald, and Luzia S. Rehmann (London: T&T Clark, 2012), 119–22; Peter S. Zaas, "Paul and the Halakhah: Dietary Laws for Gentiles in 1 Corinthians 8–10," in *Jewish Law Association Studies VII: The Paris Conference Volume*, ed. S. M. Passamaneck and M. Finley (Atlanta: Scholars, 1994), 239.

38. Markus Bockmuehl, *Jewish Law in Gentile Churches: Halakhah and the Beginning of Christian Public Ethics* (Edinburgh: T&T Clark, 2000), 43.

39. Gary Steven Shogren, "Is the kingdom of God about eating or drinking or isn't it? (Romans 14:17)," *NovT* 42, no. 3 (2000): 246–47.

40. James Crossley, *The New Testament and Jewish Law: A Guide for the Perplexed* (London: T&T Clark International, 2010), 109; Charles H. Cosgrove, "Abstention from Wine by the 'Weak' in the Roman Church: A Dietary Practice Addressed by Paul in Romans 14" (paper presented at the Annual Meeting of the Society of Biblical Literature, Pauline Epistles Section, Baltimore, 23 November 2013), 1–8.

41. E. P. Sanders, *Jewish Law from Jesus to the Mishnah: Five Studies* (London: SCM, 1990), 281. See Karl-Gustav Sandelin, "Jews and Alien Religious Practices During the Hellenistic Age (2006)," in idem, *Attraction and Danger of Alien Religion: Studies in Early Judaism and Christianity* (Tübingen: Mohr Siebeck, 2012), 1–26; Karin Hedner Zetterholm, "The Question of Assumptions: Torah Observance in the First Century," in *Paul within Judaism: Restoring the First-Century Context to the Apostle*, ed. Mark D. Nanos and Magnus Zetterholm (Minneapolis: Fortress Press, 2015), 91–103.

42. See also Tomson, *Paul and the Jewish Law*, 217–18.

43. Magnus Zetterholm, "Purity and Anger: Gentiles and Idolatry in Antioch," *Interdisciplinary Journal of Research on Religion* 1 (2005): 15. Cf. M. Isenberg, "The Sale of Sacrificial Meat," *CP* 70 (1975): 272; John Fotopoulos, *Food Offered to Idols in Roman Corinth: A Social-Rhetorical Reconsideration of 1 Corinthians 8-10* (Tübingen: Mohr Siebeck, 2003), 188.

44. Paul also uses the term πρόσκομμα (stumbling block) in Rom. 14:20. The LXX translates מכשול (Lev 19:14) and מוקש as σκάνδαλον or πρόσκομμα. They are used synonymously in the New Testament (Guhrt, *NIDNTT* 2:705, 707–08; Stählin, *TDNT* 7:341).

45. Stählin, *TDNT* 7:340.

46. Ibid., 344.

47. For a discussion of the metaphorical use of the *skandalon* command in Second Temple Jewish literature, see Rudolph, *A Jew to the Jews*, 104–6.

48. Hershey H. Friedman, "Placing a Stumbling Block Before the Blind Person: An In-Depth Analysis," 2002, 1–2. www.jlaw.com/Articles/placingstumbling.html.

49. *b. Pesaḥ.* 22b. See Num. 6:3; Gen. 9:4; *b. Ned.* 81b; *b. Pesaḥ.* 50b–51a; *y. Ber.* 8, 12a.

50. Michael B. Thompson, "Stumbling Blocks and Snares: The Context of Romans 14.13b" (Cambridge University: unpublished, 1985), 40. Cf. idem, *Clothed with Christ*, 181.

51. Cf. Josh. 23:13; Judg. 2:3; Hosea 4:17; Ps. 105[106]:34–36.

52. The non-ontological view is attested in the Torah. For example, bread made with yeast is forbidden during the festival of unleavened bread, but eaten during the rest of the year (Exod. 12:14–20). The substance of the food does not change, only its designation as forbidden or permitted for Israel.

53. See *m. Ḥul. 7; b. Ḥul.* 96-100; *Shulchan Aruch/Tur, Yoreh De'ah* 109; 99.5.

54. Binyomin Forst, *The Laws of Kashrus: A Comprehensive Exposition of Their Underlying Concepts and Applications* (Brooklyn: Mesorah, 2004), 52–75; Zushe Yosef Blech, *Kosher Food Production* (London: Wiley-Blackwell, 2008), 29–31.

55. *Bitul b'rov* applies to cold, dry foods.

56. *Bitul b'shishim* applies to foods that are blended or cooked together.

57. Forst, *The Laws of Kashrus*, 52–53. Cf. *Pischei Teshuvah* 116.10.

58. See *Shulchan Aruch* 434.2–4.

59. See Sanders, *Jewish Law from Jesus to the Mishnah*, 32–33; Jordan D. Rosenblum, *Food and Identity in Early Rabbinic Judaism* (Cambridge: Cambridge University Press, 2010), 177–78.

60. A. Andrew Das, *Solving the Romans Debate* (Minneapolis: Fortress Press, 2007), 53–114, makes a compelling case that the weak were gentiles. Contra Mark Reasoner, *The Strong and the Weak: Romans 14.1–15.3 in Context* (Cambridge: Cambridge University Press, 1999), 224; Toney, *Paul's Inclusive Ethic*, 193. Nanos, *The Mystery of Romans*, 85–165, argues that the weak were non-Christian Jews. For a response, see Das, *Solving the Romans Debate*, 115–48; Robert A. J. Gagnon, "Why the 'Weak' at Rome Cannot Be Non-Christian Jews," *CBQ* 62 (2000): 64–82, and Nanos's 2003 rejoinder ("A Rejoinder to Robert A. J. Gagnon's 'Why the "Weak" at Rome Cannot Be Non-Christian Jews,'" www.marknanos.com/ Gagnon-rejoinder-6-20-03.pdf).

61. Fredriksen, "How Later Contexts Affect Pauline Context," 32n40.

62. See Rom. 2:25–27; Michele Murray, *Playing a Jewish Game: Gentile Christian Judaizing in the First and Second Centuries CE* (Waterloo: Wilfrid Laurier University Press, 2004), 35–36. This dynamic is commonplace in the modern Messianic Jewish community and leads to the same kind of weak-strong polarities caused by gentile purists about purity that I propose Paul addresses in Romans 14.

63. "A handful of scholars—Stanley Stowers, Neil Elliott, and Runar Thorsteinson—have contended that Romans addressed an entirely or almost entirely gentile audience...the answer to the problem of Paul's apparent 'obliqueness' in Rom 14:1—15:13 lies in recognizing (with Stowers against Nanos) that both the strong and the weak are *gentiles*; (with Nanos against Stowers) that the weak are observing Jewish cultic practices. . . . The content of Rom 14:1—15:6 is completely comprehensible if the audience included current or former God-fearers alongside non-Law-observant gentiles. . . . God-fearers would have been uncomfortable as well around non-God-fearers and their meat and wine. This would have led to tensions . . . [Paul's] goal is to facilitate a healthy relationship between the non-Law-observant gentiles and the Law-observant gentiles in the Roman Christian congregations" (Das, *Solving the Romans Debate*, 53, 109, 113–14). I concur with Das that Jewish law observance by gentiles is in view in Romans 14. However, I depart from his assumption that the strong were all *non-Law-observant* Gentiles. Some of the strong may have been Torah-observant, but not as scrupulous as the weak (Bolton, "Who Are You Calling 'Weak'?," 621), or they may have been scrupulous, but not as prone to stumble because of their non-ontological view of ritual purity and their conviction that gentiles were not obligated to keep Israel's food laws. The Corinthian "weak" (1 Cor. 8:7–12) were likely gentiles.

64. See *Pesiq. Rab Kah.* 4:7; Ehrensperger, "'Called to be Saints'," 94–97.

65. Douglas J. Moo, *The Epistle to the Romans* (Grand Rapids: Eerdmans, 1996), 852–53.

66. Heikki Räisänen, *Jesus, Paul and Torah: Collected Essays*, trans. David E. Orton (Sheffield: Sheffield Academic Press, 1992), 140, 142.

67. Some exegetes suggest that Rom. 14:14, 20 reflects a tradition redacted by Luke that Jesus declared all foods clean. In Acts 10, Peter sees a vision of various kinds of animals, and Jesus instructs Peter three times to kill and eat. The traditional interpretation assumes that Jesus' command to eat unclean animals (Acts 10:13; 11:7), and his words to Peter—"What God has made clean (ἐκαθάρισεν), you must not call profane (κοίνου)" (Acts 10:15; 11:2)—imply a divine revocation of Israel's food laws. However, a more contextually supported reading of the text is that *the vision concerned men, not the menu*. Consider the following: (1) Three times Peter rejects Jesus' instruction to eat profane (κοινόν) and unclean (ἀκάθαρτον) animals (Acts 10:14–16). This implies that Peter had not previously received a teaching or example from Jesus that all foods were now clean; (2) The meaning of the vision was not immediately clear to Peter. He was "greatly puzzled about what to make of the vision" (Acts 10:17). When Peter saw the vision, he did not understand it to mean that Israel's dietary laws had been abolished; (3) Luke repeatedly indicates that the meaning of the vision concerned men, not the menu (Chris A. Miller, "Did Peter's Vision in Acts 10 Pertain to Men or the Menu?," *BSac* 159 [2002]: 317; J. R. L. Moxon, "Peter's Halakhic Nightmare: The 'Animal' Vision of Acts 10.9–16 in Jewish and Graeco-Roman Perspective" [PhD diss., Durham University, 2011], i, 6–7; David B. Woods, "Interpreting Peter's Vision in Acts 10:9-16," *Conspectus* 13 [2012]: 171–214; Oliver, *Torah Praxis after 70 CE*, 240–45). When Peter arrived at Cornelius's house, he interpreted the meaning of the vision: the profane (κοινόν) and unclean (ἀκάθαρτον) animals symbolized profane (κοινόν) and unclean (ἀκάθαρτον) people (a likely reference to God-fearers and pagans respectively). In keeping with Jewish "taboo" (ἀθέμιτος [Acts 10:28], not νόμος), Peter had avoided contact with gentiles. But through the vision, God informed Peter that he was no longer to view gentiles in this way, "God has shown me that I should not call anyone profane [κοινόν] or unclean [ἀκάθαρτον]. So when I was sent for, I came without objection. . . . I truly understand that God shows no partiality, but in every nation anyone who fears him and does what is right is acceptable to him" (Acts 10:28–29, 34–35). His decision to associate with gentiles did not overturn biblical law since the Torah does not prohibit Jews from associating with gentiles. Peter's earlier perspective that Jews should not visit or eat with gentiles because they are profane (κοινόν) or unclean (ἀκάθαρτον) was a traditional expansion of the Torah (Hannah K. Harrington, *The Purity Texts* [London: T&T Clark, 2004], 112; Christine E. Hayes, *Gentile Impurities and Jewish Identities: Intermarriage and Conversion from the Bible to the Talmud* [Oxford: Oxford University Press, 2002], 19–44); (4) Peter reiterated the symbolic meaning of the vision to the "circumcised believers" in Jerusalem. After he recounted the vision, his response to it, and the Lord's

admonition—"What God has made clean (ἐκαθάρισεν), you must not call profane (κοινοῦ)" (Acts 11:9)—Peter explains that the vision concerned men: "The Spirit told me to go with them and *not to make a distinction between them and us*" (Acts 11:12). At the Jerusalem Council, Peter once again alludes to the symbolic meaning of the vision. The gentile believers are clean, for "in cleansing [καθαρίσας] their hearts by faith *he has made no distinction between them and us*" (Acts 15:9); (5) No indication exists in Acts that Peter understood the vision literally. There is no example of him eating unclean food or encouraging other Jesus-believing Jews to eat unclean food; (6) The Jerusalem Council decision in Acts 15 centered on the question of whether Jesus-believing *gentiles* were exempt from Mosaic law. If the Torah's dietary laws had been abrogated as early as Acts 10, and Jesus-believing Jews were now exempt from the requirements of Mosaic law, there would be no reason to debate whether the law was binding on Jesus-believing gentiles. Acts 15 implies that Peter's vision in Acts 10 concerned men, not the menu (cf. Acts 15:9). The apostolic decree was only addressed to "Gentile believers" and clarified the "requirements" (including certain minimal food restrictions) that were incumbent upon the "Gentile believers" (Acts 15:19–20, 23). The presupposition throughout Acts 15 is that Jesus-believing Jews like Peter should continue to observe Mosaic law.

68. Ottenheijm, "Impurity Between Intention and Deed," 146.

69. Cf. Yair Furstenberg, "Defilement Penetrating the Body: A New Understanding of Contamination in Mark 7.15," *NTS* 54 (2008): 182–84, 186. See Friedrich Avemarie, "Jesus and Purity," in *The New Testament and Rabbinic Literature*, ed. Reimund Bieringer, Florentino García Martínez, Didier Pollefeyt, and Peter J. Tomson (Leiden: Brill, 2010), 271–75; James Crossley, "Mark 7.1–23: Revisiting the Question of 'All Foods Clean'," in *The Torah in the New Testament: Papers Delivered at the Manchester-Lausanne Seminar of June 2008*, ed. Michael Tait and Peter Oakes (London: T&T Clark, 2009), 8; idem, *The Date of Mark's Gospel: Insights from the Law in Earliest Christianity* (London: T&T Clark, 2004), 192–93.

70. See Mark 7:8–13; Matt. 15:3–6. "So really what the Gospel describes is a Jesus who rejects the pharisaic extension of these purity laws beyond their original specific biblical foundations. He is not rejecting the Torah's rules and practices but upholding them. . . . It was thus against those pharisaic innovations, which they are trying to foist on his disciples, that Jesus railed, and not against the keeping of kosher at all. This is a debate between Jews about the correct way to keep the Torah, not an attack on the Torah" (Daniel Boyarin, *The Jewish Gospels: The Story of the Jewish Christ* [New York: The New Press, 2012], 116–18).

71. David Rudolph, "Jesus and the Food Laws: A Reassessment of Mark 7:19b," *EvQ* 74, no. 4 (2002): 291–311.

72. Jesper Svartvik, *Mark and Mission: Mk 7:1-23 in Its Narrative and Historical Contexts* (Stockholm: Almqvist & Wiksell International, 2000), 344–48, regards Mark as a "Pauline Gospel." Joel Marcus ("Mark—Interpreter of Paul," *NTS* 46 [2000]:

477) concurs that "there might be good reasons why a later Paulinist such as Mark might want to anchor Pauline theology in traditions about the earthly Jesus. . . . Paul's theology was controversial; Mark, therefore, may have been trying to defend it against its detractors by demonstrating its conformity with the authoritative Jesus tradition." See Paula Fredriksen, "Did Jesus Oppose the Purity Laws?," *BRev* 11, no. 3 (1995): 25; Barnabas Lindars, "All Foods Clean: Thoughts on Jesus and the Law," in *Law and Religion: Essays on the Place of the Law in Israel and Early Christianity*, ed. Lindars (Cambridge: James Clarke, 1988), 69. "It seems to me much more likely that Mark is influenced by the insights gained in the Gentile mission, expressed by Paul in Rom. 14.14, 20, than that Paul is dependent on Jesus" (Räisänen, *Jesus, Paul and Torah*, 145).

73. "It appears that Leviticus 19 and Deuteronomy 22 were the most significant biblical law codes [in Second Temple Judaism]. Leviticus 19 was of fundamental importance for these authors as a counterpart to the Decalogue. Writing about its importance for Pseudo-Phocylides, Pieter van der Horst [*The Sentences of Pseudo-Phocylides: With Introduction and Commentary* (Leiden: Brill, 1978), 67] said: 'One might tentatively conclude that in Judaism at the beginning of our era Lev. XIX was regarded as a central chapter in the Torah.' Leviticus 20 is also significant. It is part of the sexual code in Leviticus 18 and 20. . . . These chapters appear to have formed the basis for ethical instruction in the Diaspora" (Gregory Sterling, "Was There a Common Ethic in Second Temple Judaism?," in *Sapiential Perspectives: Wisdom Literature in Light of the Dead Sea Scrolls. Proceedings of the Sixth International Symposium of the Orion Center for the Study of the Dead Sea Scrolls and Associated Literature, 20-22 May, 2001*, ed. John J. Collins, Gregory E. Sterling, and Ruth A. Clements [Leiden: Brill, 2004], 186).

7

The Pauline 'Ἐκκλησίαι and Images of Community in Enoch Traditions

Kathy Ehrensperger

Theories concerning a community, communities, or a movement behind Enoch traditions abound, and I am not going to add to the debate in this contribution.[1] I am rather interested here in images and characteristics attributed to an ideal eschatological community in some exemplary Enoch traditions, and to what extent or not such images resonate with characteristics of Pauline ἐκκλησίαι. Numerous scholars have noted that significant parallels and analogies may be identified between the Pauline Letters and Enoch traditions.[2] Such parallels and analogies are identified with regard to a number of topics, such as Adam/second Adam typology, new creation language, the role and function of the Torah, the perception of the ideal eschatological community, and universalism. I will focus here on the latter two aspects and explore to what extent analogies between the two collections of literature may provide insights into the existence of a shared pool of traditions in Second Temple Judaism. Since Paul's letters are perceived as addressing non-Jewish Christ-followers, there may be indications for the cultural translation process discernable through such a comparison, which could provide insights into the developing identity/self-understanding of the Pauline ἐκκλησίαι. The chapter explores the issue in four steps: first, I will explore designations used for community members in *1 Enoch* and in Pauline literature; second, I will consider particular characteristics of such communities; third, a brief survey of Paul's perception of unity of Jews and gentiles in Christ will be presented; and lastly, I will focus on the perception of the ideal community in the *Animal Apocalypse*, particularly in *1 En.* 90:37–38.

Designations for Community Members

The traditions collected in *1 Enoch* use a number of peculiar designations for community members addressed or in focus of the visionary accounts, such as "the righteous," "the chosen," "the chosen righteous ones," "the faithful," and "holy ones."[3] The latter two are highlighted by Paul Trebilco as evidence for Paul sharing in a Jewish vocabulary, especially when addressing his communities with these designations. In his brief discussion of Enoch traditions, Trebilco notes that οἱ ἅγιοι refers to humans (as distinct from the more frequent designation for angels) once in the *Epistle of Enoch* (*1 En.* 100:5) and twelve times in the *Similitudes* (*1 En.* 37–71) in eschatological contexts, thus serving as a designation for eschatological communities.[4] There is no doubt that in the *Similitudes*, οἱ ἅγιοι is used for humans, but it is one designation among others for those of the eschatological community and it occurs alongside the continued use of the term for angels there (for example, *1 En.* 39:5; 47:2). The data for a distinctive use of οἱ ἅγιοι in *1 Enoch* as a designation for the eschatological community is, thus, rather slim in my view, especially when only what are considered early Enoch traditions (*1 Enoch* 1–36, 83–90, 92–107)[5] are taken into account, where οἱ ἅγιοι, except in *1 En.* 100:5, coherently refers to angels.[6] While πιστεύοντες and πιστ-related terminology is prominent in Paul, the one reference to "the faithful" in the last chapter of *1 Enoch* (108:13) can also hardly serve as an indication of a Jewish vocabulary shared between Paul and *1 Enoch*.

The predominant terms used for those envisaged to be part of the ideal community in the early Enoch tradition are "the righteous," "the chosen," or the combination of the two in "the chosen righteous." These designations are hardly found in the Pauline Letters, with the "chosen" (οἱ ἐκλεκτοί) only occurring in Rom. 8:33, and with reference to Rufus in Rom. 16:13, and οἱ δίκαοι as a designation for the members of the ἐκκλησία being completely absent. In the early Enoch tradition, however, the "chosen" (οἱ ἐκλεκτοί) appears frequently and prominently as designating either the envisaged audience or the ideal community. It is often paired with "righteous" (δίκαιος), and significantly, is prominent in the opening verse of *1 Enoch*, thus clearly setting the tone as to who is in focus in this literature ("The words of the blessing with which Enoch blessed the righteous chosen who will be present on the day of tribulation, to remove all the enemies; and the righteous will be saved"[7]). Similarly, the *Apocalypse of Weeks* refers to the addressees as "the children of righteousness . . . the chosen of eternity/the world" (93:2), thus indicating that this vision concerns a "righteous community."[8] As Trebilco has noted, community language in *1 Enoch* has a clear focus in eschatological terms, but certainly, in the early Enoch tradition, this is expressed not via holiness terminology, but rather, the terminology of election and righteousness. It need not be doubted that Paul was familiar with election language as well as with the terminology of righteousness (I will come back to this below), but he clearly does not address his ἐκκλησίαι in election terminology. The closest in this respect may be Paul's "calling" (καλ-) language (Rom. 9:24; 1 Cor. 1:9; 7:22; Gal. 1:6; 5:13; 1 Thess. 2:12; 4:7; 5:24). There may be a number of reasons for Paul's choice of address, but I cannot discuss this in detail here. Since Paul is addressing Christ-followers from the nations (gentiles), it could be that he considered election language inappropriate for them, a terminology reserved for Israel only (as is certainly the case in the Psalms, Prophetic traditions, and Wisdom literature [Pss. 105:6, 43; 106:5; Isa. 42:1; 43:20; 45:4; 65:15, 23; Wis. 3:9; 4:15).[9]

It thus appears that in terms of specific designations for community members, no parallel use between significant parts of *1 Enoch* and Paul can be identified. Paul sometimes uses the designation οἱ ἅγιοι when referring to or addressing his communities—a term not used in early Enoch tradition as a designation for the members of the ideal community. On the contrary, Paul does not use the Enochic designations οἱ ἐκλεκτοί, and οἱ δίκαιοι when addressing or designating members of the ἐκκλησίαι. There could be a number of reasons for this, but before speculating about these, it is necessary to explore whether there might be other indicators, such as specific characteristics of the perception of the ideal community, which are shared between particular Enoch traditions and Paul.

Characteristics of Communities and Community Members

The communities addressed by Paul and addressed or envisaged in *1 Enoch* are not only designated with particular labels, but also are supposed to have, or are envisaged to have, specific characteristics.

Although the early Enoch traditions do not refer to the members of the ideal community as "the holy ones," the notion of purification as a decisive step in the eschatological events is clearly present. The concepts of holiness and purity are, of course, not identical; however, they are closely intertwined in scriptural perception.[10] Thus, prior to the transformation of "all the sons of men" to righteousness, the earth needs to be cleansed "from all impurity [ἀκαθαρσία] and from all wrong and from all from all lawlessness and from all sin . . . and all the earth will be cleansed from all defilement and from all uncleanness [ἀκαθαρσία]" (*1 En.* 10:20, 22). Although the "plant of righteousness" does appear after the power of violence and destruction is overcome by the intervention of Michael ("Destroy all perversity from the face of the earth and let every wicked deed be gone and let the plant of righteousness and truth appear and it will become a blessing, (and) the deeds of righteousness and truth will be planted forever with joy" [1 En. 10:16-19]), the transformation of all the sons of men can only happen after the earth has been cleansed entirely. The transgression of the created order—that is, the boundaries between heaven and earth—by fallen angels (1 En. 7:1)[11] leads to violence and bloodshed (teaching humans "to make swords of iron and weapons and shields and breastplates and every instrument of war" [1 En. 8:1]), and to idolatry ("and there was much godlessness on the earth" [1 En. 8:2]). These transgressions lead to the defilement of the earth ("and all the earth was filled with the godlessness and violence that had befallen it" [1 En. 9:1]).[12] In consequence, the defiled earth is unfit as the place where the God of Israel can be worshipped.

The sequence of eschatological events is not always perceived in the same way throughout the different stages of the early Enoch tradition. Jerusalem and the temple play a specific role as the place to which the people Israel returns in 1 En. 90:37-38, whereas in the Book of Watchers, in 10:16-22, Israel, the plant of righteousness, is restored before the transformation of "all the sons of men" without any reference to Jerusalem or the temple. The restoration of Israel and the transformation of "all the sons of men" can only happen after the cosmological cleansing has taken place, thus setting the stage for Israel and the nations to worship God in truth and peace (1 En. 11:2). The joint worshipping of Israel and the nations is one of the key aspects of the eschatological transformation envisaged in the early Enoch traditions, as Stuckenbruck has clearly demonstrated.[13] I will come back to this aspect below (3.3 and 4.4).

For now, the focus remains on the issue of cleansing and purity, which, I think, is also in view in the color white that plays a prominent role in the Animal Apocalypse (1 Enoch 85–90).[14] White in scriptural tradition is occasionally the color of purity and sinlessness or purification, as for example, in Ps. 51:7 ("Purge me with hyssop and I shall be clean, wash me and I shall be whiter than snow") or Isa. 1:18 ("though your sins are like scarlet they shall be like snow"). It possibly is the color of the garments priests wore on the Day of Atonement (Lev. 16:4). It certainly is the color of festivals and celebrations in ancient Rome, and, according to Plato, the color of the gods.[15] More striking than the actual role of the color white in the Scriptures, however, is the frequent requirement of washing and cleansing when cult activities are in view. It is not surprising that a preponderance of occurrences of respective passages and terms is found in Leviticus and Ezekiel (LXX Lev. 8:6 [λούω]; 11:25, 28; 13:34 [πλύνω]; 13:35, 37, 59; 14:4 [καθαρίζω]; 14:8 [καθαρίζω, λούω]; 14:9 [πλύνω, λούω]; 14:11, 14, 17, 18, 19 [καθαρίζω]; 16:26 [λούω]; 16:28 [πλύνω]; 22:6 [λούω]; LXX Ezek. 16:9 [λούω]; 24:13 [καθαρίζω]; 36:25, 33 [καθαρίζω]; 37:23 [καθαρίζω]; 39:12, 14, 16; 43:26; 44:26 [καθαρίζω]).[16] In order to be able "to come near" the "Holy One," one had to be in a status of holiness—that is, a member of the holy people Israel (as distinct from the nations who were profane), as well as in a state of sanctification and purity, having undergone processes of purification. The significance of this can be seen in a scene mentioned almost by chance. In retelling a scene in the context of Hezekiah's invitation to all Israel and Judah, including Ephraim and Manasseh, to celebrate Passover in Jerusalem in 2 Chron. 30:17-19, it is noted that "there were many in the assembly (ἐκκλησία/קהל) who had not sanctified (ἡγνίσθη/התקדשו) themselves; therefore the Levites had to slaughter the Passover lamb for everyone who was not pure, to make it holy (ἁγιασθῆναι/הקדישלה) in the Lord" (2 Chron. 30:17). The LXX makes a terminological distinction not made in the Hebrew text, indicating that the sanctification required here was a state of temporary dedication achieved through purification rituals and dedication prayers, as distinct from the permanent status of holiness expressed in the LXX by the Greek term ἅγιος and related terminology.[17] According to this passage, everybody in the assembly had to be in a temporary state of sanctification, which included purification, in order to bring an offering to the Lord. The notion of temporary sanctification in a cultic context is inherently bound up with purity and a process of purification. The high frequency of washing and cleansing language in Leviticus and Ezekiel is due to the crucial concern of these books with the state in which members of the people Israel could "come near" the Holy God. By analogy, the color white in the *Animal Apocalypse* may well indicate such a status of purity of those patriarchs envisaged as white bulls, with an analogous status of the eschatological community of white sheep and white cattle. Cleansing/purification is a core aspect in the early Enoch traditions, and although the designation "holy ones" is not used for the community of "the righteous," it is evident in the images of purification and the prominence of the color white that aspects of the notion of sanctification as an aspect of the status of holiness are not alien to this tradition.

The Pauline use of the designation οἱ ἅγιοι for his ἐκκλησίαι resonates with the Enochic emphasis on purification in that the status of holiness which is intertwined with, although not identical with a state of sanctification, is core to the characteristic of the Pauline ἐκκλησίαι. Consistent with scriptural and Second Temple traditions, the status of holiness and the state of sanctification are inherently bound up with processes of purification/cleansing for Paul. Contrary to the assumption that, for Paul, purity issues were of no concern as they were supposedly overcome in Christ, such issues were core to the vision and perception he had for the ἐκκλησίαι τοῦ θεοῦ.[18] As assemblies that related to the God of Israel through Christ, their transformation into a status of holiness was vital. The question here was not *whether* this was essential for those assemblies of Christ-followers from the nations, but *how* they could acquire such a status without becoming Jews—that is, part of the people Israel. The core question for them was how they could be purified, and thus, rendered holy so as to be in a status that allowed them to come near and be loyal to the one Holy God, and to worship him without becoming Jews. The connection between purification and holiness is explicit in 1 Cor. 6:11: ἀλλὰ ἀπελούσασθε ἀλλὰ ἡγιάσασθε ἀλλὰ ἐδικαιώθητε ἐν τῷ ὀνόματι τοῦ κυρίου Ἰησοῦ Χριστοῦ καὶ ἐν τῷ πνεύματι τοῦ θεοῦ ἡμῶν ("But you were washed, you were *rendered holy*, you were justified in the name of the Lord Jesus Christ and in the Spirit of our God").[19] Paul addresses the Corinthians explicitly as "those who are rendered holy in Christ Jesus" (ἡγιασμένοις

189

ἐν Χριστῷ Ἰησοῦ, 1 Cor. 1:2). The intrinsic link between purity and holiness is also evident in 1 Thessalonians 4, where Paul reminds the members of the ἐκκλησία about the will of God for them as their holiness (ὁ ἁγιασμὸς ὑμῶν, 4:3), which requires from them to abstain from "fornication" (πορνεία: most likely understood not primarily as sexual promiscuity, but rather, as expression of loyalty to other deities). After some further clarification, Paul emphasizes that "God did not call us to impurity but into holiness" (οὐ γὰρ ἐκάλεσεν ἡμᾶς ὁ θεὸς ἐπί ἀκαθαρσίᾳ ἀλλ' ἐν ἁγιασμῷ, 4:7).

Paul's letters deal with the implications of this status of holiness for Christ-followers from the nations as they arise from the practicalities of everyday life. This is evident in Romans 12–15, for example, and already earlier in Rom. 6:19, where he clarifies "[f]or just as you once presented your members as slaves to impurity and to greater and greater iniquity so now present your members as slaves to righteousness for holiness" (ὥσπερ γὰρ παρεστήσατε τὰ μέλη ὑμῶν δοῦλα τῇ ἀκαθαρσίᾳ καὶ τῇ ἀνομίᾳ εἰς τὴν ἀνομίαν οὕτως νῦν παραστήσατε τὰ μέλη ὑμῶν δοῦλα τῇ δικαιοσύνῃ εἰς ἁγιασμόν). He more explicitly explains what this encompasses in Romans 12. There is clearly a connection between issues concerning purity and the status of holiness in Paul's notion of what ought to characterize the ἐκκλησίαι τοῦ θεοῦ he had founded. In addition, Rom. 6:19 indicates a further connection between these two aspects and issues concerning righteousness/justification (δικαιοσύνη). I cannot elaborate on the links between these here, but I just note that they are obviously not detached, purely theological notions, but inherently intertwined in the form of a web or rhizome,[20] rather than in a linear vein of cause and effect. The mentioning of δικαιοσύνη here in one sweep with an admonition to avoid ἀκαθαρσία for the purpose of ἁγιασμός demonstrates that what is of high importance in the early Enoch tradition—that is, δικαιοσύνη and the perception that the members of the eschatological community are δίκαιος—is not out of view in the Pauline letters either.

The analysis of specific community-related designations in 1 Enoch and the Pauline letters provides an indication, if not for a shared terminology, then nevertheless, for a shared pool of perceptions of an eschatological community in Second Temple Judaism, involving notions of purification, purity, sanctification, holiness, and righteousness. It is expressed differently in that the groups directly in view are addressed or labeled differently (ἅγιοι in Paul, δίκαιοι in 1 Enoch). A further detailed study is needed to critically analyze possible reasons for this, but it is evident that Paul embodies, is embedded in, and draws on Jewish traditions that had circulated for some centuries before his time.

The analogies in the use of these designations and characteristics between Pauline and Enochic literature are significant in my view and point to a perception of ideal communities, distinct from Greek and Roman community traditions. Although notions of purity and holiness are evidently also of decisive importance and permeate all aspects of life in Greek and Roman tradition,[21] to attribute respective designations to an entire community, even if only an ideal one of the end time, is rather peculiar. A status of purity, or holiness, was, no doubt, required of certain cult adherents or at moments of cult performance in Greek and Roman cults, but these would be individual attributes or attributes of groups of particular people, such as priests rather than attributes of entire communities. No voluntary association would require purity or holiness, or righteousness per se from its members. They may call themselves brothers,[22] but hardly "holy ones" or "the righteous." Thus, what emerges is clear evidence that Paul's perception of the core characteristics of his ἐκκλησίαι was primarily rooted in Jewish traditions—both scriptural and others such as Enochic traditions—whether there exists a direct link between these or not. The shared terminology indicates shared cultural perceptions. Holy, cleansed, and righteous: this is what these ἐκκλησίαι as ἐκκλησίαι τοῦ θεοῦ ought to be. The designations and characteristics clearly originate from the pool of Jewish eschatological expectations and hopes. They refer not just to a state, but a status to live by: a way of life in light of eschatological events. Paul's letters witness to the fact that the implications of being called into a community perceived to be characterized by such Jewish core values were not self-evident for Christ-followers from the nations. These designations and required characteristics were not easily integrated by people who formerly were pagans and who were, or continued to be, embedded in Greek and Roman, Galatian, and Macedonian culture. Although the designations and characteristics as such were most likely familiar to them, their perception of what these encompassed were shaped by their experiences from within their particular cultural and social contexts, rather than from a Jewish context. Thus, what it means to live a life in holiness, purity, and righteousness is culturally and socially conditioned, culturally coded, and thus, embodied in different ways. The understanding of these designations and characteristics is decisively shaped by this pre-conditioning or, as Bourdieu would have it, by the respective *habitus* of Jewish and non-Jewish Christ-followers. To mediate these designations and characteristics of an eschatological community (or, in Paul's case, a community in anticipation of the *eschaton*) involves a complex translation process beyond linguistic terms: it involves a cultural translation process with all its challenges for understanding, transformed understanding, and misunderstanding.[23]

Commonality or Sameness: This is the Question

As demonstrated above, there are characteristics used by Paul for his ἐκκλησίαι that clearly originate from the pool of Jewish eschatological expectations, even though specific designations may differ between different textual traditions. The question that needs to be addressed now is who the people were who gathered as ἐκκλησίαι τοῦ θεοῦ—and who are envisaged/imagined to be the bearers of these designations and characteristics in *1 Enoch*. One core difference needs to be kept in mind at the outset here: while Enoch traditions present images of ideal communities in the context of final eschatological events at the consummation of history, the Pauline Letters address communities that are living in the here and now in anticipation of the "final days." The Christ event has initiated the eschatological process, but not concluded it. Thus, it could be said that the communities envisaged by the Enoch traditions and by Paul—although both are seen in light of eschatological events—are located at a different point on the eschatological calendar: the Pauline ἐκκλησίαι τοῦ θεοῦ at the very beginning, those of the Enoch traditions at the very end. One thus has to be careful not to overstate both the commonalities and differences between Pauline and Enochic perceptions of communities. The temporal difference in terms of what is envisaged has to be kept in mind.

Commonality in Sin in Pauline Perspective

It is evident that Paul includes Jews and non-Jews in the designation of "holy ones," that the emphasis on righteousness concerns both Jews and non-Jews, and that the purification from sin also applies to Jews as well as to non-Jews. It is evident that Paul stresses commonality between Jews and non-Jews in Christ when he uses terms and characteristics that he applies to all of those who are in Christ.

Thus, the designation "holy ones," which is inherently linked with cleansing and purity, indicates that Paul considers both Jews and non-Jews in need of release from contamination by sin. In Rom. 3:9–18, he emphasizes that all are affected by the power of sin, and thus, there is commonality between Jews and non-Jews in that no one escapes from the all-pervasive power of sin. But *how* they are affected by sin may nevertheless be different. To be affected by sin is something they have in common, but it does not render them the same. The citations in Rom. 3:9–18 from the Psalms and Isaiah (Pss. 5:9; 10:7; 14:1–3; Isa. 59:7) are expressions of Israel's anguish in the face of oppression, crying to God for deliverance. The all-pervasive power of sin does not render all the same: it affects people differently, distorts their lives in different ways. The scriptural citations imply situations of abusive power and violence. It is not the same to be a violent perpetrator as to be the victim of violence. Although this distortion of what it means to be human distorts everyone involved, and does not render victims righteous per se, the effects of sin are terrible and enclose all in an inescapable circle. But this does not render all who are trapped under the power of sin the same.[24] This negative differentiation is evident in other passages such as Rom. 2:12, where Paul certainly affirms that both those without the law and those under law, have sinned, but precisely here, the commonality is qualified by difference in that it is clarified that those who sin apart from the law will perish while those who sin under the law will be judged by the law. Thus, the difference between Jews and those from the nations is maintained in the commonality of life under the power of sin, including its effects when it comes to judgment.

This emphasis on abiding difference is, of course, also the emphasis of Paul's passionate arguments against the conversion of Christ-followers from the nations to Judaism (as in Galatians) as well as the cause of his passionate concern for the abiding value, and thus, required recognition of, and respect for, Jewish identity in or without Christ. Paul's perception of the ἐκκλησίαι τοῦ θεοῦ does not arise in a vacuum, as we have already seen above. He shares in a pool of Jewish eschatological traditions. But as someone who lived under the omnipresent power of Rome, Paul was certainly affected by its reality and ideology as well. Thus when it comes to his perception of how Israel and the nations will relate to each other in anticipation of "the world to come," it is difficult to envisage that the grand Roman imperial enterprise of the unification of the nations under its power would not have had some influence on him.

The Roman Program of the Unification of the Nations

The Augustan program of peace and justice (*pax et iustitia*), supported by the introduction of a number of laws (*leges*) was officially hailed as the inauguration of an age of salvation for all peoples, a Golden Age of prosperity. At a formal and military level, there were no substantial internal challenges to the system of Roman domination at that time, although in specific contexts and at the boundaries of the empire, of course, things would not look as settled as at, and from, the center. This military and political domination, accompanied by the respective ideological underpinnings, could not and did not intend to override or eradicate diversity in cultural, ethnic, and linguistic terms.[25] The Roman Empire, rather than eradicating difference, operated through accentuating, even stereotyping the difference of conquered peoples and nations. Thus, there were the "effete Persian," the "educated Greek," the "painted Gaul," and the "circumcised Jew," marked out as those who were not civilized and who, by nature, had to be subjugated under Rome. Roman domination and wide-ranging diversity under its rule, and the multilayered negotiations between these dimensions, are the decisive contexts of the early Christ movement.[26] This was not an encounter between equals, but between those who ruled and those who were ruled. Even the encounter between Romans and Greeks, despite some recognition and admiration of Greek traditions and practices on the part of the Romans, was never an encounter of equals—certainly not from a Roman perspective. It was in admiration of *Graeca capta*, as Andrew Jacobs in his recent study maintains, that the "Greek language and literature became the cultural spoils of Rome, but were never fully internalized—that is, Greek culture had to remain legibly 'Greek' in order to retain value within the logic of Rome's empire."[27] All other traditions and peoples under Rome and beyond its borders were beyond the "benefits" of civilization: that is, barbarian. The world of Greece and Rome was divided into two categories: civilized and uncivilized. Although it was not a hermetically sealed world and the boundaries could be crossed, this was only possible if one was willing to become like them, that is, civilized according to Greek and Roman perception.

Paul and his people were not one of "them." He was one of those others, ruled, and not really civilized, despite speaking Greek. According to the perspective of the civilized, Greece and Rome, Paul, like all other members of peoples who were not part of the latter, was part of a non-civilized nation. He was a member of a barbaric people, as Josephus's reference to his own people in Roman perspective discloses.[28] He was one of those who were circumcised, bearing the mark of Jewish distinction as a mark of cultural difference, which was already an overdetermined symbol in Roman elite literature and a mark of general ridicule (Horace considers the superstition of "clipped Jews" a social nuisance: [*Sat.* 1.9.69–70]; Martial is jealous of the sexual prowess of foreskinless Jewish men [*Epig.* 7.30.5]; and Juvenal refers to the weird Jews who "worship the sky" and "by and by shed their foreskins" [*Sat.* 14.99]).[29]

The division of the world in Roman (and Greek) perspective into "us and them," despite the recognition of diversity, emerged according to criteria which were not negotiated between the subjugated peoples, but dictated by those in power. Although the Romans could grant different status to different conquered peoples, as *colonia, amici,* or *confoederati,* they could also enslave them, and none of these turned the conquered nation into an equal partner of Rome.[30] Any status attribution was granted by the mercy (*clementia*) of Rome. The options available to those included under Roman rule by conquest were, if one was part of the provincial elite, to eventually join them in becoming "civilized" or to submit, the latter being the only option available if you were not a member of the elite. Submission was required in economic and military terms even where partial autonomy in civic and cultic affairs might have been granted. Cultural, military, economic, and cultic domination were intertwined. The power asymmetry in the relationship between Rome and the provinces should not be underestimated. Rome's territorial expansion and domination was built on military violence even where the mere threat of such violence achieved its goal. To become part of the empire was not a democratic process, but involved "intrusion, exploitation, violence, and coercion."[31] The provincial voices we know of are mostly those of the elite "who had aligned themselves with Rome and had taken their place in delivering Roman government and justice."[32] But even those voices would not be able to claim equal standing with the Roman elite during the first century CE, much as they might have aspired to such recognition. They were representatives of conquered peoples, accepted as useful tools of Roman power.[33] To be recognized by the Roman elite rulers in the first century CE, if not as equal, then at least as "civilized" and "human," was only possible on the condition that the conquered nations accepted this "civilizing" force and turned "human" according to the Roman concept of *humanitas*—that is, by becoming Roman, accepting the *pater patriae* as their Father, and embracing Roman ideology.[34] It meant copying the Roman way of life in a discourse of sameness.

Conquered nations were united under Roman control; they were united in their defeat, and in their status as enslaved, marginalized others.[35] Unity between these peoples could only consist in unity under Rome, in submission to Roman law and order. Any unity between these ἔθνη/*gentes*, which would have emerged from their own initiative and been based on their self-perception as peoples distinct from Rome, was considered to mean trouble for Rome, and thus, needed to be prevented.[36]

Unity in Christ

Paul's letters are predominantly addressing people from these ἔθνη/nations, and he himself refers to his calling experience as a commissioning to proclaim good news among the nations (Gal. 1:16). This includes the call for unity and solidarity in Christ among peoples who, at that time, were under Roman control and domination. Distinct from the Roman program, the template of his perception of the ἐκκλησίαι τοῦ θεοῦ has its roots in scriptural traditions of the unification of Israel and the nations and their interpretation in the first century. Whether there are trajectories of commonality also between Paul and early Enoch tradition will be explored below.

Paul's perception of the association of the nations/ἔθνη to the God of Israel is interpreted from within existing Jewish traditions and is neither novel to nor inconsistent with it. Israel's narrative of belonging begins with God's creation and humankind as a whole. All peoples, rather than only a few, are seen as related to each other after the flood through their common descent from Noah, according to this narrative tradition. The genealogies of Genesis 10 and 2 Chron. 1:1–2:2 connect Israel and the nations in a web of interrelations.[37] The election and particularity of one people, Israel, is seen in conjunction with openness to other nations. The particular relationship of God with this people through election, covenant, and guidance through the Torah, and the perception of "the other" as part of God's creation and divine economy, are not seen as being in contradiction with each other in significant trajectories of this tradition. Although enmity between Israel and the nations forms part of the tradition as well, this is not the only way they are perceived to interact with each other. The nations have never been out of view in Israel's narrative, and form part of the visions of the "world to come" inasmuch as they are there after the flood. When "the world to come" is envisioned, people from the nations—rather than joining Israel, that is, a socio-ethnic group, through conversion—are seen as joining themselves to the Lord as "others" (cf. Zech. 2:11–12; 8:22–23; Isa. 66:18–20).[38]

These people are not seen as becoming part of Israel, but they worship God as foreigners because God's house is now a house of prayer for all peoples (Isa. 56:7).[39] By joining in worship the distinctions between, and diversity of, Israel and nations/ἔθνη are maintained, and so is their specific way of life, and of relating to God.[40]

It cannot be discerned precisely which specific traditions of this narrative were influential for Paul's understanding of his call to the nations. But it can hardly be envisaged that such traditions were not of some importance for his understanding of his call to bring about the obedience of faith among all the nations (Rom. 1:5). These traditions of a unification of Israel and the nations to jointly worship the God of Israel, in themselves, present an alternative scenario to the scenarios of united nations under a dominating force.[41] Admittedly, not all of these Jewish traditions envisage a peaceful relationship between Israel and the nations. There are those traditions that, rather than presenting an alternative, merely present inversions of the domination-subjugation scheme, with the non-Jewish nations being subjugated now under the rule of Israel or violence exercised against them.[42]

Paul's arguments concerning the relationship of Israel and the nations, however, resonate with those traditions which envisage the unification of the nations not by force, but by them responding to the call to serve the God of Israel (cf. Tob. 14:6). The earliest Christ-followers saw this call actualized in and through the Christ event, that is, through the implications of the death and resurrection of Jesus Christ. In the first century CE, to envisage a nonviolent unification of the nations presented a powerful alternative to the notion of their unification under the dominating, "civilizing" force of Rome.

Unlike the Roman perception, where a degree of equality could only be achieved by assimilation—that is, by the adoption of the Roman way of life—the scriptural traditions of the nations joining Israel in glorifying their God do not presuppose such assimilation: in these visions, the nations are not required to become the same, that is, Jews, nor does Israel become like the nations in this process of united glorification of God. For Paul, the already of the "world to come," seen as revealed in the Christ-event, actualized such visions rather than initiating them. Based on these, the envisaged unity presupposes and actually supports the diversity and particularity of these nations, and of Israel. The nations/ἔθνη are precisely *not* to become the same as Jews: they are not to convert to Judaism, nor is Israel to become like the nations and give up its Jewish identity.

This is evident in passages such as Gal. 5:2: "Listen! I, Paul, am telling you that if you let yourselves be circumcised, Christ will be of no benefit for you" (Ἴδε ἐγὼ Παῦλος λέγω ὑμῖν ὅτι ἐὰν περιτέμνησθε Χριστὸς ὑμᾶς οὐδὲν ὠφελήσει). Here, Paul sums up his passionate plea to the Galatians to maintain their identity as Galatians and not become Jews. He argues for the necessity for these Galatian Christ-followers to be just that: *Galatian* Christ-followers. Through Christ, they are now heirs to the promises of Abraham, related to the people Israel, and as such, called to glorify the God of Israel as the God of all creation—all without becoming Jews, that is, without becoming part of the people Israel. They become part of God's people: a diverse people, not a uniform people of sameness. No one shall compel these Christ-followers from a conquered nation to assimilate and become the same as Jews. Thus, Galatians concludes with a blessing for all, for those from the nations and for Israel, rather than with a blessing for a new Israel or a new humanity (Gal. 6:16).[43]

In 1 Cor. 7:18-24, we find a strong affirmation of the identity of both Jews and people from the nations in Christ. They are both confirmed in what they are, their transformation in Christ does not lead to a mutual assimilation into some generic undifferentiated humanity—those who are circumcised (that is, Jews) remain Jews when called in Christ; those who are not circumcised (that is people from the nations), will also retain their identities. The main issue is to remain with God: ἕκαστος ἐν ᾧ ἐκλήθη ἀδελφοί ἐν τούτῳ μενέτω παρὰ θεῷ ("In whatever [condition] you were called, brothers and sisters, there remain with God," 1 Cor. 7:24).

In Romans, Paul sees a need to address issues concerning the identity of Jews and attitudes that denigrate their particular way of life. As passionately as Paul defends the identity of the Galatians in Christ, he here defends the identity of the Jews, and their ongoing bond with their God, whether they are in Christ or not (it is worth noting that no such defense is made for people from the nations who are not in Christ). Romans 9–11 clarifies Paul's position in this respect. If, as it has been argued, Jewish issues concerning food are involved in some of the problems in the Roman ἐκκλησίαι, then Paul in Rom 14:1–15:14 does not argue for assimilation toward each other, but rather, for the accommodation to the needs of the weaker partners in the debate.[44] To accommodate is not the same as to become the same. Accommodation recognizes abiding difference. Here, the difference between those who eat meat and those who eat vegetables remains and no argument is made that this should change over the course of some development. Paul merely admonishes the "strong" to accommodate the needs of the weak on occasions where the unity of the community is at stake. No requirement is made that they should change their practice entirely, but only in particular circumstances.

The key issue again is that Christ-followers from the nations glorify the God of Israel in their diversity together with Israel (Rom. 15:9–10). The paradigm of sameness promoted by the imperial power is precisely *not* what these people from the nations and the people Israel were to follow as followers of Christ. The nations do not become the same as Israel nor are they integrated into Israel or become a new Israel. If they were to become part of Israel, their identity as those from the nations would be assimilated to, and thus, lost in Israel. If Israel were to cease to be Israel, Jewish identity would be assimilated to, and thus lost, in the identity of the nations. Either way, the particularity of those in Christ is lost in a paradigm of assimilation or sameness. The nations are to join Israel in the praise of God as the nations/ἔθνη; they are related to Israel, but the distinction between circumcision and uncircumcision is not obliterated in Christ, but maintained.[45] Unity is not achieved by the eradication of cultural and ethnic distinctions, but by affirming their validity and value in Christ.[46]

Paul's strong arguments for respect for people in their difference in the exemplary passages mentioned above set out an alternative discourse to the Roman imperial ideology of sameness. It is, if not an explicit, then certainly an implicit, challenge to the prevalent Roman paradigm.

The Unification Vision in *1 Enoch* 90:37–38

Similarities or Differences to Paul?

In light of Paul's vision of unity in diversity, what are we to make of the unification vision in *1 En.* 90:37–38? As noted above, analogies between Paul and early Enoch traditions have been affirmed, particularly in interpretations of the concluding section of the *Animal Apocalypse*: "And I saw a white bull was born and its horns were large. And the wild beasts and all the birds of heaven were afraid of it and made petitions to it continually. And I saw until all their species were changed and they all became white cattle. . . . And the Lord of the sheep rejoiced over it and over all the cattle" (*1 En.* 90:37–38). Thus, Daniel Olson finds striking similarities between Paul and the *Animal Apocalypse* in their perception of the relationship between Jews and gentiles[47]/people from the nations and the future of Israel. His perception of this similarity is based on the interpretation of *1 En.* 90:37–39 as indicating that "God's purpose in human history is not to glorify the nation of Israel but to abolish all nationalities entirely and return all humanity to single, Adamic state. . . ."[48] The transformation into white cattle is understood by Olson in the vein of a new creation where there is neither Jew (sheep) nor gentile (wild animals). Paul is interpreted similarly as arguing that the division between Jew and gentile is to be abolished and those in Christ are a new creation, that is, "a kind of third race."[49] George Nickelsburg argues slightly differently that "in the end all the species representing the diversity of nations and people return to the primordial unity from which they diverged."[50] This seems to imply that the problem that needs to be overcome consists in the diversity of nations and peoples, although Nickelsburg places the emphasis on the unity of people rather than explicitly on the overcoming of diversity as God's purpose in the eschatological events. It is the violence of the nations against Israel that comes to an end, and only thus is peace and unity between them rendered possible.

The similarities seen between *1 En.* 90:37–38 and Paul's vision here of the unity of Jews and people from the nations in Christ is based on an interpretation of the Pauline Letters that assumes that Paul advocates the obliteration of difference between Israel and the nations. A variation of this theme is the assumption that gentiles will become part of a new or true Israel—a notion that is also identified in Aaron Sherwood's interpretation of *1 En.* 90:37–38 and the *Animal Apocalypse*. Although noting that the key focus is on Israel's restoration, Sherwood argues that ". . . prior to all humanity being Israel (v. 38a), Israel is given primacy. But ultimately the nations shed their identity and share Israel's and so implicitly share in their worship."[51] While in the previous trajectory of interpretation, the identity of Israel is lost, here, the identity of the nations is annihilated. In both interpretative scenarios, unity and peace are achieved at the expense of diversity. This is a questionable interpretation of Paul, as demonstrated above, and if the final vision of the *Animal Apocalypse* does envisage the abolition of all "nationalities"[52]—that is, distinct collective identities of peoples, either at the expense of Israel or of the nations—then Paul's notion of unity could not be more different. If this is the vision of the *Animal Apocalypse* and other early Enoch traditions, then there is no similarity to Paul in this respect. In that case, their respective perceptions of eschatological communities differ fundamentally. However, in light of the unity in diversity advocated by Paul for his eschatological communities argued above, I propose to reread the two verses of the *Animal Apocalypse* in question afresh.

Aspects of Sin in the *Animal Apocalypse*

Interestingly, Nickelsburg, in his introduction to Enoch's "Second Dream Vision' (*1 Enoch* 85–90), identifies the all-permeating presence of sin as a dominant feature in this vision in a vein rather similar to Paul. As in Rom. 2:12 and 3:9–18, this all-permeating presence does not affect Israel and the nations in the same vein. Humans are either victims or perpetrators of sin, with violence being the core sin here. Nickelsburg concludes that "[s]ins of violence . . . are not attributed to Israel. The Israelites are victims of Gentile violence, which is usually punishment for another kind of sin committed by Israel . . . this sin is caused by blindness and involves the flocks straying from the path that God had shown them."[53] He thus identifies a clear difference between Israel and the nations with regard to sin in the section of the Enoch tradition in question here. I have not found any interpretation that attributes the origin of sin to the mere fact that peoples are different. The diversity of peoples is not the cause of sin, nor does sin cause the emergence of a diversity of peoples.[54] The sin of Israel is to turn away from their God; the sin of the nations is to violently oppress Israel. These aspects are multifaceted and intertwined, but this does not render them the same. There is a commonality in sin between Israel and the nations, according to the *Animal Apocalypse*, but not sameness. This perception of sin certainly resonates with aspects of what we found above as characteristic of Paul's notion of sin.

The Animal and Color Symbolism

A number of interpretations consider the animal and color symbolism in the *Animal Apocalypse* as referring to the diversity of peoples per se, the nations on the one hand and Israel on the other.[55] The transformation of the nations—or of Israel and the nations—into white cattle (90:38) is interpreted as the overcoming of the diversity of peoples.[56] It appears to be assumed that the unity of peoples who worship God requires that they all become the same. However, I am not convinced that the different animals and colors in the *Animal Apocalypse* actually represent the diversity of peoples as such. If we consider the animals mentioned, then a common characteristic appears, which is also clearly expressed in the wording of the text. Almost all of them are *wild* animals, or, more precisely, predators, and no *domesticated* animals are included in this zoological park, with the exception of sheep, bulls, and cows. In light of the diversity of creation, this is quite a limited selection of creatures. No reasons are given for the emergence of cattle of different colors (*1 En.* 85:3; 89:9). The animals emerging after the flood are not just any kind of wild animals, but rather, they are characterized or caricatured in a specific way and for a specific purpose: lions, leopards, wolves, dogs, hyenas, wild boars, foxes, conies, pigs, falcons, vultures, kites, eagles, and ravens (*1 En.* 89:10). Distinct from domesticated animals, these wild animals are not guarded or guided by a fence or shepherd, but they are roaming wild. They exert destructive power when in contact with domesticated animals. Thus, the core aspect they represent is conflict, mostly violent conflict against the domesticated sheep and cattle.[57] What we find in the *Animal Apocalypse* is not an image of the diversity of peoples, but a scenario of violent conflict, allegorized in the destructive encounter between predators and domestic animals. Moreover, the colors of the cattle and sheep do not represent the full spectrum of colors, but typified white, black, and red. It has been noted that black most likely here indicates destructive power, whereas red is the color of the victims (as in the case of the black and red calves, Cain and Abel respectively, in *1 En.* 85:3). The diversity of these animals hence cannot mean the diversity of peoples per se, but a diversity of violence and enmity against Israel. The colors may also be indicative of the relationship of these animals to God, with white expressing the faithful and pure bond of humans to God and black and red, and the absence of the color white of the sheep after Jacob (*1 En.* 89:12), perhaps indicating the strained relationship between Israel and her God.[58] Oppressive violence against Israel is a core emphasis in this vision, set "in the broader context of humanity's story," as Nickelsburg has convincingly argued.[59] If the animals and the colors do not represent diversity per se, it is rather difficult to envisage that the overcoming of diversity, or the abolition of "nationalities," should be the aim of eschatological transformation. In light of this, it needs to be considered what could be implied with the image of the transformation into white cattle in *1 En.* 90:38 if it does not refer to the overcoming of difference and the transformation of all peoples into the same.

The color white certainly indicates purity, as noted above.[60] The white of the bulls, Adam, Seth, Noah, Shem, Abraham, Isaac, and of the ram, Jacob, at the beginning of the vision may indicate closeness to God in a relationship that is not estranged by sin through forsaking the ways of the Lord and by the exercise of violence. Whether these white bulls are mentioned here in an anticipatory vein, pointing to the eschatological white of the white bull at the end of the vision—and these primordial bulls are typologically depicted in relation to the messianic white bull, as Rivka Nir has recently argued—or whether the messianic white bull and the white cattle are referring to the restitution of the primordial intimate relationship with God has to remain open, in my view.[61] But certainly, in both periods, the color white indicates an ideal state in relation to God with the period in between being characterized by the absence of white.[62] The color white refers to a core characteristic in the relationship between God and humans in the absence of violence and destruction (black and red). Thus, the color white of the bulls of primordial times may refer to them being in tune with the order of creation, whereas the white of the ram

(Jacob) may indicate his obedience to the specific order given to (the people) Israel, the Torah.[63] The color white is not associated with a general notion of overcoming difference, but rather, with the absence of violence and destruction. The color white disappears, according to the vision, when God's guidance for life through creation and the Torah is abandoned. Only through this deviation perpetrators and victims emerge, symbolized in the respective species and colors. The deviation affects both perpetrators and victims, but in different ways.

The Scenario(s) of Transformation

There is a consensus that the eschatological events in the scenario of the *Animal Apocalypse* begin with the restoration of the relationship between God and Israel, that is, the restoration of the white sheep (1 *En.* 90:6, 32). While initially, they are still under attack, the flock of white sheep with their thick and pure wool[64] eventually all return to the renewed temple. The text seems unclear, according to Nickelsburg, who is of the view that the following verse, 1 *En.* 90:33, cannot possibly mean that all the predators and birds of prey were also gathered in the temple together with the sheep, because it could not be said of them that they had *returned* to that house (the temple).[65] He therefore argues that "and all" (*wa-kʷellu*) should be translated as "by" or "among." If Nickelsburg is correct, then 1 *En.* 90:32–36 only say something about the sheep (Israel). The nations (predators and birds of prey) only appear on the scene again (after having paid respect to the sheep and submitted to them in 1 *En.* 90:30) in 90:37, where they pay respect to the white bull, and then, are transformed into white cattle. In this reading, there remain two species involved: white sheep and white cattle. The white sheep comprise both, the sheep who had been resurrected and those who had returned, and are now all together in the temple. They sealed the sword that had been given to them and are now so numerous that the temple cannot hold them all. The eyes of all of them are now opened "and they saw good things; and there was none among them that did not see. And I saw how that house was large and broad and very full" (1 *En.* 90:35–36). Upon his appearance, the white bull is recognized and respected by the predators and the birds of heaven, which leads to their transformation into white cattle (90:37–38a). There is no mention that the sheep respect or fear the white bull or that they "make petition to him." There is also no mention of a further transformation of the sheep in this reading: those who had been destroyed had been resurrected to life and those who had been dispersed re-gathered (90:33a). They were already pure (white), their relationship with God restored in their turning away from "straying away": they were healthy sheep who lived in abundance (thick wool). Only the predators and birds of prey are still in need of transformation at this point, to reestablish their relationship with God. They all, white sheep and white cattle, recognize the one God, thus "the Lord of the sheep rejoiced over it" (90:38). But they recognize and worship God in their difference as sheep and cattle. The unity is a unity for the purpose of worshipping the Lord of the sheep. With the return of the sheep to the temple—that is, to their restored relationship with God—their sin is overcome. The sword is now being sealed in that Israel is not being punished anymore for going astray, the violence of the predators against Israel has no foothold anymore, and with the sheep's return to the ways of the Lord, they do not need to defend themselves anymore with the sword. Thus, the violence and enmity between Israel and the nations is overcome and with the sealing of the sword, violence and enmity have come to an end. The different species do not represent the diversity of people and nations, but the horror of violence and oppression. White sheep and white cattle represent people who, in their diversity, respect and worship the one God, and thus, can live in peace and harmony, in and with their difference.

If wa-kʷellu is translated as "and all" or "along with," then the scenario is slightly different. The white sheep and the predators and birds of heaven are then seen as all being in the temple, "and the Lord of the sheep rejoiced greatly because they were all good and had returned to that house" (1 En. 90:33). Thus, Stuckenbruck concludes that "[t]he inclusion of Gentiles with the statement 'they had all become good' ensures that, alongside Jews to be restored, Gentiles will be the object of divine joy."[66] The sealing of the sword and the open eyes still refer specifically to the resurrected and regathered sheep (1 En. 90:34-35). Difference remains: the only question concerning the interpretation under the presupposition that the predators and birds of prey are also in the temple is *whether the transformation into white bulls also includes the white sheep.* The text as such does not solve this issue. Even when the predators and birds are considered to be in the temple, it remains unclear who precisely is being transformed. The fact that no role for the white bull is mentioned in relation to the white sheep gives credit to the interpretation above, of the abiding difference of white sheep and white cattle.[67]

But even if we were to assume that "all the species" in 1 En. 90:37 includes all—the white sheep and the predators and birds of prey and that they were all transformed into white cattle—the overcoming of diversity seems the unlikely eschatological goal here. Since, as argued above, the problem prior to the transformation is not diversity, but violence and destruction between the animals concerned, the overcoming of the diversity in the process of transformation would present a solution to a problem that does not exist. The animal and color symbolism needs to be seen in relation to the problem of sin, or of violence and destruction, as depicted in the vision. As mentioned above, hostile gentile nations are depicted as threatening straying Israel. The overcoming of violence and destruction is symbolized through the transformation of the predators and the change in color of all animals. This is not identical to indicating the overcoming of diversity. Since neither the colors nor the animals symbolize diversity, but violence, on the one hand, and destruction, on the other, neither cattle and sheep nor the color white can symbolize the overcoming of diversity. The transformation of the predators and the birds of prey—the hostile gentile nations—happens after the sheep have turned back to the "ways of the Lord," expressed in their return to the "house." Since the sheep have turned white—have turned back to God—the punishing function attributed to gentile nations by God has come to an end. The return of the white sheep is, thus, the presupposition of the transformation of the predators (the gentile nations) into white cattle. Their transformation is a direct result of the sheep's return, and the color white, together with predators' transformation into domesticated cattle, should be seen as indicating the power and strength emerging from seeing with open eyes and from being in the right relationship with God. Neither the color white nor the species of bulls/cattle should be taken as symbols of uniformity or the abolition of difference.[68] The emphasis in this symbolism is not on the one species, but on the strength and prosperity cattle represent, with the color white indicating the cleansing from sin. Both are rooted in and represent a close and intimate relationship with God, recognizing his guidance, which empowers all—in their diversity—to life.

Conclusion

The interpretation of the final verses of the *Animal Apocalypse* argued for here presents an image of an eschatological community that is characterized by the overcoming of violence and enmity between Israel and the nations. Inasmuch as the vision depicts difference in sin, there is also difference in the restoration of the relationship with God. The human predicament is not diversity, but violent oppression and abandoning the ways of the Lord. Thus, restoration cannot consist in the overcoming or abolition of the difference between Israel and the nations, but rather, in analogy with the restoration of their respective relationships with God, the relationship between Israel and the nations is restored from destruction to peace and life in abundance. The emphasis in the symbolism of transformation in the *Animal Apocalypse* is on the strength and abundance of life in a life lived in relation to God, rather than on uniformity.

Despite their difference in terms of language and imagery, we thus find, in the *Animal Apocalypse*, analogies and parallels to Paul's perception of the ἐκκλησίαι τοῦ θεοῦ. Paul's at times passionate defense for the retention of the identities of Jews and those from the nations in Christ resonates with the differentiated scenario concerning Israel and the nations in the *Animal Apocalypse*. The unity of "Jew and Greek" in Christ so that they may jointly worship the God of Israel (Rom. 15:9–11) has strong analogies, not only with the ending of the *Animal Apocalypse*, but with other aspects of this vision as well.[69] The nations' transformation does not mean that they are transformed into Israel; it is, rather, an image that indicates that they join Israel in worship. The culmination of events in *1 En.* 90:37–38 in the temple clearly indicates that the worshipping of Israel and the nations in peace and unity is what is envisaged as the goal of the restoration of Israel, as well as of the nations, to their true calling, not in a assimilative move to sameness, but in diversity. Paul and the Enoch traditions, thus, seem to have significant aspects in common, drawing on a shared pool of traditions that envisage the eschatological events as leading to the overcoming of enmity and the joint worshipping of all peoples in unity in diversity. It is a pool of traditions that decisively differs from that of dominating imperial powers, in its vision in Enoch and in its actualization in the Pauline communities.

Notes

1. Although I doubt that a specific group or movement behind this cluster of texts and traditions can be identified, there must have been groups of people who transmitted these traditions—in my view, complementary, rather than alternative to Mosaic traditions. Cf. Paul Heger, "1 Enoch: Complementary or Alternative to the Mosaic Torah?," *JSJ* 41 (2010): 29–62; see also the discussion by Anathea Portier-Young, *Apocalypse Against Empire: Theologies of Resistance in Early Judaism* (Grand Rapids, MI: Eerdmans, 2011), 294–307.

2. Cf. e. g., George W. E. Nickelsburg, *1 Enoch 1: A Commentary on the Book of 1 Enoch Chapters 1–36; 81–108* (Minneapolis: Fortress, 2001), 445; Daniel Olson, *A New Reading of the Animal Apocalypse of 1 Enoch: 'All Nations Shall Be Blessed'* (Leiden: Brill, 2013), 242–43; Aaron Sherwood, *Paul and the Restoration of Humanity in Light of Ancient Jewish Traditions* (Leiden: Brill, 2013), 14–16; Paul Trebilco, *Self-Designations and Group Identity in the New Testament* (Cambridge: Cambridge University Press 2012), 122–26.

3. Cf. Nickelsburg who notes that "[c]ollective terms like the 'righteous,' the 'chosen,' the 'holy' indicate a consciousness of community though without any

indication that the community had concrete manifestations in specific places" (*1 Enoch 1*, 64).

4. Trebilco, *Self-Designations and Group Identity*, 125.

5. Cf. Loren Stuckenbruck, *1 Enoch 91-108* (Berlin, New York: DeGruyter, 2007).

6. On the designations for the heavenly entourage, see Nickelsburg, *1 Enoch 1*, 43–45.

7. Translation taken from George W. E. Nickelsburg and James C. VanderKam, *1 Enoch: A New Translation* (Minneapolis: Fortress, 2004), 19.

8. Cf. Portier-Young, *Apocalypse Against Empire*, 324. She further notes that the phrase "children of righteousness" identifies "the community's defining characteristic as righteousness or justice entailing righteous deeds, "order of life," and participation in the outworking of divine justice (93.2)."

9. On election, see Joel S. Kaminsky, *Yet I Loved Jacob: Reclaiming the Biblical Concept of Election* (Nashville: Abingdon, 2007).

10. Although the concepts of holy/profane and pure/impure are not the same, there is some overlap and interrelationship between them. The cultic categories of pure/impure did not apply to gentiles/the nations since they were considered profane, and thus, could not come close to the Holy One due to their profane status. Cf. Paula Fredriksen, "Judaizing the Nations: The Ritual Demands of Paul's Gospel," *NTS* 56 (2010): 232–52. The prerequisite in antiquity, generally, for approaching any deity's sphere was a status of purity, achieved through the performance of purification rituals. Cf. Andreas Bendlin, "Purity and Pollution," in *A Companion to Greek Religion*, ed. Daniel Ogden (Oxford: Blackwell, 2007), 178–89, and Jonathan Klawans, *Impurity and Sin in Ancient Judaism* (Oxford: Oxford University Press, 2000). Cf also Beate Ego, "Purity Concepts in Jewish Traditions of the Hellenistic Period," in *Purity and the Forming of Religious Traditions in the Ancient Mediterranean World and Ancient Judaism*, ed. Christian Frevel and Christophe Nihan (Leiden: Brill, 2014), 477–92.

11. Note the Greek here that qualifies this transgression as an act of defilement by the transgressors: μιαίνεσθαι. Stuckenbruck notes that "the angels have breached the boundaries that distinguish the heavenly from the earthly sphere" ("The Eschatological Worship of God by the Nations: An Inquiry into the Early Enoch Tradition," in *With Wisdom as a Robe: Qumran and Other Jewish Studies in Honour of Ida Fröhlich*, ed. Károly Daniel Dobos and Miklós Köszeghy [Sheffield: Sheffield Phoenix, 2009], 189–206).

12. Note that it is the earth here that "raises the voice of their cries to the gates of heaven" (9:2; cf. Rom. 8:19–22).

13. Stuckenbruck, "Eschatological Worship," 189–91.

14. Cf. also Rivka Nir, ""And Behold Lambs Were Born of Those White Sheep" (1

Enoch 90:6): The Color White and Eschatological Expectation in the Animal Apocalypse," *Henoch* 35, no. 1 (2013): 50–69.

15. For further examples and discussion, see ibid., 51–52.

16. The Greek terms consistently translate respective Hebrew terms in Leviticus and Ezekiel, thus λούω, which denotes the washing of the body, translates רחצ and πλύνω translates כבס, whereas καθαρίζω translates טהר.

17. No such distinction is made in the Hebrew that refers to both aspects with the term קדש. Cf. Tessa Rajak, *Translation and Survival: The Greek Bible and the Ancient Jewish Diaspora* (Oxford: Oxford University Press, 2009), 165; also Kathy Ehrensperger, "Called to be ἅγιοι but without εὐσέβεια?: Peculiarities of Cultural Translation in Paul," forthcoming.

18. See my "'Called to be saints': The Identity Shaping Dimension of Paul's Priestly Discourse in Romans," in *Reading Paul in Context: Explorations in Identity Formation, Essays in Honour of William S. Campbell*, ed. J. Brian Tucker and Kathy Ehrensperger (London, New York: T&T Clark 2010), 90–109, and my *Paul at the Crossroads of Cultures: Theologizing in the Space Between* (London, New York: T&T Clark 2013), 175–213; also Pamela Eisenbaum, *Paul was Not a Christian: The Real Message of a Misunderstood Apostle* (New York: HarperOne 2009, 153–67), and Paul Fredriksen, "Paul, Purity and the Ekkelsia of the Gentiles," in *The Beginnings of Christianity: A Collection of Articles*, ed. Jack Pastor and Menachem Mor (Jerusalem: Yad Ben-Zvi Press, 2005), 205–17.

19. The traditional translation of ἡγιάσασθε with "sanctified" is unclear as it does not render the distinction made by Paul's use of respective terminology (rooted in the LXX use) between temporary dedication—thus, a state of sanctification expressed by ἁγνίζω and related terminology—and the permanent status of holiness expressed by ἅγιος and related terminology; cf. above and n. 17.

20. Cf. Gilles Deleuze and Felix Guattari, *Rhizome: Introduction* (Paris: Editions du Minuit, 1976).

21. See Ehrensperger, *Paul at the Crossroads of Cultures*, 178–86; also the volume of essays *Purity and the Forming of Religious Traditions*, ed. Frevel and Nihan.

22. Cf. Reidar Aasgard, *"My Beloved Brothers and Sister": Christian Siblingship in Paul* (London, New York: T&T Clark, 2004), 107–16, 196–99.

23. For a detailed discussion, see my *Paul at the Crossroads of Cultures*, 39–62, 131–39.

24. For a more detailed discussion, see my "Reading Romans "in the Face of the Other": Levinas, the Jewish Philosopher, Meets Paul, the Jewish Apostle," in *Reading Romans with Contemporary Philosophers and Theologians*, ed. David Odell-Scott (Romans Through History and Cultures Series, vol. 7; London, New York: T&T Clark, 2007), 115–54 (133–36).

25. Cf. my *Paul at the Crossroads of Cultures*, 72–97.

26. For the impact of imperial ideology and domination, see e. g., Richard Hingley,

Globalizing Roman Culture: Unity, Diversity and Empire (London: Routledge, 2005); David J. Mattingly, Imperialism, Power, and Identity (Princeton: Princeton University Press, 2011); also Neil Elliott, The Arrogance of Nations: Reading Romans in the Shadow of Empire (Minneapolis: Fortress, 2008), Ian E. Rock, Paul's Letter to the Romans and Roman Imperialism: An Ideological Analysis of the Exordium (Romans 1:1-17) (Eugene, OR: Wipf & Stock, 2012).

27. Andrew Jacobs, Christ Circumcised: A Study in Early Christian History and Difference (Philadelphia: University of Pennsylvania Press, 2012), 9.

28. Josephus B. J. 1.3. Evidence for this perception can still be found in the third-century writings of Clement of Alexandria who refers to part of the Christian tradition as the "barbaric philosophy": see Eric Osborn, Clement of Alexandria (Cambridge: Cambridge University Press, 2005), 92–93.

29. Jacobs, Christ Circumcised, 16.

30. Dmitriev, Sviatoslav, The Greek Slogan of Freedom and Early Roman Politics in Greece (Oxford: Oxford University Press, 2011), 260; also Christian Strecker, "Fides-Pistis-Glaube. Kontexte und Konturen einer Theologie der "Annahme" bei Paulus," in Lutherische und Neue Paulusperspektive, ed. Michael Bachmann (Tübingen: Mohr Siebeck, 2005), 223–50, (236–39), and Ehrensperger, Paul at the Crossroads of Cultures, 167–72.

31. Mattingly, Imperialism, Power, and Identity, 94. This is the case even when the initiative for a treaty came from the non-Roman side, as in the case of the Jews. Cf. also my Paul and the Dynamics of Power: Communication and Interaction in the Early Christ-Movement (London, New York: T&T Clark 2007), 9; Ernst Baltrusch, Die Juden und das Römische Reich: Geschichte einer konfliktreichen Beziehung (Darmstadt: Wissenschaftliche Buchgesellschaft, 2002), 137–41.

32. Mattingly, Imperialism, Power, and Identity, 26.

33. Cf. Tacitus's description of the adoption of Roman practices by elite Britons: "They descended to the seductions to our vices, to porticos, baths and the refinement of dinners. This was called humanitas, civilization amongst the ignorant, although it was an aspect of their enslavement" (Agr. 4.21).

34. Pace e. g., Thorsteinsson who maintains that "[t]he sources reveal clearly how basic the tenet of universal humanity was to the Stoic moral teaching, and how strongly the Stoics emphasised impartiality in human relations [cf. Seneca, Clem. 1.11.2] . . . With this teaching, Seneca and his fellow Stoics sought to point out to people something that was inherent in human life itself, something that already existed as part of the creation of the world. According to the Stoics, then, if properly informed and motivated, people will (re)discover their true nature as human beings and act accordingly" (Runar M. Thorsteinsson, Roman Christianity and Roman Stoicism: A Comparative Study of Ancient Morality [Oxford: Oxford University Press, 2010, 191]). Thorsteinsson seems to overlook the significance of one detail here: that human beings had to be "properly

informed and motivated" in order to "discover their true nature." This information and motivation consisted in nothing other than the Roman perception of *humanitas*. Rather than being evidence for the recognition of a common human nature of all, the concept of *humanitas* attributes to all peoples the potential of being able to conform to the Roman elite way of life. This is far from any recognition of other peoples as human in their particularity and difference. It universalizes an imperialist concept, which is actually very particular.

35. Davina C. Lopez, *Apostle to the Conquered: Reimagining Paul's Mission* (Minneapolis: Fortress, 2008), 172.

36. As Tacitus's comment illustrates: "May the nations retain and perpetuate, if not an affection for us, at least an animosity against each other! Since, while the fate of the empire is thus urgent, fortune can bestow no higher benefit upon us, than the discord of our enemies" (*Maneat, quaeso, duretque gentibus, si non amor nostri, at certe odium sui, quando urgentibus imperii fatis nihil iam praestare fortuna maius potest quam hostium discordiam*; *Germ.* 33.2).

37. James M. Scott, *Paul and the Nations: The Old Testament and Jewish Background of the Nations with Special Reference to the Destination of Galatians* (Tübingen: Mohr Siebeck, 1995), 5–56.

38. Cf. also Isa. 56.6, where we read: "and the foreigners [ἀλλογενής; נכר: "one from a foreign land"] who join themselves to the Lord, to minister to him, to love the name of the Lord, and to be his servants." Similar traditions of a clear distinction between Israel and the nations can be found in Isa. 2:3 (ἔθνη as distinguished from the house of Jacob); Mic. 4:2 (גוים; ἔθνη); Ezek. 47:22–23 (גוים); Ezra 6:21 ("It was eaten by the people of Israel who had returned from exile, also by all who had joined them and separated themselves from the pollutions of the nations of the land to worship [דרש] the Lord, the God of Israel"). Terence L. Donaldson also refers to the narratives of Ruth and Jonah, Solomon's prayer (1 Kgs. 8:23–53), Ps. 96 and, as a peculiar example, Naaman (2 Kgs 8:15; Donaldson, *Judaism and the Gentiles: Jewish Patterns of Universalism* [Waco: Baylor University Press, 2007], 478). Cf. also Frank Crüsemann, ""Ihnen gehören... die Bundesschlüsse" (Röm 9.4). Die alttestamentliche Bundestheologie und der christlich-jüdische Dialog," *Kirche und Israel* 9 (1994): 21–38.

39. Kaminsky is of the view that even a text like Lev. 24:22, that refers to "one law for natives and resident aliens" implies "that the group boundaries remain intact" ("Israel's Election and the Other in Biblical, Second Temple and Rabbinic Thought," in *The "Other" in Second Temple Judaism: Essays in Honor of John J. Collins*, ed. D. C. Harlow et al. (Grand Rapids: Eerdmans, 2011), 17–30, esp. 20.

40. Stuckenbruck notes that "[i]t is not clear . . . that any of these passages refer to a "conversion" of the nations, especially if we define the term "conversion" as the complete transfer from one religion to another" ("Eschatological Worship," 192).

41. James Harrison, *Paul and Imperial Authorities at Thessaloniki and Rome* (Tübingen: Mohr Siebeck, 2011), 36; Brigitte Kahl, *Galatians Re-Imagined: Reading with the Eyes of the Vanquished* (Minneapolis: Fortress, 2010), 242–43.

42. As e. g., Isa. 14:2–9; 29:5–8; 34:1–4; 60:11–16; Jer. 10:25; 25:31–38.

43. Cf. also William S. Campbell, *Unity and Diversity in Christ: Interpreting Paul in Context* (Eugene, OR: Cascade Publishing, 2013), 209–12; Susan Eastman, "Israel and the Mercy of God: A Re-reading of Galatians 6.16 and Romans 9–11," *NTS* 56, no. 3 (2010).

44. Cf also Troels Engberg-Pedersen, ""Everything is Clean" and "Everything that is not of Faith is Sin": The Logic of Pauline Casuistry in Romans 14.1—15.13," in *Paul, Grace, and Freedom: Essays in Honour of John K. Riches*, ed. Paul Middleton et. al. (London, New York: T&T Clark, 2008), 22–38.

45. On distinction, see William S. Campbell, "No Distinction or no Discrimination? The Translation of Διαστολή in Romans 3:22 and 10:12," in *Erlesenes Jerusalem: Festschrift für Ekkehard W. Stegemann*, ed. Lukas Kundert and Christina Tuor-Kurth (Basel: Friedrich Reinhardt, 2013), 353–71.

46. Cf. also Ehrensperger, *Paul and the Dynamics of Power*, 22–24; also William S. Campbell, *Paul and the Creation of Christian Identity* (London, New York: T&T Clark, 2006), 149.

47. Olson's terminology.

48. Olson, *New Reading*, 242.

49. Ibid.

50. Nickelsburg, *1 Enoch 1*, 406, also 40.

51. Aaron Sherwood, *Paul and the Restoration of Humanity*, 200. He concludes that "from *Urzeit* to *Endzeit*, humanity consists of Israel alone, over whom Israel's God ultimately rejoices (*1 En.* 90:38b)." This is matched by his interpretation of Gal. 6:16 by which he affirms that "the ἔθνη audience are definitively and christologically re-identified as Ἰσραὴλ τοῦ θεοῦ" (ibid., 229).

52. Of course, not understood in the modern sense of nation states.

53. Nickelsburg, *1 Enoch 1*, 355. Nickelsburg notes the core significance of the cultic dimension in the narrative here. This is an important aspect of comparison with Paul that cannot be pursued here further.

54. The problem in the Tower of Babel story (Gen. 11:1-9) is uniformity not diversity.

55. Nickelsburg, *1 Enoch 1*, 406, Sherwood, *Paul and the Restoration of Humanity*, 190–91.

56. Olson maintains that ". . . since both sheep and wild animals disappear into a uniform race of white cattle, it is reasonable also to conclude that the *An. Apoc.* expects "Israel" as a distinctive political or ethnic category to evaporate in the

Eschaton" (*New Reading*, 21). See also Sherwood, although differently (*Paul and the Restoration of Humanity*, 200).

57. Clearly noted by Nickelsburg, who in his comment on 89:10–12 writes that "the author has drawn on the animal imagery here from Ezekiel 34, where the wild animals . . . representing the nations, prey on the sheep of Israel . . . ," and further: "Thus the author introduces here the antagonists in the central drama of the Vision: the struggle between Israel and the Gentiles who prey on them, disperse them, and destroy them" (*1 Enoch 1*, 377, also 358).

58. Cf. also Olson, *New Reading*, 76–78.

59. Nickelsburg, *1 Enoch 1*, 356, also 63.

60. Ibid., 371.

61. Nir, "'Behold Lambs'," 50–69.

62. Nir argues that the reappearance of the color white in 90:6 "indicates inauguration of a new period, namely that the eschatological-apocalyptic has dawned" (Ibid., 58).

63. I would like to thank Bill, who has drawn my attention to this aspect of the image.

64. The reference to thick and pure wool indicates that these are strong and healthy sheep nurtured on good pastures, an image that is contrasted by the earlier images of violent destruction, where the seer sees the sheep being "devoured by the dogs and by the eagles and by the kites. And they left them neither flesh nor skin nor sinew, until only their bones remained" (*1 En.* 90:4).

65. Nickelsburg, *1 Enoch 1*, 403; for a discussion of the issues involved here, see also Olson, *New Reading*, 19–22.

66. Cf. Stuckenbruck, "Eschatological Worship," 204.

67. Although Stuckenbruck translates *wa-k*ᵂ*ellu* as "alongside," and thus, sees gentiles included in the gathering in the temple, he seems to imply that only the predators and birds mentioned in v. 37 are being transformed into white bulls, although there is some ambivalence in his statement. Cf. "Eschatological Worship," 204.

68. The argument that the transformation of all into white cattle—that is, into the image and likeness of the white bull—is analogous to Adam, who is created in the image and likeness of God, cannot serve as an argument for the overcoming of difference as in Gen. 1:27. Adam is created male and female, and thus, diversity is inherent in the creation of humankind.

69. Although of course the order of events is reversed in Paul's scenario.

PART IV

Paul between Empire and Jewish Identity

8

Engendering Judaism

Paul, Baptism, and Circumcision

Joshua Garroway

Though he is hardly the first to express it, Andrew Jacobs, in his new volume *Christ Circumcised: A Study in Early Christian History and Difference*, provides a compelling description of the role played by circumcision in the imperial Roman effort to surveil its diverse population.[1] For Roman writers, circumcision became the Jewish stereotype par excellence, the mark that signified Jewishness. Alongside the "effete Persian," the "educated Greek," the "painted Gaul," and other stereotyped ethnic minorities stood the "circumcised Jew," and over all of them was perched the Roman Empire exercising what Jacobs calls "epistemological colonial control," or "optical dominance."[2] Moreover, Jacobs contends—as the mark by which the empire identified Jews—circumcision became a matter around which Jews debated their own understanding of Jewish identity, a debate ranging from, on one extreme, the rejection of circumcision by the so-called radical allegorists of Alexandria, to, on the other, the "rabbinic mania for circumcision."[3] Circumcision, thus, stood at the crossroads between imperial domination and Jewish self-understanding.

Paul, of course, also has much to say about circumcision. In some way or another, that Jewish ritual occupies his attention in portions of Romans, Philippians, and First Corinthians, while his polemic against it constitutes the focus of his Epistle to the Galatians. Before addressing Paul's view of circumcision, however, it is worth considering one further observation by Jacobs about Jewish circumcision in antiquity. The Romans, he notes, could hardly have chosen a less practical mark through which to express their ocular dominance over Jews. On the one hand, Jews were not the only circumcised population in the empire; on the other, circumcisions are concealed beneath clothing, thus obscuring the Roman gaze and prompting bizarre juridical situations such as that of the accused tax-dodger who, according to Suetonius's famous report, was required to disrobe before a procurator.[4] This inspection naturally raises an even more glaring flaw in circumcision as a stereotypical marker—that only about half the Jewish population was circumcised! A tax-dodging Jewess, Jacobs observes, might never have been detected.[5] As a concealed marker executable on male bodies only, circumcision was a deficient object of imperial surveillance.

The maleness of circumcision posed limitations from the Jewish perspective too, at least in certain situations. As the symbol of the Abrahamic covenant and a sine qua non for (male) Jewish identity, circumcision, by the imperial period, had come to mark the ontological transition through which a male gentile became a proselyte. Circumcision was the transformative final step in a male gentile's becoming a Jew: male gentiles, but obviously, not women. Absent circumcision, what was the transformative final step in a female's becoming a proselyte? Immersion would become that ritual in the rabbinic period, but there is no evidence to suggest that proselyte Baptism was practiced by Jews in the first century CE. Yet, ample evidence indicates that women of that era were interested in Judaism, with some of them going to great lengths to observe Jewish customs or participate in Jewish communities. The silence of ancient texts regarding a transformational ritual for female proselytes has bewildered even the best historians and led at least one to conclude that, except through marriage, it was simply not possible for a woman to convert to Judaism in the same sense that a man could.[6] An interested gentile woman might exhibit sympathy for Jews, adopt Jewish customs, or participate in a Jewish community, but joining the Jewish community in the capacity of a proselyte was inconceivable.

Accordingly, Paul's apparent repudiation of circumcision in favor of Baptism has often been understood as a triumph for egalitarianism over discrimination. Certainly, ancient Christian polemicists understood it that way, but so have many modern commentators. Troy Martin, for example, writes that "whereas not everyone in the Jewish community is circumcised, everyone in the Christian community is baptized. Thus, baptism into Christ provides for a unity that cannot be realized in a circumcised community."[7] Elizabeth Schüssler Fiorenza similarly notes that "if it was no longer circumcision but baptism which was the primary rite of initiation, then women became full members of the people of God with the same rights and duties."[8]

While these assessments of Paul are correct inasmuch as they note that Baptism was more universally executable than genital circumcision, my own reading of Paul varies slightly, but importantly. I have argued that Paul does not repudiate circumcision in favor of Baptism; he does not replace circumcision with Baptism as the mode of entry into God's covenant people. Rather, Paul retains circumcision as the initiatory Jewish rite, but reinterprets it so that, in the wake of Christ, circumcision is achieved *through* Baptism. As Paul (or a later disciple) observes in Col. 2:11-13, Baptism provides gentile initiates with a putative flesh-shedding circumcision, such that they are regarded, as Paul puts it in Rom. 2:26, as having a circumcised glans despite empirical reality. They have been transformed ontologically so as to bear the mark of penile circumcision necessary for inclusion in the Abrahamic covenant. Far from replacing the discriminatory circumcision with the universalizing Baptism, Paul universalizes circumcision itself, making it possible for all people to be circumcised. Thus, he can exhort his Philippian community—some of whom are circumcised, some of whom are not (and cannot be)—with the bold proclamation that "we are the circumcision" (Phil. 3:3). Circumcision for male initiates in Philippi, as in Galatia or elsewhere, is therefore unnecessary because, as a result of their Baptism, they have already been circumcised, as have their female counterparts.[9]

Why Paul understood Baptism as a putative circumcision is difficult to determine. In Romans, Paul suggests that Christ-mediated circumcision constituted a fulfillment of the covenantal promises to the patriarchs. Abraham had been promised that he would become a father of many nations, a forbear whose diverse descendants would inherit the world (Rom. 4:13–18). The Christ event made the creation of such a family possible, for by being baptized into Christ's death and resurrection, gentiles could acquire the circumcision required to join. Thus, Paul could call Abraham "the father of the circumcised": a constituency that includes both circumcised Jews and uncircumcised, yet baptized, gentiles (Rom. 4:12). Paul could also celebrate Christ as an "agent of circumcision" who welcomes gentiles into the covenant (Rom. 15:7–13).

Romans is possibly Paul's latest extant epistle, however, and I wonder whether the theological explanation for circumcision qua Baptism expressed in that letter is his only or even his original rationale. Presently, I would like to explore the possibility that at least one of Paul's motivations for interpreting Baptism as a stand-in for circumcision—perhaps even the original one—was the need to overcome the impossibility of circumcision for women. In short, I will suggest that Paul's unprecedented, apocalyptic mission to the gentiles called on him, more so than any Jew before him, to resolve the "woman question" in ancient Jewish proselytism. Tasked with bringing droves of gentiles—both men and women—into God's people before the imminent return of Christ, and knowing fully well that circumcision was the rite of entry into that people, Paul had to conceptualize a way for women to become circumcised. He surmised that the initiatory rite of Baptism was tantamount to circumcision. In so doing, one might contend, Paul founded the very idea of female conversion to Judaism.

The Woman Question in Ancient Jewish Proselytism

The when, where, and why of the emergence of conversion to Judaism remain elusive.[10] Cohen's well-known proposal—that conversion arose during the Hasmonean period when, for various reasons, Jews began to understand Jewishness as more an ethno-religious complex than an ethnicity—has been warmly received, notwithstanding Seth Schwartz's concern that the account is "too simple, monocausal and starkly binary."[11] However it emerged, a welter of evidence reveals that conversion was an established institution in most Jewish circles by the high Roman Empire.[12] Ongoing debate surrounds the extent to which proselytes became Jews *stricto sensu* (that is, *Ioudaioi*) as a result of conversion, but no one disputes that proselytes were among the Jewish ranks by the first century CE.

Circumcision was the mark that distinguished proselytes from sympathizers, as numerous sources indicate: (1) the earliest (albeit fictitious) accounts of conversion feature circumcision (Achior the Ammonite in Jth. 14:10 and Antiochus IV Epiphanes in 2 Macc. 9:12–17); (2) the mass conversions of the Idumeans and Itureans, reported by Josephus, were effected by circumcision (*A. J.* 13:257–58, 318–19); (3) circumcision was apparently expected of gentiles prior to marriage with Jewish royals (e. g., *A. J.* 20:139, 145–46); (4) in the tale of Izates, circumcision distinguishes between adherence and conversion (*A. J.* 20:17–48); and (5) countless non-Jewish authors express the belief that circumcision indicates a convert.[13] There is no disputing that circumcision, as Wolf Liebeshuetz puts it, "was of course the decisive step in the making of a Jewish proselyte."[14]

The conundrum, then, is what to make of the apparently large number of gentile women interested in Judaism around the turn of the millennium: women so often identified by historians as proselytes. If circumcision was the "decisive step" in conversion for men, what was the transformational rite for these women? Judith Lieu captures the dilemma when she writes:

> It has frequently been noted that before the end of the first century CE it is obscure what conversion meant for a woman, and how a woman convert differed from a female firm sympathizer (or God-fearer). In most cases, perhaps, inclusion in the community was simply through marriage to a Jewish husband, or—more ambiguously—adoption as a slave; but for other women, particularly those who remained married to their pagan husbands, with all the consequences that might entail for possible observation of the commandments, there was, as far as we can tell, no clear ceremony and perhaps no clear agreed idea of conversion. This accords oddly with the fact that both literary and inscriptional evidence indicates that there were women who were reckoned by some or by themselves to be proselytes, and that we are often told in the secondary literature that Judaism was attractive for women.[15]

As Lieu observes, Jewish communities incorporated women through marriage or possibly slavery, a tradition probably extending as far back as the biblical period. But how did women unaffiliated with Jewish men become proselytes? Only meager evidence supports the claim that the ritual immersion described in rabbinic literature had its origin in the first century CE or earlier.[16] Yet, there is no report of any other conversionary rite for women, giving historians over to the conclusion reached by Lieu that "there was . . . no clear ceremony and perhaps no clear agreed idea of conversion."[17]

Lieu, nevertheless, refers to the "literary and inscriptional evidence" that indicates that, despite the lack of evidence describing a formal rite of conversion, there were women in antiquity who saw themselves or were seen by others as proselytes. I am not certain the evidence is so clear. Lieu cites Bernadette Brooten's *Women Leaders in the Ancient Synagogue*, in which Brooten contends that "scholars have recognized for some time that women proselytes are mentioned relatively frequently in ancient sources."[18] But the sources Brooten adduces as proof are hardly unambiguous references to female proselytes. She mentions the wives in Damascus who, according to Josephus, "with few exceptions had been drawn away to the Jewish religion" (*J. W.* 2:560), but nothing in that description requires one to assume that Josephus means anything other than affection for Jewish rites. The same can be said of Brooten's next two examples: Helena of Adiabene and Fulvia the Roman matron. The former is said to have been "instructed by some other Jew and gone over to their laws" (A. J. 20:35); the latter "went over to the Jewish laws" (A. J. 18:82). Neither expression necessarily distinguishes these women from Jewish sympathizers. Brooten also refers to five inscriptions from Italy, allegedly indicating female proselytes, but as Margaret Williams notes, "Noy's dating of these inscriptions to the third to fourth century CE means that they cannot be used as evidence for the first century."[19] It is, therefore, debatable whether there are *any* unambiguous references to female proselytes before the rabbinic period. That many gentile women expressed a commitment to Judaism—in some cases, a profound commitment—is indisputable, but there are grounds for supposing that, without the possibility of circumcision, even the most committed gentile woman could not become a proselyte.

As far as I can tell, only one historian has said as much. Cohen reveals that view over the course of his groundbreaking study on ancient Jewish identity, *The Beginnings of Jewishness*. At first, he expresses uncertainty regarding the matter of female conversion. Having asked hypothetically whether a woman could convert to Judaism outside of a marital setting before the second century CE, Cohen writes, "if the answer is yes, how should a female convert be distinguished from a female 'Godfearer' or 'sympathizer'? The answer is not clear."[20] Yet, later, he appears more certain that the answer to the first question is "no," noting in his discussion of the rabbinic conversion protocol that "the emergence of immersion as a conversion ritual is no doubt to be connected with the emergence of the possibility that women too could convert to Judaism, not merely through marriage to a Jewish spouse but in their own right."[21] At book's end, Cohen reaffirms the linkage of immersion with female conversion:

> . . . the idea of conversion to Judaism . . . is a creation of the Hasmonean period. At first it was an option only for men; its ritual was circumcision. . . . Gradually, however, conversion for women was

introduced; its ritual was immersion (a practice that also became part of the conversion ritual for men).[22]

Such a historical connection between immersion and female conversion suggests that, lacking evidence for proselyte immersion before the second century CE, it is reasonable to assume that female conversion was also not conceptualized until then.

To buttress that point, consider the two fullest accounts of alleged female conversion in Greek literature. The accounts of Helena and Asenath are routinely adduced as the surefire proof of female proselytism. I suspect they might demonstrate the opposite. Josephus reports that Helena of Adiabene, along with her son Izates, "changed their life to the customs of the Jews" (A. J. 20:17). Helena encounters Judaism through an unnamed teacher while Izates resides at Charax-Spasini, a sojourn during which he himself comes under the tutelage of the teacher Ananias and also embraces Jewish ways. Upon returning to Adiabene to claim his throne, Izates is pleased to learn that his mother shares his affinity for Judaism and he hastens to become circumcised, thinking it is the only way he can become "certainly a Jew" (βεβαίως Ἰουδαῖος; A. J. 20:38). Terence Donaldson offers a savvy way to read this scene as indicating that Josephus considers Helena to be a full-fledged proselyte.[23] He notes that the action of Izates is introduced by the Greek αὐτός, suggesting that Izates wishes to do what his mother has also done. Since Izates pursues full proselytism by means of circumcision, Josephus must have understood his mother, too, as a full proselyte.

I wonder whether this reading begs the question, however. If one assumes that a first-century Jew such as Josephus recognized the possibility of female proselytism, then the sentence may well indicate that Josephus considers Helena to have converted fully already. If one assumes that female proselytism was as yet unimaginable, then Josephus could merely be saying that Izates wished to follow his mother's lead in Judaizing to the greatest extent possible. For a woman, that meant the most thoroughgoing commitment in the capacity of a sympathizer; for a man, commitment to the point of circumcision as a proselyte. In this regard, Josephus's description of the Roman commander Metilius might be apposite. His garrison having been (unscrupulously) butchered by Jewish rebels, Metilius saves his own hide by agreeing "to Judaize as far as circumcision" (μέχρι περιτομῆς ἰουδαΐζειν; J. W. 2:454). Is it possible that, in the view of Josephus, a man such as Izates or Metilius can Judaize to the point of circumcision—to wit, to the point of conversion—whereas a woman can merely Judaize?

Another wrinkle in the account of Adiabene leads me to suspect that Josephus believes just that. Helena admonishes Izates against circumcision out of fear that his subjects will resent being ruled by a Jew. So long as he remains in the capacity of a sympathizer, she reckons, Izates will be safe. A question I have never seen raised with respect to this detail in the story is why Helena, the supposed convert, does not worry about her own safety just the same? If she has indeed become a full convert, would not her subjects resent being ruled by a "foreign" queen? Granted Helena is not a queen regnant and does not, technically speaking, rule her subjects, but Josephus makes clear that she is a public figure with at least some measure of power, especially after the death of her husband. It is she who gathers the nobles, governors, and generals of the kingdom and exhorts them by a speech to honor the dead king's plan for succession. Why would such leaders honor the request of this proselyte queen if they might be expected to balk at the succession of a proselyte king? One possibility is that Josephus envisions Helena not as a proselyte, but as a sympathizer, safe from the accusations of foreignness Izates will face if he becomes a proselyte through circumcision.[24]

Unlike Josephus, the author of *Joseph and Asenath* does describe the elaborate process by which his female protagonist joins the Jewish people. First, Asenath undergoes the sort of theological transformation one imagines Helena, Fulvia, or other Jewish sympathizers experienced, as she acknowledges the vanity of idols, repents of her sins, and confesses loyalty to the God of Israel. Then, comes the mysterious rite by which she is "made new, and refashioned, and given new life" (*Jos. Asen.* 15:3). In the presence of an angel, Asenath eats from a celestial honeycomb and is enveloped temporarily by a swarm of bees. Whatever the source of the peculiar bee imagery, the ritual is clearly meant to describe Asenath's transition from her own people to the Jewish people, a conversion necessary before she weds the pious Joseph.[25]

Does that mean Asenath is represented as a full proselyte, a genuine initiate into the covenant of Israel? I think the answer is yes. Does that mean female proselytism was a real possibility in the time and place in which the author of *Joseph and Asenath* lived?[26] On that score, I am not so sure. The remarkable nature of Asenath's conversion may indicate, rather, that the author is at a loss to explain how a gentile woman might actually cross the boundary and become a proselyte. She can repent, change her behavior, or swear allegiance to God, but such is the conduct of any devoted sympathizer. If she is to marry Joseph, she must be transformed ontologically into a Jew. Unable to conceive of a mundane act through which that transformation might be depicted (for example, by circumcision or immersion), the author draws upon celestial imagery. God's own representative confirms Asenath's new status by allowing her to consume heavenly food. In other words, the author wants readers to appreciate that Asenath has become a Jew, but in the absence of any discourse governing female proselytism, the only recourse is to a dramatic, miraculous, divinely-mediated ritual.

As such, that ritual features a suggestive peculiarity. At one point, the man from heaven touches first the easternmost, and then, the northernmost corner of the honeycomb, and, while doing so, "the path of his finger became like blood" (16:10). If this image represents the Christian cross, as Rivka Nir has proposed, then the scene stems from the second century CE or later and is not relevant to a study of Jewish proselytism in any case.[27] If the image is at home in an earlier Jewish setting, I am not sure what to make of it. I do find it fascinating, though, that the shedding of blood is an integral part of the rite. If, as I am conjecturing, the scene results from a Jewish author's quandary over how to represent the seeming impossibility of a female conversion, then the blood might be explained as analogous to the blood shed by gentile men at conversion. That is highly speculative, of course, but so are all other interpretations of this mysterious narrative.

In any case, the miraculous nature of Asenath's conversion suggests that—if the work is to be regarded as Jewish—female conversion to Judaism may not have been an actual possibility in the author's community. Nor was it necessarily a possibility in the eyes of Josephus. As Cohen correctly observes, "at first [conversion] was an option only for men" because circumcision was its definitive rite. Some Jewish communities in the first century CE may have conceptualized female proselytism and developed criteria for distinguishing a convert, but their innovation has not left any significant mark in the historical record—one notable exception notwithstanding.

Paul understood Baptism into Christ as just that sort of conversionary rite. Through it gentiles, both men and women, became circumcised and joined the covenant of Israel, thereby preparing themselves to stand in judgment before Christ at his imminent return.

The Woman Question in Earliest Christianity

Like the origin of Jewish conversion, the origin of the gentile mission is obscure. Paul's uncontested epistles provide a glimpse of that mission as it existed in the 50s, by which time, it had been under way for a while. Hints about what happened in the past crop up periodically in the Pauline corpus, but such references are limited and prejudicial. Acts, on the contrary, offers a detailed account of the church's first decade, but the historical reliability of that narrative has been frequently (and, in my opinion, appropriately) questioned. Acts is not a transparent window into events as they really happened. Then again, even if Acts were reckoned a straightforwardly reliable historical report, Luke is far from clear about when, where, and how the gentile mission commenced. Arguments could be made that it starts with the conversion of the Ethiopian eunuch (8:26–40), with the conversion of Cornelius (10:1–11:48), with Peter's defense in Jerusalem (11:1–18), with the turning of the Cypriot and Cyrenean Jews to Greeks in Antioch (11:19–20), with Paul's first declared "turn to the gentiles" in Antioch of Pisidia (13:46), or with the authorization of the mission at the Jerusalem conference (15:1–35).

This study makes two assumptions about the earliest gentile mission. One is so widely accepted that it can be proposed without argument; the other is controversial and will be defended at length. First, I contend, the earliest gentile mission was apocalyptic in character. Whenever and wherever the first concerted overtures to gentiles were made, the missionaries doing so expected Christ to return soon. Such eschatological anticipation on the part of the earliest Christians is confirmed by evidence in the Gospels, Acts, and of course Paul, so that there is every reason to believe that the first gentiles were baptized into the movement with the expectation that they would encounter Christ before their end.

Second, I propose that most, if not all, of the first wave of male gentiles to be baptized also became circumcised. Such is not the *communis opinio*, which holds that most, if not all, gentiles were brought aboard from the start without circumcision.[28] There is no explicit evidence one way or the other. The best reason for supposing that the earliest outreaches to gentiles required circumcision is that Paul—who fashions himself an apostle to the gentiles (Rom. 11:13), entrusted with the gospel for the gentiles (Gal. 2:7), commissioned by God to preach Christ among the gentiles (Gal. 1:16), and acknowledged by his colleagues as a co-steward of the mission to the gentiles (Gal. 2:9)—says that he used to require circumcision. Amidst his rebuke of the Galatians for abandoning his "persuasion" in favor of his rivals, Paul defends himself against an accusation that he thinks has been leveled against him in his absence: "Brethren, if I am still preaching circumcision, why am I still being persecuted?" (Gal. 5:11) Paul's apology is curious. One wonders on what basis Paul was being accused of preaching, or having preached, circumcision. All the more so does one wonder why Paul concedes that the accusation, while it no longer holds water, would have been true in the past. His twofold use of ἔτι implies that he did indeed "preach circumcision" at an earlier point, and that the proof he no longer preaches so is to be found in his ongoing persecution. The difficulty of Gal. 5:11 thus boils down to two vexing questions: Why would anyone accuse Paul of preaching circumcision, currently or ever, and why would Paul concede that he once preached it?

Two solutions have dominated. Some insist that "preaching circumcision" refers to Paul's life prior to his revelation of Christ, perhaps even as a full-fledged Jewish missionary.[29] As Douglas A. Campbell observes, however, Paul's opponents would not have been likely to invoke such activity because the accusation would lack rhetorical punch in the Galatian situation.[30] Why would Paul's opponents base an accusation on Paul's Pharisaic past, knowing that Paul could, and would, admit to that period in his life, yet disregard it as irrelevant (Gal. 1:13–14; Phil. 3:7–8)? Moreover, a significant amount of time had passed since Paul's days as a Pharisee. The other solution considers a more recent event, the circumcision of Timothy, to be the basis of the opponents' accusation. Knowing that he had demanded that particular circumcision, Paul's adversaries alleged—honestly or disingenuously—that Paul advocated circumcision at least in some cases, if not more broadly. While it is defensible, this interpretation relies entirely on the historicity of Acts 16:1–3; Paul himself says nothing about circumcising Timothy. It also militates against the plain sense of Paul's apology, which sounds as if Paul concedes to having preached circumcision on more than one occasion.

The apology makes most sense, as Campbell puts it, "only if Paul really did preach circumcision at some previous point in his life as an apostle to the pagans," not simply on one extraordinary occasion (that is, with Timothy).[31] Further evidence, admittedly circumstantial, supports this conclusion. First, there is the chronology of Paul's career. In Gal. 1:11–16, Paul mentions two prior revelations, one in which he received his gospel (1:11–12) and one in which he received his commission to preach to gentiles (1:16). It is possible that Paul describes one and the same revelation,[32] but just the same, he could be referring to two discrete events. Paul makes no mention of the gospel when describing his initial revelation of Christ (1:16); moreover, what follows in Gal. 1:17–2:10 makes it more likely that, if Paul's gospel preaches salvation without circumcision, then it was not delivered to him in that first encounter. Paul admits to having spent a fortnight in Jerusalem three years after that revelation, during which visit, he interacted with Cephas and James (1:18–19). Unless Paul simply fails to mention it, Paul's circumcision-free preaching was not then an issue. Given the tremendous controversy over circumcision some fourteen years later, it is striking that a discussion did not surface at all in Paul's first consultation with the Jerusalem authorities.[33] Possibly, Paul withheld his view of circumcision from Cephas and James, or, alternatively, muted a preliminary conflict with the pillars when communicating with the Galatians, but in either case, it remains perplexing that the issue of circumcising gentiles, which reached such a fever pitch seventeen years after Paul's first revelation, took so long to boil. The delayed emergence makes sense if Paul was not yet preaching a circumcision-free gospel when he first visited James and Cephas—that is, if Paul's opposition to circumcision emerged sometime between his first and second visits to Jerusalem. Paul's autobiographical remarks, thus, accommodate the view that Paul advocated circumcision for gentiles before he opposed it.

The customary dating of Paul's epistles provides more circumstantial evidence for that view. If, as the majority of scholars contends, all of Paul's undisputed letters were composed after the meeting described in Gal. 2:1–10—between the late 40s and the early 60s—then more than a decade of Paul's career remains unaccounted for. Without resorting to Acts, we know only that some (or all) of that murky period was spent in Syria, Cilicia, Arabia, and Damascus, from which city he escaped in a basket during the reign of King Aretas (2 Cor. 11:32–33). Did Paul compose epistles during this time? If so, why have they not survived? Why have seven of Paul's epistles from the latter half of his career survived—in fact, more than seven, seeing as the Corinthian correspondence comprises at least three discrete letters—when nothing survives from Paul's campaigns in the 30s and early 40s? Any attempt to account for this phenomenon will constitute an argument from silence, but some such arguments are better than others. It is certainly plausible that remnants of Paul's early career vanished because the initial collector(s) of Paul's epistles was a partisan of the "latter" Paul—the Paul who opposed circumcision—and any material that advocated circumcision was disregarded (or discarded).

There is no way to know whether Paul founded the mission to the gentiles or whether he joined such a movement soon after it was afoot, as Acts 11:19-26 suggests. In either case, Paul was an early principal in the movement. If he was "preaching circumcision," there is reason to believe his colleagues were preaching similarly,[34] and if so, what precipitated his and/or their eventual change of heart? Why did Paul, who once preached circumcision, become so vociferous an opponent of circumcision for gentiles by the time he penned Galatians, Philippians, and Romans?

In fact, the "why" question is thorny, no matter when and where one places the decision not to circumcise baptized gentiles. If the majority is right and the first missionaries to the gentiles—be they Paul, Barnabas, or other "Hellenists" in Antioch—did not circumcise their charges, why did they not? So, James D. G. Dunn understandably asks: "When circumcision was so integral to the being of a Jewish male, why did the other Jews involved in the new sect as it began to reach out to Gentiles not simply assume that circumcision was, of course, the rite of entry into the people of God?"[35] Accordingly, he describes (what he calls) the fact that the first missionaries did not demand circumcision from gentiles as "shocking to almost any Jewish sensibility."[36] The reason they did not circumcise, he goes on to allege, is that they were awestruck by the demonstration of the Spirit evident in the baptized gentiles, and thus, concluded that circumcision would be superfluous. God obviously had accepted them already. Others have proposed alternative explanations for the presumed reluctance to circumcise. Martin Hengel, in his famous reconstruction of the early church, based on Acts 6, contends that the Hellenists were attuned to a universalist trajectory in Judaism that already had them criticizing the Law and the temple even before they first reached out to gentiles.[37] Paula

Fredriksen emphasizes the eschatological expectations among Jews during the Second Commonwealth, the texts expressing which do not suggest that gentiles at the end of time will become Jews through circumcision.[38] All these explanations assume that the first missionaries to the gentiles were content to let their charges remain gentiles. I agree with Dunn that such a decision would have been "shocking to almost any Jewish sensibility"; indeed, too shocking to any Jewish sensibility, which is why Paul and his colleagues preached circumcision to gentiles before they did not.

That being the case, what caused these missionaries, or at least Paul, to change course? I suspect that one significant factor in that decision was the theological problem posed by the admission of women. The earliest gentile mission was a movement to secure proselytes to the Jewish covenant, and, as such, it had to deal with the impossibility of circumcising women. In fact, the gentile mission was a unique and unprecedented phenomenon in Jewish history that demanded a resolution to the "woman question," for the gentile mission was both proselytizing and apocalyptic—something that had never been seen before. Jews of ages past had proselytized gentiles, even in large numbers. A case in point is the conversion of the Idumeans and Itureans during the reign of John Hyrcanus, when probably thousands upon thousands of gentile men were circumcised. No source indicates that Idumean or Iturean women underwent any sort of conversionary rite, however, because their inclusion in the Judean state was irrelevant in the eyes of their conquerors. On the contrary, before Paul, there had been apocalyptic movements among Jews—the ministry of John the Baptist, for example, or the rebellion of Judas the Galilean, or even the ministry of Jesus himself—but none of these appears to have taken an interest in the eschatological status of gentiles, men or women. Preparing Jews for the end of times was the order of the day.

As such, the gentile mission blazed a new trail. It was an apocalyptic movement intent on preparing individuals for the imminent culmination of history by securing their standing in God's covenant; it was also a proselytizing movement intent on introducing gentiles into the covenant alongside Jews. Whereas the Hasmoneans did not confront the impossibility of incorporating Idumean women into the covenant presumably because such inclusion was irrelevant, missionaries such as Paul and Barnabas assumed that women, just as men, would soon face judgment before Christ. Rectifying their covenantal status was, therefore, of utmost importance. As the author of *Joseph and Asenath* had to determine a way to make Asenath Jewish enough to marry Joseph and did so by putting her conversion in the hands of God, the early Christian missionaries had to figure a way to make gentile women Jewish enough to pass muster at the end—but a mundane ritual would have to suffice.

Paul formulated the elegant solution to the dilemma, or at least, it is in his letters in which the solution is articulated. Baptism, Paul argues, is tantamount to circumcision. It is a virtual enactment of genital circumcision. Women baptized into Christ, therefore, become reckoned as though they possess a penis that has had its foreskin removed—that is to say, reckoned as though they are entrants to the Abrahamic covenant. Paul expresses this view several times in his epistles, most notably at the end of Romans. In Rom. 15:7–13, Paul exhorts his gentile audience to "welcome one another, just as Christ welcomed you into the glory of God" (verse 7). Christ welcomed them, Paul goes on to say, by becoming a "διάκονος περιτομῆς on behalf of the truth of God" (verse 8). While διάκονος περιτομῆς has traditionally been rendered "servant of the circumcision," suggesting an allusion to Jesus' ministry among Jews during his lifetime, I have argued that a preferable translation is "agent of circumcision," suggesting an allusion to the circumcision experienced by Roman gentiles at their Baptism.[39] Paul's imagery in Rom. 2:26 indicates that their baptismal circumcision was not merely one of the heart, but also of the penis, as it causes a foreskinned penis (and, I am assuming, a woman's non-penis) to be reckoned as a circumcised glans.[40] Colossians 2:11 speaks similarly, describing the "circumcision not wrought by hands" undergone by the Colossians at their Baptism, a circumcision achieved by "stripping off the body of the flesh." Because baptized gentiles have been circumcised in this manner, Paul can suggest that Abraham is, for them, a "father of circumcision" (Rom. 4:12) and include them in his declaration that "it is we who are the circumcision" (Phil. 3:3).[41]

Admittedly, more than a decade separates the penning of Romans and Philippians from the time when Paul will have stopped demanding circumcision, and in those letters, his equating of Baptism with circumcision comes in the context of the debate over circumcising men. Against missionaries who would claim, or are claiming, that baptized men require circumcision, Paul contends that Baptism already provides such men the genital circumcision needed to the enter the Abrahamic covenant. To circumcise them (again) would constitute mutilation (Phil. 3:2) and would deny the effect of Christ's death and resurrection (Gal. 5:11). While women, too, were certainly included among those putatively circumcised Romans and Philippians, Paul never says explicitly that the extension of covenantal status to women was one of the reasons for his initial abandonment of circumcision. That said, the gentile mission's unique and unprecedented combination of aims—both apocalyptic and proselytizing—lays the foundation for at least a circumstantial case.

There is other circumstantial evidence as well. First and foremost is the famous formulation of pairs in Gal. 3:28. Paul's inclusion of male-female and slave-free alongside Jew-gentile remains one of the more nagging difficulties in Pauline interpretation. Determining how these former pairs relate to Paul's argument is no easy task. Most commonly, it is suggested that Paul is invoking a baptismal formula in which these pairs appear, but Troy Martin has argued convincingly for interpreting Gal. 3:28 in conjunction with the institution of circumcision in Gen. 17:9–14.[42] That foundational passage explains which persons are obligated to be circumcised: Jews (not gentiles), slaves (not free foreigners), and men (not women). By including those pairs at the conclusion of his argument in Galatians 3, Paul shows that the covenant of Baptism does not discriminate as does the covenant of circumcision: Baptism is available to Jews and gentiles, slaves and free persons, men and women. Based on what I have argued above, I would adjust that claim slightly: the covenant of circumcision, when effected through Baptism, becomes available to Jews and gentiles, slaves and free persons, men and women. Paul's point is that Baptism into Christ makes any person—whether Jew, Greek, slave, free, man, or woman—into a descendant of Abraham and an heir, according to the promise, and as such, circumcised. That is why Galatian men, to whom the epistle is implicitly addressed (see Gal. 5:2), should not pursue (empirical) circumcision, for to do so would be to acknowledge a conception of circumcision that cannot incorporate all persons into the Abrahamic covenant. Assuming that Paul is not here, for the first time, correlating Baptism with Gen. 17:9–14 and with the discriminatory nature of circumcision, there is reason to suppose that the "woman question" had already crossed Paul's mind in the past.

No less suggestive is the manner in which Acts describes the introduction of gentile women into the movement. That women were among the first worshippers of Jesus in the wake of his execution is emphasized by Luke in an almost heavy-handed way. "Certain women" accompany the apostles already in Acts 1:14, while "both men and women" are said explicitly to receive God's spirit in the passage from Joel quoted at Pentecost (Acts 2:18), to be among the converts at Solomon's portico (5:18), to be pursued by Saul (8:3; 9:2; 22:4), and to be converted by Philip in Samaria (8:12). These women, however, are Jewish (or Samarian). No gentile women appear in the narrative until Acts 13:50, in which case they are arrayed *against* Paul and Barnabas. The Jews of Pisidian Antioch request the assistance of prominent gentile women sympathetic to Judaism in casting out the apostles from the city. Yet, the next one reads of gentile women, they are the targets of Paul's missionizing in his very first stop following the Jerusalem conference. Paul seeks out women gathered by the river in Philippi, among whom is the gentile sympathizer Lydia. Lydia and her household are promptly baptized, as are leading gentile women in Thessaloniki (17:4), Beroea (17:12), and Athens (17:34). To be sure, it is possible that Luke understands women to have been included in the group to whom Peter preached in the house of Cornelius, among the

Greeks to whom the Cypriot and Cyrenean Jews preached in Antioch (11:20), or among the gentiles converted in Pisidian Antioch (13:48) and Iconium (14:1). But Luke makes no mention of women in those cases—a stark contrast to the explicit mention of women from the start of Paul's ministry in Macedonia and Achaea. It is no less possible, then, that Luke sees the confirmation of Paul's circumcision-free gospel at the Jerusalem conference as the decision that enabled missionaries to conceptualize the inclusion of gentile women in the movement. This reading would cohere felicitously with Luke's description of the Pharisaic objections that trigger the conference, which appear to assume that the gentile converts under discussion are men (Acts 15:5).

A final circumstantial factor is the prominent role of women in Paul's ministry. How many women there were and just what roles they played is difficult to determine, but the uncontested epistles make clear that many of Paul's colleagues were women. Junia (Rom. 16:7), Phoebe (Rom. 16:1-2), Prisca (Rom. 16:3-5), Euodia and Syntyche (Phil. 4:2-3), and Chloe (1 Cor. 1:11) seem to have been especially integral. To some degree, the extensive involvement of women may trace back to the first churches in Judea or even to the ministry of Jesus himself, though it should be noted that, while Luke counts "both men and women" among the earliest converts, all of the original apostles are men, as are all of the leaders selected in Acts 6. The importance of women in Paul's cohort may also be related to the spread of the gospel into Asia and Macedonia, where women often held prominence in religious life and organizations.[43] There is no way of knowing whether Paul's enlisting the aid of Phoebe and other (gentile) women was the direct result—or cause—of his decision to interpret Baptism as an enactment of circumcision, though their influence in western cities such as Philippi, Cenchreae, Corinth, and Rome may suggest that they emerged during the later, non-circumcision phase of Paul's ministry.

Conclusion: Engendering Judaism

The reconstruction for which I have argued is speculative, though, to be fair, all efforts to envision events in the first two decades of the church require a measure of imagination. As I see it, the earliest overtures to gentiles, which may have occurred among gentile sympathizers in Antioch, in Samaria, or perhaps even in Jerusalem itself just months after the crucifixion, were, for all intents and purposes, a Jewish mission. The objective was to share the report of Christ's death and resurrection with gentiles as it was being shared with Jews, and to baptize gentiles into that death and resurrection *as Jews*, which is to say, with circumcision. As such, the gentile mission confronted the Jewish dilemma regarding the possibility of female conversion. Pressed by apocalyptic anticipation and/or by the need to make sense of Christ's death and resurrection, Paul resolved the dilemma by determining that Baptism into Christ was tantamount to circumcision. Gentile men and women, therefore, could be brought into the Abrahamic covenant, still as Jews, but Jews circumcised by Christ rather than by a human hand. In this way, Paul "engendered" Judaism in two respects: he engendered the spread of Judaism by opening it up to a new constituency, and this he did by in-gendering Judaism through the incorporation of gentile women.

Considering the weight given to circumcision by the Romans in their exercise of ocular authority over their subjects, Paul's simultaneous embrace and rejection of circumcision makes his response to Roman power difficult to assess. To the extent that Paul rejects empirical circumcision of gentile men, Jacobs is right to argue that Paul "may be viewed as resisting Roman power."[44] Yet, to the extent that Paul embraces circumcision by attributing that status to gentile men and women baptized into Christ, one might say Paul accommodates Roman hegemony no less than the Judaizers of Galatia or the later rabbis. The doubled nature of Paul's response to Roman power is, thus, both savvy and vigorous. It expands circumcision to include all Jews (properly understood in terms of Christ), while at the same time, cloaking the circumcisions of all Jews, both male and female.[45]

Notes

1. Andrew Jacobs, *Christ Circumcised: A Study in Early Christian History and Difference* (Philadelphia: University of Pennsylvania Press, 2012).

2. Ibid., 17.

3. Ibid., 21.

4. Suetonius, *Dom.* 12.2.

5. Jacobs, *Christ Circumcised*, 18.

6. Most notably, Shaye J. D. Cohen, *The Beginnings of Jewishness* (Berkeley: University of California Press, 1999), 169, 223. Others have expressed uncertainty about the possibility of female conversion or about the form it might have taken; e. g., Judith M. Lieu, "Circumcision, Women and Salvation," *NTS* 40 (1994): 358–70; Paula Fredriksen, "Judaism, the Circumcision of Gentiles, and Apocalyptic Hope: Another Look at Galatians 1 and 2," *JTS* 42 (1991): 536, 546; Martin Goodman, *Mission and Conversion: Proselytizing in the Religious History of the Roman Empire* (Oxford: Clarendon, 1994), 62, 169; Shelly Matthews, *Rich Pagan Women and the Rhetoric of Mission in Early Judaism and Christianity* (Stanford: Stanford University Press, 2001), 99.

7. Troy W. Martin, "The Covenant of Circumcision (Genesis 17:9-14) and the Situational Antitheses in Galatians 3:28," *JBL* 122 (2003): 124.

8. Elisabeth Schüssler Fiorenza, *In Memory of Her: A Feminist Theological Reconstruction of Christian Origins* (New York: Crossroads, 1994), 210.

9. Joshua D. Garroway, *Paul's Gentile-Jews: Neither Jew nor Gentile, but Both* (New York: Palgrave-Macmillan, 2012).

10. I want to make it clear that I am considering the "woman question" *only* with regard to Jewish proselytism—that is to say, the capacity of a gentile woman to become a proselyte. Whether or not circumcision as the mark of the Abrahamic covenant prevented women born into Jewish families from being reckoned full Israelites will not be an issue here.

11. Cohen, *Beginnings of Jewishness*, 109–39; Seth Schwartz, "Conversion to Judaism in the Second Temple Period: A Functionalist Approach," in *Studies in Josephus and the Varieties of Ancient Judaism: Louis H. Feldman Jubilee Volume*, ed. S. Cohen and J. Schwartz (Leiden: Brill, 2007), 223.

12. Which is not to say that all Jews embraced circumcision, especially within priestly circles—a point made most recently by Matthew Thiessen, *Contesting Conversion: Genealogy, Circumcision, and Identity in Ancient Judaism and Christianity* (New York: Oxford University Press, 2011). He was preceded in this regard by Gary G. Porton, *The Stranger within Your Gates: Converts and Conversion in Rabbinic Literature* (Chicago: University of Chicago Press, 1994); Daniel R. Schwartz,

Studies in the Jewish Background of Christianity (WUNT 60; Tübingen: Mohr Siebeck, 1992); and Cohen, *Beginnings of Jewishness*.

13. For a listing of many examples, see Fredriksen, "Judaism, the Circumcision of Gentiles, and Apocalyptic Hope," 536 and n. 12 above.

14. Wolf Liebescheutz, "The Influence of Judaism among Non-Jews in the Imperial Period," *JSJ* 52 (2001): 239. Notwithstanding the several historians who have argued, usually based on the tale of Izates, that conversion without circumcision was occasionally possible; e. g., Peder Borgen, "Militant and Peaceful Proselytism and Christian Mission," in *Early Christianity and Hellenistic Judaism* (Edinburgh: T. & T. Clark, 1996), 53; Gary Gilbert, "The Making of a Jew: 'God-Fearer' or Convert in the Story of Izates," *Union Seminary Quarterly Review* 44 (1991): 299–313.

15. Lieu, "Circumcision, Women and Salvation," 364.

16. Even recently, a few have argued that immersion does trace back to an earlier period; e. g., David Daube, "Conversion to Judaism and Early Christianity," in *Ancient Jewish Law: Three Inaugural Lectures* (Leiden: Brill, 1981), 7; Lawrence H. Schiffman, *Who Was a Jew? Rabbinic and Halakhic Perspectives on the Jewish-Christian Schism* (Hoboken, NJ: KTAV, 1985), 25–30. A prominent defender in the previous generation was Joachim Jeremias, *Infant Baptism in the First Four Centuries* (trans. D. Cairns; Philadelphia: Westminster, 1960), 24–29.

17. Lieu, "Circumcision, Women and Salvation," 364.

18. Bernadette J. Brooten, *Women Leaders in the Ancient Synagogue* (Chico, CA: Scholars, 1982), 144.

19. Margaret H. Williams, *Jews in a Graeco-Roman Environment* (WUNT 312; Tübingen: Mohr Siebeck, 2013), 68n32.

20. Cohen, *Beginnings of Jewishness*, 171.

21. Ibid., 223.

22. Ibid., 306.

23. Terence L. Donaldson, *Judaism and the Gentiles: Jewish Patterns of Universalism (to 135 CE)* (Waco: Baylor University Press, 2008), 335.

24. Alternatively, it might be that Josephus presents Helena as being afraid that, in the wake of a circumcision, the Jewish identity of Izates would be confirmable upon examination, if that were ever required. As a sympathizer, his Jewish observances could remain private and inscrutable.

25. For a sampling of different interpretations of the honeycomb and the bees, see John J. Collins, *Between Athens and Jerusalem: Jewish Identity in the Hellenistic Diaspora* (2d ed.; Grand Rapids: Eerdmans, 2000), 235–36; Ross S. Kraemer, *When Asenath Met Joseph: A Late Antique Tale of the Biblical Patriarch and His Egyptian Wife* (New York: Oxford University Press, 1998), 166–69; Gideon Bohak, *Joseph and Asenath and the Jewish Temple in Heliopolis* (Atlanta: Scholars, 1996), 8–14;

Randall D. Chesnutt, *From Death to Life: Conversion in Joseph and Aseneth* (JSPSup 16; Sheffield: Sheffield Academic, 1995), 114; Marc Philonenko, *Joseph et Asénath: Introduction, Texte Critique et Notes* (Leiden: Brill, 1968), 65–66, 96.

26. For a sampling of the wide range of views regarding date and provenance, see the concise summary in Collins, *Between Athens and Jerusalem*, 103–8.

27. Rivka Nir, *Joseph and Aseneth: A Christian Book* (Sheffield: Sheffield Phoenix, 2012), 88–89. That the work is of Christian origin is also the view of Kraemer, *When Asenath Met Joseph*, and has advocates as far back as Pierre Batiffol, "Le Livre de la Prière d'Aseneth," in *Studia Patristica: Études d'ancienne literature chrétienne* (Paris: Leroux, 1889-90), 1–115.

28. It was declared the *communis opinio* long ago by Ernst Haenchen, *The Acts of the Apostles: A Commentary* (trans. R. McL. Wilson; Oxford: Blackwell, 1971), 365n6. More recently, see James D. G. Dunn, *Beginning From Jerusalem: Christianity in the Making* (Grand Rapids: Eerdmans, 2009), 2:301. See also Martin Hengel, *Between Jesus and Paul: Studies in the Earliest History of Christianity* (Philadelphia: Fortress, 1983), 13, 56.

29. Ernst Barnikol, *Die vorchristliche und frühchristliche Zeit des Paulus* (Kiel: Walter G. Mühlau, 1929), 18–24; Hans-Joachim Schoeps, *Paul* (Philadelphia: Westminster, 1961), 64, 219; Terence L. Donaldson, *Paul and the Gentiles: Remapping the Apostle's Convictional World* (Minneapolis: Fortress, 1997), 275–84. Richard N. Longenecker, *Galatians* (WBC 41; Nashville: Thomas Nelson, 1990), 233, says that Paul refers to his "pre-Christian life and activities," but falls short of identifying him specifically as a Jewish missionary.

30. Douglas A. Campbell, *The Deliverance of God: An Apocalyptic Rereading of Justification in Paul* (Grand Rapids: Eerdmans, 2009), 157.

31. Ibid. According to Francis Watson, *Paul, Judaism and the Gentiles* (Cambridge: Cambridge University Press, 1986), 28–38, Paul "preached circumcision" to Jews following his conversion, a proposal that Donaldson, *Paul*, 269–72, thoroughly examines and dismisses.

32. On which assumption Donaldson, ibid., 270–71, rejects the present view.

33. So Campbell, *Deliverance of God*, 155–56.

34. Here, I part ways with Campbell (ibid., 157–58), who believes Paul abandoned circumcision upon encountering other missionaries in Antioch.

35. Dunn, *Beginning From Jerusalem*, 442.

36. Ibid.

37. Hengel, *Between Jesus and Paul*, 56–58.

38. Fredriksen, "Judaism, the Circumcision of Gentiles, and Apocalyptic Hope," 544–48.

39. Joshua D. Garroway, "The Circumcision of Christ: Romans 15.7-13," *JSNT* 34 (2012): 303–22.

40. For a rabbinic expression of the idea that Jewish women and uncircumcised hemophiliac men are reckoned as though they are genitally circumcised, see *b. 'Abod. Zar.* 27a, and the analysis of that passage in Shaye J. D. Cohen, *Why Aren't Jewish Women Circumcised: Gender and Covenant in Judaism* (Berkeley: University of California Press, 2005), 93–101. See also Garroway, *Paul's Gentile-Jews*, 115–17.

41. On this reading of Romans 4:12, see Garroway, ibid., 81–113.

42. Martin, "The Covenant of Circumcision (Genesis 17:9–14) and the Situational Antitheses in Galatians 3:28."

43. For a brief discussion, see Ben Witherington III, *The Acts of the Apostles: A Socio-Rhetorical Commentary* (Grand Rapids: Eerdmans, 1998), 334–39.

44. Jacobs, *Christ Circumcised*, 23.

45. The title of this chapter is borrowed from my colleague Rachel Adler's pioneering work in Jewish theology, *Engendering Judaism: An Inclusive Theology and Ethics* (Boston: Beacon, 1999).

9

———

Paul's Jewish Identity in the Roman World

Beyond the Conflict Model

Jeremy Punt

Interpreters within the Christian tradition have often anachronistically read Paul's letters in the New Testament as if Paul were a "Christian" standing outside the Jewish tradition, with the focus on his thoughts probably distracting any serious attention from his Jewish identity.[1] His letters were dealt with in ways that prejudiced their religious and confessional interpretation in a narrow sense of these terms, disallowing the recognition of their political and ideological dimensions. More recently, the study of the Pauline letters has seen various important changes, not unrelated to shifts in academic inquiry within biblical studies and the guild as a whole. Following the centuries-long tradition of interpreting the letters in individualistic, spiritualizing, and denominational ways—as three not unrelated aspects (the so-called Lutheran approach)—important interpretive changes came to fruition in what eventually came to be known as the New Perspective on Paul (NPP).[2] While the traditional

Paul was understood as a religious innovator who broke with his Jewish life, the new Paul is seen now as addressing issues of social, ethnic, and cultural difference and group identity and solidarity from his Jewish perspective.[3] This new take on Paul and acknowledgment of his Jewishness should not be divorced, of course, from the first-century sociopolitical context.[4]

In the first-century CE Mediterranean context, the very existence of life in its various forms was determined by the seemingly omnipresent and omnipotent Roman Empire in its various guises, not only in imperial ideology. Reigning emperors and current and past imperial families made their presence felt in Rome and in the provinces through the "mass media" of the time that included statues, coins, monuments, and temples. Material items made the imperial presence clear, exuding power and control.[5] Paul lived under the reign of this empire, as did those communities who received, and then, distributed his letters. His letters were created, circulated, and read within this sociohistorical setting of empire as not merely one element, but a setting informed and constituted by empire. It was a reign that expanded beyond military domination, including sociopolitical notions, systems, and structures.

However, the hope that the Jewishness of Paul, on the one hand, and his imperial setting, on the other, could be treated as mutually advantageous for studying each other has not yet fully materialized.[6] This is somewhat surprising, since the two foci can be reciprocally beneficial for Pauline interpretation: in fact, the new emphasis on Paul's Jewishness requires more attention for the reigning political context than was common in the past, and so too does studying his imperial context require more appreciation for Paul's Jewish frame.[7] This chapter is a brief attempt to investigate possible intersections of Paul's Jewishness and imperial location. To be clear, my investigation here is not a historical (re)construction attempt, such as to construct the situation of Jews in empire already before the first- and second-century Jewish revolts. Then also, acknowledging connections as suggested here are all too often approached with limitations imposed by rather blunt adversarial terms, situated in alterity and a fair amount of antagonism.[8] My investigation wants to steer clear from a simple (simplistic?) conflict model. In short, it explores intersections between appreciation of Paul's Jewishness and locating Paul within empire, and wants to consider the mutually beneficial hermeneutical impact of the two on each other in our continuing investigations.

Paul and Second Temple Judaism

Paul's Jewish identity is, as a topic, a subsidiary of the larger question: who and what was a Ἰουδαῖος in the middle of the first century CE.[9] Nevertheless, Paul's Jewishness is evident from claims he made in his authentic letters, as for example in Rom. 11:1b: καὶ γὰρ ἐγὼ Ἰσραηλίτης εἰμί, ἐκ σπέρματος Ἀβραάμ, φυλῆς Βενιαμίν—and in 1 Cor. 11:22: Ἑβραῖοί εἰσιν; κἀγώ. Ἰσραηλῖταί εἰσιν; κἀγώ. σπέρμα Ἀβραάμ εἰσιν; κἀγώ. Paul's claims upon and association with a strong Jewish identity and heritage are clear. And in Phil. 3:5, Paul also refers to himself as a Pharisee (κατὰ νόμον Φαρισαῖος).[10] Even if passages such as Gal. 1:11–17 and Phil. 3:4–6 have been interpreted such that Paul distanced himself from his Jewish culture and heritage,[11] Romans 11 and 1 Corinthians 11 stand as clear indications of Paul's unqualified, strong, and positive association with his Jewishness.

Newer perspectives on Paul were necessary to come to terms with Paul's Jewishness, and managed to bring about some much needed correctives—particularly about the understanding of Paul's Jewish setting, if not necessarily understanding Paul as a Jew.[12] The deeply embedded, F. C. Baur-inspired template of Christian universalism versus Jewish particularism in Pauline studies skewed interpretation in the modern era.[13] Scathing criticism of the dominant modern construction of Judaism versus Christianity, in vogue since the nineteenth century, challenged scholars for not living up to their convictions:

> Despite widespread admission of the anachronism involved (for both!), use of the constructs continues. However much the concepts may have been changing, the dichotomy, enshrined in standard studies and

reference works in the field, still carries the connotations of Christian 'universalism' and transcendent spirituality versus (a divinely rejected) Jewish particularism and legalism. Numerous recent studies have demonstrated that key aspects of these pretentious, all-encompassing constructs have no basis in Pauline and other literature, including the Book of Acts, which is of questionable validity as a historical source.[14]

Correctives from the NPP fray included, for example, an emphasis on the collective setting of first-century life and the Pauline letters that rejects a modern, Western introspective conscience;[15] renewed appreciation for the role of the covenant in relation to the Torah in Second Temple Judaism (for example, covenantal nomism à la Sanders[16]); and acknowledgement of Second Temple Judaism as a religion—or maybe better, composite religious tradition—of grace that posited a faithful and gracious God.[17]

Counter-criticism did not stay out. Almost right from the start, questions were asked about the NPP, both from scholars defending the traditional interpretation of Paul as well as scholars arguing that neither Paul nor Second Temple Judaism were adequately accounted for by the NPP. Not discounting the efforts to critique traditional but skewed interpretations of Paul's relationship to Judaism, scholars have questioned whether much has changed: a deep-set, traditional, supersessionist interpretation often still holds sway[18] (for example, Wright's "fresh" perspective,[19] Segal,[20] and others);[21] New Perspective scholars (for example, Dunn) tend to presuppose a Pauline path parallel to Judaism; and others interpret Paul as proposing different, unique, and separate soteriological pathways for Jewish and gentile believers (for example, Gaston, Gager, Stowers, and Marshall).[22] The NPP's "rediscovery" of Paul's Jewishness clearly needs much further work.[23]

Jewish life in Palestine and the Diaspora during the Hellenistic and Roman periods was characterized by pluriformity and diversity.[24] Recent scholarship questions and deconstructs the dichotic divide between Judaism and Hellenism.[25] The at times almost venerated distinction between Hellenistic and Palestinian Judaism as separate entities in themselves is patently false, given the pervasive influence of

Hellenism[26] even within Palestine.[27] At the time, all forms of Judaism were Hellenistic,[28] and Judaism in Palestine was just as Hellenistic as the Judaism in the Western Diaspora.[29] Two other developments further eroded the notion of Hellenism and Judaism as two isolated entities. The first is awareness of the fallacious postulate of a "rationally superior out-going Greek or 'Western' culture and the justly submitting 'Oriental' cultures conquered by Alexander." This has led to research which shows the "initial insularity of the Greek conquerors in the conquered lands" and the consistent influence of Greek culture in the Mediterranean area long before Alexander's conquests.[30] Secondly, generalizing claims about Diaspora Judaism versus Palestinian Judaism are questioned, and similarities and differences accounted for in a more cautious way.[31]

In short, first-century boundary lines between Jewish and non-Jewish identity appear to be less than rigid and even blurred.[32] This realization can lead to one of two contentious conclusions. Relaxed "border control" in the first century probably initiated more cordial relationships between Jews and non-Jews, and such interaction was likely to generate one of two reactions (and some positions in between): mutual acceptance of Jewish and non-Jewish bona fides, or alternatively, a more determined effort—at least from Jewish hardliners—to re-establish social (and political) control by insistence on adequate lines of demarcation.[33]

Such was the nature of the Jewish context for interpreting Paul's letters and within which Paul and his communities's identity was framed. And so, besides Paul's claims in, for example, Rom. 11:1 and 2 Cor. 11:22, his apparent dismissal of his Jewish heritage in Phil. 3:5 may not be that at all. In Phil. 3:5–6, Paul refers to himself in the present tense as a Jew, listing many attributes in support, but concluding in Phil. 3:7 [ἀλλὰ] ἅτινα ἦν μοι κέρδη, ταῦτα ἥγημαι διὰ τὸν Χριστὸν ζημίαν. Segal's observation is typical: "As is quite clear from his rhetoric, he has thrown this all [that is, his Jewish and Pharisaic identity] over to be *in Christ* and this is a mark of derision."[34] But the interpretive framework is not different religious paradigms, but rather, a polemic between Paul and his adversaries. So, as is clear from his other letters, Paul is not ditching his Jewish credentials, but he indicates that he no longer bases his status claims on them.[35]

Paul's apparent description of the Jews (Ἰουδαῖοι) as those τὸν κύριον ἀποκτεινάντων Ἰησοῦν καὶ τοὺς προφήτας and who θεῷ μὴ ἀρεσκόντων καὶ πᾶσιν ἀνθρώποις ἐναντίων (1 Thess. 2:15; see 1 Thess. 2:14–16) is another text often cited in negation, or even condemnation, of Paul's Jewish identity. Scholars have shown how a particular historical framework and reading stance support such anti-Jewish interpretation. At the same time, reflection about the perspectival and ideological nature of language emphasizes the function of construing a particular version of Jesus' death by casting a negative light on an author's adversaries. First Thessalonians 2:14–16 reflects the Israelite prophetic tradition to make sense of senseless violence.[36] First Thessalonians 2 provides no indication that Paul distanced himself from his Jewish heritage, and the harsh words in 1 Thess. 2:14–16 again are better understood therefore as intra-Jewish critique.

Does an approach to Paul's relationship with Judaism that does not rest on Christian supersessionism, or on parallel paths for Jews and gentiles, or on separate but equal soteriological conduits, look different from traditional approaches, and even the NPP? A number of so-called Radical New Perspective on Paul scholars,[37] some of whom were cited above, suggest that a number of important changes are indeed issued in. The newer perspective on Paul's Jewishness can largely be encapsulated in a number of principles:[38] Paul addressed gentiles in his letters, and did not make categorical, generalizing claims about Judaism or the law.[39] He spoke of the Torah in the context of God's gift to Jews, which, as a standard for all humankind, proved too high a hurdle for gentiles and saw Christ as sacrificial atonement.[40] For Paul, the Torah functioned as an instrument through which Jews lived out their relationship with God;[41] therefore, doing good works did not stand in opposition to having faith, and Paul's notion of justification by faith referred to Jesus' faithfulness, established gentiles in the proper relationship to God, and included them into God's family.[42] How, then, does a renewed appreciation of Paul's Jewishness relate to an appreciation for the imperial context in which he functioned?

Paul, Jewishness, and the Roman Empire

Another recent development that has garnered some disparate interest is the variegated effort to account for the Pauline letters in the context of the Roman Empire. As mooted above, locating Paul in terms of the empire potentially enriches our understanding of Paul's Jewishness, and vice versa. Ironically, and with a few (at times much maligned) exceptions, the intersection of Pauline studies and work on empire remains undervalued, though.[43] Notwithstanding that the imperial context, arguably, was the more pervasive and stringent presence in first-century Mediterranean life, ironically, this deficit still reigns.[44] As the very fabric of that society, the Roman Empire's ubiquity included, but also reached further than, the impact of philosophical contexts, religious formations, local power plays, and so on. But, and perhaps explaining the irony somewhat, empire encapsulated all: philosophical schools, religious groups, and powerful patrons in one way or another were co-opted and included in imperial structures and ideology. Given the first century's integrated and holistic life (versus a modernist compartmentalization of life) and the minimal direct engagement reflected between Paul and the empire in his letters, the intertextuality between them requires harder work and probably a different approach—also in our focus on Paul's Jewishness.[45]

A number of obstacles have hindered explorations of the intersection between Paul's Jewishness and imperial context. One, attempts to account for empire in the Pauline documents at times have been portrayed somewhat rigidly, engaging empire as a material and almost organizational structure, such as in terms of his ostensible Roman citizenship status, missionary travels, or confrontation with authorities.[46] And two, the intersection between Paul and empire was conceptualized in stark adversarial terms, including Paul versus the Emperor, or Jesus believers (including Jewish believers) versus the Romans. Certain events in the ancient world, such as the mob uprisings against the Jews since 38 CE in Alexandria,[47] may suggest an oppositional relationship between Jews and Empire—at best.[48] But, as Fredriksen suggests, "the tendencies of imperial law, the eruptions of anti-Jewish (and anti-pagan, and anti-heretical) violence, the increasingly strident tone and obsessive repetition of orthodox anti-Jewish rhetoric" may lead to misinterpretation. Rather than a consistent program of Roman persecution, or a separation between the ways of Jews, on the one hand, and all others, on the other hand, such instances show imperial ideology's dissatisfaction with the extent to which Jewish people integrated in society.[49] In short, anti-Jewish sentiments found in ancient accounts are often testimony to the close relationships between Jewish and other communities, notwithstanding a Jewish sense of exclusivity and even seclusion.

Moreover, various sources attest to special privileges given to Jewish communities in the Roman Empire.[50] Since political and religious powers were inextricably linked in ancient times, all were expected to demonstrate their loyalty to the politico-religious system. However, "Jews as a rule were exempt from the obligation to participate in Greco-Roman religious feasts and other such rites."[51] Jewish historian Josephus (B. J. 7.45; C. Ap. 2.282) claims that Judaism was quite trendy in first-century Rome, to the extent that non-Jews adopted Jewish customs and names. Indeed, so-called God-fearers even participated in synagogue activities;[52] on the other hand, various ancient sources indicate that Jews were given concessions that allowed them to largely maintain their customs and beliefs, so that they, notwithstanding occasional outbreaks of violence against them,[53] were relatively settled during imperial times. The early followers of Jesus who were Jewish or associated with Jews shared in these privileges. Tensions between Jesus believers and other Jews also showed, as has been the case quite often, that the greatest danger to any community or organization was often perceived as the danger from within.[54]

The accommodating stance of the Roman toward Jews did not mean the absence of diverging views among Romans in this regard in the first century. A double emotional response that consisted of dislike and fear characterized some anti-Jewish traditions, for which Schäfer proposed the term "Judeophobia."[55] Opponents such as Cicero, Juvenal, and Tacitus[56] saw Judaism as the typical *barbara superstitio*, by its very nature ill-disposed toward Roman "*religio*, the latter being the essence of the political, cultural, and religious ideals of ancient Rome."[57] However, Judaism evidently exercised a strong appeal as well.[58] Until Christianity, conversion to Judaism and the non-observance of other cults were for Romans, in a certain way, betrayal of the *patria nomima*. Joining another people in the worship of its god, the God of Israel, was seen in some circles as *maiestas*, high treason.

Three, it should be mentioned that the subtle or overt anti-imperial sentiment, as far as scholars detect it in the Pauline letters, at times, is accompanied by an anti-Jewish sentiment, or at least, an attempt to purge Paul's Jewishness. Dissatisfied with his anti-empire reading, McKnight complains about "Wright [who] routinely observes that Paul plays a new music in the echo chamber and this music subverts the music of Rome and revises the music of Judaism."[59] Such criticism, which tends to align the disavowal of an anti-imperial tone in Paul's writings with a perceived non-Jewish or at least Jewish-supersessionist tone in his writings, confirms the intersectionality of Paul's Jewishness and an imperial awareness. Maybe the connection is simply the continuing anachronistic spiritualization so typical of much Pauline scholarship?[60] Or, maybe there is something more to it? It remains interesting to see how scholars who acknowledge the political dimension of Paul's letters, ranging from Dunn (justice) to Horsley, Elliott, and Wright (anti-empire), typically and differently, brought Paul's Jewishness into the discussion. However, the relationship between Paul the Jew and the Roman Empire still tended to be scripted as essentially based on opposition and even animosity, that is, a conflict model.[61] A good example is found in Elliott's work.

Neil Elliott has done much to argue that Paul, in the Letter to the Romans, is not simply treating Jews and non-Jews alike with reference to their position before God. From Elliott's perspective, Paul insisted that non-Jews did not buy into imperial propaganda in the wake of the return of Jews after the edict of Claudius in 49 CE banished them from Rome. Paul, in fact, was challenging imperial propaganda for its negative influence on gentile Jesus followers and ensuing poor reflection on their fellow Jewish believers. Paul was intent on the congregation being able to distinguish between imperial justice and God's justice, between *clementia* and divine mercy.[62] The bigger scope of Elliott's argument is that the Romans letter does not succumb to imperial propaganda or boil down to theological criticism of Judaism in favor of a new vision for the salvation of humankind.[63]

The extent to which such interpretations are persuasive will probably be debated further in the years to come. But what emerges is that while a reconsideration of Paul's Jewishness is a priority, so too is rethinking empire in Paul, which starts with rethinking *empire* as such. Without discounting other approaches to empire, it can be theorized as a structural, differentiated, influential, negotiated concept.[64] First, the structural and material reality of empire is difficult to deny; it is composed of, and operated, in terms of a principal binary of center and margins, where the center is often symbolized by a city and the margins are those that are subordinated to the center—at a political, economic, or cultural level.[65] But second, empire structurally was not a uniform phenomenon in the temporal or spatial sense, but differentiated in constitution and deployment, regardless of many remaining similarities.[66] Third, the reach and power of empire was of such an extent that it influenced and impacted on people in direct and indirect forms, in overt and subtle ways: on all aspects of life, the lives of the powerful as well as of the subalterns. This unrelenting material presence and ideological influence, traversing other dimensions of first-century life across a geographical spread of communities, encompasses two further claims about empire. Fourth, empire was primarily a *conceptual entity* to which its material form(s) attest—even admitting mutuality between structure and idea does not reverse the conceptual *primacy*![67] And finally, contrary to restrictive, essentialist understandings of empire,[68] it can be theorized as dynamic, and primarily, a process, in its conceptualizing as well as its constant fabrication: a negotiated concept! Positions toward empire were dynamic—not naive, static positions "for" or "against"—as people's responses to and interactions with empire were infinitely more complex and hybrid than merely those of singular support or opposition.[69]

The connections between a Jewish and imperially situated Paul can be illustrated in the two passages from 1 Thessalonians 2 and Philemon 3 referred to above. Since 1 Thess. 2:14–16 cannot be considered a blunt condemnation of Jews from an ostensibly "Christian" position, this allows one to appreciate the typical imperial strategy of divide and rule at play.[70] Invoking the Jewish tradition where God's judgment is passed on Israel for killing her prophets, and of Jewish suffering as a result of rejecting God's prophets (for example, Neh. 9:26; Jer. 2:30; 2 Chron. 36:16; cf. *Jub.* 1.12; *T. Levi* 16.2 and Luke 11:49–51; Matt. 23:34–36), Paul engages in typical Jewish rhetoric. Paul's point is that the Thessalonian Jesus believers, like their Judean counterparts, suffered at the hands of their own people. First Thessalonians 2 attests neither to an imagined Jew–Christian divide nor to some narrow religious (as separated from social, political, and economic) aspects. As much as Paul blames some Jews for killing other Jews (Jesus and the prophets), he accuses the Thessalonians of oppressing other, Jesus-believing Thessalonians. But in so doing, in a context where crucifixion was the prerogative of the imperial powers, Paul also reminds of empire's power to multiply divisiveness among subject peoples.[71]

Past interpretations of Phil. 3:2–9 have often emphasized that Paul's earlier life was inextricably linked to Judaism and Jewish practice, which was, on the one hand, connected with his past persecution of Jesus followers, and, on the other, with a sinful past life of which Paul was ashamed. In contrast, Paul's post-Jesus life was marked by redemption. What is telling, though, is that in Philemon 3, as in Romans 11 and in 2 Corinthians 11, Paul applied Jewish descriptions to his own life in the present tense and not simply as bygone labels of a past life; in fact, Paul used the Jewish identity labels as indicators of status and not shame. Moreover, adequate explanations of Paul's earlier persecution of Jesus followers have not been forthcoming;[72] in contrast, more evident solutions have largely been ignored, starting with Jesus' execution as criminal because he was perceived to be a political threat. So, too, as far as the persecution Paul suffered consequently, his message could easily be interpreted as anti-imperial, or at least, critical of the empire.[73]

A major historical source for the relationship between Jews and the Roman Empire—Josephus's *Jewish War*—demonstrates the complexity of the relationship. Rather than a facile Jew versus Roman or Judaism versus Roman Empire contrast and conflict, Josephus's work underlines both the tension between various Jewish groupings, on the one hand—doing the Romans' work for them (for example, *J. W.* 5.11.4; see also Tacitus *Hist.* 5.12.4)—but also, on the other, the ambivalence of many Jews toward the Empire.[74] Sources such as Josephus, whose own tolerance of the Romans may be reflected in his assessment of the relationship between empire and Jewish groups, considered a group such as the Pharisees as tolerant, even if not accommodating of Roman colonial rule. The potential negative spin-offs for all Jews when a small minority among them referred to Jesus with imperial titles—"Lord" and "Messiah," coming to establish a "kingdom"—may have driven Paul the Pharisee to pursue and prosecute Jesus followers. Ascribing Paul's actions against Jesus followers to confessional, dogmatic differences subscribe to the cloak of traditionalism obscuring Paul.[75] But so, too, reading Paul the Jew as standing simply in an adversarial position against Rome does not do justice to the complexity of empire and life in empire. One final example will have to suffice.

Paul's mapping out of identity in Galatians learns from imperial practice. The Jerusalem proclamation (Gal. 2:6–9) not only reversed the reigning cartography by making lands beyond the center into territories to be claimed and filled out by missionaries,[76] but was also a subjugated people's audacious attempt at reversing the imperial order by privileging the Jesus movement's position and status.[77] The Jerusalem Jesus movement did, however, at the same time adjust and appropriate Roman imperial discourse for its own purpose.[78] Paul's rhetorical use of an allegory derived from his Jewish heritage—Abraham's two women companions and sons (Gal. 4:21—5:1)—is another indication of how Jews remain incorporated in the newly constituted Israel defined by Paul. His argument resembles imperial language of subjugation of foreign nations for the sake of their incorporation into empire. Jews fit the mold of subjugated nations of imperial Rome, particularly when Paul ascribes to them the status of slavery, and so, confirms their need for subjugation. In a similar vein, barbarism, effeminacy, intemperateness, and other negative qualities ascribed to the nations were presented (with divine imperative) as legitimate reasons for subjugating foreign nations. In fact, Paul made a female slave the norm for the identity of "Jew." Jews are now defined through the image of Hagar as Abraham's companion and no longer as legitimate descendants of the original divine promise. At the same time, though, the argument's logic sanctioned the inclusion also of Jews (as the descendants of a slave mother who now found themselves in a liminal position) into Jesus-follower circles.[79]

Conclusion:
The Weight of Reception on Paul the Jew and the Romans

Identifying the interpretation of Paul as the weather vane of New Testament scholarship may be the result of more than what his letters themselves offer to theologians and historians alike.[80] Strong interpretive processes have, over a long time, constructed a history that celebrates and amplifies Paul's view, equating it with "the Christian view."[81] Tradition influences how a reader constructs history, and that history, in turn, shapes the interpretation of Paul's letters. The understanding of, or rather, lack of accounting for both Paul's Jewishness and his imperial social location were detrimentally prompted by the confessional, spiritualizing, and individualist reading of the letters. Paul's co-optation in Christianity has led to the essentialization, individualization, and depoliticization of the Bible in ecclesial and academic circles.[82] Moreover, under the weight of the accumulated Western exegetical tradition thus informed, the letters were deprived of various crucial dimensions, including the Jewishness of Paul and the imperial context in which his letters were composed. Avoiding the older temptation to reduce the Jewishness of a text or group to some point along an imagined axis of reaction to the "Greco-Roman context"[83] should not result in easy recourse to more recent truisms concerning identity as constructed through the discourse of alterity.[84] The value of interpreting Paul with full consideration of his Jewishness and imperially inscribed social location[85] is varied, but interconnected. At a hermeneutical level, such interpretations undo traditional heuristic frameworks, exposing their commitment to ideals and ideologies of earlier times, informed by ecclesial politics and theological strategy. At an historical level, such interpretation puts the Pauline letters into proper contextual perspective, alert to the sociopolitical and cultural dimensions that informed the letters at different levels.

Notes

1. See J. D. G. Dunn, "Who Did Paul Think He Was?: A Study of Jewish-Christian Identity," NTS 45, no. 2 (1999): 174–93.

2. Dunn's eponymous article published in 1983 is commonly seen as the provenance for the NPP. Subsequently, many scholars invoked the so-called New Perspective, and the NPP label soon found many different applications. Cf. R. B. Matlock, "Almost Cultural Studies?: Reflections on the "New Perspective" on Paul," in Biblical Studies/Cultural Studies: The Third Sheffield Colloquium, ed. J. C. Exum and S. D. Moore (Gender, Culture, Theory vol. 7; Sheffield: Sheffield Academic Press, 1998), 433–59, and B. Worthington, "Alternative Perspectives Beyond the Perspectives: A Summary of Pauline Studies That Has Nothing to Do with Piper or Wright," CurBS 11, no. 3 (2013): 366–87 for different forms of meta-critique directed at the NPP.

3. M. Johnson-DeBaufre, "Historical Perspectives: Which Past? Whose Past?," in Studying Paul's Letters: Contemporary Perspectives and Methods, ed. J. A. Marchal (Minneapolis: Fortress Press, 2012), 19. Even if written for a different purpose and specific audience, see Johnson-DeBaufre's valuable chapter on historical approaches to the Pauline letters, emphasizing how language's reality-shaping

role and perspectival perception and history as interpretive venture assist in recognizing Paul's Jewish context (ibid., 13–23).

4. A point implicitly acknowledged, but not argued by Johnson-DeBaufre, when she refers to recent approaches to Paul having become more attuned to his repoliticizing (political and economic dimensions of his letters) and decentering (toward a people's history), while acknowledging how a monolithic and retrospective Christian interpretation has skewed Pauline studies over centuries (ibid., 13–23). Scholars tend to introduce a choice between dealing with the Jewish orientation and the so-called Greco-Roman context of the NT, implying that recognition of the one excludes the other (cf. S. E. Porter and A. W. Pitts, "Greco-Roman Culture in the History of New Testament Interpretation: An Introductory Essay," in *Christian Origins and Greco-Roman Culture: Social and Literary Contexts for the New Testament*, ed. Porter and Pitts [Texts and Editions for New Testament Study vol. 9; Early Christianity in Its Hellenistic Context, vol. 1; Leiden: Brill, 2013], 2). For criticism and comment on the term *Greco-Roman*, and particularly for its masking of the ubiquity of the Roman Empire, cf. A. Y. Reed and N. B. Dohrmann, "Introduction: Rethinking Romanness, Provincializing Christendom," in *Jews, Christians, and the Roman Empire: The Poetics of Power in Late Antiquity*, ed. Dohrmann and Reed (Philadelphia: University of Pennsylvania Press, 2013), 4–9.

5. See C. Ando, *Imperial Ideology and Provincial Loyalty in the Roman Empire* (Classics and Contemporary Thought, vol. 6; Berkeley: University of California Press, 2000); P. Zanker, *The Power of Images in the Age of Augustus*, trans. A. Shapiro (Jerome Lectures, series 16; Ann Arbor: University of Michigan Press, 1990).

6. "[J]ust as Jews are frequently dismissed as atypical by scholars of Roman history, so Rome still remains invisible or occluded in a surprising proportion of studies on Jewish materials written under Roman rule and/or by Roman citizens" (Reed and Dohrmann, "Rethinking Romanness, Provincializing Christendom," 4).

7. Unfortunately, the opposite seems to prevail. Pauline scholars who investigate a nexus of some sort or other between the letters and empire may tend to drown out Jewish in favor of Roman notions, as McKnight rightly complains about Wright (S. McKnight, "Empire Criticism and N. T. Wright," 2013, http://www.patheos.com/blogs/jesuscreed/2014/02/11/empire-criticism-and-nt-wright).

8. "With the *contra Iudaeos* tradition, [scholars] have treated polemics as the central engine of both Christian and Jewish identity formation" (Reed and Dohrmann, "Rethinking Romanness, Provincializing Christendom," 21); cf. T. Wiley, "Paul and Early Christianity," in *Empire and the Christian Tradition: New Readings of Classical Theologians*, ed. D. H. Compier, Pui-lan Kwok, and J. Rieger (Minneapolis: Fortress Press, 2007), 47–61.

9. The wide-ranging debate includes whether the term Ἰουδαῖος should be

understood as geographical term, i. e., as *Judean* (cf. Malina and others) or as *Jew* (cf. C. Johnson Hodge, *If Sons, Then Heirs: A Study of Kinship and Ethnicity in the Letters of Paul* [Oxford; New York: Oxford University Press, 2007], and others). Cf. also D. M. Miller, "The Meaning of *Ioudaios* and Its Relationship to Other Group Labels in Ancient 'Judaism'," *CurBS* 9, no. 1 (2010): 98–126; idem, "Ethnicity Comes of Age: An Overview of Twentieth-Century Terms for *Ioudaios*," *CurBS* 10, no. 2 (2012): 293–311; idem, "Ethnicity, Religion and the Meaning of *Ioudaios* in Ancient 'Judaism'," *CurBS* 12, no. 2 (2014): 216–65; P. Eisenbaum, *Paul Was Not a Christian: The Original Message of a Misunderstood Apostle* (San Francisco: HarperCollins, 2009), 99–115.

10. A notion for which space does not allow discussion here; cf. A. F. Segal, "Paul's Jewish Presuppositions," in *The Cambridge Companion to St Paul*, ed. J. D. G. Dunn (Cambridge Companions to Religion; Cambridge: Cambridge University Press, 2003), 159–72. Segal's position is clear—"Paul is almost certainly the only New Testament writer to represent Pharisaic Judaism, though he gives us the view of someone who left it unconditionally" (ibid., 162)—but qualified: "Paul left Pharisaism for his own brand of Christianity, but he did not leave Judaism and he did not forget his Pharisaic training" (ibid., 163).

11. E. g., Dunn, "Who Did Paul Think He Was?," 184, 186; but cf. Eisenbaum, *Paul Was Not a Christian*, 132–49.

12. E. g., Segal therefore argues that Paul's "basic assumption" in his letters is not a "critique of works centered righteousness", which Segal rightly calls a concern "characteristic of a later time" (idem, "Universalism in Judaism and Christianity," in *Paul in His Hellenistic Context*, ed. T. Engberg-Pedersen [Minneapolis: Fortress Press, 1995], 1–29 [23–25]). But then he insists that Paul's primary concern is with "the process of transformation by faith that brings justification," a universal process for both Jewish and gentile converts to Christianity.

13. F. C. Baur's postulation of the universality of Christianity versus the exclusivity of Judaism has proven difficult to eradicate. With the origin of Paul's shift from Judaism to "Christianity" located in the Damascus road events, he moved "from the bodiliness of genealogy to the pure spirituality of faith, from the particularity of 'peoplehood' to the universality of multiculturality, from the locality of land to the globality of the world" (M. Volf, *Exclusion and Embrace: A Theological Exploration of Identity, Otherness, and Reconciliation* [Nashville: Abingdon, 1996], 43–50; cf. e. g., D. Boyarin, *A Radical Jew: Paul and the Politics of Identity* [Critical Studies in Jewish Literature, Culture, and Society vol. 1; Berkeley: University of California Press, 1994], 228–60; J. D. G. Dunn, *Romans 9-16* [WBC vol. 38b; Dallas: Word Books, 1988], 72). However, the presence of both universalist and particularist sentiments in most religious and other institutions were common in the first century, as were the ensuing tensions (E. C. Park, *Either Jew or Gentile: Paul's Unfolding Theology of Inclusivity* [Lousville:

Westminster John Knox, 2003], 3). For the recent invocation of universalist categories in Pauline literature, cf. Worthington, "Alternative Perspectives Beyond the Perspectives," 268–71 on Badiou, Žižek, and other continental philosophers.

14. R. A. Horsley, "Innovation in Search of Reorientation: New Testament Studies Rediscovering Its Subject Matter," *JAAR* 62, no. 4 (1995): 1153.

15. K. Stendahl, "The Apostle Paul and the Introspective Conscience of the West," *HTR* 56 (1963).

16. E. P. Sanders, *Paul and Palestinian Judaism: A Comparison of Patterns of Religion* (Philadelphia; London: Fortress Press; SCM, 1977).

17. E. g., J. D. G. Dunn, "The New Perspective on Paul," *Bulletin of John Rylands Library* 65 (1983); E. P. Sanders, *Paul, the Law, and the Jewish People* (Philadelphia: Fortress Press, 1983). In the words of Dunn (ibid., 97): "If Stendahl cracked the mould of twentieth-century reconstructions of Paul's theological context, by showing how much it had been determined by Luther's quest for a gracious God, Sanders has broken it altogether by showing how different these reconstructions are from what we know of first-century Judaism from other sources."

18. Segal argues that with the growing majority of gentiles in the church, which included Jewish "Christians," Paul wanted to avoid two classes of "Christians," and "separate covenants" for Jews and gentiles, as all need to be "transformed by their faith in the risen, spiritual Christ." Paul's emphasis on "the centrality of faith, his insistence that all need transformation, and his specific language for flesh and spirit" are different from the positions of other Hellenistic Jewish writers (Segal, "Universalism in Judaism and Christianity," 23).

19. N. T. Wright, *Paul: In Fresh Perspective* (Minneapolis: Fortress, 2005).

20. "For Jews it is right action which brings righteousness" (Segal, "Paul's Jewish Presuppositions," 167). Segal has written extensively on the relationship between Pauline and Jewish thought on universalism and particularism in the first-century Jewish-Hellenistic world (*Paul the Convert: The Apostolate and Apostasy of Saul the Pharisee* [New Haven: Yale University Press, 1990]; "Universalism in Judaism and Christianity," 1–30). Segal's arguments are in line with the increasing tendency to explain Paul's mission to the gentiles, both in his own perception of it and in the presentation thereof, against the background of a revisioned Jewish pattern of universalism, rather than of the rejection of Jewish particularism (T. L. Donaldson, "'The Gospel That I Proclaim Among the Gentiles' (Gal. 2:2: Universalistic or Israel-Centred?," in *Gospel in Paul: Studies on Corinthians, Galatians and Romans for Richard N. Longenecker*, ed. L. Ann Jervis and P. Richardson [JSNTSup 108; Sheffield: Sheffield Academic, 1994], 166–93). Segal argues from the perspective of the Jewish environment, and the different models of incorporating gentiles into the Jewish tradition. A basic distinction in first-century Judaism that Segal insists upon is the difference between conversion and salvation: the former entails the law, the

latter not necessarily, as in the case of "righteous Gentiles" ("Universalism in Judaism and Christianity," 5–6; cf. Boyarin, *A Radical Jew*, 299–300n1). Cf. also R. Goldenberg, *The Nations That Know Thee Not: Ancient Jewish Attitudes Towards Other Religions* (Biblical Seminar 52; Sheffield: Sheffield Academic, 1997), 99–107 who emphasizes the diversity in Jewish attitudes to gentiles and their religious practices, including high levels of tolerance.

21. Volf, *Exclusion and Embrace*, 43–50 argues for retaining the traditional view of the "universality of Christianity" versus the "exclusivism of Judaism." In this argument, Volf aligns himself closely with Boyarin, who, in turn, finds his starting point in Dunn's thesis that Paul's polemic directed at the law was an attempt to address Jewish nationalism and ethnocentrism which effectively excluded "gentiles" from the covenantal relationship with God. Boyarin, however, criticizes the coercive "universalizing" or multicultural transformation of the Jewish tradition (*A Radical Jew*, 228–60).

22. Cf. L. Gaston, *Paul and the Torah* (Vancouver: University of British Columbia Press, 1987), J. Gager, *The Origins of Anti-Semitism: Attitudes Towards Judaism in Pagan and Christian Antiquity* (New York: Oxford University Press, 1983) and, of course, Stendahl who holds that Paul thought that salvation was wrought for the Jews on basis of the law and for Christians on basis of Christ. Cf. M. Bockmuehl, "The Noachide Commandments and New Testament Ethics: With Special Reference to Acts 15 and Pauline Halakah," *RB* 102, no. 1 (1995): 100 who contends that Paul attempted "to forge a united body of Jewish and Gentile Christians in a fellowship of equals, in which the former continue to live by the special laws and the latter merely by the Noachide laws."

23. One direction in which such work has to develop further is to account for the damage done to the proper understanding of Paul's Jewishness through the "parting of the ways" model (cf. P. Fredriksen, "What "Parting of the Ways"?: Jews, Gentiles, and the Ancient Mediterranean City," in *The Ways That Never Parted: Jews and Christians in Late Antiquity and the Early Middle Ages*, ed. A. H. Becker and A. Y. Reed [Minneapolis: Fortress Press, 2007]; P. Schäfer, *Judeophobia: Attitudes Towards the Jews in the Ancient World* [Cambridge; London: Harvard University Press, 1997]); space prevents discussion here.

24. E. g., A. J. Bij de Vaate and J. W. Van Henten, "Jewish or Non-Jewish: Some Remarks on the Identification of Jewish Inscriptions from Asia Minor," *BO* 53, nos. 1–2 (1996): 27–28; M. Goodman, *Judaism in the Roman World: Collected Essays* (Ancient Judaism and Early Christianity; AGJU vol. 116; Leiden: Brill, 2007), 146. In the first century, there was no authoritative or normative Judaism: Judaism was a *pluriform* phenomenon. This is borne out by the different categories of Judaism(s) during the first century, i. e., rabbinic (or Palestinian), Hellenistic (or Diaspora), and apocalyptic (cf. e. g., Don N. Howell Jr., "Pauline Thought in the History of Interpretation," *BSac* 150, no. 599 [1993]: 317).

25. A. Gerdmar, *Rethinking the Judaism-Hellenism Dichotomy: A Historiographical Case*

Study of Second Peter and Jude (Coniectanea Biblica: New Testament Series 36; Stockholm: Almqvist & Wiksell International, 2001); T. Engberg-Pedersen, *Paul Beyond the Judaism/Hellenism Divide* (Louisville: Westminster John Knox, 2001).

26. In the sense of "the mixed culture that developed in the various parts of the eastern Mediterranean area before, during and after the Hellenistic period proper," and thus, distinct from the Hellenistic period of "political dominance" (cf. T. Engberg-Pedersen, Introduction to *Paul in His Hellenistic Context*, ed. Engberg-Pedersen [Minneapolis: Fortress, 1995], xviii n. 5).

27. R. Murray, "Jews, Hebrews and Christians: Some Needed Distinctions," *NovT* 24, no. 3 (1982): 196, 201–2.

28. M. Hengel, *The Cross of the Son of God: Containing The Son of God, Crucifixion, The Atonement* (London: SCM, 1986), 26–28). Contrary to his position on the pervasiveness of Hellenism, Hengel here argues that the earliest Christ followers' use of the title *Son of God* was largely independent of Hellenistic influence. L. H. Feldman, *Jew and Gentile in the Ancient World: Attitudes and Interactions from Alexander to Justinian* (Princeton: Princeton University Press, 1993), 19–25, however, cautions against reading too much into Greek inscriptions found in the land of Israel, suggesting that widespread communication in the Greek language may not have been so common during NT times. The land of Israel was called Judea in Persian times, Coele Syria in Hellenistic times, Judea in early Roman times, and Palestine after the defeat of Bar Kokhba (S. J. D. Cohen, *From the Maccabees to the Mishnah*, ed. W. A. Meeks [Library of Early Christianity; Philadelphia: Westminster, 2006], 99).

29. M. Hengel, *Judaism and Hellenism: Studies in their Encounter in Palestine During the Early Hellenistic Period* (London: SCM, 1981), 311–12.

30. "Hellenistic culture" is a term indicating "the culture that results from mixing *originally* Greek cultural elements with *originally* non-Greek cultural elements. It is *the mixture* (in a given time and place) that constitutes Hellenistic culture proper (in that place)" (Engberg-Pedersen, Introduction to *Paul in His Hellenistic Context*, xvii–xviii; emphasis in original).

31. Ibid., xvxiv–xix. Supposed differences between Palestinian and Hellenistic Judaism are questioned in light of recent research (cf. e. g., J. Lieu, J. North, and T. Rajak, Introduction to *The Jews Among Pagans and Christians*, eds. Lieu, North, and Rajak [London and New York: Routledge, 1992], 1–8; Murray, "Jews, Hebrews and Christians," 194–208), although e. g., L. H. Feldman, "How Much Hellenism in Jewish Palestine?," *Hebrew Union College Annual* 57 (1986): 83–111 argues that there was a distinction in the *degree* of hellenization between Jewish groups in the Diaspora and those in Palestine. Harsh distinctions often forced on different forms of Judaism during the first century—as, for example, in Montefiore's work—have been questioned, especially the notion that Hellenistic and Palestinian Judaism were two quite different and even opposing movements (e. g., W. D. Davies, *Paul and Palestinian Judaism: Some Rabbinic*

Elements in Pauline Theology [4th ed.; Philadelphia: Fortress, 1980], 1–16). The presumed distinctions have been questioned increasingly since the discovery of the Dead Sea Scrolls and the continuing investigation of early Jewish literature (Howell, "Pauline Thought in the History of Interpretation," 322).

32. Bij de Vaate and Van Henten, "Jewish or Non-Jewish," 28.

33. An awareness of separation, even a principled insistence upon separation, seems clearly attested in some early to mid-second-century writers (Ignatius, Marcion, Justin); equally clearly, we see strong indications of persistent, intimate interactions (Fredriksen, "What 'Parting of the Ways'?," 61). "Judaism in the Second Temple Period was not very rigid, and was constantly changing. These changes can only be understood as being the result of an awareness and openness found in certain groups in Judaism during their ambivalent and continuous rapport with the Gentiles" (D. Mendels, *Identity, Religion and Historiography: Studies in Hellenistic History* [JSPSup 24; Sheffield: Sheffield Academic, 1998], 33).

34. Segal, "Paul's Jewish Presuppositions," 159.

35. Eisenbaum, *Paul Was Not a Christian*, 140.

36. Johnson-DeBaufre, "Historical Perspectives," 23–26.

37. Radical NPP scholars include e. g., Eisenbaum, Fredriksen, Hodge, Nanos, and Zetterholm (cf. Zetterholm's helpful guide of 2009, *Approaches to Paul: A Student's Guide to Recent Scholarship* [Minneapolis: Fortress Press]).

38. Space does not allow for attempting to describe Second Temple Judaism here; suffice it to refer to Casey who lists eight identity factors of Second Temple Judaism: ethnicity, Scripture, monotheism, circumcision, Sabbath observance, dietary laws, purity laws and major festivals (idem, *From Jewish Prophet to Gentile God: The Origins and the Development of New Testament Christology: The Edward Cadbury Lectures at the University of Birmingham, 1985–86* [Cambridge; Louisville: James Clarke; Westminster John Knox, 1991], 12). The priority for ethnicity is shared by Barclay: "it was ethnicity—precisely the combination of ancestry and custom—which was the core of Jewish identity in the Diaspora" (J. M. G. Barclay, *Jews in the Mediterranean Diaspora: From Alexander to Trajan (323 BCE—117 CE)* [Berkeley and Los Angeles: University of California Press, 1996], 404), cf. Dunn, "Who Did Paul Think He Was?," 180–82.

39. Even if, as Boyarin, *A Radical Jew*, 204, contends, "[Paul's discourse on the Law and Judaism is] forever caught in a paradox of identity and difference." Cf. Matlock, "Almost Cultural Studies?," 450.

40. Segal underscores the widespread primacy of the Torah among the various, divergent Jewish groups, and then stresses that "[t]he only question for him [i. e., Paul] was in what way the Torah needed to be practised by Christians" ("Paul's Jewish Presuppositions," 161).

41. Segal is a good example of scholars who distinguish between "fleshly and

spiritual observances," or, in his words, between "ceremonial" and "moral" law. Keen to argue for Jewish universalism and for toleration of differences within monotheistic religion, under the influence of Hellenism and dominant cultural forces of the day ("Universalism in Judaism and Christianity," 29), the particularity of Judaism disappears. Like Dunn, Segal claims that "works of the Law" *denotes* the effects of ceremonial laws in the community, but adds that it *refers* to ceremonial laws as such, as well: "Paul is saying that the special laws of Judaism are not relevant for salvation" (ibid., 23–24). The special or ceremonial Jewish laws are not nullified, but relativized by faith in Christ: they are now voluntary, "and at best practiced for the sake of church unity." It meant that "[t]he effect of Paul's preaching and his vision of a new, unified Christian community was the destruction of the *ritual* distinction between Jew and Gentile within the Christian sect" (ibid., 27; emphasis in the original).

42. See Eisenbaum, *Paul Was Not a Christian*, 216–49; idem, "Jewish Perspectives: A *Jewish* Apostle to the Gentiles," in *Studying Paul's Letters: Contemporary Perspectives and Methods*, ed. J. A. Marchal (Minneapolis: Fortress Press, 2012), 135–50.

43. Cf. the work by Blumenfeld; Carter; Elliott (*Liberating Paul: The Justice of God and the Politics of the Apostle* [The Bible & Liberation, vol. 6; Maryknoll: Orbis, 1994]; *The Arrogance of Nations: Reading Romans in the Shadow of Empire* [Paul in Critical Contexts; Minneapolis: Fortress, 2008]); Harrington; Horsley (ed., *Paul and Empire: Religion and Power in Roman Imperial Society* [Harrisville: Trinity Press International, 1997]; idem, ed., *Paul and Politics: Ekklesia, Israel, Imperium, Interpretation: Essays in Honor of Krister Stendahl* [Harrisville: Trinity Press International, 2000]; *Paul and the Roman Imperial Order* [Harrisville: Trinity Press International, 2004]); Wright; and a few others. Cf. my longer argument in this regard ("Paul's *Imperium*: The Push and Pull of Empire, and the Pauline Letters [forthcoming]).

44. "The modern scholar trained in Jewish Studies might thus find himself [*sic*] in a position like that of Josephus, who writes of Roman power and politics in relation to war but tackles questions of culture with primary reference to 'the Greeks'" (Reed and Dohrmann, "Rethinking Romanness, Provincializing Christendom," 7).

45. The literary argument is that ancient Jewish literature tends to map Roman rule on biblical models, or onto the historical precedents provided by Assyrian, Babylonian, Achaemenid, Ptolemaic, or Seleucid rule. The specificity of Roman rule is typically smoothed away, e. g., when apocalyptically Rome is folded into Babylon or when in midrash, Jewish life in the Empire fades into the Deuteronomistic dichotomy of Israel and the nations. Glimpses of Jews' engagement with Rome's distinct imperial power are found e. g., in the *Kittim* of the Qumran literature or the (still fuzzy) Babylon-and-Rome of *4 Ezra* and Revelation (Reed and Dohrmann, ibid., 1).

46. Scholars often perceive Paul's relationship to Empire in narrow, individual terms: e. g., "one thing seems sure in the mystery which is Paul's life: he was a member of a client group beholden to but quite different from the Roman administration. As we know from modern examples, this predicament yields a very complex and difficult kind of doublemindedness, a combination of pride and shame at one's past, depending on the context" (Segal, "Paul's Jewish Presuppositions," 160).

47. See Feldman, *Jew and Gentile in the Ancient World*, 113–17; E. M. Smallwood, *The Jews Under Roman Rule: From Pompey to Diocletian* (Leiden: Brill, 1976), 144–209.

48. Such animosity often came from the Roman intelligentsia and the violence caused by localized tensions, and it was the Jewish success in attracting both converts and sympathizers that often aggravated Roman antipathy (S. G. Wilson, "Jewish-Christian Relations 70-170 CE," *ABD* 3.835). N. R. M. de Lange reckons that is only with the reign of Hadrian that Romans are seen as persecutors of Jewish religion: "The image of Rome in the subsequent rabbinic literature is predominantly a negative one" ("Jewish Attitudes to the Roman Empire," in *Imperialism in the Ancient World: The Cambridge University Research Seminar in Ancient History*, ed. P. D. A. Garnsey and C. R. Whittaker [Cambridge Classical Studies; Cambridge; London: Cambridge University Press, 1978], 269).

49. Fredriksen, "What "Parting of the Ways"?," 61.

50. E. g., exemption from military duty and the emperor cult, the right to keep the Sabbath and to collect the temple tax, cf. P. Perkins, *Reading the New Testament: An Introduction* (rev. ed.; Mahwah: Paulist, 1988), 28. C. D. Stanley ("Paul the Ethnic Hybrid?: Postcolonial Perspectives on Paul's Ethnic Categorizations," in *The Colonized Apostle: Paul through Postcolonial Eyes*, ed. Stanley [Paul in Critical Contexts; Minneapolis: Fortress, 2011], 125) argues that Roman anxiety about their status in comparison with the revered histories of the Egyptians and Greeks, and the special privileges accorded to Jews in many parts of the Empire, are testimony to Roman lenience regarding identity categories. By the fourth century the privileged position of the Jews in the Roman Empire changed with the political triumph of Christianity (de Lange, "Jewish Attitudes," 281).

51. Zetterholm, *Approaches to Paul*, 7.

52. E. g., ibid., 5.

53. Such animosity mainly came from the Roman intelligentsia and the violence caused by localized tensions, and it was the Jewish success in attracting both converts and sympathizers that often aggravated Roman antipathy (Wilson, "Jewish-Christian Relations," 835). And ambiguity reigned in any case, "The tension between pro-Roman and anti-Roman sentiment comes to be characteristic of Jewish attitudes in the following years. Prayers for the welfare of the empire stand side by side with prayers for its overthrow and the establishment of the messianic empire" (de Lange, "Jewish Attitudes," 266).

54. W. S. Green, "Otherness Within: Towards a Theory of Difference in Rabbinic Judaism," in *"To See Ourselves as Others See Us": Christians, Jews, "Others" in Late Antiquity*, eds. J. Neusner and E. S. Frerichs (Chico: Scholars, 1985), 49–69; Simmel, quoted in S. Matthews and E. L. Gibson, Introduction to *Violence in the New Testament*, ed. Matthews and Gibson (New York and London: T & T Clark International, 2005), 4; D. Frankfurter, "Violence and Religious Formation: An Afterword," in *Violence in the New Testament*, ed. Matthews and Gibson, 142.

55. "[T]he peculiarity of the Roman attitude toward the Jews seems better expressed by the term 'Judeophobia' in its ambivalent combination of fear and hatred. [. . .] [T]he Roman fear is peculiar not only in that it projects onto the Jews an irrational feeling of being threatened by some mysterious conspiracy but also, and mainly, in that it responds to the very real success of the Jews in the midst of Roman society, that it is the distorted echo of sympathy" (Schäfer, *Judeophobia*, 210–11).

56. "They [i. e., the Greco-Roman and Greek authors] turned Jewish separateness into a monstrous conspiracy against humankind and the values shared by all civilized human beings, and it is therefore *their* attitude which determines anti-Semitism" (ibid., 208).

57. Ibid., 181.

58. "Proselytism is a subject only in Roman, not in Greek literature" (ibid., 193). If Schäfer's reconstruction of Domitian's motives for prosecuting the *fiscus iudaicus* is reliable, enough Romans were drawn to conversion that their forced inclusion onto the tax roll might have significantly increased government revenues (ibid., 183; cf. 106–18).

59. McKnight's misleading objection that Wright's concerns with empire blurs his (Wright's) ability to place Paul in terms of his Jewish context ("when the empire temptation presents itself with one or more terms, the Jewish music is turned down or off so the Roman music can be given full play"; McKnight, "Empire Criticism and N. T. Wright"), succumbs to an inappropriate choice between Paul's Jewishness or embeddedness in Empire.

60. Even in his recent defense of the new perspective, Dunn is at pains to patch up differences with the "old" and "new" perspectives, and his interest is clearly in doctrinal matters: "The 'new perspective' simply asks whether all the factors which made up Paul's doctrine have been adequately appreciated and articulated in the traditional reformulations of the doctrine" (J. D. G. Dunn, "A New Perspective on the New Perspective on Paul," *Early Christianity* 4 [2013]: 157).

61. To group empire studies or anti-empire approaches under the rubric of "postcolonial" (Zetterholm, *Approaches to Paul*, 200–209) tends to blur the boundaries between such approaches by assigning a one-dimensional relationship to a much more complex and intricate set of relations between the empire and people in the first century CE.

62. Elliott, *Liberating Paul*.

63. See Zetterholm, *Approaches to Paul*, 200–209.

64. See Punt, "Empire and New Testament Texts: Theorising the Imperial, in Subversion and Attraction," *HTS Teologiese Studies/Theological Studies* 68, no. 1 (2012): 1–11, http://dx.doi.org/10.4102/hts.v68i1.1182.

65. On this key binary or "binomial" (Segovia) other binaries follow: civilized/uncivilized; advanced/primitive; cultured/barbarian; progressive/backward; developed/undeveloped or underdeveloped. In the discussion of Rome and its role and impact on the communities of the early followers of Jesus, the city of Rome constitutes such a metropolitan or rather imperial center, and areas such as western, and in particular, eastern parts of the ancient world, including subcontinents such as Asia, were peripheral areas (S. J. Friesen, *Imperial Cults and the Apocalypse of John: Reading Revelation in the Ruins* [Oxford: Oxford University Press, 2001], 17).

66. Every empire is imperial in its own distinctive way since "[t]here are empires such as the Ottoman, based on a common religious faith, and there are religiously tolerant, pagan, and even largely secular empires, such as Rome became in its grandest centuries. There are short-lived empires, based, like that of Alexander the Great, upon raw military power. And there are empires that thrive for centuries, usually because, like Rome and Carthage, they achieve commercial prosperity that can enlist the allegiance of far-flung economic elites, or because they establish a professional civil service, an imperial governing class" (M. Walker, "What Kind of Empire?," *The Wilson Quarterly* 26, no. 3 [2002]: 40).

67. Studies of the modern phenomenon of empire also focus on empire as construct, a *concept*, not a nation, and thus, without boundaries. Applying requisite caution, the recent studies (e. g., *Empire* [Cambridge and London: Harvard University Press, 2000] and *Multitude: War and Democracy in the Age of Empire* [New York: Penguin Books, 2004]) by literary scholar Michael Hardt and political theorist Antonio Negri on empire, nevertheless, add some valuable theoretical resources for theorizing (about) ancient empires.

68. Choosing against essentializing empire does not imply a disavowal of real life and flesh and blood entities (so e. g., J. K. Roth, "Response: Constructing and Deconstructing Empires," *JAAR* 71, no. 1 [2003]), but points to the illusionary nature of sure categories (essentialism) and certain grounds (objectivity) (cf. M. J. Brown, "Paul's Use of DOULOS CRISTOS IHSOU in Romans 1:1," *JBL* 120. no. 4 [2001]: 44), i. e., to view social phenomena in terms of transhistorical essences, independent of conscious beings, disallowing the notion that society or people determine the categorical structure of reality.

69. Modern empire theory provides further useful categories for theorizing the Roman Empire of the first century, but space does not allow much further discussion here; suffice it to mention the importance of borderlessness,

psychological impact, and claims upon world peace (Hardt and Negri, *Empire*, xv). At the heart of imperial peace is violence, ably supported by the military and various other structures, systems and manifestations of violence (cf. Punt, "Violence in the New Testament and the Roman Empire: Ambivalence, Othering, Agency," in *Coping With Violence in the New Testament*, ed. P. G. R. de Villiers and J. W. van Henten [STAR 16; Leiden: Brill, 2012]), and the position of Roman emperors and the elite depended on their *perceived ability* to inflict violence (S. P. Mattern, *Rome and the Enemy: Imperial Strategy in the Principate* [Berkeley, Los Angeles, and London: University of California Press, 1999]).

70. Demanding tribute and material from the "colonized," Jerusalem is portrayed in Galatians as the center defining the symbolic universe to which all colonies are mere extensions, on the periphery. The use of ethnic binarism, courtesy of the myths of homogeneity (gentiles as a collective sameness) and of difference (with ontological essentialisms used for polarizing gentiles and Jews in opposing camps), and also settler colonialism, aided the discursive onslaught of Jerusalem (S. Wan, "The Letter to the Galatians," in *A Postcolonial Commentary on the New Testament Writings*, ed. F. F. Segovia and R. S. Sugirtharajah [The Bible and Postcolonialism; New York: T & T Clark, 2007], 253).

71. Cf. Johnson-DeBaufre, "Historical Perspectives," 28; also M. Desjardins, *Peace, Violence and the New Testament* (Sheffield: Sheffield Academic, 1997), 66–68; Frankfurter, "Violence and Religious Formation," 140–52., esp. 142). Strife and fighting among Jewish revolutionary groups themselves were common (L. L. Grabbe, *Judaism from Cyrus to Hadrian* [London: SCM, 1992], 449–500; W. J. Heard, "Revolutionary Movements," in *DJG*, 696–97), and can, apart from other considerations, be related to the conflicting aspirations of groups that, while oppressed by a superior military power, were aimed at strengthening their own positions.

72. Claiming the scandal of a crucified Messiah, or proselytizing competition (admission of uncircumcised gentiles into the fray, or blurring the sociological divide) as basis for Jewish persecution of Jesus followers, does not hold water: Deut. 21:23 (in Gal. 3:13) contemplates someone executed for a capital offense, and first-century Jewish groups simply were not as exclusivist as the parting of the ways model suggests. Cf Eisenbaum, *Paul Was Not a Christian*, 142–46.

73. Eisenbaum, ibid., 137.

74. See P. R. Davies, "Life of Brian Research," in *Biblical Studies/Cultural Studies: The Third Sheffield Colloquium*, ed. J. C. Exum and S. D. Moore (Gender, Culture, Theory vol. 7; Sheffield: Sheffield Academic Press, 1998), 401.

75. See Eisenbaum, *Paul Was Not a Christian*, 145–47.

76. "Paul's elaborate allegory of heavenly and earthly Jerusalem in 4.21–5.1, if it was to retain any irony at all, assumed an unstated and hitherto unchallenged centrality of Jerusalem" (Wan, "The Letter to the Galatians," 254).

77. Ibid.

78. "Jerusalem arrived at its new position by first destabilizing the imperial discourse, casting doubt on Roman homogeneity by differentiating the circumcised from the uncircumcised, thereby contesting the imperial and dominant centre" (Ibid., 255).

79. See Punt, "Identity Claims, Scriptures and Rome in Galatians," *AcTSupp* 19 (2014): 81–104.

80. So R. Morgan, "New Testament," in *The Oxford Handbook of Biblical Studies*, ed. J. W. Rogerson and J. M. Lieu (Oxford; New York: Oxford University Press, 2006), 39.

81. "The valorization and magnification of Paul's view as *the* Christian view is the result of the interpretive process of history, not a fact of history" (Johnson-DeBaufre, "Historical Perspectives," 19).

82. R. A. Horsley, "Submerged Biblical Histories and Imperial Biblical Studies," in *The Postcolonial Bible*, ed. R. S. Sugirtharajah (The Bible and Postcolonialism 1; Sheffield: Sheffield Academic, 1998), 162.

83. In short, neither of the three options often exercised are sufficient: it was not simply Paul the Jew vs. the Romans (anti-empire readings); nor simply Paul the Jew and other Jews vs. the Romans (anti-empire readings of a historicist bent); nor simply Paul the Jew vs. other Jews because of the Romans (adjusted traditional approach).

84. See Reed and Dohrmann, "Rethinking Romanness, Provincializing Christendom," 3–4.

85. What Reed and Dohrmann (ibid., 2) call "the simultaneous Romanness and Jewishness of ancient Jews in the Roman Empire."

PART V

Paul beyond Judaism?

10

Paul the Jew Was Also Paul the Hellenist

Anders Klostergaard Petersen

Wie alles sich zum Ganzen webt,
Eins in dem Andern wirkt und lebt!
    —Goethe, *Faust*, v. 447f.

Initially, it may appear rather banal—verging on a tautological statement—to proclaim that Paul the Jew was also Paul the Hellenist.[1] After all, have we not—following in the aftermath of Martin Hengel's erudite work, *Judentum und Hellenismus*, and the scholarly discussions it gave rise to, also with respect to the interpretation of the emergence of formative Christ-religion and its texts—had almost half a century of studies that have been careful to highlight how Paul's Judaism should not be understood as exclusive of his Hellenism and vice versa? Nevertheless, the argument that I shall develop in this chapter may not be as trivial as it sounds on a first hearing. Despite the fact that we have had almost fifty years of discussion pertaining to the

Judaism/Hellenism debate and thirty years of intense scholarly exchange on Paul's respective Hellenism and Judaism,[2] I do not think that we have come far enough in terms of the theoretical underpinning and methodological subtlety that the question demands. Although scholars are often prone to emphasize the necessity of moving beyond the conceptualization of the problem in terms of a dualism, or, worse, a dichotomy, the binary formulation—still coming close in many cases to a dichotomization of the two entities—still characterizes much current work.[3] Paul the Jew is frequently played out against Paul the Hellenist and the other way around.

Some of this may have to do with difficulties pertaining to an inescapable "aspectualism": a study focused on Paul's relationship to Stoicism or Greco-Roman philosophy of a popular kind will find it hard to place simultaneous emphasis on Paul's Jewishness. Owing to the perspective one projects onto the world, there is a certain and obvious limit to how much one can encapsulate. That said, however, I think there is more to the question than having to make an inevitable choice when selecting a particular empirical focus for one's study. It is not only a matter of choosing sides or refraining from doing so, but a far more thorough question with important theoretical ramifications for how we ultimately understand culture and the relationship between different cultural entities—whether in the current world or in that of antiquity. In addition, this initial question also determines the methods to be applied in order to make the simultaneous double movement from the theoretical perspective to the empirical matter segmented by that particular view and back again. This also has significant consequences and implications for the models to be used, whether they are of a more abstract (for instance, culture or religion perceived as a system) or a more concrete nature (culture or religion understood in terms of a kinship metaphor).[4] It is through such models that we filter the theoretical perspective (see the figure below, which is meant as an iconic representation of the ideal relationship between theory, method, models, and empirical matter).

Theory, Model, Method and Empirical Matter

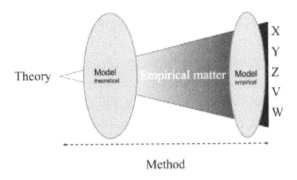

Method

Due to space constraints, I shall confine my discussion to three aspects with respect to which I want to provide a rejoinder to the current debate on Paul's relationship to Judaism and Hellenism or Greco-Roman culture. The three aspects are intrinsically related in terms of overall theoretical perspective. Additionally, I have decided to direct my attention to issues of a more theoretical nature, important for the discussion of Paul's relationship to Hellenism and Judaism. Since I got the impression that the first papers circulated at the conference underlying this volume were predominantly focused on empirical matters, I thought it beneficial to also have a contribution that concentrated more specifically on the discussion of various theoretical matters pertinent to the comparison between Paul's purported Hellenism and Judaism and the manner of staging the problem. It is to this question that I devote the rest of my chapter.

Provisional Sketch of the Three Main Issues

First, I think it is pivotal to explore how we may possibly refine our thinking about culture. Such an endeavor is crucial in order to develop a terminology and a concomitant manner of conceptualizing the relationship between what appear to us as different cultural trajectories, and to avoid the problem of turning Paul's alleged Judaism and Hellenism into a zero-sum game. Despite all allegations to the opposite, it is hard to avoid the impression that this is, in fact, the practical upshot of numerous studies in which the demonstration of one cultural entity is ultimately conceived of as a corresponding lack of the other.[5] Similarly, and as a reasonable objection to my line of thought, it may be argued that if we turn Judaism and Hellenism into excessively general, and, therefore, fuzzy categories, we are no longer able to make crucial, and finer, cultural differentiations and gradations. In fact, we especially risk emptying the category of Hellenism so that it is used in an extremely general and superfluous manner, as a floating signifier; thereby, it no longer comes to mean anything to designate one form of Judaism as being of a particularly Hellenistic nature. Perhaps there is a more theoretically appropriate manner of conceptualizing the relationship between cultural entities by which we shall, at one and the same time, be able to steer past the Scylla that turns Paul's Judaism and Hellenism into a binary choice and the Charybdis that makes the two of such a comprehensive nature that the differentiation between them loses its value. I concur with the astute observation of Erich Gruen when he endorses the view that:

> We avoid the notion of a zero-sum contest in which every gain for Hellenism was a loss for Judaism or vice-versa. The prevailing culture of the Mediterranean could hardly be ignored or dismissed. But adaptation to it need not require compromise of Jewish precepts or practices... Ambiguity adheres to the term "Hellenism" itself. No pure strain of Greek culture, whatever that might be even in principle, confronted the Jews of Palestine or the Diaspora. Transplanted Greek communities mingled with ancient Phoenician traditions on the Levantine coast, with powerful Egyptian elements in Alexandria, with enduring Mesopotamian institutions in Babylon, and with a complex mixture of societies in Asia Minor. The Greek culture with which Jews came into contact comprised a mongrel entity-or rather entities with a different blend in each location of the Mediterranean. The convenient term "Hellenistic" employed here signifies complex amalgamation in the Near East in which the Greek ingredient was a conspicuous presence rather than a monopoly.[6]

Second, I will attempt to sketch a taxonomy that will enable us not only to distinguish between different analytical levels, but also—and perhaps more importantly—to enhance our awareness of the analytical levels at which we, in a particular study, may operate with the

Hellenism/Judaism distinction. I think there are different levels of analysis to which this conceptual scheme may advantageously be applied, but it is important also to acknowledge the particular level at which one is working in a specific study of Paul's respective Judaism and Hellenism, whereby I do not mean to say, obviously, that one is excluded from operating simultaneously with different aspects as long as the pertinent levels are made theoretically and methodologically lucid.

Third, in continuity with recent work in the field of the study of religion, I suggest that it may be advantageous to extend the debate of Paul's Judaism and Hellenism to a level of analysis that, for a long period of time, has been neglected in the humanities and the social sciences: that is, that of cultural evolution. Needless to say, I acknowledge the contentious nature of this form of thinking, but I nevertheless find it imperative—for reasons that will hopefully become clear—to revitalize a manner of thinking that has been banned for almost a century. Evolutionary reasoning had its heyday from the Enlightenment to around 1920, when the experience of World War I made it intellectually impossible to uphold a form of thinking that had turned Western culture into the apex of civilization and Christianity into the zenith of the history of religion. Although there was a horrendous political aftermath of this type of thinking with the rise of the extreme right-wing political movements of the 1930s, it is fair to say that in intellectual circles, this form of reasoning came to a halt around 1920. In retrospect, though, we may have thrown the baby out with the bathwater: it may be useful to stop neglecting the evolutionary perspective and the scope of questions implied by it and to apply it to the field of problems pertaining to the relationship between Hellenism and Judaism in Paul's thought world. For this reason, I shall—despite potential problems in taking it up again—argue that we may benefit considerably from the evolutionary perspective when, for instance, we focus on the Hellenism/Judaism field of problems. In fact, the application of this perspective may—in line with my previous point—enable us to refine our discussion of the set of problems involved. However, it is pivotal to specify the manner according to which such a viewpoint may be assumed, since it should only be taken up again if it is possible to do so in a way that avoids the problems of previous, outdated, and politically highly dubious ways of endorsing evolutionary thinking.

Point One: Providing a Model for Thinking About Culture

By way of my endorsement of the quote from Erich Gruen above, I have indicated the problems that emerge if Paul's dependence on Judaism is turned into a zero-sum game in which placing focus on one cultural entity leads to a corresponding downplaying of the other. In order to move forward with the argument, however, it is obviously crucial to document how Paul's engagement with Hellenism did neither exclude nor reduce his belongingness to Judaism. There are several ways of looking at this question, but a pivotal point of departure is to decide the manner according to which we shall examine the categories. One reasonable way to scrutinize the problem is by adopting the emically abstract or second order perspective by which we would have to examine how Paul could possibly have understood his relationship to the entities "Judaism" and "Hellenism." In this context, however, I am not sure that such an approach would work, since I do not see how Paul could have used the concept of "Hellenism." After all, the way in which we use the term today is a reflection of a third-order or etic type of thinking, completely at odds with Paul's world. A different manner of proceeding, then, is to transfer the field of problems to the third-order or etic level of analysis. In this manner, I shall pose the question of how Paul may be seen to relate to the two cultural entities that we, for conventional reasons, have come to designate "Judaism" and "Hellenism."

In addition to making a choice with respect to the overall theoretical perspective, we also need to make it clear that when we are talking about the relationship between different cultural entities, we are providing a *Stillleben Bild* of culture that never existed in reality. There is not a 1:1 relationship between described and actual culture, as

Korzybski made patently clear by his distinction between map and territory. Although the map is an iconic representation of the territory, it would be a great mistake to conflate the one with the other.[7] The territory is only accessible to us by means of our specific approach that already calls for a particular manner of conceptualizing culture. So, let us begin here: how shall we understand culture in framing the question pertaining to Paul's relationship to Judaism and Hellenism and the intertwinement between them?

For good conceptual reasons, culture is often thought of in terms of a container that, by virtue of itself, is of a homogenous nature, but at the same time is open to influence from the outside. That is, cultural change is understood as a matter of foreign influence, or, alternatively, as a rejection of becoming susceptible to external impact, but even the latter choice is already, in itself, an exhibition of outside influence. Even the deliberate choice to reject foreign influence is, of course, also a way of coming under this influence, since it comes to determine what one sees oneself in need of discarding. In the wake of this tradition of conceptualizing culture, it is common to use terminology such as syncretism, bricolage, assimilation, and so on: concepts that imply the idea of pure entities. In the context of studies of the ancient world, this trajectory of scholarship has frequently been supplemented by the assertion that unlike the current world, ancient cultures were less complex, and therefore, less prone to cultural blending or amalgamation. The same idea is often transferred to the level of selves who are understood to be far more homogenous in terms of worldview than inhabitants of contemporary Western cultures.[8] From such a viewpoint, Paul—the advocate of virtues and vices of a Greco-Roman popular moral-philosophical nature—is seen by his use of catalogues of vices and virtues to detract from his corresponding Judaism.[9] From the perspective of this line of thinking, Paul the "user" of Stoic *peristaseis* catalogues, for example, is seen to be less "Jewish" than Paul the unremitting adherent of Jewish law.[10] Similarly, Paul, who, according to such a conceptual scheme, is turned into the prototypical exponent of the Jewish Diaspora, is held to be less "Jewish" than representatives of Palestinian forms of Judaism.[11] The underlying assumption, of course, is that Paul's Christ-determined Judaism should be measured on a scale that operates with a frequently underdetermined model of a normative Palestinian version of Judaism as the most genuine type of Judaism (that, of course, gives rise to another unspoken problem: that of which Palestinian Judaism should be conceived of as being the prototypical version of the category—Sadduceean or Pharisaic Judaism, for instance).

I do not underestimate or ignore the differences that exist between current Western culture and the ancient Mediterranean world, but I think it is a gross mistake to impute cultural homogeneity to the cultures of the past, and, corollary with such a view, to attribute uniformity with regard to worldview to particular persons of the ancient Mediterranean world. If, for a moment, we return to the previous quote from Gruen's *Heritage and Hellenism: The Reinvention of Jewish Tradition*, I even think that Gruen's argument here is not radical enough in terms of acknowledging the interweaving and crisscrossing of the different traditions with each other. Although our texts may, for rhetorical purposes, promulgate such a strong contrast between, say, Paul's Christ-adhering movement and the Greek world as found in 1 Cor. 1:22–24, the same texts embrace terminology, categories, structures, and rhetorical, intellectual, and ideological elements that blatantly reveal them to be part and parcel of the very same world that they rhetorically denigrate and deny belonging to. Provisionally, therefore, I think it is fitting and apt to conceptualize the relationship between different cultural/religious entities in terms of concentric circles that differ from each other only by virtue of their cultural extension and the degree to which one entity overdetermines the other.

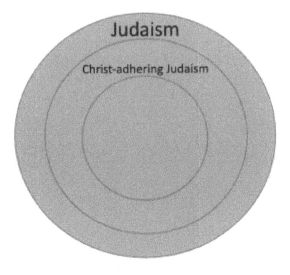

From the perspective of intellectual history, the different cultural entities of the epoch and the area they covered were different manifestations of similar and comparable structures. Needless to say, this observation is made from the etic perspective located at the highest level of abstract analysis. None of the texts would themselves have made such a contention. In addition, I shall emphasize that the more we focus on singular cultural entities and on the texts belonging to them, the more apparent the differences become between entities belonging to individual units of a more general cultural character.

Although the figure evokes a response from an etic perspective and has a bearing on the analytical level of a highly generalized concept of culture, it contradicts not only the ancient texts, but also conventional wisdom where differences between the individual manifestations are patently obvious. Despite similarities between singular traditions belonging to different cultural entities, the differences between them are also conspicuous. The figure below is meant to correct the deficiencies of the first figure by conveying a model that, on the one hand, defies a conceptualization of culture in terms of homogenous, pure entities, and, on the other hand, acknowledges and maintains the differences that, undoubtedly, remain between various cultural entities.

Cultural *koinē* of the Mediterranean World during the Hellenistic Period

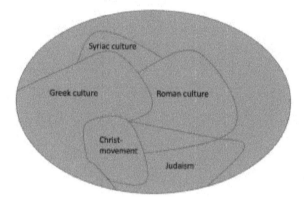

Apart from the overall circle that iconically signifies the common cultural koine of the different traditions (the basic point of the first figure), the inner part of this second figure is drawn as a Venn diagram. This type of diagram has the advantage of enabling one to point to identical, similar, or overlapping traditions (*per genus proximum*), and at the same time, to emphasize traditions particular to the cultural entity under scrutiny (*per differentiam specificam*).[12] By depicting the relationship between different cultural entities in terms of a Venn diagram, I hope to convey the insight voiced by Marshall Sahlins that culture, in general, although foreign in origin, is always distinctively local in pattern.[13] If cultural crisscrossing and perpetual interchanges between individual traditions are the norm rather than the exception, it is, of course, crucial that we do not understand the relationship between Paul and traditions of an allegedly other Greco-Roman, Hellenistic world in terms of culturally distinct and homogenous entities. It is more adequate and historically more appropriate to think of the relationship between the various traditions—that, due to a particular *Wirkungsgeschichte*[14] already initiated by the texts themselves, have led us into thinking of them in terms of culturally distinct and separate entities—in the light of such notions as "passing" and "hybridity."[15]

In order not to be misunderstood, I shall underline that I am not talking about a reciprocal relationship between the early Jewish traditions pertaining to the Christ movement and those that we traditionally think of as Greco-Roman (that is a problem beyond which I have not yet succeeded in moving in my iconic representations). During the earliest period of the Christ movement, there is no evidence that representatives of this group exerted any influence on elite traditions of the Greco-Roman world. Whereas we may find elements borrowed from different trajectories of Greco-Roman philosophy of a popular kind in early Christian writings, such as the Pauline Letters, we do not find Christian traditions in Greco-Roman philosophy during the period in which the earliest writings of the Christ movement were composed. This observation points to an important fact: talk about hybridity and passing in this context refers primarily to the minority or the culturally subordinated group. Instead of interpreting the elements in Paul known from Greco-Roman philosophical traditions as essentially foreign elements, however—whether one is talking of them in terms of borrowing or taking over—they ought to be understood as means by which a culturally subordinated group attempted to gain a position within the discourses of the dominating culture. It is in this particular context that scholars of postcolonialism have used the term *passing* to designate "the successful participation by individuals in multiple layers of dominant and dominated culture, especially the attempt by 'outsiders' to master attributes or tools of 'insiders' in order to gain recognition and power through the hegemonic culture itself."[16]

We need, however, to be careful about the inferences we draw from this vocabulary. If we do not interpret the terminology in the light of the previous theoretical reflections, we may, once again, fall prey to misunderstandings of an essentializing nature with respect to the conception of culture, since the terms highlighted may convey the impression that not only are we talking about essentially different traditions, but also that the "exploitation" of the dominant culture by dominated and largely "foreign" segments were of a deliberate character. Although the situation on an etic view may be interpreted in this manner, can we be sure that this was really the way according to which Paul, for instance, conceived of his use of traditions originating in popular Greco-Roman philosophical traditions?[17] In the Pauline Letters, traditions that we tend to think of as different in terms of origin are closely intertwined. Paul inhabited what, to our analytical categories, may appear as distinctively different worlds, but Paul apparently had no problem in passing from one to the other. He was a Jewish immigrant—although, perhaps, of Roman citizenry—to the communities he founded in the West, but he was also a newcomer to a persecuted cult. At the same time, however, he was the embodiment of a relatively advanced Hellenistic education (presumably the second level in terms of the three levels of Greek philosophical and rhetorical elite education), which allowed him to "vacillate" or commute between several worlds.[18] Different cultural traditions were intertwined with each other. Hence, it is reasonable to think of Paul not as a cultural bricoleur who, equipped with an Olympian overview, could do as he liked with respect to the use of different cultural traditions. To Paul, ostensibly, these traditions were merely part and parcel of the cultural identity he maintained, and that, of course, he understood to be representative of true Judaism.

By saying this, I do not surmise that people of the ancient Mediterranean world were incapable of distinguishing between cultural traditions. We have already seen how 1 Corinthians 1 shows Paul's ability to differentiate between what he understood to be incompatible religious traditions. Galatians 3:26–29 is another Pauline example that evidences the fact that Paul acknowledged the existence of what he perceived as different cultural and religious traditions. However, there is a huge difference with respect to the way people of the ancient world differentiated between various cultural traditions and the manner according to which modern scholarship makes such distinctions. I shall close this section by referring to a thought-provoking statement of John Barclay. Although formulated in a slightly different context, Barclay espouses a view that, undoubtedly, also applies to Paul's relationship to Judaism and Hellenism:

> But was there a clearly bounded cultural entity called "Judaism" to which various aspects of Hellenistic culture could be added, or was "Judaism" itself (and, for that matter, "Hellenism") in continual cultural flux, and thus creatively adopting different forms and expressions of itself? The concept of "hybridity", developed in post-colonial studies, may be of benefit here. In the mixing of indigenous and dominant cultures, we should not assess the resulting cultural cross-breeds by criteria of "authenticity", but expect both cultures to be transformed in continuing, and never static, processes of self-reinvention. The crucial questions here are not genetic (what element is taken from what traditions?), but strategic: whose interests are being served and at what cost to whom? In this light it is unhelpful to speak of "striking balances", as if some proportional calculus is to be applied (a bit of Judaism and a bit of Hellenism, in varying degrees).[19]

Point Two: Taxonomical Considerations in Discussing Paul's Relationship to Judaism and Hellenism

I hope to have made it clear that thinking about culture in terms of blending, as conceptualized by means of a Venn diagram—rather than thinking of it in terms of cultural borrowing, syncretism, bricolage, and so on—is a theoretically superior way of approaching the problem of Paul's relationship to various cultural traditions. In addition to the crucial insight of Sahlins that all cultures are hybrid by nature and that they are, therefore, foreign in origin but distinctively local in pattern, we may add another important point to the discussion formulated by Shils. He emphasizes how an important drive in the development of traditions is the interaction with other traditions that involves acts of imitation, borrowing, and differentiation.[20] I concur with Shils, but, once again, I shall have to express a reservation in order to pinpoint the perspective from which Shils's insight has particular relevance. Alternatively, due to the terminology involved, we may risk relapsing into a form of thinking about culture that, in light of my previous discussion, appears dubious. On the one hand, it would be presumptuous to deny Paul the possibility of having absorbed traditions from the surrounding cultural world and having integrated them into his own thinking. On the other hand, we shall have to be careful in formulating this form of cultural integration so that we avoid the risk of conceptualizing it from an emic point of view, and consequently, ascribing to Paul the Olympian ability of picking and choosing from his cultural surroundings. We may be helped in clarifying what we are talking about when discussing Paul's relationship to Hellenism and Judaism if we can make some simple taxonomical differentiations. We should be able to distinguish between different analytical levels at which the different exchanges with traditions of the Greco-Roman world could have taken place. Whereas the first three levels in the scheme below are of a relatively accessible nature, the fourth level is rather more imperceptible, wherefore I shall return to it in more detail in the next section.

Taxonomy of analytical levels for comparison

Level 1:	Direct historical relationship: x exerts influence on y.	A) Quotations → Direct / Indirect B) Particular motifs C) Clusters of motifs D) Larger patterns of thought
Level 2:	Indirect historical relationship: x exerts influence on y via z.	
Level 3:	Direct general historical relationship in terms of general mediation: x, y, and z belong to what from an etic perspective may be designated a shared pool of traditions.	
Level 4:	Indirect general historical relationship in terms of convergent cultural evolution: x, y, and z are comparable in terms of intellectual history and, occasionally, by virtue of social profile.	
Level 5:	Relationship in terms of cognitive and behavioral shared features.	

The first three levels depicted in this scheme should come as no surprise to scholars of late Second Temple Judaism. It is fairly easy to provide examples that comply with the various analytical levels from, for instance, at level one, Paul quoting in 1 Cor. 15:32, the general

Greek tenet of "Let us eat and drink for tomorrow we shall die" to level two Paul echoing basic ideas about virtues and vices shared by wide currents of the Greco-Roman and Jewish world. Similarly, it is easy at level three to think of Paul's understanding of, for instance, *epithumia* as expressed in Romans 6–7 as an example of a direct historical relationship between various cultural entities elicited by means of a general form of mediation.[21] Although a few colleagues come close to arguing that Paul has adopted his notion of *epithumia* from the Greco-Roman moral philosophical tradition,[22] I find it more accurate to conceive of the relationship with respect to this concept in terms of general mediation. There is nothing in Paul's discussion in Romans 6–8 to indicate the more specific notions found in the Greco-Roman moral tradition, nor is there anything to suggest that we have moved outside the realms of a form of late Second Temple Judaism exclusive to parallel interlacing with strands of the Greco-Roman world.

Point Three: Discussing Paul's Relationship to the Greco-Roman World in Terms of Cultural Evolution

As indicated in the introductory part, it remains contentious to endorse a cultural evolutionary perspective, given the strongly negatively loaded past of such a view. It is, therefore, imperative to make it patently clear that I do not discuss evolution in light of either truth or ethics, in contrast to previous forms of evolutionary thinking. I do not, with respect to the examined texts and cultures, assert that one manner of thinking is superior to another form in terms of truth.[23] Nor do I argue that one type of culture is ethically superior to another. I subscribe to the perspective of cultural evolution in the context of aesthetics only: that is, with respect to the question of higher or lesser degrees of cultural complexity. Since it is likely to cause misunderstandings, I want to emphasize that in the current debate about cultural evolution, nobody is raising the question in a manner that implies the superiority of one cultural entity over and against another with respect to either the true or the good. In that sense, the contemporary discussion is not a revitalization of the former debate, but in my view, it would be naive and scientifically unsatisfactory if we are no longer able to make distinctions between different forms of culture in terms of complexity.

The emergence of philosophical discourse with the pre-Socratic philosophers, for instance, marked the introduction of a form of thinking that, compared to previous types of religiosity, was more complex due to the fact that it added on to or extended the previous cultural strata, and yet, was unthinkable without them. Similarly, the appearance of various types of Judaism subsequent to older and more archaic forms of Israelite religion was unthinkable without the existence of the former ones that they, in a simultaneous process, both presupposed and polemicized against. This is the manner in which aesthetic complexity may be discussed with respect to the question of cultural evolution.[24]

Additionally, ongoing and vibrant research in the field of cognitive science has made it inevitable in the humanities and social sciences to reflect upon the relationship between nature and culture and not only upon their interactions. In terms of brain size, according to cognitive scientist and psychologist Merlin Donald, not much has changed over the past two million years. Donald divides the evolution of humankind into a three-stage theory that allows for gradual transitions taking place between four phases. The first decisive change took place when our bipedal but apelike ancestors acquired the ability to communicate via voluntary motor acts—that is, with the transition from episodic to mimetic culture. The next significant change took place with the emergence of mythic culture approximately thirty thousand years ago, when our predecessors, *Homo sapiens sapiens*, obtained the ability to communicate by means of linguistic signs—that is, by spoken language. According to Donald, the final crucial evolutionary transition occurred with the appearance of literate or symbolic culture that considerably enhanced the possibilities of external memory storage. This has been a process of increasing acceleration that has not yet come to an end. One of the things that this new research in the field of cognitive studies forces us to do is to rethink the relationship between culture and nature, and especially, those intermediary layers with regard to which it is difficult to ascertain the precise influence of biological and cultural components. Of utmost importance, additionally—on the basis of Donald's theory that constitutes the framework for the late Robert Bellah's work on cultural evolution—is the insight that the modern mind comes forward as a hybrid structure, built from vestiges of earlier biological stages as well as new external symbolic memory devices that have radically altered its organization. This has given rise to Bellah's now famous tenet that when it comes to the question of cultural evolution, nothing is ever lost—or nothing decisive, that is. Bellah and Donald's assumption, with which I concur, implies that all human culture should be conceived of in relation to and built upon older biological and cultural layers of memory. Implied in their view is also the fact that cultural evolution is not of a peremptory, irreversible nature. Things may, by virtue of being built on older cultural strata, be rolled back, just as the cultural evolutionary development Bellah envisages is based on the Durkheimian idea that symbolic culture can only persist by means of underlying biological and cultural layers. One may ask, however: what has this to do with the question of Paul's relationship to Judaism and Hellenism?

Much, indeed. If one places the discussion in the wider context of the emergence of axial-age culture, much of the difference between the Greco-Roman world and Judaism fades away, in the sense that the question cannot now be reduced to a contrast between Hellenism, on the one hand, and Judaism, on the other. The developments in ancient Greece and Israel may be seen as embedded in a larger and far more comprehensive process of transition that occurred in a number of Eurasian cultures during the late-sixth century BCE, and, subsequently, from China in the far East to India, from the Near Oriental world with ancient Israel as a prominent example to ancient Greece in the West (see level four of my fourth chart above). In China, the change was personified by renouncers and thinkers such as Confucius, and later, Mencius and Xunzi. In India, this development was embodied by Gautama Siddharta, the Buddha to be; it was epitomized in Israel by the prophets and in Greece by the pre-Socratic philosophers and Socrates and Plato some years later. Needless to say, this development was not only of an intellectual character.

As Jared Diamond, among others, has argued, there were good reasons why this development took place in this specific geographical area and during this particular period. Natural presuppositions contributed to social processes such as the increased urbanization that was conducive to the scientific inventions and better exploitation of natural resources that simultaneously and reciprocally gave rise to new forms of thinking. Although these intellectual manifestations were individually very different from each other, there are also conspicuous similarities when one compares them. They all mark an important transition in terms of thinking with respect to previous forms of religion, which continued, but at the same time, were extended and fed by the new types of discourses; this led, in turn, to continuous interchanges between the two, in positive, but also—frequently—negative ways. In this manner, the whole question of the relationship between Hellenism and Judaism in the ancient world should not be confined to the Greco-Roman part of the Mediterranean basin and Israel only. We need to situate the development of the two cultural spheres in the wider context of axial-age types of culture/religion.[25] Thereby, we shall be able to see how the time-honored dualism between Hellenism and Judaism disappears, since discourses of the two cultures of the axial-age type may better be understood as an alternative form of cultural-evolutionary development within the context of ancient Eurasian religion. There are five elements that come to the fore in the context of religious changes in the transition from archaic to axial-age forms of religion.[26] First, the latter exemplify the emergence of thinking about thinking: that is, contrary to previous forms of religion, they are characterized by a growing utilization of self-reflexivity frequently expressed as second-order concepts and by the ability to understand one's own thinking and practice from an ostensibly external perspective. Second, this form of self-reflexivity, which amounts to a foundational epistemology, is often voiced in spatial categories whereby differences between opposing views are projected onto a vertical structure that frequently manifests itself as the contrast between the heavenly view over and against the earthly. Congruent with this staging of the dualism is its projection onto an axis of depth. The contrast is here extended as a difference between the interior and the exterior, the soul and body, corresponding to the location of heaven and earth on the vertical scale. Sometimes, the ascription of values to these two axes is correlated with a horizontal, temporal scale where the difference is voiced in terms of a contrast between past and present. This may take several forms in which the difference can be assigned to a negative past vs. a positive present and vice-versa. It may also manifest itself—as is well-known from Pauline eschatology—as the difference between a negative past and a positive present (that of the Christ adherents) that simultaneously corresponds to a positively ascribed true past (for instance, the Abraham tradition) that predates the negatively assigned past (for instance, the Moses tradition). Third, the transition from archaic to axial-age forms of religion is characterized by the development toward heno- or monotheism: that is, by the reduction of the divine pantheon of archaic types of religion. Fourth, axial-age forms of religion are typified by a strong awareness of the existence of rivaling worldviews that need to be denigrated to substantiate the truth of one's own worldview. Fifth, the axial-age forms of religion are distinguished from archaic ones by the idea that the adherents shall emulate the godhead to such an extent that they eventually transgress the ontological differentiation between the divine and human realms so characteristic of archaic types of religion, whereby they are transformed into the same material as the deity, and in some cases, even transferred to the place of the godhead.

Once again, I shall underline, in order not to be misunderstood, that I am not attempting to conceal obvious differences between the various cultural manifestations of the different cultural/religious entities involved in my comparison. However, what I do claim is that behind these occurrences, we find a number of striking similarities that are best explained in terms of convergent evolution. Although the early Christ movement, in terms of origin, is considerably later than the emergence of the first axial-age forms of culture, I think it is obvious to conceive of it as a post-axial phenomenon, which is to say that it presupposes the first axial transition. There are other types of late-Second Temple Judaism not only in the Diaspora, but also in the land of Israel that testify to the influence of axial-age thinking, but the early Christ movement is a prominent example. This is evident in our earliest sources: the Pauline Letters. The pervasive apocalyptic worldview that permeates Paul's thinking is, obviously, of a distinctively Jewish nature, but this manner of conceptualizing the world also bears witness to striking similarities to the basic cognitive scheme of Platonism and subsequent forms of Hellenistic transcendental philosophical movements—as has been persuasively demonstrated by Henrik Tronier in several publications.[27]

Contrary to traditional ways of discussing this relationship, however, we need not surmise a historical relationship in which Platonism exerted direct influence on Paul's thinking. I think the theoretical model presented here is superior to a strong causal-historical one, since the latter suffers from the difficulty of substantiating Platonic influence on Paul in any direct manner. The point here is that the two cultural manifestations are exemplary of what we may dub convergent cultural evolution: that is, the fact that comparable cultural developments are likely to occur if certain social and basic biological and nutritional presuppositions are present. In this sense, both may be understood as different representatives of two types of axial-age thinking. The same holds true for many of the resemblances between Paul and Stoicism that have been brought forward in recent years, not least by my Copenhagen colleague Troels Engberg-Pedersen.[28] Rather than seeing Paul as the Jewish pursuer of Stoicism that Engberg-Pedersen, in some of his works, comes close to depicting, I find it more persuasive to account for the demonstrable similarities between Paul and Stoicism in terms of convergent evolution. Such a perspective has the great advantage of enabling us, on the one hand, to acknowledge similarities while we retain, on the other hand, those aspects of Paul's worldview that make it very different from an exclusively Stoic one. Similarly, a number of resemblances highlighted by scholars in recent years between Paul's social-moral inculcations and those found in the popular Greco-Roman moral-philosophical tradition would, in my view, benefit from being discussed in terms of convergent evolution, rather than, as has been the case, in terms of a predominantly genealogical frame of reference. I do not think that it is coincidental that it has been difficult to substantiate such similarities when one has recourse to a model focused on direct historical influence only.

A Brief Conclusion

Rather than having examined some specific Pauline passages or having discussed Paul's basic worldview compared with that of advocates either of the Greco-Roman or the Jewish thinking of the era, I have moved in a slightly different direction. In this chapter, I have been mostly concerned with a number of theoretical issues that, in my view—and if we want to advance the discussion in the future—should be considered particularly relevant to the question of Paul's relationship to Judaism and Hellenism. Apart from the fact that this time-honored debate has suffered from numerous ideological biases, I think it has also been incomplete, owing to its overwhelming focus on a "strong" model of historical influence and a concomitant incapacity to differentiate between the different analytical levels at which Paul's relationship to Judaism and Hellenism may be discussed. What I have suggested in this chapter is a new manner of resuming the Hellenism/Judaism debate with respect to Paul.

I have concentrated on three issues of general interest. First, I have briefly sketched a model of thinking about culture that should help us to avoid the risk of making Paul's relationship to Judaism and Hellenism a zero-sum game in which the demonstration of Hellenistic elements would imply the view of a negatively-corresponding absence of Jewish elements. Second, I have sketched a taxonomy that could enable us to differentiate between four levels (some of them involving sublevels as well) of analysis at which Paul's relationship with Judaism and Hellenism may be fruitfully discussed. Third, in line with the recent resurgence of cultural evolutionary theory, I have proposed a manner of thinking in which the discussion of the Judaism/Hellenism debate in the context of Paul may benefit from the inclusion of such a perspective that involves the idea of convergent evolution. The overall point is that such a perspective has the potential of bringing the debate forward in a way in which we may finally move beyond the Judaism/Hellenism divide not only at the empirical level of analysis but also at the underlying theoretical level.[29]

Notes

1. Some of the arguments presented in this article have also been developed in my "Alexandrian Judaism: Rethinking a Problematic Cultural Category," in *Alexandria. A Cultural and Religious Melting Pot*, ed. George Hinge and Jens A. Krasilnikoff (Aarhus: Aarhus University Press, 2009), 115–43; "Reconstructing Past (Jewish) Cultures," in *With Wisdom as a Robe. Qumran and Other Jewish Studies in Honour of Ida Fröhlich*, ed. Károly Dániel Dobos and Miklós Kőszeghy (Sheffield: Sheffield Phoenix, 2009), 365–83; and "Finding a Basis for Interpreting New Testament Ethos from a Greco-Roman Philosophical Perspective," in *Early Christian Ethics in Interaction with Jewish and Greco-Roman Contexts*, ed. Jan Willem van Henten and Joseph Verheyden (Leiden: Brill, 2013), 53–81.

2. That is, if one takes the modern scholarly discussion of Paul—dating back to E. P. Sanders's *Paul and Palestinian Judaism* from 1977 which, in hindsight, has been reckoned as the beginning of the so-called New Perspective on Paul—as one's point of departure. Needless to say, there is an extensive trajectory of scholarship predating the contemporary debate. This current of scholarship dates at least as far back as the emergence of the *Religionsgeschichtliche Schule* in Göttingen at the end of the 1880s, when the second wave pertaining to the question of the relationship between Christ religion and Judaism and Hellenism respectively took its beginning. At that time, the differentiation of "Jewish" and "Hellenistic" components of early Christ religion became a crucial question and syncretism a catchword in the appraisal of the formative Christ religion; on this, see my forthcoming essay "Franz Cumont and the History of Religions School," in *The Christian Mystery. Early Christianity and the Pagan Mystery Cults in the Work of Franz Cumont (1868-1947) and in the History of Scholarship*, ed. Annelies

van Lannoy and Danny Praet (Turnhout: Brepols, 2016). Prior to that, however, the question had already loomed large in, for instance, the philosophy of Hegel and among a number of prominent Enlightenment thinkers. Therefore, and though the assertion is common, it is not correct to see Droysen as the originator of the modern concept of Hellenism, even if he, in continuity with the Tübingen school, came to exert strong influence on the subsequent debate on Hellenism: on this see Arnaldo D. Momigliano, "J. G. Droysen. Between Greeks and Jews," in *A. D. Momigliano: Studies on Modern Scholarship*, ed. Glenn W. Bowersock and Tim J. Cornell (Berkeley, Los Angeles and London: University of California Press, 1994), 147–61, and for the older discussion, Reinhold Bichler, '*Hellenismus'. Geschichte und Problematik eines Epochenbegriffs* (Darmstadt: WBG, 1983).

3. This also applies to the magnum opus of my former teacher Martin Hengel, as has been pointed out by John Collins in his retrospective review (John J. Collins, "Judaism as *Praeparatio Evangelica* in the Work of Martin Hengel," *RSR* 15, no. 3 [1989]: 226–28). Collins criticizes Hengel's depiction of the relationship between Judaism and Hellenism for creating a narrative that ultimately serves to pave the ground for the emergence of Christianity. For the ideologically-loaded nature of the Hellenism/Judaism debate, see Troels Engberg-Pedersen, "Introduction: Paul Beyond the Judaism/Hellenism Divide," in *Paul Beyond the Judaism/Hellenism Divide*, ed. Engberg-Pedersen (Louisville: Westminster John Knox, 2001), 1–16; Dale B. Martin, "Paul and the Hellenism/Judaism Dichotomy: Toward a Social History of the Question," in ibid., 29–61; and Philip S. Alexander, Philip S., "Hellenism and Hellenization as Problematic Historiographical Categories," in ibid., 63–80.

4. To the best of my knowledge, the importance of models in the filtration of the theoretical perspective has been especially well highlighted and elaborated upon by Jeppe Sinding Jensen. See his *The Study of Religion in a New Key: Theoretical and Philosophical Soundings in the Comparative and General Study of Religion* (Aarhus: Aarhus University Press, 2003); and "Conceptual Models in the Study of Religion," *The Oxford Handbook of the Sociology of Religion*, ed. Peter B. Clarke (Oxford: Oxford University Press, 2009), 245–62; as well as the more accessible volume for scholars not trained in the philosophy of science *What Is Religion?* (Surrey: Acumen, 2014).

5. This also pertains to the proponents of the self-acclaimed Radical New Perspective on Paul. In a recent essay, a leading advocate of this viewpoint, Mark Nanos, has dubbed this current of scholarship "Paul within Judaism" to emphasize the precise nature of the shared conviction among scholars belonging to this trajectory. By virtue of the emphasis they place on Paul's Jewishness, however, they come to pay very little attention in reality to those currents in Paul that, from an etic point of view, appear to be of a Greco-Roman nature. This is also evident in Nanos despite his argument to the contrary in his "Introduction" to the volume *Paul within Judaism: Restoring the First-Century*

Context to the Apostle, ed. Nanos and Magnus Zetterholm (Minneapolis: Fortress, 2015), 1–29: "Of course, Judaism—that is, the Jewish way(s) of life—was also an expression of Greco-Roman culture that included a great deal of diversity, not least in the Diaspora where Paul was active. These scholars [i. e., those working within the perspective—AKP] work from the presupposition that Judaism, as a multifaceted, dynamic cultural development, took place within other multifaceted dynamic cultures in the Hellenistic world, and thus that there is a lot more interaction and combining of cultural ideas and behavior than categorical distinctiveness or social separation, as scholars traditionally supposed. They want to avoid perpetuating the usual habits of scholarship that implicitly, when not explicitly, represent Paul as engaged in creating an entirely new and different culture, new communities, and even a new religion; moreover, that he was doing so specifically in conflict with Judaism." There are at least three elements in this quote that call for further consideration: 1), the theory of culture implied by the quote; 2), the implicit assumption that Diaspora Judaism in toto should be more prone to influence from the Hellenistic world; and 3), the theoretical ambiguity pertaining to the use of the notion *newness*.

6. Erich Gruen, *Herritage and Hellenism: The Reinvention of Jewish Tradition* (Berkeley: UCL Press, 1998), xiv.

7. See Alfred Korzybski, "A Non-Aristotelian System and its Necessity for Rigour in Mathematics and Physics," in id., *Science and Sanity. An Introduction to Non-Aristotelian Systems and Semantics* (4th ed.; Englewood, NJ: Institute of General Semantics, 1958), 747–61, which, contrary to common practice, deserves to be quoted at length. Korzybski originally presented the paper before the American Mathematical Society at the New Orleans Meeting, American Association for the Advancement of Science, 28 December 1931. In it, he includes the perspicacious analogy to map and territory with respect to which he subsequently develops his argument about language and mathematical language: "If we consider an actual territory (*a*) say, Paris, Dresden, Warsaw, and build up a *map (b)* in which the order of these cities would be represented as Dresden, Paris, Warsaw; to travel by such a map would be misguiding, wasteful of effort. In case of emergencies, it might be seriously harmful. We could say that such a map was 'not true', or that the map had a *structure not similar* to the territory, structure to be defined in terms of relations and multidimensional order. We should notice that: A) A map may have a structure similar or dissimilar to the structure of the territory. (1) B) Two similar structures have similar 'logical' characteristics. Thus, if in a correct map, Dresden is given as between Paris and Warsaw, a similar relation is found in the actual territory. (2) C) A map *is not* the territory. (3) D) An ideal map would contain the map of the map, the map of the map of the map, endlessly." In the study of religion, Korzybski's insight has been elegantly applied by Jonathan Z. Smith ("Map Is not Territory," in id., *Map Is not Territory: Studies in the History of Religion* [Leiden:

Brill, 1978], 289–309) to whom the map/territory distinction is now commonly ascribed.

8. See the discussion in my forthcoming article "The Use of Historiography in Paul: A Case-Study of the Instrumentalisation of the Past in the Late Second Temple Period," in *Historiography and Religion*, ed. Jörg Rüpke, Susanne Rau, and Johannes Bronkhorst (Berlin: De Gruyter, 2015), 63–92.

9. The classic treatment of this subject is Anton Vögtle, *Die Tugend und Lasterkataoge des Neuen Testaments: Exegetisch, religions-, und formgeschichtlich untersucht* (Münster: Aschendorff 1936), but see also the still very readable treatise of Adolf Bonhöffer, *Epiktet und das Neue Testament* (Gießen: Alfred Töppelmann, 1911) and the more contemporary studies of Abraham J. Malherbe, "Hellenistic Moralists and the New Testament," *ANRW* 2.26.1: 267–333; and David C. Aune, "Passions in the Pauline Epistles: The Current State of Research," in *Passions and Moral Progress in Greco-Roman Thought*, ed. John T. Fitzgerald (London and New York: Routledge, 2008), 221–37.

10. See, for instance, Martin Ebner, *Leidenslisten und Apostelbrief. Untersuchungen zu Form, Motivik und Funktion der Peristasenkataloge des Apostels Paulus* (Würtzburg: Echter Verlag, 1991); and John T. Fitzgerald, *Cracks in an Earthen Vessel: An Examination of the Catalogues of Hardships in the Corinthian Correspondence* (Atlanta: Scholars Press, 1988), who show in detail the close correspondences between Pauline lists of sufferings and those found in Stoic and popular philosophical sources.

11. As I have argued in a recent paper ("New Testament Traditions in the Context of Judaism: a Humpty-Dumpty Take on a Moot and Ideologically Skewed Way of Phrasing a Problem" [presented at the Nordic New Testament Conference, Aarhus, 29 May–2 June 2015]), such an understanding is also reverberated by Nanos's otherwise perspicacious view in Nanos, ibid., 9f. (cf. my footnote above where the full quote is given). This is noteworthy since Nanos is one of the leading proponents of the so-called Radical New Perspective on Paul, or what Nanos rightly prefers to designate the "Paul within Judaism" Perspective.

12. As is evident from the iconic representation, I have made no attempt to adjust the size of the individual entities of the diagram to the actual percentage-wise relationship between them in terms of area, particular time period, and cultural impact. The diagram serves merely as an illustration of a more basic theoretical tenet pertaining to the underlying conceptualization of culture that I espouse. In addition, the entities featured in the diagram serve to illustrate the theoretical point; it does not make any claim to comprehensiveness. Hence, the circle denoting indigenous Syriac culture has been arbitrarily picked to illustrate the overall point of different cultural entities characterized, on the one hand, by their share in a common pool of traditions, and, on the other hand, by their cultural distinctiveness.

13. Marshall Sahlins, "Two or Three Things that I Know about Culture," *The Journal of the Royal Anthropological Institute Incorporating Man* 5, no. 3 (1999): 399–421.

14. I use the German term *Wirkungsgeschichte* in this chapter since the English category "history of reception" does not denote the precise nature of what I intend to encapsulate by the German term. The English word is equal to German *Rezeptionsgeschichte*, but this category implies an individual, subjective element of receiving tradition and making it one's own. *Wirkungsgeschichte*, in contrast, denotes the sheer development of traditions as chains of continuous sign productions.

15. For the notion of hybridity in postcolonial theorizing, see among others Robert J. C. Young, *Postcolonialism: An Historical Introduction* (London: Blackwell, 2001), 345–47; and Ania Loomba, *Colonialism/Postcolonialism* (London: Routledge, 2005), 145–53.

16. Rebecca Lyman, "The Politics of Passing: Justin Martyr's Conversion as a Problem of 'Hellenization'," in *Conversion in Late Antiquity and the Early Middle Ages: Seeing and Believing*, ed. K. Mills and A. Grafton (Rochester: University of Rochester Press, 2003), 37.

17. The problems pertaining to developing a language that moves beyond the deliberate and acknowledged oscillation between different cultural traditions are conspicuous in this regard. Even such a careful analysis as that of James Constantine Hanges has serious problems in moving beyond a language that imputes a high degree of deliberate choice to Paul's vacillation between different traditions: see, for instance, Hanges, *Paul, Founder of Churches. A Study in Light of the Evidence for the Role of "Founder-Figures" in the Hellenistic-Roman Period* (WUNT 1.292; Tübingen: Mohr Siebeck, 2012), 451.

18. Cf. Ronald Hock, "Paul and Greco-Roman Education," in *Paul in the Greco-Roman World: A Handbook*, ed. J. P. Sampley (Harrisburg: Trinity Press, 2003), 198–227.

19. John M. G. Barclay, review of John J. Collins, *Between Athens and Jerusalem: Jewish Identity in the Hellenistic Diaspora*, *JJS* 52 (2001): 363–68; cf. the quote above from Erich Gruen.

20. Edward A. Shils, *Tradition* (Chicago: Chicago University Press, 1981).

21. For an extensive discussion of this topic, see Emma Wasserman, *The Death of the Soul in Romans 7: Sin, Death, and the Law in Light of Hellenistic Moral Psychology* (WUNT 2.256; Tübingen: Mohr Siebeck, 2008), and for the notion of *epithumia* as a central concept in Graeco-Roman moral philosophy, see the true masterpiece of Martha Nussbaum, *The Therapy of Desire: Theory and Practice in Hellenistic Ethics* (Princeton: Princeton University, 1994).

22. See, for example, Stanley K. Stowers, *A Re-Reading of Romans: Justice, Jews, and Gentiles* (New Haven and London: Yale University Press, 1994).

23. Needless to say, I am only making the argument with respect to the texts and cultures under scrutiny. In terms of different interpretations of the examined

texts and cultures, one should, of course, distinguish between higher and lesser degrees of plausibility pertaining to different interpretations.

24. See my forthcoming essays "The Use of Historiography in Paul" and "Zur Zeit wird hier das Raum: A Cultural Evolutionary Perspective on Paul and His Religion as Epitomised by His Letters," in *Spatialising Practices*, ed. Gerhard van den Heever (Leiden: Brill, 2016).

25. Until recently, culture and religion were identical or overlapping entities: it is only since the Enlightenment that the two have moved apart and it has become possible to distinguish between them, even if this development pertains predominantly to the Western part of the world. Of course, it was possible in the ancient world to differentiate between different degrees of sacrality, wherefore we also have the distinction between *sacrality* and *profanity*. The point here, however, is that the notion of secularity is unthinkable prior to Enlightenment traditions at the earliest. Phenomena such as theatre, sports, eating, visits to the toilet, etc., were to greater or lesser degrees, in the ancient world, all part of that which we, from a modern etic perspective, designate by the category *religion*.

26. See my essay "Attaining Divine Perfection through Different Forms of Imitation," *Numen* 60, no. 1 (2013): 7–38.

27. See, for instance, Henrik Tronier, "The Corinthian Correspondence between Philosophical Idealism and Apocalypticism," in *Paul Beyond the Judaism/Hellenism Divide*, ed. Engberg-Pedersen, 165–96.

28. See, for instance, Engberg-Pedersen, *Paul and the Stoics* (Edinburgh: T&T Clark, 2000), and id., *Cosmology & Self in the Apostle Paul. The Material Spirit* (Oxford: Oxford University Press, 2010).

29. I think that at least some of the essays in the edited book by Troels Engberg-Pedersen (*Paul Beyond the Judaism/Hellenism Divide*) do, in fact, bring us forward at the empirical level of analysis with respect to the field of problems under scrutiny. However, the book is slightly disappointing when it comes to the overall discussion of making progress at the theoretical level and at the corollary levels of methodology and applied models.

11

Paul, Antisemitism, and Early Christian Identity Formation

William S. Campbell

The letters and reported activities of Paul have been used both negatively and positively in relation to the topics of anti-Judaism/antisemitism—thus there is a somewhat ambivalent attitude to his legacy. As Lloyd Gaston has noted, "[W]hatever the effect of the Gospels, it is Paul who has provided the theoretical structure for Christian anti-Judaism from Marcion through Luther and F. C. Baur down to Bultmann, in a manner even more serious than Ruether indicates in her brief discussion of Paul."[1] I will begin, therefore, by looking at Paul's contribution in both its positive and negative aspects to consider how this should be evaluated, but first, I will consider briefly some aspects of the history and origin of anti-Judaism/antisemitism.[2]

Continuity in Theological Traditions:
Historic Animosity in Christian Tradition
and the Legacy of Antisemitism in the Drive to De-Judaize

In my opinion, it is not entirely unjustified to describe the basic drive in modern antisemitism as being to rid the world of Judaism, in all its forms and influences.[3] This goal is supported both by pseudoscientific racial groupings, entirely without rational support, and by a prejudice against Judaism, both in itself (but particularly, as it emerges within Christianity) and because of its supposedly tribalistic/particularistic tendencies. Historically, prior to the emergence of Christianity, there had existed a form of anti-Judaism/antisemitism in the Roman Empire: a prejudice against Jews because of their distinctive view of God and way of life. Such attitudes can legitimately be viewed as part of a general distinction between Greeks and barbarians—that is, toward those who differed from the pan-Hellenic ideal, especially as such attitudes often coexisted alongside a respect for Judaism's ancient cultural, and particularly, its legal, heritage. However, this form of anti-Judaism has been considered by some as both the forerunner and origin of anti-Judaism/antisemitism in its more developed forms. Thus, Peter Schäfer argues that there was "hostility directed at the Jews which distinguishes the Jews from other ethnic groups. . . . '[T]he' Jews are identified as the outcasts of human civilization."[4] It is

> . . . the phobic mystification of the out-group which distinguishes the "anti-Semitic" from the "anti-Jewish" attitude. Since it is the peculiar result of the amalgamation of Egyptian and Greek prejudices, one might argue that only the idea of a world-wide Greco-Hellenistic civilization made it possible for the phenomenon we call anti-Semitism to emerge.[5]

Despite its existence prior to the New Testament era, which must certainly be acknowledged, the vital question to be faced is how or whether this prejudice relates to the anti-Judaism of the post-New Testament era. The balance of opinion appears to lie with the view that it was only after the emergence of the gentile mission, and later than the fall of the temple, that we can talk of an anti-Judaism proper, sourced in and arising from the emergent Christian movement.[6] With Paul, I will maintain, it is still possible to have a real dialogue concerning Judaism, because "he faces Jewish issues within a Jewish framework."[7] But within Christianity in its early expressions and through the centuries prior to the full-blown emergence of antisemitism in the nineteenth century, there existed varied forms of animosity toward Jews.[8] This increased considerably with the growth of gentile Christianity, and the eventual elevation of Christianity to a state religion, when Judaism itself, and all forms of following Christ in its Jewish expressions, were marginalized or even persecuted.

The primary reason for animosity against Jews in the earliest period of Christian origins concerned the unwillingness of many Jews to acknowledge Jesus as the Messiah. On the Jewish side, messianic claims were not unknown, nor were they necessarily a cause for division or persecution.[9] But, for some Christians, the failure to recognize their Messiah was tantamount to questioning, and thus, destabilizing their symbolic universe.[10] Thus, the relation of Christianity to contemporary Judaism and its debt to its Jewish roots became an early source of internal debate as evidenced, for example, in the exaggerated views of Marcion, which, though rejected, persisted only to reappear occasionally as a radical option in the modern period, especially when the identity of the church was in dispute.[11]

As the *Adversus Judaeos* literature indicates, rivalries had existed as early as the beginning of the second century between Jewish and Christian groups—the latter becoming increasingly gentile-dominated, and anti-Jewish.[12] Such rivalry, as in any groups competing for the allegiance of people, accentuated the differences and minimized the commonality between these two entities, leading to negative self-definition and consequent increasing divergence.[13] However, the real and genuinely sibling rivalry was an internal one about how Jewish or un-Jewish the new faith should become.[14] This internal division was fueled both by its parallel existence alongside Judaism and by political factors such as Roman legislation that, in its effect, was more favorable to one or the other group, and varied according to local circumstances as to which was in the majority or minority.[15] But the most serious consequence of this internal dispute about the Jewishness of Christianity was that it eventually reflected negatively on Jews external to the church. An internal identity dispute was externalized, and eventually, led to a negative self-definition over against Jews and Judaism[16] that, beginning in the post-Pauline era, was destined to become the badge of Christianity as a whole. The other aspect of this concern for internal conformity was that Jews, as a whole, necessarily had a negative identity foisted upon them that was determined by the Christian need for a foil against which to negatively define themselves.

When Judaism continued to exist long after the fall of the temple, and in some places, to flourish, to certain Christian leaders at least, from Ignatius to John Chrysostom, it was perceived as a real threat, against whose attractions their flock had to be protected. The friendly association between Jews and Christ followers continued in some regions for several centuries at least.[17] Augustine was one of the first Christian theologians to credit Judaism with any religious value in itself.[18] But throughout the centuries that followed, even until the Reformation, relations between Jews and Christians—though often peaceable—were seldom cordial, and were frequently punctuated by periods of political instability in which Jews sometimes flourished financially because of laws against usury, but were generally used as scapegoats in every situation of crisis. In order to survive, they were forced to migrate frequently across the centuries, hence the origin of the myth of "The Wandering Jew."[19]

The negative stereotyping of Jews and Judaism had become enshrined in Western culture and tradition to the extent that it affected not only how contemporary Jews were regarded, but even how the period of Christian origins was and is to be interpreted. Luther, though initially more favorable, eventually turned strongly against the Jews, regarding their faithfulness to the Torah as the negative reflex of the contemporary church with its emphasis on merit.[20] Yet again, as in the case of Ignatius and Chrysostom, the reaction to Judaism was triggered by an inner Christian debate, rather than from a genuine interest in Jews. There was little or no interest in Judaism as such, but only in its use for polemical or apologetic purposes. Overall, the Reformation did little to change the prospects of Jews, but the Enlightenment enabled them in some places to flourish, and the possibility of fully integrating in society became a reality in nineteenth-century Europe. Significantly, it was at this period, when Jews were becoming more fully involved in European culture, that modern, fully developed antisemitism appeared.[21] The emergence of racial theories[22] had already taken place in late medieval Spain. The ideology of "purity of blood" (*limpieza de sangre*) was introduced by the Spanish church as an indirect result of the forced conversion of many Spanish Jews as an alternative to expulsion. The threat caused by the sudden influx of ex-Jews (*conversos*) into the higher echelons of Spanish society led to the promulgation of a series of statutes to limit the influence of the "new Christians," supposedly because of their liability to infidelity. But, though scholars disagree, it appears that this early racist ideology was not "the ancestor of the Nazi Nuremberg laws," or a "dress rehearsal for the nineteenth century," as some claimed it to be.[23] In his critique of Ruether, Alan Davies notes that the Spanish precedent was not imitated by the Germans, and insists that modern racial antisemitism arose out of the alienated spiritual condition of modern humanity, and not—as Ruether maintained—as a secular mutation of a more ancient prejudice. Thus, racial antisemitism based on the use of pseudoscientific theories functioned in support of treating the Jews as a separate, foreign entity; not only did it not allow them the opportunities for equality that the Enlightenment had seemed to guarantee, but it served as a rationale for further discrimination against them.[24]

A pattern of anti-Jewish interpretation was integral to Christianity throughout a great deal of its history. In some respects, this paralleled the treatment of other minorities, but differed in its communal depth and theological support. Popular anti-Jewish prejudice was imbibed with mothers' milk, and the churches' teaching—whether in sermons, liturgy or creeds—offered an ongoing theological tradition that allowed or even ensured that anti-Judaism was endemic in European society. An early example of the church's involvement in anti-Jewish legislation with a racial component is provided, as noted above, in late medieval Spain. In the modern period, the tragedy of anti-Judaism, already a horrific evil in itself, was that it also contributed to and was involved in the rise of secular antisemitism.[25] As Alan Davies summarizes,

> Indisputably, the religion which watered the cultural soil of the West throughout the centuries with its negative myth of Jewish existence was no minor factor in the success of Nazi propaganda, because of its grip on the popular as well as the ecclesiastical mind right down to our own generation. But it was not the *only* force at work for ill.[26]

Thus, however we attribute the relative blame, Christianity, in its social history—while not being *solely* guilty of the production of antisemitism—demonstrates a complicity in the prejudice that assisted its persistence.[27]

But if it is concluded that Christianity, however substantial the role it played, is not to be regarded as the sole originator of antisemitism, an attribution of blame to another source is demanded. Although Greek xenophobia certainly existed, can it be argued that a pre-existing prejudice against Jews or Judeophobia *as such* was a sufficient cause to explain the origin of antisemitism? Hannah Arendt has made a strong case that modern antisemitism should be regarded as a completely new entity.[28] John Gager rightly views the confusion around this issue as partly being due to the use of terms such as *antisemitism* or *anti-Judaism* in a global manner, as if they encompassed the full range of interactions between Jews and Christians in antiquity.[29] He insists,

> Our study has led to the conclusion that neither in paganism nor in Christianity is there evidence for a consistently negative understanding of Judaism. All of the surviving testimony—including the most vigorously anti-Jewish and anti-semitic examples—suggests that Judaism provoked among Christians and pagans alike profound *internal* divisions.[30]

Gager retains the term *antisemitism* to designate hostile statements about Jews and Judaism on the part of gentile outsiders—these showing little real knowledge of Judaism and being based on sweeping generalizations. For early Christian judgments against Judaism, he uses the term *anti-Judaism* because these are primarily a matter of religious and theological disagreement.[31] Whether there can be any general consensus is debatable, but it appears that a good case can be made for a latent antisemitism, probably intermittent in its effects, that existed primarily in literary form in the pre-Christian era.[32] What is significant, in my view, in deciding that this attitude to Jews differs from normal forms of xenophobia is its almost mythical dimension—the exaggeration and distortion of the significance of Jews as a constant threat to the civilized world. Thus, Alan T. Davies combines anti-Judaism and antisemitism in the German term *Judenhass*,[33] but perhaps more appropriate is Peter Schäfer's preference for *Judeophobia*: "On the whole, . . . the peculiarity of the Roman attitude toward the Jews seems better expressed by the term 'Judeophobia' in its ambivalent combination of fear and hatred."[34]

In this long period of history, there can be no doubt that even though the anti-Judaism that many perceive in the remainder of the New Testament played a dominant role, and was complicit in the rise of modern antisemitism, the interpretation of Paul's letters and the reports of his activities also played a significant role in a variety of ways. We will first consider the negative effect of these.

Aspects of Paul's Gospel that Seem to Threaten the Status of Israel: Accusations Against Paul

At the commencement of this section, I wish to stress that in my opinion, although Paul's rhetoric and situational context lends itself to enormous diversity in interpretation, *his role in relation to anti-Judaism has been accentuated most seriously by the presuppositions of his interpreters.* It is a most difficult enterprise to attempt to separate the "historical Paul" from the Paul of New Testament reception history.[35] This is not to suggest that past interpreters should have been capable of entirely transcending their own social locatedness, but rather, that, even allowing for historical factors, more accuracy could have been exercised.[36] As noted above, the prevailing tendency of interpreting Paul as the heroic emancipator of gentiles from the "bondage" of Jewish law made it difficult to view the apostle in any kind of positive relation to Peter and the (Jewish) "Christian"/apostolic leadership in Jerusalem. The *adversus Judaeos* materials simply presumed that Paul, like the other New Testament authors, was an enemy of Judaism; by the second century, moreover, they came to regard Jewish indifference or contempt for the gospel as a permanent condition. Their function was to secure Christian identity for gentiles. As Paula Fredriksen notes, "[a]rguments *adversus Judaeos* served to confirm certain constructions of gentile Christian identity against many challengers. . . ."[37] On the contrary, it is quite clear that Paul was much more difficult to "gentilize" than even the image of Jesus. Both Johann Gottlieb Fichte and Paul de Lagarde greatly disliked the apostle Paul because of his ineradicable Jewishness and its subsequent legacy in Christian theology.[38] The latter was a very different image from the Paul of the church fathers, who used real or imagined Pauline arguments in order to denigrate Judaism.[39]

Behind most of modern New Testament interpretation lies the almost all-pervasive influence of F. C. Baur, the great Tübingen scholar. More than most of his contemporaries, Baur clearly recognized the tendency of Lutheran dogma to dominate the interpretation of Paul. Baur was extremely innovative in that he took as his starting point not the framework of Christian theology, as was customary, but a historical focal point where the dynamics of the tension between Jew and gentile offered the option of a new perspective. His concern with the *Sitz im Leben* provided a new and lasting historical-critical potential for understanding the New Testament and Paul in particular. Baur, despite emphasizing historical origins, was strongly influenced by a particular Hegelian philosophy of history that was greatly to hinder his attempt to historically contextualize, especially with respect to Judaism.[40] We will return to Baur's perspectives and influence from time to time in our subsequent discussion. We will now consider five aspects of Paul's gospel that have been perceived as threatening the status of Israel.

Paul's Self-Designation as Apostle to the Nations:
An Indication of a Lack of Hope for Israel?

First, Paul's role as apostle to the nations is frequently assumed to mean his abandonment of his "previous" Jewish identity, and his call and subsequent concentration on the gentile mission is considered to be evidence that he no longer saw any value in Israel or her Torah. Some scholars, such as Rosemary Ruether, accentuate Paul's contrasts between flesh and spirit to give a dualistic interpretation. However, Paul's dualism—if we can use the term at all in relation to his thought—is an *ethical* dualism, not an ontological one.[41] Unfortunately, when Paul is interpreted in binary categories, Jews and Judaism are usually assigned to the negative category—as, for example, in the faith/works antithesis.[42] Ruether—though by no means totally unjustified in her various critiques of traditional Christianity—is too extreme in depicting Paul as accentuating the eschatological division of the ages in a dualistic pattern that allows no positive value of any kind to Torah religion, and, by extension, even to Israel. Paul can refer to his kin according to the flesh in a purely neutral sense without pejorative overtones. Since gentiles do not enter the scene until Rom. 9:24—and, at this point in the chapter, Paul is discussing calling only with respect to Israel—we should translate Rom. 9:8 as "for it is not those of fleshly descent *alone* who are the children of God, but those of fleshly descent and of promise who are Abraham's seed."[43] Paul's discussion in Romans 9–11 does concede ongoing validity to Judaism, rather than assuring only the ultimate vindication of the church. Ruether neglects the full impact of Romans 9–11 for understanding Paul's relation to his ancestral faith, and thus—wrongly, in my opinion—assigns to him the stance of anti-Judaism, thereby missing the unique perspective within the New Testament of his concern for God's purpose with Israel.[44] Paul's concern for the gentile mission should not be viewed as antipathy toward Israel, but rather, as evidence of his parallel concern for her ultimate restoration. Both of these perspectives emerge out of his zeal for the glory of God.

Paul's Critique of the Function of the Law—a Critique of Israel?

One aspect of Paul's gospel that was particularly obnoxious to Jews is his apparent denigration of the law, especially in such strong language as "ministry of death" (2 Cor. 3:7), "children of slavery" (Gal. 4:24f.; Rom.7:21–24), and so on. In my opinion, Paul's view is significantly debased when scholars take individual statements from differing letters, addressing differing contexts, and assemble them together in a thematic, systematic relation as if Paul were outlining his general theological stance on particular topics.[45] The resultant "theology" is a selective, decontextualized, generalized amalgam of ideas that Paul never actually expressed in any one letter.

Apart from this criticism, another factor not sufficiently recognized is that Paul's letters are all addressed to gentiles, and his reporting on, and views of, the law are therefore specifically directed to *the law as it affects gentiles*, whom he is desperately trying to discourage from attempting to follow this. Even though this explanation does not solve all our problems with Paul's discussion of the law, it at least helps to explain why the content of his letters would, in this aspect, seem very foreign to Jews, and likewise, why his interpreters find apparently anti-Jewish elements within them (especially when the addressees are not explicitly identified as gentiles). In any case, when it is not assumed that Paul's letters are addressed to both Jews and gentiles, reading them as addressed to gentiles offers a radically different hermeneutical key to his thinking.

Another contextual factor that helps to explain how Paul's statements were decontextualized to sometimes give them an anti-Jewish function is relevant here. When Paul argued fiercely for the equality of gentiles in Christ, he did so to prevent them yielding to pressure to also become Jews and to keep the law. In so doing, he produced arguments against gentile Judaizing that were intended to protect gentiles in a minority situation. But later, when his letters were read in a new context dominated by gentiles, the arguments against Judaizing—arguments for equality—became interpreted against Jews and Jewishness of any kind, in a manner entirely atypical of the apostle. Here again, as previously noted, we find an example of how internal Christian discussions were reapplied externally with disastrous consequences.

The Universal Emphasis of Paul's Gospel: Favoring Gentiles and Disadvantaging Jews?

Yet another emphasis in Paul that appears to threaten Jewish identity is the universal aspect of his gospel. His frequent stress upon πᾶς and πάντες, "all," includes and seems to categorize together both Jew and gentile. Some interpreters use this apparent universalism to draw a contrast between Judaism as narrow, tribalistic, and exclusive, in comparison with a (theoretically) all-embracing Christianity. Granted, it is a common feature of Paul to speak of Jew and gentile in the same sentence, suggesting that one major feature of his message is a removal of the distinction between two entities historically distinguished by the covenant. But this universalism has to be interpreted within the framework of a Jewish understanding of creation that is inclusive of all humanity, whether Jewish or gentile. It is inclusive in terms of diversity, not via an imposed sameness that denies or seeks to overcome the diversity of creation.[46] Despite occasional voices denigrating the gentile overlords and persecutors of Israel, Israel's peculiar vocation is to be a light to the gentiles: a vocation that is to bind Jew and gentile in mutual relation within the ongoing purpose of Israel's God. As Terence Donaldson summarizes this form of universality: "Israel's story is thus set within the universal story of God's dealings with the whole human race, rather than over against it."[47] From this perspective, the more typical emphasis of Paul is expressed as "not to the Jew only, but also to the gentile" (Rom. 3:29–30, 4:9), since this form of expression, though inclusive, encapsulates the abiding difference while resisting polarity.

Behind the problems in interpreting the universal aspects of Paul's gospel lies an assumed philosophical contrast between the universal and the particular. This is a modern assumption that owes much to the tendency toward binary thinking and shows the influence of Hegel's form of philosophy, as exemplified in the thought of F. C. Baur.[48] Baur claimed that though "Judaism and Christianity stands in a narrow and unmediated relationship. . . . the Old Testament concept of God has, on the other side, also such a genuinely nationalist imprint that the whole stands in its particularism in the most distinct opposition to Christianity."[49] Such a contrast usually has the effect of denigrating Judaism by comparison with Christianity, and it seems to be a comparison that is obviously valid. That is primarily because it arises from a modern contrast. As Johannes Munck has asserted, "[t]he opposition between universalism and particularism is the product of a modern cosmopolitan outlook and has nothing to do with the biblical concept of the mission [of the early church]."[50] Thus, contrary to our preconceptions, universalism and particularism need not be opposing ways of viewing the world, but can, in Jewish thought—of which, in this respect, Paul is a good exemplar—be rather understood as complementary, the universal operating via the particular, so that particularity and universality are both intelligible and relevant in understanding the vocation of Israel (and by implication, also in relation to Paul).[51]

A secondary outcome of a perceived universalism in Paul's pattern of thinking is the tendency to universalize his statements made within a limited, specified context—to apply them generally or universally.[52] As noted above with reference to Paul's critique of the law in relation to gentiles, this decontextualizing arises especially when Paul's audience is perceived to comprise both Jews and gentiles—his statements addressing humanity in general, the common needs of all people. Thus, what Paul says in Galatians can be imported into Romans without adjustment[53]; what he says to the Galatians about circumcision must be construed as concurring with statements on this same topic elsewhere. The result is that Paul appears to contradict himself (especially in the discussion of Jewish issues), or, alternatively, that some texts are simply ignored in favor of others.[54] I do not wish to deal further with this theme, but I simply note that it is a presupposition of Paulinism that Paul's statements must have a universal application, thus rendering the Pauline *sine qua non* distinction between Jew and gentile effectively redundant and meaningless. Paradoxically, this widely pervasive presupposition is often not even discussed even among those deeply indebted to the Pauline framework inaugurated by F. C. Baur, whose most important contribution was to read Paul strictly and critically in his historical context.

Call: A Conversion Out of Judaism into Christianity?

We now turn to the issue of whether or not Paul abandoned his previous Jewish identity on becoming apostle to the gentiles. Paul's statements certainly stress his ongoing adherence to this ancestral faith: "I also am [not *was*] an Israelite" (Rom. 11:1); "Are they Israelites? So am I" (2 Cor. 11:22). Such clear, specific identifications must take precedence over other texts, which can be interpreted as indicating otherwise, but *which need not necessarily be thus interpreted*. The KJV translation of Gal. 1:13 indicates how this verse is viewed as problematic: "For ye have heard of my manner of life in time past in the Jews' religion." This translation, with its emphasis on the otherness of the religion of the Jews, shows how this verse can easily be taken to demonstrate that Paul abandoned Judaism for the sake of following Christ. But the best understanding of this statement is that Paul is simply referring back to a previous period in his life, prior to his Damascus road experience. If he had said something such as "my way of life when I lived in Damascus," this backward reference would carry merely a neutral reference to a previous historical period without such overtones of dismissal or abandonment as are sometimes read into the verse.

Some problems arise specifically because Paul's Damascus road experience is interpreted anachronistically in the framework of modern conceptions of conversion, leading to the view that he had to be *either* Jewish or Christian due to the conversion requirements. But at the period Paul received his call/vision, Christianity did not exist as a separate entity, but was a messianic movement within the diversity of contemporary Judaism. To view Paul as called is not to deny the reality of his experience, but only how it is to be interpreted. Other Jews also became followers of Christ, but they did not become members of a new religion. The peculiarity in Paul's instance is partly due to the fact that he was called not to be a reformer within Judaism, but to be apostle to the gentiles, thus lending more credence to the view that Paul must have turned away from Judaism. Once again, we see how a binary form of thinking leads to the erroneous conclusion that Paul could not be both Jewish and follow Christ.

In the same vein, 1 Cor. 9:19ff. suggests, on Paul's part at least, a limited or only occasional observance of Jewish patterns of life. Paul asserts that though he was free from all men, he put himself under bondage to all, so that he might win the more. Surprisingly, he says "[t]o the Jews I became as a Jew" (1 Cor. 9:20), as if he were, in fact, no longer a Jew. But the succeeding verses indicate that Paul's rhetorical flourishes demonstrate that he accommodates to diverse groups of people for the sake of the Gospel,[55] rather than that he lived out a series of contradictory life patterns in succession.[56]

Similarly, in Phil. 3:1–8, Paul seems to declare that all Jewish things are completely worthless: like rubbish, in fact. But, when we read carefully, we find that Paul states that he counts all things, gentile as well as Jewish, as loss. In an image of profit and loss—in accountancy imagery, not toilet imagery—Paul asserts that in comparison with Christ, all else is as nothing, but not that these things, in and by themselves, have no value. Apart from the comparison with Christ, whom Paul regards as the Messiah of Israel, the items compared retain their own inherent value, and, even within the Christ comparison, it could be argued that *in Paul's perspective*, this is certainly not an anti-Jewish stance. Likewise, the rhetorical claim in 1 Corinthians 7 and Gal. 5:19 that circumcision is nothing and uncircumcision is nothing is another way of saying that, in and by itself, simply to be Jewish or to be gentile does not make one closer to God or his purpose. Ethnicity, in and by itself, is not decisive in the divine evaluation of all things.[57]

Decontextualized Pauline Rhetoric: A Criticism of Judaism?

As our consideration of these verses indicates, part of the problem faced by Paul's interpreters is that Paul's rhetoric is challenging. He exaggerates to emphasize. He strategically plays the fool in order to shame his boasting opponents and converts.[58] In his Letter to the Romans, he relates Jew and gentile to one another to stress both equality in Christ, and yet, abiding difference. Having insisted on their equality, he proceeds in Romans to allow a certain advantage (not privilege)[59] to the Jews according to their covenant heritage, Scriptures, and so on. Having acknowledged the sinfulness of all of humanity, he then introduces the possibility that Israel has been rejected and may be no different from gentiles, but then goes on to claim that though, at the present, there is only a remnant that responds positively to the message of the Christ movement, eventually "all Israel will be saved." So, Paul's rhetorical strategies are themselves confusing, and admittedly, part of the problem faced by his interpreters—rather than, in my view at least, his use of weak arguments or contradictions in his thinking.

Again, Paul's challenging arguments stem, partly at least, from the fact that he was addressing letters to gentiles[60] to, in some sense, Judaize them,[61] without—at the same time—allowing them to become proselytes to Judaism. In fact, he faces a well-nigh impossible task: to relate gentiles to Judaism and its symbolic universe without—at the same time—giving an adverse picture of Judaism as a possible reason for not going the whole way to becoming proselytes. If Paul had held a derogatory view of Judaism as an inferior religion, as in Baur's assessment it had to be, he could have won converts much more easily. Again, if he himself had really turned his back on Judaism, he could have said so as a warning to others. His real problem was how to explain why gentiles should not become Jews—and yet, develop a self-understanding of what it means to be a non-Jew within a Jewish framework of understanding. For converts to learn to be a gentile was no easy task.[62]

This apparent ambivalence may have been sensed by members of Paul's ἐκκλησίαι and exploited by his opponents. It is characteristically demonstrated by the fact of Paul's own consistent affiliation to the practice of Judaism. If he had really lived like a gentile, he would have offered a living gentile model, in whose life and practice, a mirror was held up in which others could see clearly both themselves and their calling. But Paul did continue to live Ἰουδαϊκῶς ("Jewishly," Gal. 2:14), and the way he related his life and practice to gentile Christ followers was to teach them to "remain as they were when called" (1 Cor. 7:20), not to become Jews. He could not have taught them, thus, had he himself not remained a Jew, as he was when called. This became his acknowledged pattern in all his ἐκκλησίαι (1 Cor. 7:17).

From this perspective, we have arrived at a very good reason why Paul did not—in fact, could not—give up living Jewishly. As noted above, a common characteristic of Paul's thinking was to relate Jew and gentile—though remaining ethnically distinct—within the ongoing purpose of God, as he himself understood this to be unfolding in the Christ event. But he did not argue in binary fashion, *either* Jew *or* gentile, but in an inclusive pattern, "to the Jew (first) but also to the Greek" (Rom. 2:9-10; 9:24). And because he did not argue in binary fashion, he did not experience the contradictions that some of his interpreters can neither avoid nor resolve. Thus, some problems in understanding Paul are the problems of his interpreters, far removed from the world of the apostle. Some consider Jews as being favorites of the God of Israel,[63] and their own solution to this unfairness seems to be to displace the Jews and replace them by gentiles, who now, by a fiat of reversal, occupy the favored position—*thus, not really dealing with the issue of apparent divine favoritism, whether to Jew or gentile.*

Despite his favored title, "apostle to the gentiles," Paul himself did not envision his apostolic calling as serving a function *only* in relation to the gentiles, as if he had concluded they were to form a separate entity completely divorced from Jews and Judaism. Rather, he believed and hoped that a successful mission to gentiles would have a salvific influence on Jews, so that, together, they would then achieve the goal of the divine purpose to join in harmonious worship of the God of Israel (Rom. 15:7-13). Thus, Paul's vocation can be most accurately described, not in a one-sided partisan way as the lone, heroic apostle to the gentiles who delivered them from the bondage of the law, but rather, as apostle to the gentiles for the sake of Israel and the glory of God. Paul, unlike some of his interpreters, both ancient and modern, did not see hostility as the only and inevitable relation between Jew and gentile. Although he was frequently engaged in conflict, he did not see conflict as a necessary principle of divine evolution, but as the result of sin operating in and through human beings, whether Jewish or gentile. Thus, the obliteration of ethnicity or separation from Judaism would not necessarily solve this problem, whether for him or his converts. He did not envision his role as being the overcoming of ethnic division through the formation of non-ethnic ἐκκλησίαι—as a "third entity" neither Jewish nor gentile[64]—but as assisting in the removal of hostility through the reconciliation of Jew and gentile *as Jews and as gentiles* in the divine purpose. Paul had a very developed concern for his own people (Rom. 9:3-5), as well as for gentiles also, and thus, he can speak of "the daily pressure upon me of my anxiety for all the churches" (2 Cor. 11:23-28). He followed a vision that, though differentiated and circuitous in conception, embraced not just part, but the whole of humanity.

Aspects of Paul's Gospel and Activity that are Affirmative of the Identity of Israel

As already noted, Paul's letters have provoked differing images of him in relation to Israel. But there is no real difficulty in finding statements within them that are strongly supportive of the high status that, in my view, he still continues throughout his life to attribute to Israel.

Paul both affirmed and sought to defend Jewish identity in several ways:

Paul Never Identifies gentiles as Israel

I put this point first because it was such a central and significant aspect of Paul's mission. There was no uniformity in the early centuries of the church, and sometimes, the terminology of *new Israel* was applied to those uncircumcised, but in Christ. There is also debate about whether the New Testament is uniform in not using the terminology of *Israel* for gentiles, as in the case of Paul. But what has become increasingly clear in recent Pauline scholarship is that the term *Israel* belongs exclusively to the historic people of God. Despite ongoing attempts to somehow equate those in Christ with Israel, there is no evidence in Paul's letters of this option. The key passages, Rom. 9:24f. and Gal. 6:16, simply do not support such a view.[65] Indeed, Paul is the least likely New Testament writer to confuse the identity of circumcision and uncircumcision. Israel, κατὰ σάρκα—"according to the flesh"—is not used negatively and is never counterbalanced by a phrase such as Israel "according to the Spirit."[66]

A major problem with including Christ-following gentiles in Israel—even if were accepted that this is what Paul does—is that the division between Christ followers and the "rest of Israel," so significant for Paul that he wrote three long chapters (Romans 9–11) on the topic, is overlooked as if all of God's purpose for all humanity had now been fulfilled. That such a perception of Israel means a takeover of the inheritance of Israel is obscured by the fact of combining the uncircumcision with Jewish Christ followers. This would also have the effect that the righteous remnant—in Paul's view, obviously a remnant from the circumcision—becomes, instead, a joint remnant of Jewish and gentile Christ followers. And if both Jewish and gentile Christ followers are together combined in the term *Israel*, what proportion of this combination would be required to be Jewish in order to legitimate the term? Elijah believed that he alone of all God's prophets remained (Rom. 11:3-6). But Paul rejects Elijah's despairing estimate and cites the divine estimate, not as one only, but as seven thousand faithful (Rom. 11:4). So, neither in the time of Elijah, nor even in Paul's lifetime, would only *one* be sufficient to represent Israel. The variation of this view argued by N. T. Wright is that Christ represents Israel as the true Jew, that Israel and her function as "light to the nations" is taken over without remainder by Christ, and that "the rest" disappears because all Israel is thus redefined.[67] Such a view gives no reason for the tears Paul sheds on behalf of his "brothers according to the flesh."[68] Further, there is no New Testament text that equates Christ with Israel. For Paul, Israel is not a theological concept to be defined and redefined at will by Christian theologians; Israel is the historic people of God, but certainly never legitimately gentile, even in part.[69]

Paul Respects and Seeks to Operate in Accordance with the Jerusalem Summit Agreement of Two Distinct Missions

The significance of arguing that Paul worked in tandem with, and not in opposition to, the Jerusalem leadership is crucial in determining his attitude to Jewish identity. If he recognizes the validity of Peter's leadership of a mission to the circumcision, this means that Paul is still operating within an ethnic discourse of Israel and the nations. It means also that he recognizes that while Peter is called to lead the mission to the circumcised, he himself is not thus commissioned. Again, if Paul keeps to the Jerusalem summit agreement, then he acknowledges that his mission requires recognition from fellow Jews even while it is directed to gentiles. It also means that he has not written off Israel, or a mission to Israel. If Paul had broken relations completely with Peter at Antioch and started his own independent mission, then this action would constitute Paul as one of the best examples of the sectarian spirit, sometimes manifested in Christianity in earlier history, but especially, today. Such a spirit would have lent impetus to all the divisive tendencies of new movements, especially in respect of relations with Judaism, and could possibly have completely hindered the development and growth of Christianity. Hence, Paul's ongoing concern for unity.[70]

A serious defect in James Dunn's argument that the "Antioch incident" of an argument between Peter and Paul is that he credits Paul with "push[ing] what began as a qualification on covenantal nomism into an outright antithesis." Thus, "far from being one identity marker for the Jewish Christian alongside other identity markers (circumcision, food-laws, Sabbath), faith in Jesus Christ becomes the *primary* identity marker which renders the others superfluous."[71] By using faith in Christ both as the primary identity marker—and claiming that this, however, was not the case with Jewish Christ followers—Paul forced through his more radical opinion to produce an antithesis with Jewish identity and a break with Peter mission. These combinations render Paul anti-Jewish by producing, from his reported activity, an *antithesis* with Judaism. Granted that there are numerous ways of reading the "Antioch Incident,"[72] my main criticism of Dunn's position is that it depicts Paul as actively promoting division somewhat as if he were an enthusiastic sectarian against Judaism. Given Dunn's generally favorable attitude to Judaism, it is sad to see his use of the typically hostile, value-laden term *antithesis*, and his depiction of Paul as proactive in producing the antithesis. Not only so, but by replacing *antithesis* after, and in relation to, the pioneering rebuttal of scholarly anti-Judaism by Sanders, Dunn has actually assisted in "putting the clock back" to where we were prior to Sanders, but with added interest! Jews can now be condemned for ethnic pride, and ethnic separateness as an expression of "good works." Indeed, Sanders's achievement seems at this point to have been entirely ignored.

Paul Defended Both Jewish and Gentile Christ Followers' Distinct Identities by Stressing "Remain as You Were When Called"

In earlier research on Romans 9–11, I soon recognized that if Jewish identity were to be regarded as incompatible with being in Christ, then there could have been no real equality for Jews in emergent Christianity and no real recognition of the heritage of Israel, either then or now. Gager points out that Fichte was the first in the modern era to revive the claim of Marcion that Jesus was not a Jew.[73] And if Paul is regarded as having abandoned his Jewish heritage, Christianity is then well on the way to getting rid of its Jewish roots and becoming a gentile church. But if, as we have argued, Paul recognized and cooperated with Peter as leader of the mission to the circumcision, this means, de facto, a recognition of Judaism as fully compatible with being in Christ. If, on the contrary, a Jewish pattern of life is permissible, or, more likely, just to be tolerated for a short temporary period of transition in the early days of the church, this constitutes a denial of this compatibility, and is, in short, a failure to recognize Jewish Christ followers as authentic and valid followers of Christ. The interpretation of Romans 14–15 serves as a test case in this respect because here, Paul puts the responsibility on the "strong" to adjust to and to accept the "weak," who are not necessarily of Jewish origin, but are, in fact, practicing at least some elements of a Jewish pattern of life.[74] A careful exegesis of this passage in context demonstrates beyond doubt that living Jewishly is not, in Paul's view, a temporary weakness to be relinquished or even gradually overcome, but a pattern of life to be accepted long-term.[75] Similarly, in my book *Paul and the Creation of Christian Identity*, I have taken with the utmost seriousness Paul's thrice-repeated command to the Corinthians that they should "remain as you were when called" (1 Cor. 7:17–24), whether as circumcised or uncircumcised. Possibly, in the earliest days, the formula "remain as you were when called" was concerned to protect the equality of gentiles, but that makes no difference to its validity. Paul also thereby acknowledges and protects the retention of the identity of Jews in Christ as Jews, the necessary correlate to the retention of "in Christ" gentile identity.[76]

For Paul, Gentile "Christianity" Shares Salvation with Israel, and Has No Independent Identity

Another aspect of Paul's formulation of gentile identity is that while this is equal in Christ to Jewish identity, there can be no independent identity for gentile Christ followers, apart from Israel. We turn to Paul's famous analogy of the olive tree and its branches in Rom. 11:17–24. We note that the gentiles are termed "wild olive branches," denoting their recent addition to the olive tree, but also indicating that since branches of themselves possess no potential for permanent growth, these gentiles cannot become an independent tree, but are forever indebted to, and dependent on, the stem on which they have been grafted. This was Paul's deliberate response to conceited gentile Christ followers, puffed up with their own mistaken self-understanding. Paul is clear that, in and by themselves, these are not an independent entity—a clear pointer to his anti-sectarian, Israel-centered perspective, further demonstrated in his strong emphasis on a "saving remnant" (Rom. 9:27–30; 11:5–6) and aspirations for the salvation of "all Israel" (11:25–32). Gentiles are called to recognize that branches do not support the root, but the root supports them (11:18). Most significantly, they are called to "share the rich root of the olive tree"—not to displace others or claim it as solely their own (11:17: note the term συγκοινωνός).[77] From this, it is abundantly clear that Paul did not anticipate a gentile church as an entity separated from Israel; even if he had envisaged such a prospect, it is clear that he would have opposed it.

In Paul's View, without Israel, God's Purposes Can Never Come to Completion

Paul, in one other major aspect, also sought to protect or at least to promulgate the identity of Israel. He stresses that though, in his Gospel, God has done a new thing in Christ to provide access to salvation for gentiles, this salvation is, as yet, not fully realized, but awaits the consummation of all things, when Christ will give back the kingdom to the Father. The "not yet" of Paul's message is firmly emphasized in his letters, lest gentiles should assume that the "day of the Lord" was already present. He uses the term *affirmation* in relation to the promises, rather than *fulfillment*.[78] Thus, in addition to maintaining that he himself did not presume to have already attained, but instead still presses on toward the mark of the high calling of God in Christ, he points also to the eventual salvation of "all Israel." The implication is clear: not only do gentile Christ followers share in the salvation that, though real, is present only in hope and in anticipation, but the consummation is not merely an outcome of gentile fruition, but is dependent in the last analysis upon Israel. Until this time, nothing can be complete, so all gentile self-centered boasting is permanently eliminated. God's purpose, without Israel, cannot be completed. In this way, Paul binds gentile Christianity, not only in its roots, to Israel, but also in its destiny in which the future of both are inextricably intertwined. For this divine purpose, Christ became a servant to the circumcised that the nations might join together in glorifying God (Rom. 15:7–13).

We have looked at a number of items that demonstrate beyond reasonable doubt that Paul was firmly resolved to protect and to honor the identity of Israel as a God-given, covenantal gift. The terms "new Israel" and Israel "according to the Spirit" are not part of his vocabulary. Israel is not replaceable by any other people or theological conception.[79] No one, not even Christ himself, can take the place of, or take over, the calling of Israel. Even a holy remnant, composed only of faithful Israelites, is not sufficient to represent Israel, nor can such exist as an end in itself, but serves only as a conduit to the eventual salvation of πᾶς Ἰσραήλ. Living Jewishly is neither in opposition to following Christ nor a temporary or inferior identity soon to be relinquished, but simply, living in accordance with the covenant calling that informs Paul's abiding conception of the difference between Jew and gentile. Since it is not possible for them to take over the place of Israel, the greatest privilege open to gentile Christ followers is to "share the richness of the olive tree" into which they have been grafted through Christ.

Individually, these items we have investigated above are all significant, but, cumulatively combined, they offer well-nigh incontrovertible evidence of Paul's continuing commitment to Israel, and to the hope of Israel.

Universalistic or Particularistic Frameworks
for the Interpretation of Paul?

Peter J. Tomson argued some years ago that "[i]f it is true that a shift of paradigm is required in scholarship on Paul and the Jewish Law, we are in the situation that anomalous results which disharmonise within the established paradigm are essential indicators as well as starting points towards a more adequate paradigm."[80] John Gager echoes similar views in his critique of the traditional reading of Paul, and how it not only came into being, but also managed to survive for so long: "Put briefly, the goal of criticism at this point is to bring existence of the paradigm into conscious awareness and to demonstrate the extent to which it governs the interpretive process."[81]

The established paradigm of Paulinism seems to have such a broad general consensus that research results achieved by operating within its parameters are, in many instances, not really questioned, and alternative options are given little serious attention. But, as Tomson notes, anomalies within the established paradigm that cannot be harmonized may point the way to more appropriate conclusions. I believe that one such anomaly can be clearly identified in Paul's ongoing positive attitude to his own and Jewish Christ followers' Jewish identity. This attitude conflicts with a universalistic perspective on Christianity that operates with a hegemonic view of the church as essentially a gentile church in which uniformity is anticipated—this uniformity being, in turn, read back into the Pauline era with fatal results for any conception of real diversity in Paul's theology.[82] And from this universalistic perspective, Jewishness of any kind in the Pauline era becomes problematic. Thus, a weakness in Paulinism is easily discernible since, despite all the emphasis on Paul's universalism, Jews and Judaism seem not to be easily accommodated! Despite notable exceptions, this consensus—that is, Paulinism—has continued to be dominant from Baur's initial publications in the 1830s until the work of Sanders and others in the 1970s began to challenge its dominance, while by no means totally destroying its influence.

When Albert Schweitzer departed radically from Baur and his school, in opposition to contemporaries such as Bousset, he found no problem with seeking to understand Paul exclusively in the light of his Jewish and Jewish-Christian background, rather than from a Hellenistic or Hellenistic-Jewish perspective. This was partly because of Schweitzer's specific insight that led him to conclude that Paul himself lived as an observant Jew and expected Jewish Christians to keep the law. He based this particularly on 1 Cor. 7:17–20—"let everyone remain in their calling"— labeling it as Paul's status quo teaching. For Schweitzer, there was pluriformity in Paul as regards law observance: since believers may be "in Christ" ontologically while living "in the flesh" in the world where the law applies, the law is thus still in force.[83]

The great historian Adolf von Harnack had found a similar anomaly in understanding Paul, in that a Jewish Paul did not fit the contemporary consensus regarding the apostle and was an obstacle to the true Paulinism that Harnack himself favored.[84] The apostle Paul suffers misunderstanding, particularly in the perception of his relation to Judaism, because of the "consensus" image of him favored by his interpreters. But at least some of these have honestly pointed out anomalies in the interpretation of the apostle, and these are instructive for future directions and research. Terence Donaldson lists three assumptions as typical of a universalistic understanding of Paul[85] (which I identify as equivalent to Paulinism):

1. Paul's depiction of Torah religion as inadequate and supposedly leading to self-righteousness is assumed to be accurate also with respect to Jews;
2. Paul's conversion is assumed to be conversion from one religion to another, from one based on works to one based on faith; and,
3. Paul's interest in Israel in Romans 9–11 is viewed as inconsistent with his more fundamental conviction that ethnic distinctions are abolished and assumed to be the result of residual convictions of ethnic loyalty overriding the more fundamental convictions.[86]

It is noteworthy that all of these have to do directly with Paul's (negative) relation to Judaism, which thereby emerges as characteristic of this view of Paul. Thus, any new paradigm for understanding Paul must avoid this historic denigration of Judaism, and simultaneously, ensure a paradigm that allows for real pluriformity in his thinking. That a new paradigm is urgently required lies in the fact that (unavoidable) continuity in theological, social, and cultural understanding has to be recognized and taken seriously into account. J. C. Beker's optimistic claim that E. P. Sanders's book *Paul and Palestinian Judaism* had destroyed the anti-Jewish bias in scholarship once and for all[87] is, unfortunately, not only premature, but also still very inaccurate, especially when it is realized that even unintended bias, *in its effect*, is exactly the same as that which is explicit, if not perhaps more insidious.

The fundamental issue that has to be determined is to whom Paul addresses his letters. If these are addressed to both Jews and non-Jews, to regard them within a universalistic paradigm seems somewhat warranted. But if, as is now being recognized, the addressees are designated as gentiles, then we must be careful not to generalize or universalize the statements within them, as is still often assumed to be normal and an acceptable interpretation. The universalistic framework is deeply rooted in gentile Christianity as a whole. F. C. Baur depicted Paul as enabling humankind to break out of the bounds of Judaism to create a universal spiritual religion free of ethnic encumbrances, and so, able to flourish in a gentile world. In specific contrast, Johannes Munck, in his attempt at a refutation of Baur's views, stressed the particularity of the addressees, followed significantly by Stendahl, who popularized and extended Munck's influence. Stendahl challenged the traditional view that Paul addressed the whole of humanity rather than gentiles exclusively. For Stendahl, generalization of Paul's letters as addressing all humanity meant they were read as expressions of a timeless message about the (individual) human and her religious problems. Part of the problem here is, as Stendahl clearly recognized, Western individualism: Paul is not concerned with humanity only as individuals, or as *homo generalis*, but humanity in its collective dimension as peoples—Jews and the nations—and their relation to one another.[88]

What has not been adequately recognized is that the generic human is an abstraction that never actually exists, like the rhetorical Jew, or the (hidden) Jew in all of us![89] The latter use of the term *Jew* demonstrates a common tendency toward abstraction and idealism in scholarship, very different from Paul's concrete use.[90] Universalism sees the church as made up of *generic human beings*, and thus, from this perspective, there can be no distinction between Jew and gentile. And since salvation is potentially open to all, in Christ, it seems that this is generically universal too. But Paul's categories are male- and female-specific, Jewish and gentile—not abstractions without gender or ethnic affiliation, despite Gal. 3:28 being thus (mis)interpreted. Human beings only exist in differentiated form, even though no discrimination must be allowed against them on the grounds of difference.[91] Paul's categories are also particularistic in another sense, in that they are Israel-oriented: his thought focuses specifically on Israel and the nations.

As noted at the beginning of this section, both Albert Schweitzer and Adolf von Harnack found problems with the traditional view of Paul in relation to keeping the Jewish law. As we noted also, Augustine, centuries ago, asked Jerome why should there be a problem if the apostles Peter and Paul, as faithful Jews, continued to keep Torah.[92] My particular interpretation of Paul has followed the insights of these significant scholars through the vehicle of the modern categories of social identity theory.[93] The insights this offers are not simply another new fad to vary the scholarly discussion, but offer, instead, a real insight into the pluriformity in Paul's theologizing, thus enabling an exit from the burden of a Paulinism paradigm no longer, if ever, fit for purpose.

Paul's thought indeed is *universal* in scope, but universal via the particularity of Israel. It must be acknowledged that Jew and gentile and their relative status and relation to one another is so central a theme in Paul that his approach must be categorized as decidedly not one of uniformity, but of pluriformity, and therefore, fundamentally particularistic rather than universalistic. The unity of Jew and gentile in Paul is, thus, not a unity of sameness, but unity through diversity.[94] The correlate of this is his emphasis on reconciliation, both of Jew and gentile,[95] but also, eventually, of all things. To describe this form of theologizing from another aspect—interpreters should approach Paul from a perspective of comparison with Judaism rather than one of contrast. Only then can the anti-Jewish universalistic framework of Paulinism be overcome, or perhaps transcended, as some of its exponents propose for the Jewish Torah.

Conclusion

One question still requires some consideration: why does Christianity continue the tendency to use Jews and Judaism as a negative foil? In the changes in the reception of Paul in the last half-century, huge advances have been made in the recognition of, and legislation against, prejudice of all kinds. Discrimination on the basis of race, gender, and sexual orientation have all been highlighted, and, in theory at least, the churches have sought to make members fully aware of such inequalities and biases. Religious pluralism, as an everyday reality for many people, has helped to remove superstition and fear of the unknown. Alongside such developments, Christian–Jewish dialogue has played an active role in continued opposition to all kinds of anti-Judaism/antisemitism, and yet, anti-Judaism still continues to be prevalent (and is currently increasing in Europe) despite a more accurate understanding of Second Temple Judaism. One suggestion concerning this has emerged at several points in this study. Ruether maintained that, for Christianity, "anti-Judaism was not merely a defence against attack, but an intrinsic need of Christian self-affirmation."[96]

Although I am inclined to agree to some extent, I do not accept that Christianity is inherently and irredeemably anti-Jewish. As noted already, the existence of an alternative symbolic universe may threaten our stability, but it need not necessarily do so. Only if, in an imperialistic fashion, I wish my view of the world to be recognized as the one and only correct or viable understanding is such destabilization inevitable. This is the source of the problem. However, the Pauline view of the world included Jews who radically rejected his messianic presentation of Jesus as the Christ. But he was able to live alongside these without threatening or being threatened. In this aspect, Paul offers a non-sectarian attitude, and as such, also a model for the church today.

Also, it has to be acknowledged that the migration of peoples may actually increase rather than diminish anxiety, since migrants may also bring an alternative religion and value system with them. It seems apparent that vulnerability, whether real or imagined—especially when it is associated with diminishing resources or severe deprivation—challenges the identity of a social group or section of a society, sometimes leading this last to stereotype the group that differs from them as sub-human, demonic, or otherwise. Such a reaction represents deep insecurity such that normal reactions or responses are not perceived as adequate—partly because part of the problem is that the insecure group tends to exaggerate the potential power, influence, and urgency of the perceived threat. As noted above, Christianity ought not to feel threatened by such situations, since the God of Israel and the nations is not a God of uniformity, but of pluriformity. However, there are many Christians who do hold that their form of Christianity is the one and only true view of reality, and therefore, any alternative view—whether arising from the presence of a plurality of religions, or even secular atheism—is really threatening. In such instances, Judaism as the (perceived) initial and ongoing threat to Christianity is the primeval prototype of the enemy to the faith, and thus, antisemitism is continually nurtured. It does not seem to assist harmony with Jews that Christians share their roots with Judaism and the Hebrew Scriptures. This awareness may even cause resentment against Judaism as its ongoing presence may remind Christians that they are not totally independent of another major faith. Although I do not agree with Ruether that Christianity is fatally flawed in its inability to live with Judaism, I do recognize that there are many varieties of Christian faith, of which such an analysis is still unfortunately true.

We see, therefore, that behind the insecurity is a zeal for uniformity—accompanied by a desire to enforce it—and an unwillingness to accept the humbler position of acknowledging difference in belief and practice, and to live in peace with this. And if Christian insecurity has some connections historically to the origin of Christianity as a parallel development together with (rabbinic) Judaism, this imperialistic desire for uniformity may also have historical roots of a similar kind. Both sources of insecurity must be acknowledged, and dealt with, but not allowed to dominate the ongoing pluriformity.

Notes

1. *Paul and the Torah* (Vancouver: University of British Columbia Press, 1987), 15.

2. Since there is no such entity as "semitism," I will not include the hyphen in *antisemitism*.

3. Cf. the careful study of Anders Gerdmar, *Roots of Theological Anti-Semitism: German Biblical Scholarship and the Jews, from Herder and Semler to Kittel and Bultmann* (Leiden: Brill, 2009), esp. the chapter on "Walter Grundmann: Towards a Non-Jewish Jesus" (531–75) and his positive portrayal of Johannes Weiss as a pointer to the way forward for exegesis after Auschwitz (612–13). Gerdmar also draws attention to the power of tradition in which recurring descriptions of Jews and Judaism lived on from 1738 to the 1950s, some indeed having roots in the church fathers (577–78).

4. *Judeophobia: Attitudes towards the Jews in the Ancient World* (Cambridge, MA: Harvard University Press, 1997), 197.

5. Ibid., 206.

6. The rejection of the Christian message by Judaism and the increasing hostility between local Jewish and Christian communities turned Christian theology in an anti-Jewish direction. Cf. D. R. A. Hare, "The Rejection of the Jews in the Synoptic Gospels and Acts," in *Anti-Semitism and the Foundations of Christianity*, ed. Alan T. Davies (New York: Paulist Press, 1979), 28–32.

7. Cf. J. C. Beker, *Paul the Apostle: The Triumph of God in Life and Thought* (Philadelphia: Fortress Press, 1980), 341.

8. Marcel Simon held that Christian antisemitism, originating in the Jewish rejection of Christian claims, goes back as far as the Gospel of John (though not in Paul). He held that though the Christian expression draws in part on pagan traditions, it differs from such because of its religious and theological basis. John Gager builds on this distinction by Simon in his *The Origins of Anti-Semitism: Attitudes Toward Judaism in Pagan and Christian Antiquity* (New York; Oxford: Oxford University Press, 1983), 16.

9. Messianic claims were often met with skepticism, and Christology *alone* does not inevitably lead to anti-Judaism, as Hare argued strongly against Ruether. Hare denies that though there remains an inevitable anti-Judaism in Christianity and a parallel anti-Christianity in Judaism, the hostility displayed by a secessionist group toward that religious tradition from which it broke away need not necessarily or categorically be permanent. "It is more likely that this kind of defensiveness will recede with the passing of time unless other factors enter the situation to exacerbate the situation" ("The Rejection of the Jews," 41–43). N. T. Wright's view that Jesus Christ represents (and thus in my view replaces) Israel certainly is in its effect anti-Jewish, whether or not its author intended this, in that Paul's doctrine of "the rest" (of Israel) has disappeared (*The Climax of the Covenant: Christ and the Law in Pauline Thought* [Edinburgh, T&T Clark, 1991], 182, 237). Cf. also Terence L. Donaldson, *Jews and Judaism in the New Testament: Decision Points and Divergent Interpretations* (London: SPCK; Waco, TX: Baylor University Press, 2010), 129.

10. Cf. Peter L. Berger and Thomas Luckmann, *The Social Construction of Reality: A Treatise in the Sociology of Knowledge* (Garden City NY: Doubleday, 1966), 108.

11. Thus, Susannah Heschel notes that "calls for reviving Marcion's elimination of the Old Testament from the Christian canon can be found in 19th century German Protestantism from Friedrich Schleiermacher to Harnack" ("Quest for the Aryan Jesus: The Archaeology of Nazi Orientalist Theology," in *Jews, Antiquity, and the Nineteenth Century Imagination*, ed. Hayim Lapin and Dale B. Martin [Bethesda, MD: University Press of Maryland, 2003], 65–84 [71]).

12. Thus, Magnus Zetterholm's claim that "one theme that is specially developed in the *Adversus Judaeos* literature is that the Jews had misunderstood their own holy scriptures and as a result had lost the right to them. This right had passed over to the Christian church which now represents the true people of the God of Israel. Such tendencies are evident already in texts from the end of the first century CE, for instance, in Hebrews and *Barnabas*, but more fully developed in texts from the second century, as in Justin's *Dialogue with Trypho, Apology* and Melito of Sardis's *Peri Pascha*" (*The Formation of Christianity in Antioch: A Social-Scientific Approach to the Separation between Judaism and Christianity* [London; New York: Routledge, 2003], 220).

13. This may have resulted in a residue of sectarian attitudes to Jews which unfortunately still, even today, have not been eliminated, hence my emphasis that Paul was not sectarian. If one is secure in one's faith, the mere existence of an alternative symbolic universe is not necessarily a threat.

14. Cf. Gager, *The Origins of Anti-Semitism*, 269.

15. Cf. Mikael Tellbe, *Paul Between Synagogue and State: Christians, Jews and Civic Authorities in 1Thessalonians, Romans and Philippians* (Stockholm: Almqvist & Wiksell, 2001).

16. We will deal with this issue more fully later in relation to Paul.

17. As Chrysostom's opposition to it demonstrates: "For you fellowshipped with those who crucified Me . . . you revived festivals which I had terminated. You ran to the synagogues of the Jews . . ." (Chrysostom, *Adv. Jud.* 6.7 [PG 48,915]; Rosemary Ruether, *Faith and Fratricide: The Theological Roots of Anti-Semitism* [New York: Seabury, 1974], 176). In these well-known examples, a concern for the protection of the church and its members is primary, but this certainly does not excuse Chrysostom's intemperate attacks on Jews, which later provided the Nazis with potent examples of how to denigrate them.

18. See Paula Fredriksen, *Augustine and the Jews: A Christian Defense of Jews and Judaism* (New York: Doubleday, 2008), 290–352.

19. Cf. ibid., 302–6, 325–52. Cf. also Adolf L. Leschnitzer, "The Wandering Jew: The Alienation of the Jewish Image in Christian Consciousness," in *The Wandering Jew: Essays in the Interpretation of a Christian Legend*, ed. Galit Hasan-Rokem and Alan Dundes (Bloomington: Indiana University Press, 1986), 236–60.

20. Cf. Sanders's critique of Luther that "the supposed legalistic Judaism of scholars from Weber to Thyen serves a very obvious purpose. It acts as the foil against which superior forms of religion are described. It permits, as Neusner has said, the writing of theology as if it were history. One must note in particular the projection on to Judaism of the view which Protestants find most objectionable in Roman Catholicism: the existence of a treasury of merits established by works of supererogation. We have here the retrojection of the Protestant-Catholic debate into ancient history, with Judaism taking the role of Catholicism and Christianity the role of Lutheranism" (*Paul and Palestinian Judaism*, 57). Similarly, James D. G. Dunn, "The New Perspective on Paul," in *Jesus, Paul and the Law: Studies in Mark and Galatians* (London: SPCK, 1990), 183–206 (185).

21. See the excellent discussion by Davies, whose superb analysis of the situation in Europe notes connections and differentiates between differing periods and differing countries. He concludes that "[t]o the mass man who had suffered the loss of his identity, the architects of the new totalitarian order, borrowing from the racist pioneers of the previous century, offered a new and alluring identity: the Aryan. . . . The Aryan myth, the great myth of the European

racists, was neither a variation of the old Christian religious myth of the Jew, but a myth born of different parentage and bred in a different matrix. Its foundations are found in the romantic intuition that peoples whose languages are interrelated must possess a common racial origin. . ." ("Myths and Their Secular Translation," in *Anti-Semitism and the Foundations of Christianity*, 188–207 [200–202]).

22. The emergence of racial theories in support of antisemitism took place first in Spain, and as the first instance of institutionalized racism, this cannot be ignored. Cf. Susannah Heschel's Introduction on "Theology and Race" (1–25) and the chapter on "The Institute for the Study and Eradication of Jewish Influence on German Church Life" (67–95) in her magisterial study *The Arian Jesus: Christian Theologians and the Bible in Nazi Germany* (Princeton: Princeton University Press), 2008.

23. Davies, "Myths and Their Secular Translation," 198–99.

24. Thus, Davies criticizes Ruether in her *Faith and Fratricide* for failing to note that the conspiratorial motif of the *Protocols of the Elders of Zion* was probably inspired more by the Judeophobia of the Third French Republic that was reaching its crescendo in the Dreyfus affair than by latent medieval mysticism. "This Judeophobia . . . was prompted more by modern than medieval causes" (ibid., 198).

25. Thus, Uriel Tal's study *Christians and Jews in Germany: Religion, Politics and Ideology in the Second Reich 1870–1914* (Ithaca, NY; London: Cornell University Press, 1975) claims the existence and mutual impact of two antisemitisms, the one Christian, the other explicitly anti-Christian. The Christian variety clearly has its roots in the Christian tradition, but even the non-Christian variety borrowed heavily from Christian sources: the racial antisemites appropriated basic Christian ideas while reprobating them, and adopting them for their own purposes. "Racial anti-Semitism and traditional Christianity . . . were moved by a common impulse directed either to the conversion or to the extermination of Jews" (ibid., 304).

26. Davies is critical of Ruether's thesis that modern antisemitism is only a secular mutation of religious anti-Judaism ("Myths and Their Secular Translation," 198–203).

27. As noted above, scholars disagree concerning the link between anti-Judaism and the rise of antisemitism. John Gager thus disagrees with Hannah Arendt (*The Origins of Totalitarianism* [New York: Schocken, 1966], xi) because she considered that antisemitism is a uniquely modern phenomenon and did not posit any continuity between the two kinds of prejudice (Gager, *The Origins of Antisemitism*, 266–67). Gager concludes that Christian beliefs about Judaism are not alone responsible for modern antisemitism, and that early Christianity as such did not led to later expressions of antisemitism, whether Christian or otherwise: "Certainly for Christianity in its early stages, the real debate

was never between Christians and Jews but among Christians. Eventually the anti-Jewish side won. Its ideology became normative, not just for subsequent Christianity and Western culture but, through the formation of the New Testament, for our perception of earlier Christianity as well. The voice of the losing side fell silent" (ibid., 268–69).

28. *The Origins of Totalitarianism*, xi. See the discussion of Arendt's view by Davies, "Myths and Their Secular Translation," 188–207.

29. *The Origins of Anti-Semitism*, 9.

30. Ibid., 266-67.

31. Gager follows some of Hare's refinements within the category of Christian anti-Judaism (in his "The Rejection of the Jews in the Synoptic Gospels and Acts"), distinguishing Christian anti-Judaism and gentilizing anti-Judaism, but relabeling Hare's "prophetic anti-Judaism" as intra-Jewish polemic (*The Origins of Anti-Semitism*, 8–9).

32. As Zetterholm comments: "As early as the third century BCE, Greek authors in Egypt commented on the Jewish exodus from Egypt and various distinctive Jewish cultural features such as circumcision and the Sabbath celebration. Some of this material was included in a clearly anti-Semitic literary tradition handed down throughout history" (*Approaches to Paul: A Student's Guide to Recent Scholarship* [Minneapolis: Fortress Press, 2009], 41).

33. "Myths and their Secular Translation," 203. Davies also claims in his critique of Ruether that "an inquiry such as Ruether's into the Christian materials and their social incorporation in the Christian nations should be balanced by an inquiry into the intellectual and spiritual *pathology* of European society since the 19th century, and its supreme expression in genocide" (ibid.; emphasis mine).

34. Cf. *Judeophobia*, 210.

35. Cf. Ekkehardt Stegemann, "Der Jude Paulus und seine antijüdische Auslegung: Antijudaismus im Neuen Testament," in *Auschwitz-Krise der christlichen Theologie*, ed. Rolf Rendtorff and Ekkehard Stegemann (Munich: Kaiser, 1980), 117–39.

36. A notable example here is C. H. Dodd, in his *The Epistle to the Romans* (London: Hodder & Stoughton, 1932). Dodd recognizes the pro-Jewish impact of Romans chapter 11, but at various points, chides Paul for being too patriotic or too emotionally tied to his own people (cf. ibid., 174–83).

37. These included Jewish contemporaries, pagans sympathetic to Judaism, gentile Christian Judaizers (that is, gentile Christians who voluntarily assumed Jewish practices), and Jewish Christians (those Jews who both proclaimed Jesus and who lived according to their ancestral practices): cf. Fredriksen, *Augustine and the Jews*, 77–78.

38. Thus, Fichte was probably the first modern European to echo Marcion's suggestion that Jesus was not a Jew. His proto-racist admirer, Paul de Lagarde, "did not belong to the theological stream of Christian anti-Judaism except in the most generalized sense: his anti-Jewish sentiments were really formed out of modern German self-intoxication and xenophobia" (Davies, "Myths and Their Secular Translation," 196–97).

39. But, as Beker notes, "[o]f all the New Testament authors, it is only Paul who is passionately engaged with the Jews as the people of the promise and who, notwithstanding his radically different understanding of messianism, keeps his thought anchored in the Hebrew scriptures and in the destiny of Israel, as God's people. . . . [T]his very Jewish element of Paul made it impossible for the church to accept Paul as its 'catholic' theologian" (*Paul*, 340).

40. Baur's attempt to wrest the interpretation of Romans from the dominant Lutheran approach was a radically new historical, and potentially liberating, understanding, recognizing chapters 9–11 as central; but, as Ernst Käsemann notes, Baur's insights did not achieve their full potential because he held on to the (mistaken) view that Jewish Christians were dominant at Rome (due, I believe, to his anti-Jewish presuppositions). Cf. F. C. Baur, *Paul: His Life and Works*, trans. A. Menzies (Edinburgh: Theological Translation Fund, 1876), 313, and Käsemann, *Commentary on Romans* (London, SCM Press), 1980, 253–54.

41. Cf. Sheila E. McGinn, "Feminism and Paul in Romans 8:18-23," in *Celebrating Romans: Template for Pauline Theology. Essays in Honour of Robert Jewett*, ed. McGinn (Grand Rapids: Eerdmans, 2004), 21–38 (29).

42. On the questionable tendency to operate in binary categories in the interpretation of Paul, see Kathy Ehrensperger, *That We May Be Mutually Encouraged: Feminism and the New Perspective in Pauline Studies* (London; New York: T&T Clark, 2004), 59–67.

43. Contra the RSV, the NRSV translation has: "This means that it is not the children of the flesh who are the children of God, but the children of the promise are reckoned as descendants." This translation gives the impression that Paul denies Israelites as heirs to the promise, and that gentiles have displaced them. See also my *Paul and the Creation of Christian Identity* (London; New York: T&T Clark, 2006), 124.

44. *Faith and Fratricide*, 104–7.

45. Although not typical of C. K. Barrett's normally careful scholarship, in his comments on Rom. 9:13, he asserts "[i]t is important to recall here that the seed of Abraham contracted till it became ultimately Christ, and was subsequently expanded to include those who were in Christ." This somewhat Barthian comment is based on Christ as the one seed of Gal. 3:16, but does not take account of "all his seed" in Rom. 4:16, παντὶ τῷ σπέρματι, which Paul further

specifies as "not only (to) the adherents of the law, but also (to) those who share the faith of Abraham, for he is the father of us all" (Rom. 4:16).

46. For a critical discussion of the philosophical and hermeneutical issues in relation to unity via sameness, see Kathy Ehrensperger, "Reading Romans 'in the Face of the Other': Levinas, the Jewish Philosopher, Meets Paul, the Jewish Apostle," in *Reading Romans with Contemporary Philosophers and Theologians*, ed. David W. Odell-Scott (Romans Through History and Culture Series; London: T&T Clark, 2007), 115–54, esp. 123–32.

47. Cf. Donaldson, *Judaism and the Gentiles*, 477–82.

48. Although I cannot discuss the issue, I see here a general Hegelian influence on Baur, rather than direct dependency; cf. Anders Gerdmar, "Baur and the Creation of the Judaism-Hellenism Dichotomy," in *Ferdinand Christian Baur und die Geschichte des fruehen Christentums*, ed. Martin Bauspiess, Christof Landmesser, and David Linicum (Tübingen, Mohr Siebeck, 2014), 107–28, 123–26). The problem with Hegel's thought is that in his philosophy, every state of being brings forth its own negation, which then gives birth to a more complex unity. Every thesis generates its antithesis, and these two opposites are joined in a synthesis that necessarily should include elements of both its antecedents. Thus, in Hegel's evolutionary form of thought, nothing was, nor could it possibly be, better in former times, and because it represents an earlier stratum—an antithesis—in the divinely-controlled world order, Judaism of necessity is depicted as inferior to Christianity. Hence, Baur's adoption of aspects of Hegelian thought resulted in the antithesis between Judaism and Christianity being continually stressed, and yet, there was, surprisingly, little space for Jewish-Christian influences in Christian theology! See Zetterholm, *Approaches to Paul*, 33–40.

49. *Die christliche Gnosis oder die christliche Religionsphilosophie in ihrer geschichtlichen Entwicklung* (Tübingen: C. F. Osiander, 1835; new ed.; Darmstadt, 1967), 32. I am indebted to Susannah Heschel for this reference and, for convenience, follow her translation (*Quest of the Aryan Jesus*, 72).

50. *Paul and the Salvation of Mankind* (London: SCM, 1959), 71. Munck states, "the very opposite of Baur's view is right. The primitive Church and Paul were universalistic as Jesus was, because they knew that the Gospel was for Gentiles as well as Jews, whereas the later Catholic Church lost that universalism. It no longer divided the human race into Israel and the Gentiles, but turned with its message to the Gentiles."

51. Cf. my essay "Universality and Particularity in Paul's Understanding and Strategy of Mission," in my *Unity and Diversity in Christ: Interpreting Paul in Context* (Eugene, OR: Cascade, 2013), 187–202.

52. On the problems inherent in universalizing Pauline statements, see the section "Levinas and Universalization in Pauline Interpretation" in Ehrensperger, "Reading Romans 'in the Face of the Other.'"

53. On this, see n. 44 above.

54. Although Paul actually states that both circumcision and uncircumcision are nothing, often what he says about uncircumcision is ignored, thus perverting Paul's balanced statement into an anti-Jewish assertion; cf. my essay, ""As Having and as Not Having": Paul, Circumcision and Indifferent Things in 1 Corinthians 7:17-32a," in *Unity and Diversity in Christ*, 106–26.

55. For recent study of this theme, cf. David Rudolph, *A Jew to the Jews. Jewish Contours of Pauline Flexibility in 1 Corinthians 9.19-23* (Tübingen: Mohr Siebeck, 2011) and Mark D. Nanos, "Paul's Relationship to Torah in Light of His Strategy to Become Everything to Everyone," in *New Perspectives on Paul and the Jews: Crosscurrents in Paul Exegesis and Jewish-Christian Relations*, ed. Reimund Bieringer and Didier Pollefeyt (London: T&T Clark, 2012), 106–40.

56. As was already clearly recognized by Augustine in his reading of 1 Cor.9:20 in his correspondence with Jerome. For Augustine: "If Paul had observed these *sacramenta* (this is Augustine's term for Jewish rites) because he pretended that he was a Jew in order to gain the Jews, why did he not also offer sacrifice with the Gentiles since he became like someone without the Law for those who were without the Law, in order that he might gain them, too?" Augustine's assumption was that both Peter and Paul continued to live Jewish lives, cf. Fredriksen, *Augustine and the Jews*, 236–38.

57. This is where James Dunn makes too much of ethnicity as if all of Jewish life were determined by ethnic considerations alone. We will return to this later.

58. Cf. Larry L. Welborn, *Paul the Fool of Christ: A Study of 1 Corinthians 1-4 in the Comic Philosophic Tradition* (London: T&T Clark, 2005).

59. Cf. Arland J. Hultgren, *Paul's Letter to the Romans: A Commentary* (Grand Rapids: Eerdmans, 2011), 135, contra C. H. Dodd.

60. As I have argued, particularly in relation to Romans; cf. "The Addressees of Paul's Letter to the Romans: Assemblies of God in House Churches and Synagogues," in *Between Gospel and Election: Explorations in the Interpretation of Romans 9-11*, ed. Florian Wilk and J. Ross Wagner (Tübingen: Mohr Siebeck, 2010), 127–45.

61. Cf. Paula Fredriksen, "Judaizing the Nations: The Ritual Demands of Paul's Gospel," *NTS* 56 (2010): 232–52.

62. Cf. Stephen Fowl, "Learning to Be a Gentile," in *Christology and Scripture: Interdisciplinary Perspectives*, ed. Andrew T. Lincoln and Angus Pattison (London: T&T Clark, 2007), 22–40.

63. Somewhat surprisingly, C. H. Dodd sometimes uses such terminology: cf. *Romans*, 43, 63, and 179–83.

64. See my essay, "Unity and Diversity in the Church: Transformed Identities and the Peace of Christ in Ephesians," in *Unity and Diversity in Christ*, 127–45.

65. See my *Paul and the Creation of Christian Identity*, esp. the section entitled "The Church is not Israel (or New Israel), 129–33. Cf. also Susan Eastman, "Israel and the Mercy of God: A Re-reading of Gal. 6:16 and Rom. 9-11," in *NTS* 56, no. 3 (2010): 367–95. Eastman argues convincingly for the view I have always maintained that the Israel of God in Gal. 6:16 refers to historic Israel, not those in Christ.

66. Cf. Rom. 1:3; 4:1; 9:3; 1 Cor.10:18. Cf. Gaston, *Paul and the Torah*, 18.

67. This seems to me to be the outcome of Wright's view of Jesus as the representative and embodiment of Israel thus fulfilling Israel's vocation (*Paul and the Faithfulness of God* [Minneapolis: Fortress Press, 2013], 825–36, esp. 830.

68. Cf. Terence L. Donaldson, *Jew and Anti-Judaism in the New Testament* (London: SPCK, 2011), 129–31.

69. See my chapter "Self-Understanding and the People of God: Israel in Romans," in *Paul and the Creation of Christian Identity*, 121-39. Cf. also Kathy Ehrensperger's study of Paul's careful use of the term γένος in "Paul, His People and Racial Terminology," *Journal of Early Christian History* 3, no. 1 (2013): 17–32.

70. Cf. Kathy Ehrensperger, *Paul and the Dynamics of Power: Communication and Interaction in the Early Christ-Movement* (London: T&T Clark, 2009), 35–62.

71. "The New Perspective on Paul," in *The New Perspective on Paul: Collected Essays* (Tübingen: Mohr Siebeck, 2005), 89–110.

72. See e. g., Magnus Zetterholm's comprehensive discussion in *The Formation of Christianity in Antioch*, 129–34, 164–66.

73. See n. 37 above.

74. Cf. my chapter "The Rule of Faith in Romans 12:1—15:13," in *Unity and Diversity in Christ*, 39–66.

75. Contra John Barclay who argues that "[w]hat Paul demands of these weak Christians is their commitment to a church in which the Jewish mode of life is tolerated but not required. . . ." ("Do We Undermine the Law? A Study of Romans 14:1—15:6," in *Paul and the Mosaic Law*, ed. James D. G, Dunn [Tübingen: Mohr Siebeck, 1996], 287–308). Paul's stance is intelligible only if he is perceived as giving equal value to Jewish and gentile life patterns, otherwise, as Barclay claims, Paul would be guilty of subverting "the basis on which Jewish law is founded and creating a crisis of cultural integrity among the very believers whose law-observance he is so careful to protect" (ibid., 308). Cf. P. F. Esler's criticism of Barclay that even if this were the effect of Paul's teaching, it was not what he intended (*Conflict and Identity in Romans: The Social Setting of Paul's Letter* [Minneapolis: Fortress Press, 2003], 355).

76. *Paul and the Creation of Christian Identity*, esp. 157–58.

77. Contra the erroneous, value laden and misleading RSV and NRSV translation of ἐν αὐτοῖς as "in their place."

78. Cf. βεβαιόω to confirm in Rom. 15:8. See the excellent critique and innovative interpretation of the broken olive branches by Mark D. Nanos: "Broken Branches: A Pauline Metaphor Gone Awry? (Romans 11:11–24)," in *Between Gospel and Election: Explorations in the interpretation of Romans 9-11*, ed. Florian Wilk and J. Ross Wagner (WUNT 257; Tübingen: Mohr Siebeck, 2010), 339–76.

79. Contra C. H. Dodd's claim: "Therefore, even if the entire Israelite nation is rejected, the promise has not been broken. It has been fulfilled by God in his own way" (*Romans*, 154–55).

80. *Paul and the Jewish Law: Halakha in the Letters of the Apostle to the Gentiles* (Assen; Maastricht: Van Gorcum; Minneapolis: Fortress Press, 1990), 9.

81. *The Origins of Anti-Semitism*, 199. Gager notes also Paul Meyer's claim that all modern commentaries on Paul are governed by "decision(s) made on grounds extrinsic to the text itself," and his further question—why is it "that certain interpretations of Paul are not only very widely held but also, in some quarters, and in the commentary literature generally, firmly opposed, sometimes vehemently?" (The reference here is to Meyer's essay, "Romans 10:4 and the 'End' of the Law," in *The Divine Helmsman: Studies on God's Control of Human Events*, ed. J. L. Crenshaw and S. Sandmel [New York: KTAV, 1980], 59–78 [64]).

82. According to Anathea Portier-Young's definition, a hegemonic discourse "asserts as normative and universal what are in fact particular and contingent ways of perceiving the world" (*Apocalypse against Empire: Theologies of Resistance in Early Judaism* [Grand Rapids: Eerdmans, 2011], 11).

83. Cf. *Die Mystik des Apostels Paulus* [1930], repr. with Introduction by W. G. Kümmel (Tübingen: Mohr Siebeck 1981), 178–99.

84. Here, I follow Peter Tomson, *Paul and the Jewish Law*, 9-12. "Though more adequately expressed and historically nuanced, Harnack's view has parallels with C. H. Dodd's concern that Paul did not uniformly live out the implications of his own pattern of thought with respect to Israel, i. e., he did not conform to Dodd's perception of Paulinism." Cf. n. 35 above.

85. *Paul and Anti-Judaism in the New Testament*, 113–15.

86. This criticism is particularly characteristic of C. H. Dodd's understanding of Paul; cf. *Romans*, 183.

87. *Paul*, 340.

88. Krister Stendahl, *Paul Among Jews and Gentiles and Other Essays* (Philadelphia: Fortress Press, 1976), 5–6, 26–27, 36–40, 72–75.

89. Cf. Käsemann's horrific indictment of the devout Jew: "[T]he apostle's real adversary is the devout Jew, not only as the mirror-image of his own past—though that, too—but as the reality of the religious man. . . . [R]eligion always provides man with his most thorough-going possibility of confusing an illusion with God. Paul sees this possibility realised in the devout Jew," ("Paul

339

and Israel," in *New Testament Questions of Today* [London: SCM Press, 1969], 183–87 [184, 186]).

90. Paul's discussion in Rom. 2:17-29 is concerned with someone who calls themselves a Jew, but does not live like a Jew, not merely with a theoretical definition. When scholars move from discussing real Jews to theoretical abstractions, it is very often an indication of theology/ideology superseding historical investigation, and a failure to deal properly with Jews as a historical people.

91. I have argued the case for a new interpretation of Rom. 10:12 (and indirectly also for Rom. 3:22)—often viewed as supporting a "no distinction", non-ethnic interpretation of Paul—in my "No Distinction or No Discrimination? The Translation of ΔΙΑΣΤΟΛΗ in Romans 3:22 and 10:12," in *Erlesenes Jerusalem: Festschrift für Ekkehard W. Stegemann*, ed. Christina Tuor-Kurth und Lucas Kundert (Basel: Friedrich Reinhardt, 2013), 353–71. There is no agreed New Testament meaning for the term διαστολή. The translation of 'οὐ γάρ ἐστιν διαστολή' in this passage should not be taken as meaning "it is not that there are distinctions between Jew and Greek," but rather, as "it is not that there is discrimination between Jew and Greek"; although ethnic distinctions as Jew or Greek do exist among people(s), the phrase here in which διαστολή occurs should be rendered as "no discrimination is made" despite the distinguishing of differences (following the interpretation of Joseph Fitzmyer, *Romans*, [AB; London; New York: Doubleday, 1993], 592).

92. See n. 55 above.

93. For an up to date and comprehensive coverage of this field, see J. Brian Tucker and Coleman A. Baker, *T&T Clark Handbook to Social Identity in the New Testament* (London: Bloomsbury, T&T Clark, 2014).

94. See Kathy Ehrensperger, "Reading Romans 'in the Face of the Other'."

95. Cf. my essay, ""Let Us Maintain Peace" (Rom. 5:2): Reconciliation and Social Responsibility," in *Unity and Diversity in Christ*, 187–202.

96. *Faith and Fratricide*, 181.

12

Discussing/Subverting Paul

Polemical Rereadings and Competing Supersessionist Misreadings of Pauline Inclusivism in Late Antiquity: A Case Study on the Apocalypse of Abraham, Justin Martyr, and the Qur'an

Carlos A. Segovia

My purpose in this chapter is to explore the negative of the image this volume tries to build, for Paul was often read in antiquity as no longer being a Second Temple Jew. More specifically, Paul's Abrahamic argument in Romans 4 and Galatians 3—which he originally put forward to substantiate his core claim to the inclusion of the gentiles in God's people—was polemically reworked and reframed in a number of texts, both Christian and Muslim (or rather, proto-Muslim), to substantiate the opposite claim: namely, that Israel had been excluded from God's salvation plan. In broad terms, this is well-known to everyone, at least as regards the Christian supersessionist reworking(s) of Paul's argument, so I will focus here on its less-known quranic (or proto-quranic) reworking. Additionally, I will try to show that the quranic supersessionist reworking of Paul's argument, which has not been sufficiently analyzed to date, paradoxically drew on its polemical rereading within post-70 Judaism—to which the Apocalypse of Abraham witnesses, in my view—while simultaneously building on the traditional Christian distortion of Paul's message. Therefore, I think it is legitimate to speak of different cultural contexts that produced various intertextual reworkings of Paul's Abrahamic argument, ranging from polemical re-readings to supersessionist misreadings in early Judaism, Christianity, and Islam, respectively—reworkings whose fascinating interconnections should be examined afresh if we want to understand why and how Paul's message came to be appropriated and subverted, and thereby, neglected, as a first-century Jewish conceptual construct that we have only very recently started to unravel by questioning its ongoing traditional misrepresentation, and to which, in short, I hope to add here a new, though seldom explored, (inter)textual site: Muslim Scripture. Accordingly, I will undertake a symptomatic and intertextual rereading of several quranic verses, including verse 124 in *sūrat al-baqara* and verse 5 in *sūrat al-qaṣaṣ* (Q 28)—where Abraham is introduced as a "guide" and every guide's followers labeled as "heirs"—and verses 1 to 56 of *sūrat al-wāqi'a* (Q 56), which, in turn, display the very same spatial, numerical, and axiological distinctions set forth in the vision contained in chapters 21 and 22 of the *Apocalypse of Abraham*, but polemically contend that God's people is to be identified with the "foremost" in faith and monotheism, not with Israel. Moreover, I suggest this may contribute to explain the reason why the quranic prophet was described as الرّسول النّبي الأمّي *al-rasūl al-nabī al-ummī*—that is, "the apostle/prophet to the gentiles"—at a time when the construction of a new ethnic/cultic category (the "Arabs/Muslims") was at stake.

A Preliminary Note on Religious Identity and Discursive Practice

Religious identity making builds upon a number of peculiar power/knowledge strategies that tend both to emphasize distinctiveness as the outcome of an exceptional founding event and to heighten a group's sense of uniqueness and stability. Selective remembering of the past, mythical and hyperbolic reworking of elusive historical data, ethnic and genealogical self-legitimation, artificial distinguishing between sameness and otherness, and more or less systematic historicization of dogma conspire to inscribe religious renewal as divinely sanctioned, rather than politically achieved due to more mundane reasons, and thus, contribute to (re)present self-identity as an unproblematic notion. Likewise, the adaptation of previous textual materials in a polemical fashion often plays a particularly significant role and stands as a means to obliquely, but effectively enhance identity claims. My purpose here is to briefly analyze one such strategy, namely, Paul's Abrahamic argument in Romans 4 and Galatians 3, and to examine the different ways in which it was polemically reworked, reshaped, and reframed in post-70 Judaism, early Christianity, and proto-Islam so as to create, validate, and strengthen religious in-group/out-group discourse.

Reassessing Paul's Abrahamic Argument

In Galatians 3 and Romans 4, Paul (re)uses the story of Abraham (against those fellow Jews and/or proselytes who claimed that belonging to the γένος of Abraham was "characterized and conditioned by observance of the Mosaic law"?)[1] to provide his gentile audience with an authoritative (counter-)model for *inclusion* in the people of God.

As Caroline Johnson Hodge puts it, Paul's major argument in both sections is that "righteousness before the God of Israel depends not on practicing the Law . . . but on the faithful actions of Abraham and Christ and God's resulting promises of blessed descendants."[2] In other words, she adds,

> Paul employs the story of Abraham as a model to illustrate how the God of Israel works in the world, a model which operates within the logic of patrilineal descent: he chooses a faithful person to receive his blessings and pass them on to future generations. . . . For Abraham, this meant that

life would come to his seed and to the womb of Sarah, despite their old age. For Christ, this meant that peoples who had previously been alien to the God of Israel would become adopted sons. Abraham's faithfulness resulted in the guarantee that God's promise would come to all his descendants, both Jews and Gentiles. Christ's faithfulness implements this promise for the Gentiles.[3]

This *new* reading of Paul's Abrahamic argument challenges both the traditional interpretation of the apostle to the nations and the so-called New Perspective on Paul, for as I have elsewhere argued, Paul's views on gentile inclusion are quite well-rooted in Jewish tradition.[4] Moreover, Paul's own explicit claims that God's election of Israel is irrevocable (Rom. 11:1, 29) and that he has only been commissioned to bring the gentiles through Christ into God's allegiance (15:16, 18) are easier to understand in light of this new reading.[5]

Nevertheless, several late antique Christian authors reframed Paul's aforementioned argument in order to completely *subvert* its inclusive scope by explicitly transforming gentile inclusion into Jewish *exclusion* from God's people; thereby, Romans 4 and Galatians 3 became the cornerstone of Christian supersessionism and a major topos in Christian anti-Jewish controversy, as shown by the works of Barnabas, Aristides, and Justin Martyr. In addition, the author of the *Apocalypse of Abraham*—a Jewish pseudepigraphon written in the aftermath of the destruction of Jerusalem in 70 CE—seems to argue with Paul by reusing Abraham's story in a way that implicitly *minimizes* the significance of gentile inclusion, thus emphasizing Israel's election and physical descent from Abraham against Paul's universalistic claims.

In short, supersessionist misreadings and polemical rereadings of Paul's Abrahamic argument produced in late antiquity new interpretations and textual adaptations of the story about Abraham and the nations.[6] Occasionally, however, such reinterpretations *intertwined* with one another, and strangely enough, they *coalesced* to produce a different kind of supersessionism that opposed both Judaism (initially) and (later) Christianity. In what follows, I shall try to reread some excerpts from the Apocalypse of Abraham, Justin Martyr's

Dialogue with Trypho, and the Qur'an in light of these preliminary observations.

Answering Paul from within Judaism:
The Apocalypse of Abraham as a Test Case

The *Apocalypse of Abraham*—which is only extant in Church Slavonic after a Greek text very likely made from a now lost Hebrew (or, less probably, Palestinian Aramaic) original—divides into two main, perhaps once independent, sections: (1) chapters 1 to 8, which deal with Abraham's conversion to monotheism, and (2) chapters 9 to 31, which focus primarily on Abraham's ascent to heaven and on the visions of the cosmos and of the future of mankind that he is granted there.[7]

Its anonymous author wrote in the decades following the destruction of Jerusalem in 70 CE. Like the authors of *4 Ezra* and *2 Baruch*, he aimed at reflecting upon the causes of so profound a crisis and recalled Israel's pre-Mosaic founding myth (that is, Abraham's *election*) to give new hope to Israel and to help her overcome the present evil age. His reasoning goes as follows: Abraham searched for God and, in fact, became God's "friend." An angel called Yahoel helped him to escape from Azazel (the prince of darkness who had tried to dissuade him from offering sacrifices to God) and later assisted him in his heavenly journey. Once in heaven, Abraham sees the divine throne, the firmaments and the earth, and enquires of God the reasons for the presence of evil on earth. He is taught about the history of God's people and about what has gone wrong with them: they have gone astray because they have fallen into idolatric practices.[8] That is why their temple has finally been destroyed by the idolatrous gentiles, who, all this notwithstanding, will be delivered to eternal punishment by God's messiah in due time. Then, too, Israel will be gathered from the nations and will be restored. So, there is new hope for Israel, provided she does not err again in cultic matters. In short, Abraham's faithfulness is used by the author of the *Apocalypse of Abraham* as a refounding myth to comfort Israel (Abraham's *descendants*) in times of sorrow.

Despite their obvious differences in genre, content, and purpose, Galatians 3, Romans 4, and *the Apocalypse of Abraham* are unique among the Jewish writings from the Second Temple period and its immediate aftermath in that they *all* appeal to Abraham as the sole forefather of the faithful. This alone suffices to point out a likely thematic relationship between these three texts. Yet, while in Galatians 3 and Romans 4, Paul's Abrahamic argument entails a model for Gentile inclusion, as I have formerly argued, in the *Apocalypse of Abraham*, Abraham's model works *for Israel alone*. Although those lacking Abrahamic kinship are there divided into wicked and righteous people (*Apoc. Ab.* 22:4), the righteous among them cannot be compared to Abraham's descendants, who have been set *apart* for God (22:5). To put it differently: only Israel can be legitimately called "God's people" (22:5)—that is, gentiles should not regard themselves as Abraham's *true* sons/heirs.

While not denying righteousness and redemption to at least *some* gentiles, this overtly contrasts with Paul's claims about their inclusion in the people of God, as also with his view on Israel's sanctity/distinctiveness, yet *not* radical separateness. Hence, in my view, it would not be too adventurous to affirm that the author of the *Apocalypse of Abraham* was probably acquainted with Paul's message, which, urged on by the tragic events that had led to Israel's destruction a few decades earlier and trying to give her new hope by emphasizing her special status before God, this author tacitly intended to oppose. After all, it is hard to imagine Paul's message as an isolated phenomenon, unable to attract the attention and eventual criticism of his fellow Jews, even though most scholars have looked at it, hitherto, as though it went virtually unnoticed among his Jewish contemporaries. Elsewhere, I have tried to show that a careful "symptomatic" rereading of *4 Ezra* 8:32, 36 and Rom. 4:5; 5:6, 10 may, in fact, lead to the opposite conclusion.[9] Perhaps the same logic ought to be applied despite the fact that it cannot be fully proved here.

Transforming Paul from Without:
Christianity as a Supersessionist Misreading of Paul?

New, though obviously, different polemical readings of Paul's Abrahamic argument were produced within the earliest gentile-Christian communities as well.

Drawing on and seemingly following in the footsteps of the intra-Jewish controversy set forth in the Fourth Gospel—which presents the Johannine community as the genuine children of Abraham—two significant gentile-Christian texts written prior to Justin Martyr's *Dialogue with Trypho*, namely, the *Epistle of Barnabas* (late first–early second century) and the *Apology* of Aristides (early second century), introduce Abraham either as a Christian himself (*Barnabas*) or as the spiritual forefather of the gentile Christ-believers (Aristides), hence implicitly downplaying Israel's Abrahamic filiation. Justin goes even further: he argues that, contrary to what they claim, the Jews must not be regarded as Abraham's *true* children, and thus, expressly "renders them orphaned":[10] "We, who have been led to God through this crucified Christ are the true spiritual Israel and the descendants [γένος] of Judah, Jacob, Isaac, and Abraham, who, though uncircumcised, was approved and blessed by God because of his faith," he writes (*Dial.* 11.5), thereby transforming Paul's original concern for gentile inclusion into the banner of Jewish exclusion from the people of God—or almost.[11]

The story of early Christian supersessionism is, of course, well-documented.[12] Justin Martyr's contribution to it is no mystery, as it was he who actually coined the expression *verus Israel* as a signifier for the church.[13] Yet it is interesting to note that, quite probably, Justin's biased reading of Galatians 3 and Romans 4 is dependent upon a likewise distorted reading of Gal. 6:15–16 (where Paul simply states that in spite of their eventual ethnic differences, Christ-believers form a single community before God [verse 15] before going on to bless both them *and* Israel [verse 16])[14] and Rom. 9:6 (where, albeit somewhat ambiguously, Paul merely seems to suggest, within the overall argument of chapters 9 to 11, that those fellow Jews who refuse to admit the arrival of the messianic age and the need to carry out a mission to the gentiles in order to facilitate their ingathering refuse to fulfill Israel's role as "light to the nations," and cannot thus be counted among the spiritual leaders of *Israel*—a concept that Paul now somehow *expands* to include the faithful gentiles as well,[15] thus emphasizing the crucial role played by God's promise in the formation of *all* new lineages [Rom. 9.8–9]).[16] Be that as it may, Justin clearly betrays Paul's explicit warning against gentile boasting in Rom. 9:4; 11:1, 18, 26, and 29.

Ultimately, Paul's Abrahamic argument made good sense in the Second Temple period, for Jerusalem was physically there to eventually open its gates to the gentiles. After the destruction of the city in 68–70 and 132–35 CE, however, the ingathering of the nations became a difficult task to fulfill. Those whom Paul invited to join Israel, furthermore, became Israel's enemies. There is, to be sure, something truly awkward in this! Yet, one must understand that Paul's mission presented the risk of requiring too little from its addressees; that many gentile-Christians feared to self-represent themselves as philo-Jews in the face of Rome's overweening state power, given that Rome had successfully defeated two major consecutive Jewish revolts; and that Jews, in turn, felt the need to struggle for their own identity by increasingly differentiating themselves from the Christians. As Daniel Boyarin has thoroughly shown, rabbinic Judaism and Christianity only emerged as two separate religions around the fifth century.[17] However, hostilities on both sides commenced very early due to political reasons, and Paul's message was explicitly transformed into the keystone of the Church's supersessionist claims, which would later play a remarkable role—overlooked until now—in the shaping of Islamic supersessionism.

Abraham in the Qur'an: A Few Remarks

The fifth-century church historian Sozomen (*EH* 375) witnesses to the influence that the Jews presumably exerted upon certain pre-Islamic Arabs by *convincing* the latter of their Abrahamic lineage.[18] Islam, in turn, contributed to further develop that very notion among the Arabs of late antiquity and beyond.

As is well-known, the Qur'an makes Abraham the father of the only *true* religion that deserves such a name: Islam. Accordingly, early Muslim authors made Abraham Muhammad's spiritual forebear, and in fact, his sole complete prophetic *model*.[19] Yet, there is much more behind the quranic and early Islamic reuse of Abrahamic motifs and legends, which has been studied in recent years by Heribert Busse (1988),[20] Reuven Firestone (1990),[21] Gerald Hawting (1999, 2010),[22] François de Blois (2002),[23] Roberto Tottoli (2002),[24] Brian Hauglid (2003),[25] Shari Lowin (2006),[26] Friedmann Eißler (2009),[27] and Gabriel Reynolds (2012).[28]

It must be stressed, however, that these authors have mainly explored the biblical, rabbinic, and Christian precedents of such early Islamic and/or proto-Islamic traditions; albeit somewhat disappointing, this is just normal. When examining the Jewish and Christian connections—I would prefer to say the Judeo-Christian *setting*—of early Islam, scholars of Islamic origins have seldom paid enough attention to the Old Testament Pseudepigrapha. In fact, an analysis of the Old Testament pseudepigraphic *subtexts* of the Qur'an is still wanting. This does not only apply to the Qur'an as a whole, but to its Abrahamic and crypto-Abrahamic legends and motifs as well, although Geneviève Gobillot has rightly emphasized the role likely played by the *Apocalypse of Abraham* and the *Testament of Abraham* in the composition of several key passages of the Qur'an (for example, 17:1, 5, 7; 20:133; 53:33–41; 87:16–9)[29] and in the development of some equally significant Muhammadan legends (including Muhammad's celestial journey).

In the next section, I will try to offer an *intertextual* approach to a passage in the Qur'an (namely, 56:1–56) that I will read in light of a strikingly similar passage, contained in the *Apocalypse of Abraham*, that displays the very same spatial, numerical, and axiological distinctions. Then, I will try to show that the *Apocalypse of Abraham* may have played, together with Romans 4 and/or Galatians 3, a significant role in the founding *myth* of Islam, which, I shall argue, is also to be envisaged as a supersessionist myth.[30]

"Those on the right" and "those on the left" in Qur'an 56:1-56

Chapter 56 of the Qur'an (*sūrat al-wāqi'a*) opens with an announcement of the end of time and with a vision of the cosmic events that will follow (56:1–6). As I have argued elsewhere,[31] such a vision resembles the one contained in *Apoc. Ab.* 21:4g, which presents similar, though not identical, cosmic traits. Then, in the quranic passage, we read that on that day, mankind will be divided into "three groups" (56:7):

1. Some will be placed "on the right" (56:8) = Q G1;
2. some will be placed "on the left" (56:9) = Q G2; and
3. there shall be a third group different both from the group "on the right" and the group "on the left": "the foremost" (*al-šābiqūn*) in faith and monotheism, who will stand "near to God" (56:10–11) = Q G3.

The quranic text goes on to describe the fate of each group: in the first place, the fate of the "foremost" (56:12–26) and the fate of the righteous standing "on the right" side (56:27–40), who shall all enter Paradise; then, the fate of the wicked standing "on the left" side (56:41–56), who shall all be thrown to the Gehenna.

This clearly parallels the account in *Apoc. Ab.* 21:7 and 22:1, 3–5, where we find a similar picture and a similar group division:

- 21:7 . . . I saw there a great crowd of men, and women, and children, and half of them <on the right side of the portrayal, and half of them> on the left side of the portrayal. . . .

- 22:1 And I said, "Eternal Mighty One! What is this picture of creation?" . . .

- 22:3 ". . . Who are the people in the picture on this side and on that?"

- 22:4 And he said to me,

  "These who are on the left side are a multitude of tribes who were before and who are destined to be after you: some for judgment and justice, and others for revenge and perdition at the end of the age."

- 22:5 "Those on the right side of the picture are the people set apart for me of the people [that are] with Azazel. These are the ones I have destined to be born of you and to be called my people."[32]

Some brief remarks might prove useful at this point:

1. The quranic narrative follows the spatial order provided in *Apoc. Ab.* 21:7 (right to left) instead of the one provided in *Apoc. Ab.* 22:4–5 (left to right).

2. Those placed "on the left side" in *Ab.* (including both the "righteous" and the "wicked") are divided in the Qur'an into two separate groups: Q G1 and Q G2, which stand "on the right" side and "on the left" side of the picture, respectively.

3. In spite of this spatial shift, the twofold order present in *Ab.* 22:4 is well preserved.

4. At the same time, those labeled in *Ab.* 22:5 as "God's chosen people" are set apart as Q G3. Their designation is quite similar in both texts: they are said to be "those set apart for God" (*Apoc. Ab.* 22:5a), "God's chosen people" (*Apoc. Ab.* 22:5c), and those brought "near to God" (Q 56:11). Interestingly enough, they close the list of the different kinds of people that each text mentions.

5. As in *Ab.* 21:7 and later in *Apoc. Ab.* 22:5, there is a big line that makes such people (the "foremost," or God's chosen ones) stand apart from everyone else.

6. Yet, while in *Ab.*, God's chosen ones are said to be Abraham's descendants, the Qur'an does not further qualify them in any other way: they are simply said to be God's chosen ones, though we later read that many among the "older people" and only a few among the "later people" will join such a group (56:13–4; cf. *Apoc. Ab.* 22:4a, where a somewhat different chronological distinction is

also made). I shall examine this rather rough contrast in the next section.

7. The quranic account of the fate of each group also parallels, and expands, *Ab.* 22:4b.

8. Finally, it should also be noticed that—if we leave aside *Ab.* 21:7—both texts begin by questioning the identity of the groups standing on the right side and on the left side of the picture: in *Apoc. Ab.* 22:3, it is Abraham who asks the question about their identity. In the quranic text, the question is outlined four times—twice apropos of those standing "on the right" (56:8, 27) and twice of those standing "on the left" (56:9, 41)—without anyone actually asking the question. That is to say, the Qur'an puts it forth as an impersonal question addressed to its readers, just as the whole vision is.

Their differences notwithstanding, a similar scheme can therefore be found in both texts:

	ApAb	Q
the righteous	on the left	on the right
the wicked	on the left	on the left
God's chosen ones	on the right, apart from everyone else	apart from everyone else

It goes without saying that the central image in both—that is, the opposition between the right and the left side—is relatively frequent in early Jewish and Christian imagery. Yet, to the best of my knowledge, it is only applied to the fate of the righteous and the wicked in the *Apocalypse of Abraham*, the apocryphal *Acts of John* (second half of the second century CE), and the Qur'an. The author of the *Acts of John* used it, however, in a narrower and metaphoric way to merely announce that those on the right side would stand fast and those on the left side would be removed at the end of time (114). Unless I am mistaken, therefore, the only *authoritative* and *extensive* parallel to the quranic story is to be found in the *Apocalypse of Abraham.*

The Qur'an's Supersessionist Rereading of Paul and the Founding Myth of Islam

To sum up: in the Qur'an, "God's chosen ones" are transformed *from* Abraham's carnal descendants via Isaac (that is, from Israel) *into* a new, purely spiritual group: "the foremost" in faith and monotheism. This is to be compared with Q 2:135 and 3:67, were Abraham is presented as حنيف (*ḥanīf*) in the sense that he's neither a Jew nor a Christian (which obviously adds something to his simpler presentation as just a *ḥanīf* in 3:67, 95: 4:125; 6:79; 6:161; 16:120, 123, on the one hand, and 2:124, on the other hand). For, even if, in the latter case, he is not explicitly described as a *ḥanīf*, he is implicitly described as the father of a people that can no longer be equated with his own carnal descendants (the Jews). Now this, as we have seen, is but the typically Christian anti-Jewish supersessionist argument. To be sure, the church intended to replace Israel, whereas Muslims regard themselves as being elder than the Israelites (and the Christians) in matters of faith due to their presumed Abrahamic (that is, pre-Mosaic) lineage. If, however, one brackets this latter conviction as a mere self-legitimizing claim, one may take the founding myth of Islam to be a *supersessionist* myth as well: a *new* supersessionist myth that was polemically read backwards as a *restoration* myth.[33] Quite probably, however, the Qur'an, or at least its pre-canonical *Grundschriften*,[34] belongs to an earlier chapter in that development: a chapter that should be labeled as "proto-Islamic" rather than Islamic, a chapter *prior* to the establishment of Islam as a new religious (id)entity.[35]

Now, what was the *role* played by the *Apocalypse of Abraham* in the early proto-Islamic shaping of such a myth? In my view, the *Apocalypse of Abraham* provided the editors of the quranic text—or its *Grundschiften*—with the very *core* of the myth itself. It also provided them with its precise *apocalyptical* form. Once readapted, it offered them a *place* to inscribe their ideological construction.

It provided them, quite possibly together with Romans 4 and/or Galatians 3, with the core of the myth itself, for there is no other text—either Jewish or Christian—that presents Abraham as the sole forefather of the faithful. Obviously, the *Apocalypse of Abraham* would hardly have had such a great impact upon them, had they not been formerly inclined to read it in that way, but it seems safe to deduce that the traditional Christian interpretation of Romans 4 and Galatians 3 was already at hand to instruct them. There is, of course, no way to prove this. Yet, such a hypothesis cannot be discarded a priori in my opinion, as there is no better one that helps us make sense of why the editors of the quranic text used the Abraham story as they did.

Furthermore, Abraham's designation as "guide" (إمام, imām) in Q 2:124 might reflect an adaptation of his role as "father" of the faithful, regardless of their ethnicity, in Romans 4. We should compare here the relationship suggested in Q 28:5 between "leaders" (أئمة, a'imma) and "heirs" (وارثون, wāriṯūn). Besides, the rather unclear distinction between Q G1 and Q G3 could perhaps be reminiscent of that found in Rom. 4:11-2, where the difference between groups 1 ("all who have faith") and 3 ("those who walk . . . in faith") is likewise unclear in my view.[36] Finally, if Guillaume Dye is correct about the Christian liturgical background of Q 19:1-63[37]—and I take it he is—then it is clear that the editors of the Qur'an, or (again) its *Grundschriften*, knew of Galatians 3 and were moreover familiar with its traditional Christian reading; I would like to thank Guillaume for kindly drawing my attention to this issue.[38]

Be all of that as it may, it is clear that the *Apocalypse of Abraham* functioned as a subtext for them and as a source for—perhaps even as the main source of—their own founding myth. As said above, the *Apocalypse of Abraham* also provided the myth its precise apocalyptic form, which is, in fact, lacking both in Romans 4 and Galatians 3. The Qur'an is surely more than an apocalypse, but if it may also be defined as an apocalypse—and I think it should be, due to the revelatory and eschatological concerns that lie at its very center—then I see it as an apocalypse entirely based upon the *Apocalypse of Abraham*. For all that we can find in the Qur'an (its non-negotiable monotheistic claims and polemics, which are, in fact, traced back to Abraham; its many allusions to a revelation received from above whose first witness was Abraham; the announcement of God's judgment as inevitable; and the distinction between Abraham's followers and everyone else in both the present and the future life; and so on) is already present in the *Apocalypse*.

At first sight it would appear that the aforementioned mainstream Christian interpretation of Romans 4 and Galatians 3 contributed in some way to shape the supersessionist framework of the new myth. Moreover, the quranic reuse of *Apoc. Ab.* 22:5 shows that such a supersessionist framework, wherever it came from, resulted in a textual adaptation (and corruption) of the contents of the Jewish apocalypse: the Jews are no longer God's chosen ones (as was claimed in *Apoc. Ab.* 22:5); they have been replaced by the "foremost" in faith and monotheism (Q 56:10). Actually, this is the only verse in the Qur'an where such replacement explicitly takes place. Some may object that there ultimately is no supersessionism in the Qur'an: that the Qur'an accepts all prior revelations while simultaneously denouncing their intrinsic limitations and their eventual corruption by their own followers.[39] The Quranic reuse of the *Apocalypse* proves that this is not so: the new *Umma* is expressly said to substitute Israel. But then, it could be legitimately argued that the "sectarian milieu" out of which Islam emerged was, in fact, a Christian one.

Exploring the contour lines, intellectual background, geographical location, and time frame of this Christian milieu belongs to an altogether different study that I cannot undertake here.[40] Yet, it is fascinating to see that within a single text of as yet unclear provenance, such as is the Qur'an,[41] Paul's Abrahamic argument as reframed by the church is subliminally (re)used against the Jews in a passage that puts forth a new founding myth that literally draws upon the post-Pauline Jewish discussion of that very argument in the *Apocalypse of Abraham*, to which the quranic myth is therefore fully indebted. The quite vexing fact that the apparent distinctiveness of such a new myth conceals a Christian reinterpretation of an intra-

Jewish argument—as well as the textual corruption of the latter—prevents us from assigning too much distinctiveness to the myth itself. Hence my hesitation to label it as Islamic, for there still is nothing specifically Islamic in such a myth. Perhaps this could help us understand though, as an aside, the reason why the quranic prophet is mentioned in the Qur'an as الرّسول النّبِي الأُمّي (al-rasūl al-nabī al-ummī, 7:157–58; 62:2)—that is, the "apostle/prophet to the gentiles"![42]

Notes

1. Birgit van der Lans, "Belonging to Abraham's Kin: Genealogical Appeals to Abraham as a Possible Background for Paul's Abrahamic Argument," in *Abraham, the Nations, and the Hagarites*, ed. Martin Goodman, George H. van Kooten, and Jaques T. A. G. M. van Ruiten (Themes in Biblical Narrative 13; Leiden and Boston: Brill, 2010), 312. On proselytes as Paul's eventual opponents in Galatia, see Mark D. Nanos, *The Irony of Galatians: Paul's Letter in First Century Context* (Minneapolis: Fortress, 2002), 193–283. I find Nanos's reasoning most compelling, for who else could be "jealous" of Pauls" gentile converts (notice the wording in Gal. 4:17; 6:12–13)?

2. Caroline Johnson Hodge, *If Sons, Then Heirs: A Study of Kinship and Ethnicity in the Letters of Paul* (Oxford and New York: Oxford University Press, 2007), 86.

3. Ibid., 91.

4. Carlos A. Segovia, *Por una interpretación no cristiana de Pablo de Tarso: El redescubrimiento contemporáneo de un judío mesiánico* [*A Non-Christian Interpretation of the Apostle to the Nations: Rereading Paul as a Messianic Jew*] (published online by the author, iTunes Store, 2013), 90–106. See also Terence L. Donaldson, *Judaism and the Gentiles: Jewish Patterns of Universalism (to 135 CE)* (Waco: Baylor University Press, 2007).

5. On whose implications and context, see now Pamela Eisenbaum, *Paul Was Not a Christian: The Original Message of a Misunderstood Apostle* (New York: HarperCollins, 2009). See also Magnus Zetterholm, *Approaches to Paul: A Student's Guide to Contemporary Scholarship* (Minneapolis: Fortress, 2009). On the politically subversive aspect of Paul's message to the nations, see Neil Elliot, *The Arrogance of Nations: Reading Romans in the Shadow of Empire* (Paul in Critical Contexts; Minneapolis: Fortress, 2008); Davina Lopez, *Apostle to the Conquered: Reimagining Paul's Mission* (Paul in Critical Contexts; Minneapolis: Fortress, 2008); Brigitte Kahl, *Galatians Re-imagined: Reading with the Eyes of the Vanquished* (Paul in Critical Contexts; Minneapolis: Fortress, 2010).

6. On its progressive decline within rabbinic Judaism, see Moshe Lavee, "Converting the Missionary Image of Abraham: Rabbinic Traditions Migrating from the Land of Israel to Babylon," in *Abraham, the Nations, and the Hagarites*, ed. Martin Goodman, George H. van Kooten, and Jacques T. A. G. M. van Ruiten, 203–22.

7. On the *Apocalypse of Abraham*—its date, context, contents, versions, and manuscript witnesses—see Alexander Kulik, *Retroverting Slavonic Pseudepigrapha: Toward the Original of the Apocalypse of Abraham* (SBLTCS 3; Atlanta: Society of Biblical Literature, 2004), 1–3; George W. E. Nickelsburg, *Jewish Literature between the Bible and the Mishnah: A Historical and Literary Introduction* (2nd ed.; Minneapolis: Fortress, 2005), 285–88.

8. The *Apocalypse of Abraham* explicitly recalls Manasseh's sins (2 Kgs. 21:2–7; 2 Chron. 33:2–7). Cf. 2 Kgs. 21:10–5, whose author points to Manasseh's defilement of the temple cult as the cause of the fall of Jerusalem in 587 BCE.

9. Carlos A. Segovia, "Some Brief Suggestions for a Symptomatic Rereading of 4 Ezra in Light of P. Sacchi's and E. P. Sanders's Contributions to the Study of Early Judaism, with a Final Note on the Hodayot from Qumran and Paul" (paper presented at the 6th Enoch Seminar: "2 Baruch - 4 Ezra: 1st Century Jewish Apocalypticism," Milan, June 26 June–1 July 2011).

10. Jeffrey S. Siker, *Disinheriting the Jews: Abraham in Early Christian Controversy* (Louisville: Westminster John Knox, 1991), 163. Since they only mention Abraham occasionally, and are therefore of little relevance to this survey, I will not analyze here the two other primary sources studied by Siker, i. e., Ignatius's *Epistle to the Philadelphians* and the *Gospel of Philip*.

11. Cf. e. g., *Dial.* 119.6; 120.2, on which, see also Denise Kimber Buell, *Why this New Race? Ethnic Reasoning in Early Christianity* (New York: Columbia University Press, 2005), 105–6.

12. See for an overview, Michael J. Vlach, *The Church as a Replacement of Israel: An Analysis of Supersessionism* (Edition Israelogie 2; Frankfurt am Main: Peter Lang, 2009); Terence L. Donaldson, *Jews and Anti-Judaism in the New Testament: Decision Points and Divergent Interpretations* (London: SPCK, 2010).

13. On Justin, his world, writings, tentative project, and conceptual complexities, see Judith L. Lieu, *Image & Reality: The Jews in the World of the Christians in the Second Century* (Edinburgh: T & T Clark, 1996); William Horbury, *Jews and Christians in Contact and Controversy* (Edinburgh: T & T Clark, 1998); Timothy J. Horner, *Listening to Trypho: Justin Martyr's Dialogue Reconsidered* (Contributions to Biblical Exegesis & Theology 28; Leuven: Peeters, 2001); Tessa Rajak, "Talking at Trypho: Christian Apologetic as Anti-Judaism in Justin's *Dialogue with Trypho the Jew*" (1999), in *The Jewish Dialogue with Greece and Rome: Studies in Cultural and Social Interaction* (AGJU 48; Leiden and Boston: Brill, 2001) 511–33; David Rokéah, *Justin Martyr and the Jews* (Jewish and Christian Perspectives 5; Leiden and Boston: Brill, 2001); and especially, Boyarin, *Border Lines: The Partition of*

Judaeo-Christianity (Divinations: Rereading Late Ancient Religion; Philadelphia: University of Pennsylvania Press, 2004) and Buell, *Why this New Race?*.

14. That is, he does *not* make Christ-believers "the Israel of God" (Ἰσραὴλ τοῦ θεοῦ). See Lloyd Gaston, *Paul and the Torah* (Vancouver: University of British Columbia Press,1987; repr. Eugene: Wipf & Stock, 2006), 90.

15. Hence the assertion in v. 6b: Οὐ γὰρ πάντες οἱ ἐξ Ἰσραὴλ οὗτοι Ἰσραήλ; . . . Ἰσραιλῖται in several mss. from the 6th century onwards (see Robert Jewett, *Romans: A Commentary* [ed. Eldon J. Epp; Hermeneia; Minneapolis: Fortress, 2007], 570). Cf. the "remnant" motif in 11:5.

16. On the overall argument of Rom 9–11 see Stanley K. Stowers, *A Rereading of Romans: Justice, Jews, and Gentiles* (New Haven: Yale University Press, 1994), 285–316.

17. Boyarin, *Border Lines*.

18. On the rather uncertain pre-Islamic identity and history of the Arabs, see Jan Retsö, *The Arabs in Antiquity: Their History from the Assyrians to the Umayyads* (London and New York: Routledge, 2003). On Sozomen, see Gabriel Said Reynolds, *The Emergence of Islam: Classical Traditions in Contemporary Perspective* (Minneapolis: Fortress, 2012), 161.

19. On the making of the Islamic prophet, see Uri Rubin, *The Eye of the Beholder: The Life of Muhammad as Viewed by the Early Muslims—A Textual Analysis* (Studies in Late Antiquity and Early Islam 5; Princeton: Darwin Press, 1995); John Wansbrough, *Quranic Studies: Sources and Methods of Scriptural Interpretation* (London Oriental Series 31; Oxford and New York: Oxford University Press, 1977; repr. with a foreword, translations and expanded notes by Andrew Rippin [Amherst, NY: Prometheus Books, 2004]) 53-84; Stephen J. Shoemaker, *The Death of a Prophet: The End of Muhammad's Life and the Beginnings of Islam* (Divinations: Rereading Late Ancient Religion; Philadelphia: University of Pennsylvania Press, 2012); Carlos A. Segovia, *The Quranic Noah and the Making of the Islamic Prophet: A Study of Intertextuality and Religious Identity Formation in Late Antiquity* (Judaism, Christianity, and Islam—Tension, Transmission, Transformation 4; Berlin and Boston: De Gruyter, 2015).

20. Heribert Busse, *Die theologische Beziehungen des Islams zu Judentum und Christentum: Grundlagen des Dialogs im Koran und die gegenwärtige Situation* (Grundzüge 72; Darmstadt: Wissenschaftliche Buchgesellschaft, 1988).

21. Reuven Firestone, *Journeys in Holy Lands: The Evolution of the Abraham-Ishmael Legends in Islamic Exegesis* (Albany: State University of New York Press, 1990).

22. Gerald R. Hawting, *The Idea of Idolatry and the Emergence of Islam: From Polemic to History* (Cambridge Studies in Islamic Civilization; Cambridge and New York: Cambridge University Press, 1999).

23. François de Blois, "*Naṣrānī* (Ναζωραῖος) and *ḥanīf* (ἐθνικός): Studies on the Religious Vocabulary of Christianity and Islam," *Bulletin of SOAS* 65 (2002): 1–30.

24. Roberto Tottoli, *The Biblical Prophets in the Qur'ān and Muslim Literature* (Richmond: Curzon Press, 2002).

25. Brian M. Hauglid, "On the Early Life of Abraham: Biblical and Qur'ānic Intertextuality and the Anticipation of Muḥammad," in *Bible and Qur'ān: Essays in Scriptural Intertextuality*, ed. John C. Reeves (SBLSS 24; Atlanta: Society of Biblical Literature, 2003), 87–105.

26. Shari L. Lowin, *The Making of a Forefather: Abraham in Islamic and Jewish Exegetical Narratives* (Islamic History and Civilization 65; Leiden and Boston: Brill, 2006).

27. Friedmann Eißler, "Abraham im Islam," in *Abraham in Judentum, Christentum und Islam*, ed. Christfried Böttrich, Beate Ego, and Friedmann Eissler (Göttingen: Vandenhoeck & Ruprecht, 2009), 116–88.

28. Gabriel Said Reynolds, *The Qur'ān and Its Biblical Subtext* (Routledge Studies in the Qur'an; London and New York: Routledge, 2012).

29. Geneviève Gobillot, "Apocryphes de l'Ancien et du Nouveau Testament," in *Dictionnaire du Coran*, ed. Mohammad Ali Amir-Moezzi (Paris: Robert Lafont, 2007), 58–61. See, however, my remarks on Gobillot's cross-references, which, at times, fail to be exact, in Carlos A. Segovia, "Thematic and Structural Affinities between 1 Enoch and the Qur'ān: A Contribution to the Study of the Judaeo-Christian Apocalyptic Setting of the Early Islamic Faith," in *The Coming of the Comforter: When, Where, and to Whom? Studies on the Rise of Islam and Various Other Topics in Memory of John Wansbrough*, ed. Carlos A. Segovia and Basil Lourié (Orientalia Judaica Christiana 3; Piscataway, NJ: Gorgias Press, 2012), 237–38n41.

30. A more detailed study of such parallels can be found in Carlos A. Segovia, "'Those on the Right' and 'Those on the Left': Rereading Qur'ān 56:1-56 (and the Founding Myth of Islam) in Light of Apocalypse of Abraham 21-2," *Oriens Christianum*, forthcoming.

31. See once more, ibid.

32. Kulik, *Retroverting Slavonic Pseudepigrapha*, 26–27.

33. On the supersessionist nature of the founding myth of Islam, see Camila Adang, *Muslim Writers on Judaism and the Hebrew Bible: From Ibn Rabban to Ibn Hazm* (Islamic Philosophy, Theology, and Science 22; Leiden and Boston: Brill, 1996), 192–93; John Wansbrough, *The Sectarian Milieu: Content and Composition of Islamic Salvation History* (Oxford and New York: Oxford University Press, 1978; reprint. with a foreword, translations and expanded notes by Gerald R. Hawting [Amherst, NY: Prometheus Books, 2006]) 109–14; Guillaume Dye, "La théologie de la substitution du point du vue de l'islam," in *Judaïsme, christianisme, islam: le judaïsme entre "théologie de la substitution" et "théologie de la falsification*," ed. Thomas Gergely (Brussels: Didier Devillez EME, 2010), 83–103; Geneviève Gobillot, "Des textes pseudo clémentines à la mystique juive des premières siècles et du Sinaï à Ma'rib. Quelques coïncidences entre contexte culturel et

losalisation géographique dans le Coran," in *The Coming of the* Comforter, ed. Carlos A. Segovia and Basil Lourié, 8ff.; Aaron W. Hughes, *Abrahamic Religions: On the Uses and Abuses of History* (Oxford and New York: Oxford University Press, 2012), 39ff.

34. On which, see Wansbrough, *Quranic Studies*, 1, 12, 20–21, 33–52. See also Manfred Kropp, ed., *Results of Contemporary Research on the Qur'ān: The Question of a Historical-Critical Text of the Qur'ān* (Beiruter texte und studien 100; Beirut and Wurzburg: Orient-Institut Beirut and Ergon, 2007); Gabriel Said Reynolds, ed., *The Qur'ān in Its Historical Context* (Routledge Studies in the Qur'an; London and New York: Routledge, 2008).

35. Which, in my view, took place around the turn of the 8th century under 'Abd al-Malik b. Marwān's rule; see my essay "Identity Politics and Scholarship in the Study of Islamic Origins: The Inscriptions on the Dome of the Rock as a Test Case," in *Identity, Politics, and Scholarship: The Study of Islam and the Study of Religions*, ed. Matt Sheedy (Sheffield, UK, and Bristol, CT: Equinox, forthcoming).

36. See James Swetnam, "The Curious Crux at Romans 4:12," *Biblica* 61 (1980): 110–15; Maria Neubrand, *Abraham, Vater von Juden und Nichtjuden: Eine exegetische Studie zu Rom 4* (Würzburg: Echter, 1997), 234; Jewett, *Romans*, 319–21.

37. Guillaume Dye, "Lieux saints communs, partagés ou confiqués: aux sources de quelques pericopes coraniques (Q 19:1-63)," in *Partage du sacré: transferts, dévotions mixtes, rivalités interconfessionnelles*, ed. Isabelle Dépret and Guillaume Dye (Brussels-Fernelmont: EME, 2012), 100.

38. On Paul's Abrahamic argument in Rom. 4 and the early Islamic concept of *ḥanīf* (pl. *ḥunafāʾ*), see also de Blois, "*Naṣrānī* and *ḥanīf*," 16–27.

39. See e. g., Fred M. Donner, *Muhammad and the Believers: At the Origins of Islam* (Cambridge, MA: Harvard University Press, 2010).

40. I intend to develop this and the preceding section in a future book coauthored with my colleague from the Free University of Brussels (ULB), Guillaume Dye. It is provisionally entitled *Re-Imagining Islam in the Late 7th century*, and a preview of its contents is available at https://www.academia.edu/7050551. See also Segovia, *The Quranic Noah and the Making of the Islamic Prophet*; id., "A Messianic Controversy behind the Making of Muḥammad as the Last Prophet?" (forthcoming in *Early Islam: The Sectarian Milieu of Late Antiquity?*, ed. Guillaume Dye [LAMINE; Chicago: Chicago Oriental Institute]); id., "The Jews and Christians of pre-Islamic Yemen (Ḥimyar) and the Elusive Matrix of the Qur'ān's Christology" (forthcoming in *Jewish Christianity and the Origins of Islam*, ed. Francisco del Río Sánchez [JAOC; Turnhout: Brepols]).

41. On whose ambiguous origins, see once more Wansbrough, *Quranic Studies*.

42. Cf. the later Muslim polemics against Paul, who came to be regarded by several medieval Muslim authors as the corruptor of Christianity; see now Ryan Szpiech, "Preaching Paul to the Moriscos: The *Confusión o confutación de la secta*

Mahomética y del Alcorán (1515) of 'Juan de Andrés'," *La Corónica* 41.1 (2012): 317–43. On the designation of the quranic prophet as *rasūl al-ummī*, see Rubin, *The Eye of the Beholder*, 23–30.

Index of Names